THE FLAMENCO/ CLASSICAL GUITARTRADITION

VOLUME 2:

ADVANCED TECHNIQUES AND REPERTOIRE

BY COREY WHITEHEAD
AND RICARDO MARLOW

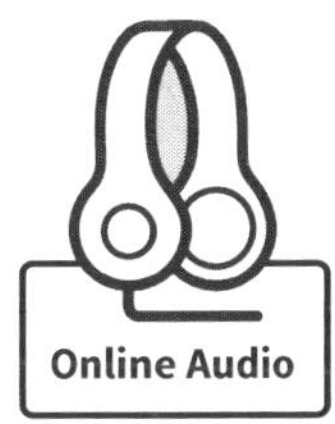

To access the online audio recording go to:
WWW.MELBAY.COM/31005MEB

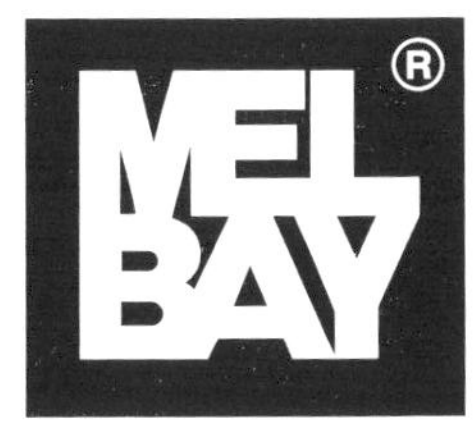

WWW.MELBAY.COM

Preface

Volumes 1 and 2 of *The Flamenco/Classical Guitar Tradition* are designed for the aspiring concert classical guitarist as well as for the serious flamenco player; they are also ideal for the seasoned professional who simply wants to acquire a deeper understanding of music notation and repertoire for the Spanish guitar of the late Classical and Romantic eras (1790 – 1910). During this period, and particularly from the mid-19th century until the present day, composer/guitarists like Aguado, Arcas, Damas, Tárrega, and Rodrigo were writing in both "classical" and flamenco styles, establishing a firm foundation for what the authors call *The Flamenco/Classical Guitar Tradition*. The resulting book series attempts to reveal and further develop the repertoire of that tradition along with the distinctive classical and flamenco guitar techniques needed to carry it forward.

Parallel to the establishment of the guitar repertoire, luthiers were making great strides in developing the instrument itself. Antoni Stradivari (1644 – 1737) is believed to have produced at least 1,116 string instruments including violins, violas, cellos, harps, and guitars. The forms for three sizes of guitar-like instruments can be seen in the Stradivarius Museum in Cremona, Italy. An internet source called "The Dutch Luthier" claims that there are five extant Strad guitars, one of which, although heavily restored can be seen under glass in the museum in Cremona; another similarly restored instrument is still playable as evidenced on The Dutch Luthier website.

Other luthiers in the Cremona area, including Amati, Guarneri, and Rugeri made string-family instruments, but relatively few were producing guitars. Prior to 1850, the standard guitar string length was 630 – 640 mm. The shape of these instruments was more like a peanut and, rather than fan-bracing, these early guitars had transverse bars or transverse bracing. The necks of these guitars met the body at the 11th fret and the fretboard did not extend onto the soundboard. Frets beyond the eleventh were placed directly on the soundboard like those of the lute. The headstock featured friction pegs for tuning. These wooden pegs are also called *claves* or *violin pegs*.

"Classical" or "classic" guitar is a generic term for the nylon or gut-string guitar, which originated in Spain and is often referred to as the "Spanish guitar". The classical guitar was modernized by Antonio de Torres around 1850 with a standardized 650 mm string length and a body a bit wider, deeper, longer, and louder. Torres used a fan-bracing technique on the interior surface of the soundboard. Although modern luthiers still experiment with double-top soundboards with lattice bracing, the fan-braced classical guitar with a 650 mm string length has remained the standard to this day. The oldest known guitar with a 650 mm string length was made in Naples, Italy in 1808 by Gennaro Fabricatore (1800 – 1853). This instrument is owned by author Corey E. Whitehead who used it to make the companion recordings for this book.

Flamenco and classical guitars were quite similar between 1850 and 1910 but, the standard string length for the flamenco guitar has changed since 1950 to at least 657 mm, i.e., 655 plus 2 mm nut height compensation. The modern flamenco guitar requires this longer string length according to Manuel Reyes Sr., as he testified to this author in an interview in his workshop in Córdoba, Spain in 2008. Flamenco and older classical guitars have a steeper neck angle in relation to the soundboard (11 degrees) to achieve the proper string height for the right hand; this angle places the strings closer to the soundboard. Both classical and flamenco guitars were known to have a *golpeado*r or tap-plate, for tapping percussive rhythms on the soundboard and to protect the wood from damage from strumming.

Along with the structure of the guitar itself, guitar technique has also evolved. Dionisio Agujado (1784 – 1849) was the first artist/composer to consistently use fingernails to enhance volume and tone. Most of his contemporaries played using calluses that developed in front of very short nails on the picking hand. Usually, the nails did not make direct contact with the strings, but rather supported the callused flesh as it crossed the strings to produce a sweet tone of limited volume.

The use of fingernails of the right hand was not standardized until the 20th century, after the death of Francisco Tárrega in 1909. According to Emilio Pujol (1886 – 1980), Tárrega disavowed the use of fingernails in playing the guitar the last seven years of his life. This was an aesthetic decision on Tárrega's part rather than the result of declining fingernail quality. The nails/no nails controversy is ongoing in some circles, chiefly fueled by students of Emilio Pujol.

The art of flamenco began with *cante jondo* or "deep song" accompanied by percussion provided by bells, anvil strikes, butter churn sticks (*palos*), hand clapping (*palmas*), the snapping of fingers, and stomping of feet—all marking the musical form and meter (*compás*). Naturally, dancing became an outward form of expression of the lyrics (*letras*) which were concerned with emotion and action, often depicting scenes of farm life, blacksmith shops, prisons, mines, mountains, smuggling, love, death, loneliness, and the glorification of God.

The guitar and perhaps the vihuela—an instrument similar to the early guitar with the third string tuned to a half-step lower—became the natural "supporting actors" in this ensemble. It was the guitar that survived, however, and became the ambassador and face of the art of flamenco that the public outside of Spain associates with flamenco, even more so than a polka dot shirt or flowered dress, fans, or castanets.

The guitar was already old by the time it became a part of the flamenco ensemble; its history logically predates the first publication of guitar and vihuela music, Luís Milan's *El Maestro*, which appeared in tablature (*cifra*) in 1536. The 16th century guitar most commonly had only four strings or *courses*—a course being either a single string or pair of strings placed close together and fingered as one. This instrument had a single high first string and three lower double courses.

It is possible that the guitar and vihuela were used to accompany songs such as *Verdiales* and *Fandangos de Huelva* for centuries before the larger 6-string model was ever invented. The 1538 publication of *Los seys libros del Delfín de la música* by Luys de Narváez contains compositions for vihuela and voice using what is called "*Rodeñas* tuning" (6-D, 5-A, 4-D, 3 F♯, 2-B, and 1-E). *Los seys libros del Delfín* is remarkable in that it presents *Romanceros, Villancicos* (Christmas carols) and *Tientos* plus the first theme and variations in print. *Seguidillas* and *Fandangos* would appear in still other 16th and 17th-century publications.

In closing, while this book series relies on standard notation to convey its information, **sight reading ability is not an absolute requirement for learning the art of playing flamenco guitar**. Flamenco comes from a long tradition of oral dissemination, and true understanding of the music comes from immersion in the culture, taking part in *juergas* (song and dance carousals) and *fiestas*, accompanying singers and dancers, listening to recordings, and watching videos. As an alternative to living in Andalucia and learning by diligent work and cultural osmosis, the authors humbly offer *The Flamenco/Classical Guitar Tradition* series.

Best of luck in your Flamenco/Classical guitar journey,
Corey E. Whitehead
Richard Marlow

Contents

Unit I, Part I

Fretboard Geography

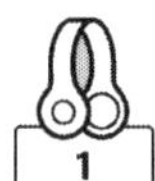

Modal Scales on Each String

Corey E. Whitehead

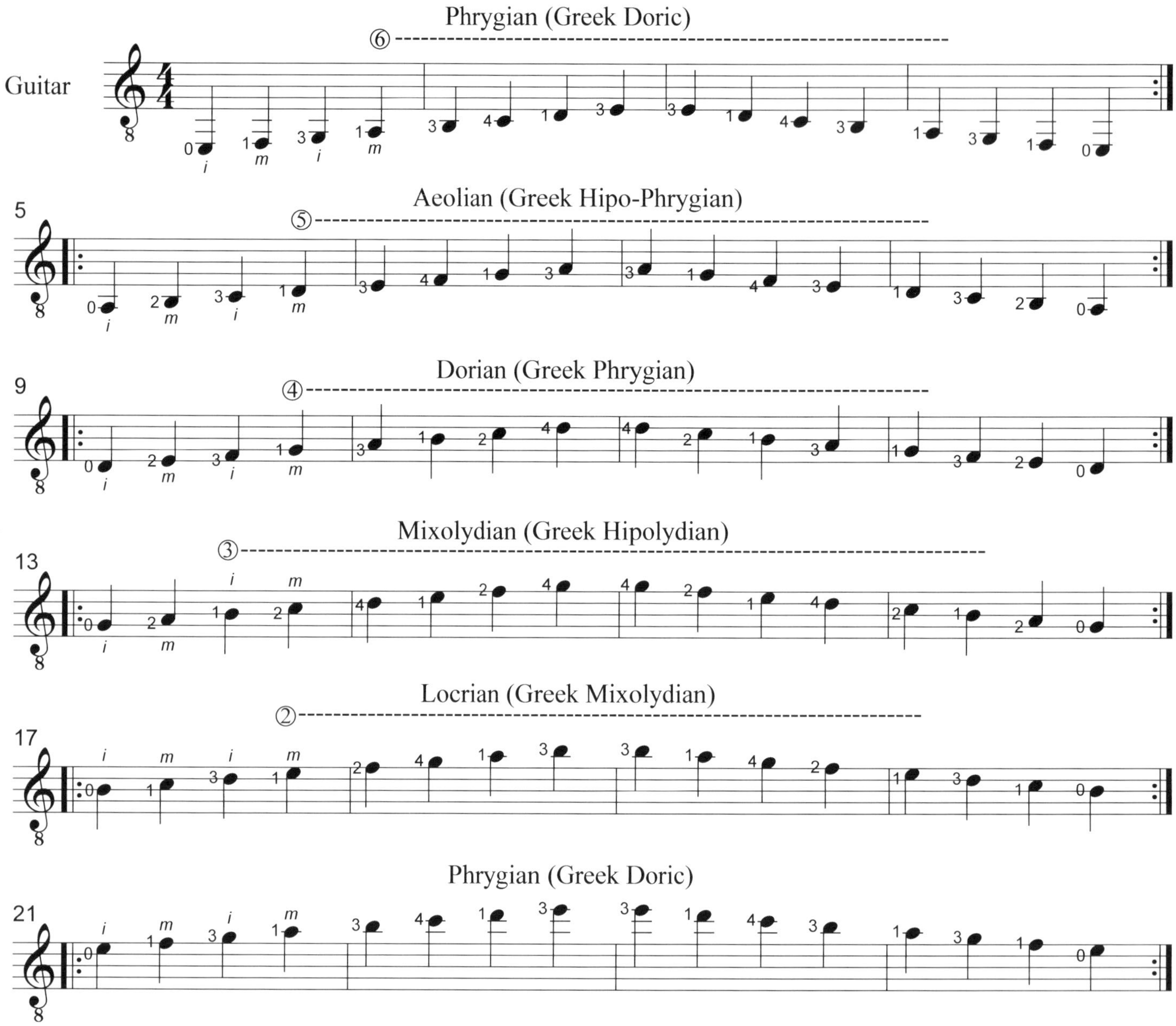

Phrygian (Greek Doric)

Guitar

Aeolian (Greek Hipo-Phrygian)

Dorian (Greek Phrygian)

Mixolydian (Greek Hipolydian)

Locrian (Greek Mixolydian)

Phrygian (Greek Doric)

Performance Notes: Both the modern Roman-ecclesiastic and ancient Greek name of the modes are given for each scale. Note that Greek musical scales are perceived only in descending order, whereas Roman modes ascend and descend.

1) Use alternation of the index and middle fingers of the right hand playing rest-stroke (apoyando).
2) Vary this study by playing each note twice, thrice, or four times using duplet or triplet 8th or 16th notes.
3) Anchor the right-hand thumb on one of the bass strings, such as the 4th string when playing picado on the first string.
4) Apply other right-hand formulas such as (i-a), (a-i), (a-m), (m-a), or (a-m-i-m) or (i-m-a-m).
5) When playing the 5th or 6th string, anchor the thumb of the right hand on the golpeador or soundboard.
6) This exercise will help you learn the names and locations of the notes in the C Major/A natural minor scales as applied to the guitar. Start by reviewing the names of the open strings. Then, realizing that B-C and E-F are naturally occurring semi-tones (also called half-tones or half-steps), say or sing the notes as you play through the modal scales on each string.

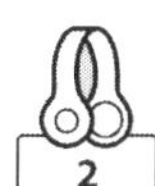

The Chromatic Scale on Each String

Corey E. Whitehead

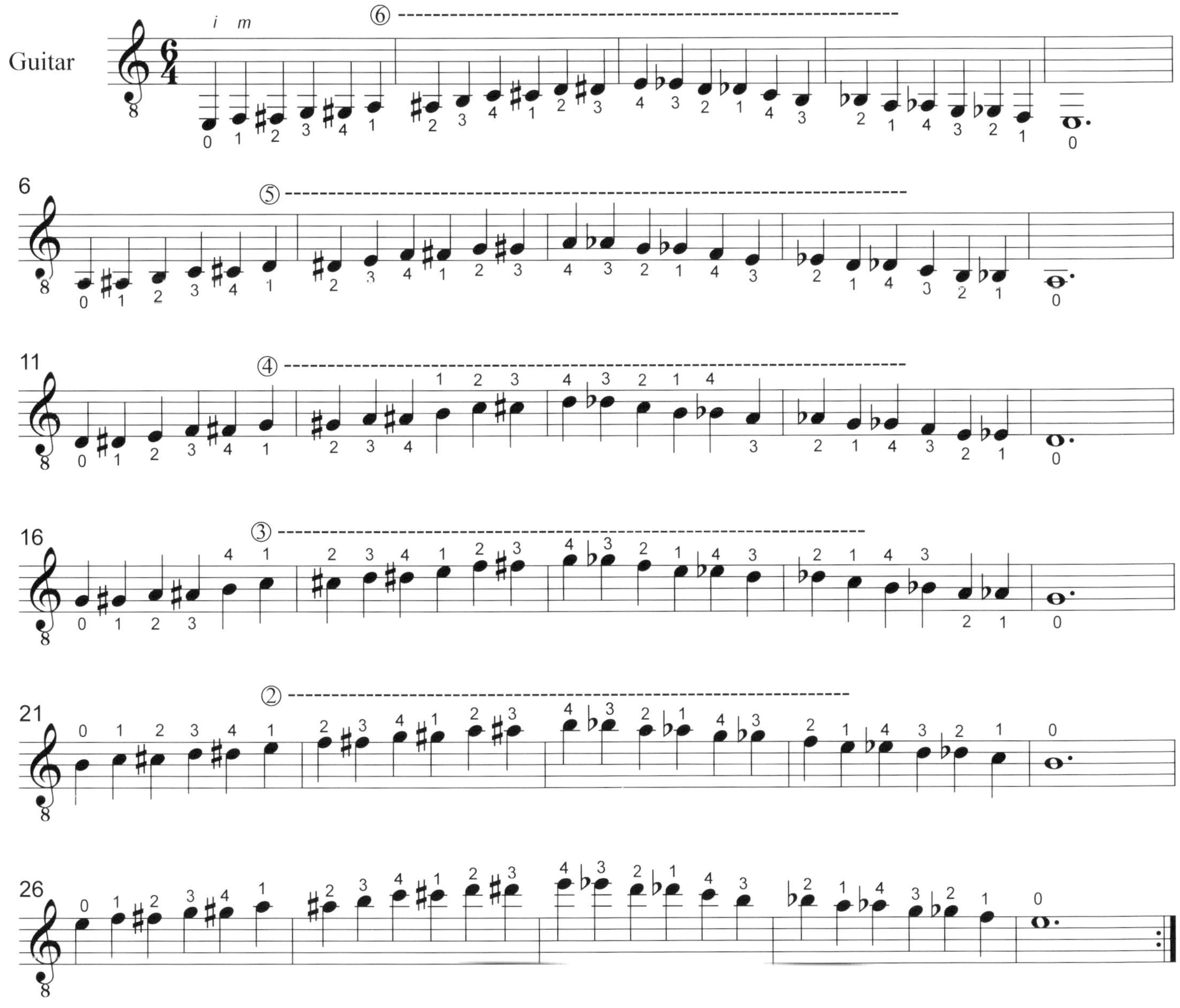

Guitar

Performance Notes

1) Use alternation of the index and middle fingers of the right hand playing rest-stroke (apoyando).

2) Vary this study by playing each note twice, thrice, or four times using duplet or triplet 8th or 16th notes.

3) Anchor right-hand thumb on one of the bass strings, such as the 4th string when playing picado on the first, etc. When playing the 5th or 6th string, anchor the thumb of the right hand on the golpeador or soundboard.

4) Apply other right-hand formulas such as (i-a), (a-i), (a-m), (m-a), or (a-m-i-m) or (i-m-a-m).

Triads and Inversions

A **chord** is defined as any three or more notes sounded together. Each tone has a specific frequency that defines it, such as A-440 with 440 cycles per second (440Hz).
An **interval** is defined as the sonic distance between two notes.

Chords are **classified** first by the types of intervals that exist between their member notes, tones, or pitches. When first learning about intervals, chords and harmony, it is convenient to think in terms of the C major scale with no sharps or flats while envisioning a keyboard. For example, a second (2nd) is the distance between any two adjacent tones of a major scale: C-D, D-E, E-F, F-G, G-A, A-B, B-C)—all white keys on a piano. Chords built on intervals of a second feature adjacent scale tones sounded together. These usually dissonant chords are often used in cinematic music and, at times, in flamenco.

The intervals E-F and B-C are both intervals of a second, a **semitone** or half-step, one fret apart. They are called the **natural half-tones**; they are the two places in every octave on the piano where there is no black key in between. The remaining pairs of adjacent scale tones in a major or natural minor scale, C-D, D-E, F-G, G-A, A-B, are also intervals of a second, but they are a **whole tone** or whole step apart from each other. Since there are seconds of a smaller size (half-steps, one fret apart) and seconds of a larger size (whole steps, 2 frets apart), it becomes necessary to distinguish between the two; the smaller intervals of a second are called **minor seconds** and the larger ones are called **major seconds**.

We've established that any two notes sounded together form an interval, i.e., not a chord; it follows that any three notes sounded together form a **triad**, the simplest, most basic type of chord used in music. In order to discuss triads or chords in general, we first need to learn about **intervals of a third**. Again, think in terms of the C-major scale: C-E, D-F, E-G, F-A, G-B, A-C, B-D, (C) or, in solfege syllables as music theory is taught in Spain and most parts of the world: Do-Mi, Re-Fa, Mi-Sol, Fa-La, Sol-Si, La-Do, Si-Re, (Do). While these intervals certainly can be found on the guitar fretboard, it's easier to envision them as they lie on the keyboard in the key of C major. To cement them in your memory, play them on a keyboard—all on white keys—and sing along using solfege syllables.

Again, we find smaller and larger intervals of a third (3rd). The smaller ones, A-C, B-D, D-F, and E-G, consist of three semitones or 1 ½ tones and are called **minor thirds** (3rds); the larger 3rds encompassing 4 semitones, C-E, F-A, and G-B (Do-Mi, Fa-La, Sol-Si)—are called **major thirds**. While you will have to expand your knowledge of intervals to include 4ths, 5ths, 6ths, 7ths, etc., we can now discuss triads with authority.
Triads containing intervals of a second are called **clusters** and may consist of two major seconds, two minor seconds, or one of each—a minor second plus a major second. A triad containing two half-step intervals (minor 2nds) is most dissonant and a triad with two whole-step intervals (major 2nds) is least dissonant.

In theory, triads consist of the **root** of the chord plus two intervals of a third. If we stack two intervals of a third over the tones of a C major scale, we get the following result:

I	ii	iii	IV	V	vi	vii°
C – E – G	D – F– A	E– G– B	F– A– C	G– B– D	A– C– E	B– D– F or in solfege syllables
Do-Mi-Sol	Re-Fa-La	Mi-Sol-Si	Fa-La-Do	Sol-Si-Re	La-Do-Mi	Si-Re-Fa
Major	minor	minor	Major	Major	minor	diminished

In the perfect keyboard world, triads can be formed and played from any tone in any key using the tonic, 3rd and 5th note of the scale. When the root of the chord, C in the C-E-G triad, is the lowest note in the chord, it is said to be in **root position**. When the 3rd of the chord is the lowest note in the chord, it's in **first inversion** and when the 5th of the chord is the lowest note, it's in **second inversion**.

Theoretically, triads can be written in **closed voicing** in root position on three consecutive lines or three consecutive spaces; on a keyboard, you can play them just like that. Due to the tuning of the guitar in Perfect 4ths and one major 3rd (G-B), it's not always possible to play triads in root position in closed voicing, so guitarists are often forced to play inversions of chords, occasionally omitting certain chord tones. With dominant seventh chords and their extensions with 4 or more chord tones, note omissions and **open voicings** occupying a range of more than an octave may be needed. This combination of factors accounts for the unique and often gracious sound of guitar chord accompaniment and melody/chord playing.

The following examples in standard notation and chord grids illustrate the major, minor, and diminished triads on adjacent strings in all possible positions and string locations.

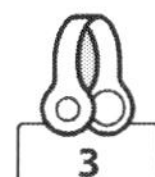

Triads and Inversions

Corey E. Whitehead

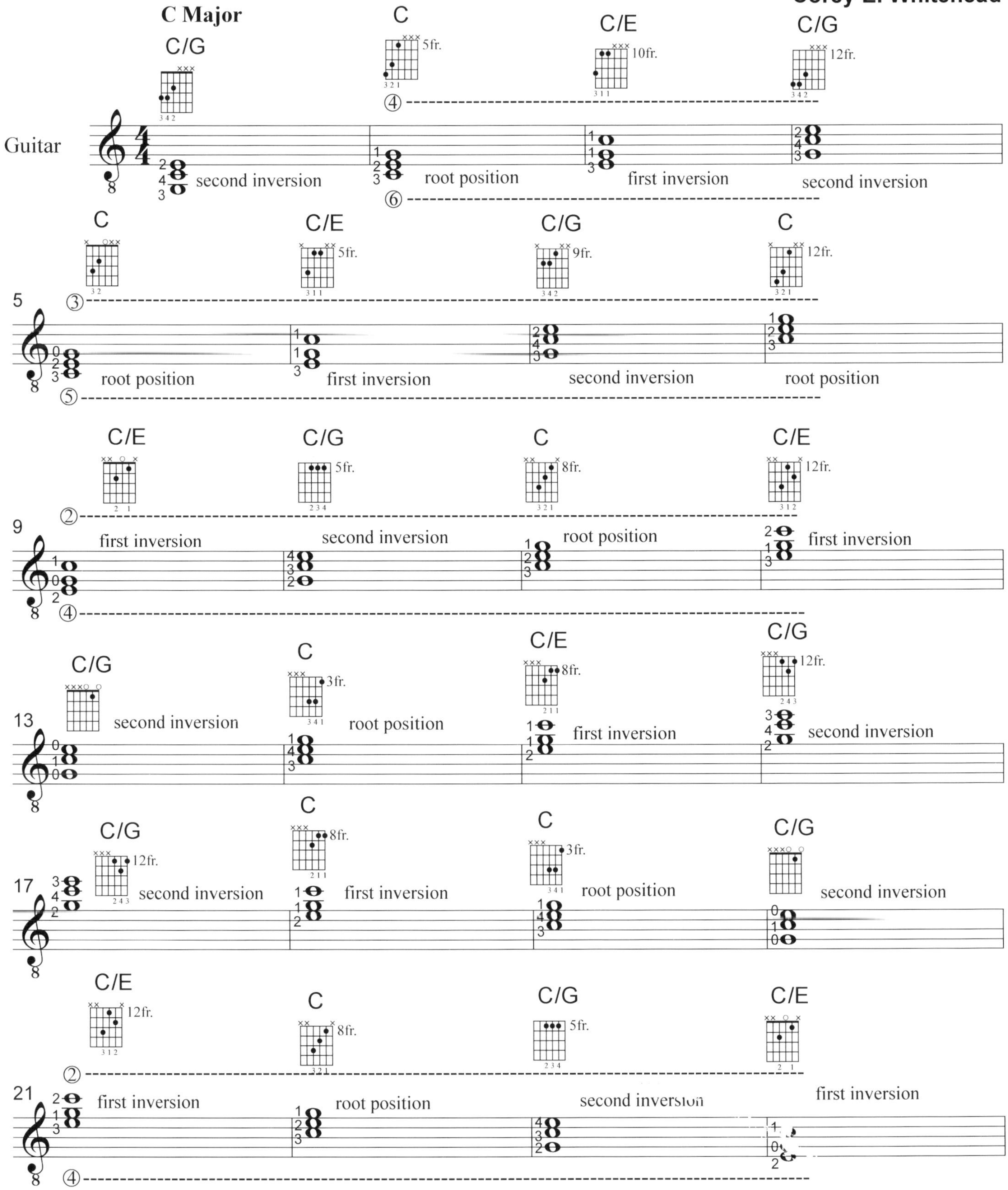

C Major

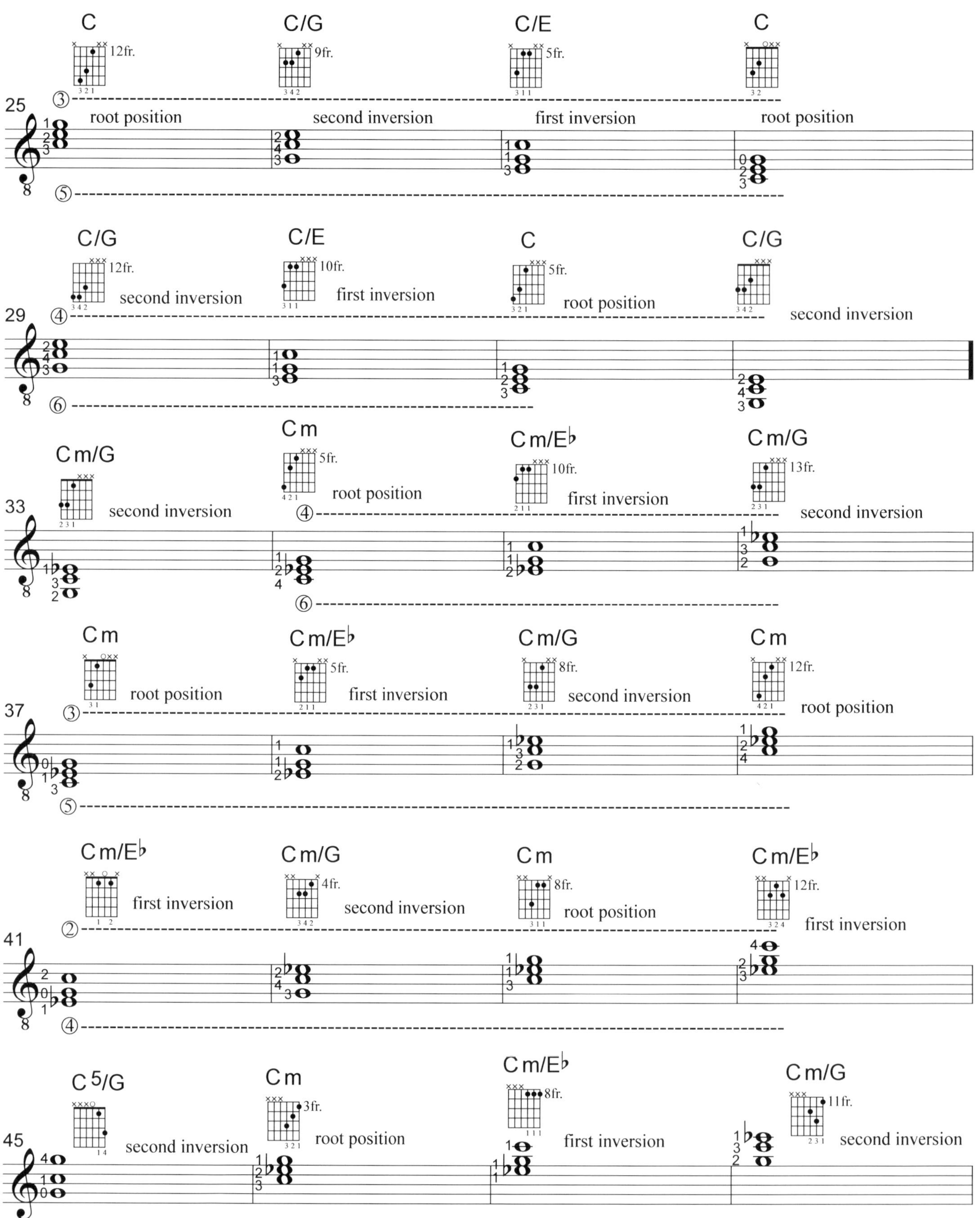
C
C/G
C/E
C
root position
second inversion
first inversion
root position
C/G
C/E
C
C/G
second inversion
first inversion
root position
second inversion
Cm/G
Cm
Cm/E♭
Cm/G
second inversion
root position
first inversion
second inversion
Cm
Cm/E♭
Cm/G
Cm
root position
first inversion
second inversion
root position
Cm/E♭
Cm/G
Cm
Cm/E♭
first inversion
second inversion
root position
first inversion
C5/G
Cm
Cm/E♭
Cm/G
second inversion
root position
first inversion
second inversion

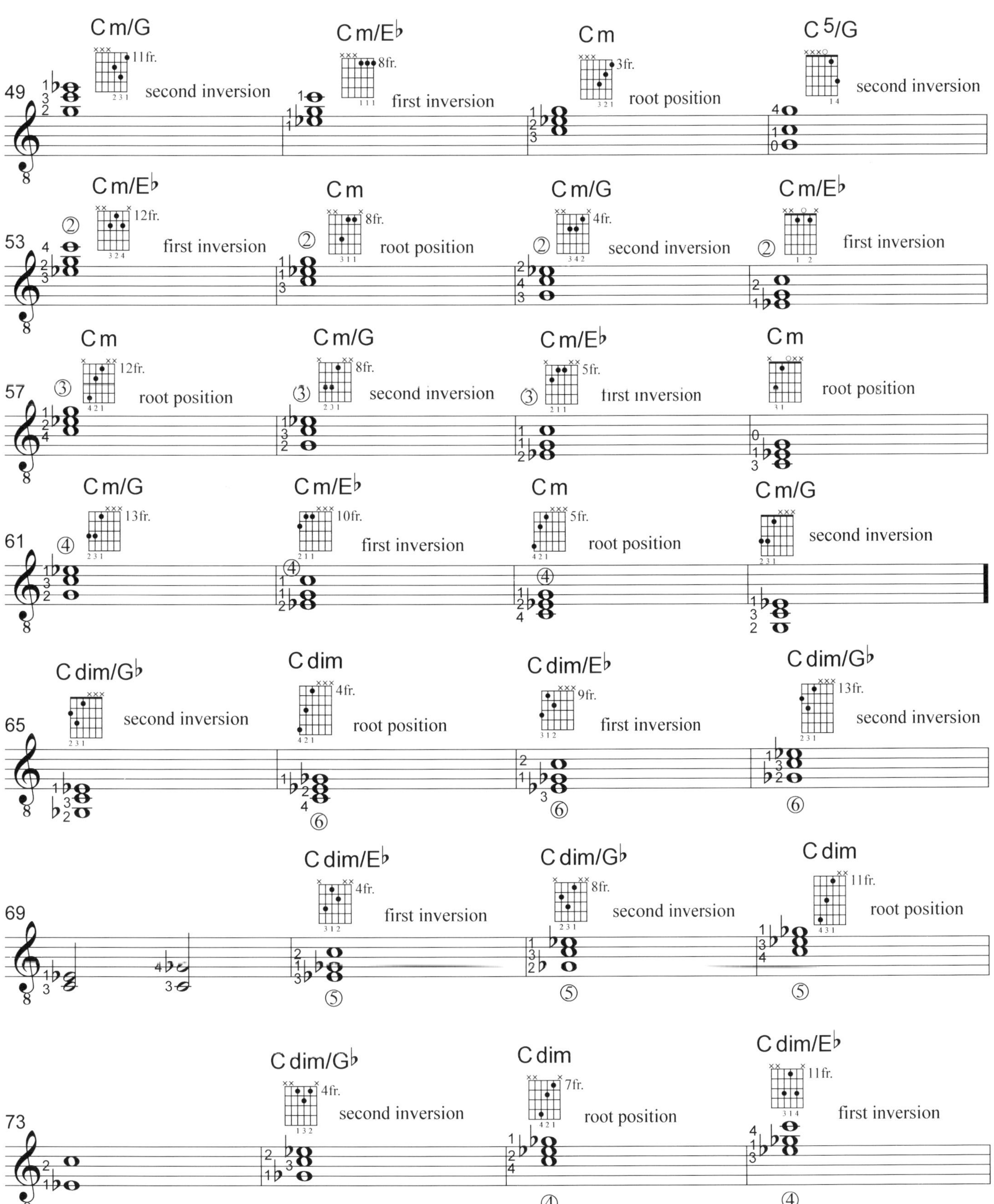
49
Cm/G
11fr.
second inversion
Cm/E♭
8fr.
first inversion
Cm
3fr.
root position
C5/G
second inversion
53
Cm/E♭
12fr.
first inversion
Cm
8fr.
root position
Cm/G
4fr.
second inversion
Cm/E♭
first inversion
57
Cm
12fr.
root position
Cm/G
8fr.
second inversion
Cm/E♭
5fr.
first inversion
Cm
root position
61
Cm/G
13fr.
Cm/E♭
10fr.
first inversion
Cm
5fr.
root position
Cm/G
second inversion
65
Cdim/G♭
second inversion
Cdim
4fr.
root position
Cdim/E♭
9fr.
first inversion
Cdim/G♭
13fr.
second inversion
69
Cdim/E♭
4fr.
first inversion
Cdim/G♭
8fr.
second inversion
Cdim
11fr.
root position
73
Cdim/G♭
4fr.
second inversion
Cdim
7fr.
root position
Cdim/E♭
11fr.
first inversion

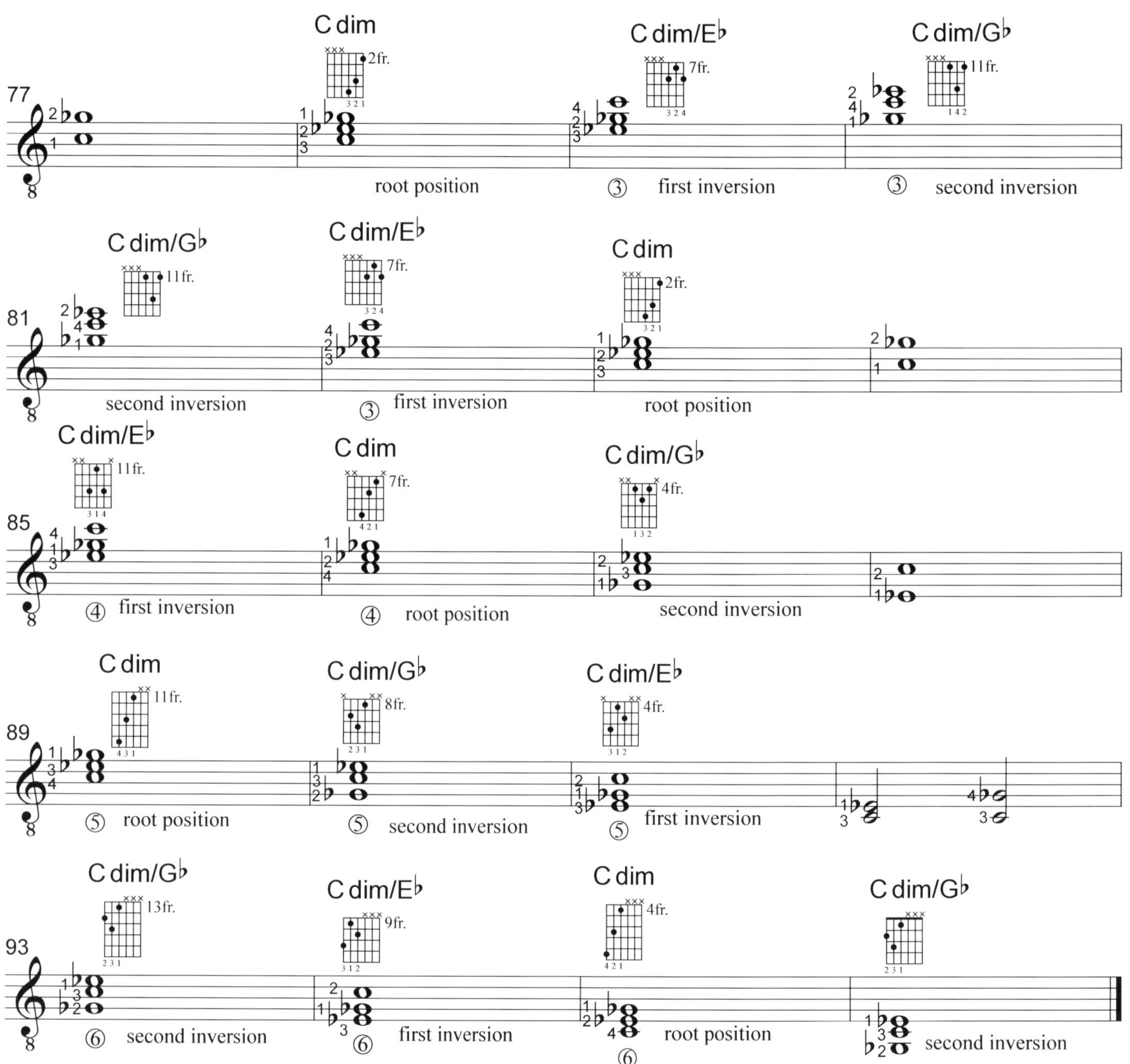

77
C dim
2fr.
root position
C dim/E♭
7fr.
③ first inversion
C dim/G♭
11fr.
③ second inversion
81
C dim/G♭
11fr.
second inversion
C dim/E♭
7fr.
③ first inversion
C dim
2fr.
root position
85
C dim/E♭
11fr.
④ first inversion
C dim
7fr.
④ root position
C dim/G♭
4fr.
second inversion
89
C dim
11fr.
⑤ root position
C dim/G♭
8fr.
⑤ second inversion
C dim/E♭
4fr.
⑤ first inversion
93
C dim/G♭
13fr.
⑥ second inversion
C dim/E♭
9fr.
⑥ first inversion
C dim
4fr.
root position
⑥
C dim/G♭
second inversion

The CAGED System (Scales and Chords)

The so-called "C-A-G-E-D System" refers to the transposition of the major chord shapes— C, A, G, E, and D— to any position on the fretboard by moving all of the pitches (notes) up an equal number of frets. That way you can play a C Major (C) chord in the open position with the C shape, at the third fret (third position) with the A shape, at the fifth position with the G-shape, at the eighth position with the E shape, or at the tenth position with the D shape.

In the following examples, the C Major chord is transposed as described above. The F Major and G Major chords are included to create I-IV and V chords in five different positions. Each of these five positions has an associated diatonic scale on the white keys of the piano—CDEFGABC.

1) Memorize the five open chord shapes and then transpose them to the five positions.
   Remember that the G shape is best used as a four-string chord when transposed; either the highest or lowest four strings make a useable chord in higher positions. It is possible, however, to transpose the entire G chord shape, depending on one's hand size and the scale length of the guitar.
2) Learn the C shape in five positions.
3) Learn the F shape and G shape in five positions.
4) Focus on the left-hand fingers creating the shape of the chord and landing at once.
5) Practice changing chords: C-F, F-C, C-G, G-C, etc.
6) Practice songs that use I-IV-V (C-F-G) chords in any order.
7) Practice the scale that goes with each chord.
8) Record yourself strumming or fingerpicking a chord for 60 seconds. Play it back and improvise over your recording using the scale for that position.
9) Repeat this exercise using a chord progression, i.e., more than one chord.
10) Repeat this routine in each of the five positions.

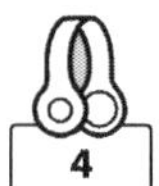

The C-A-G-E-D System

Corey E. Whitehead

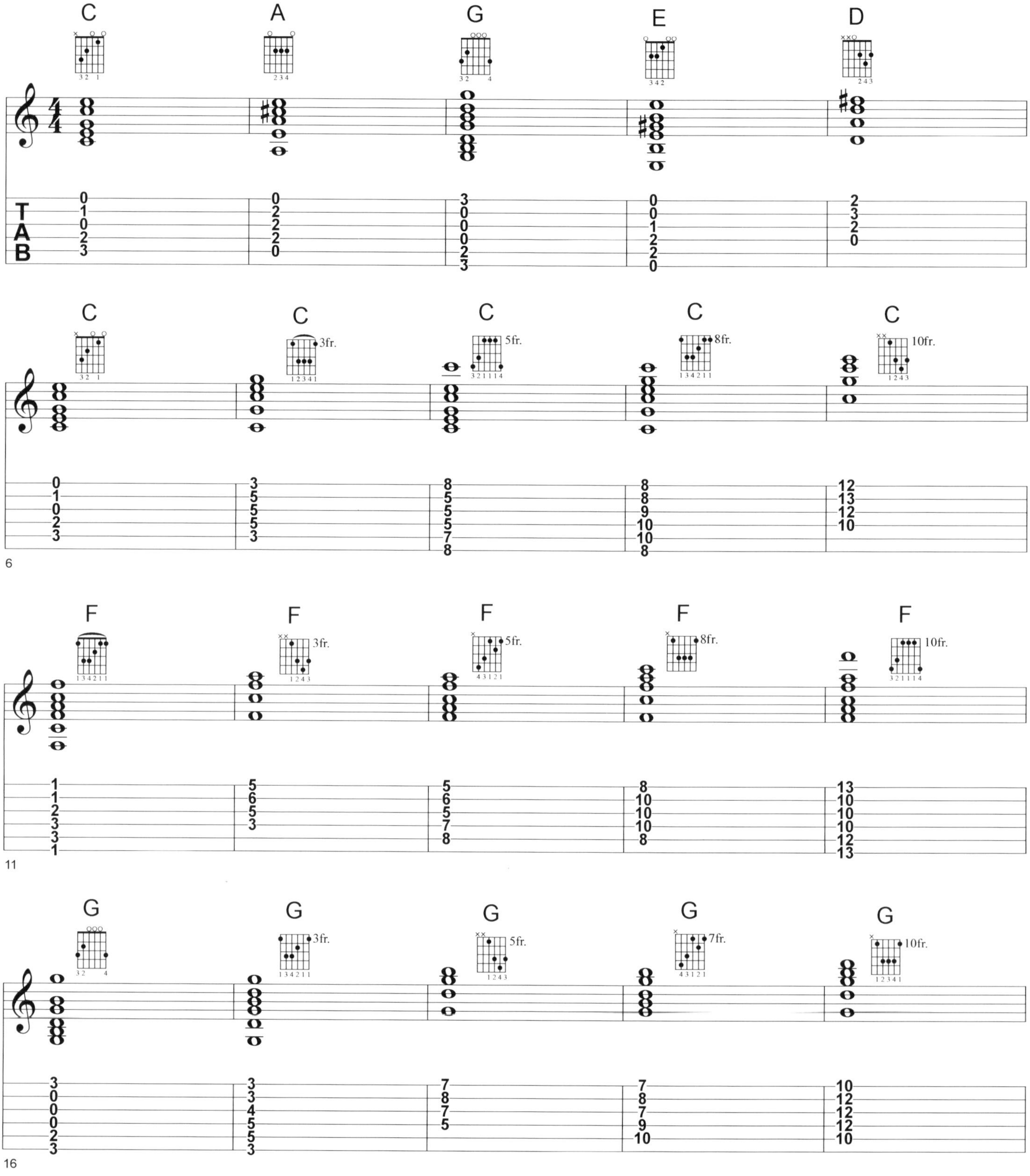

C A G E D

C C C C C

F F F F F

G G G G G

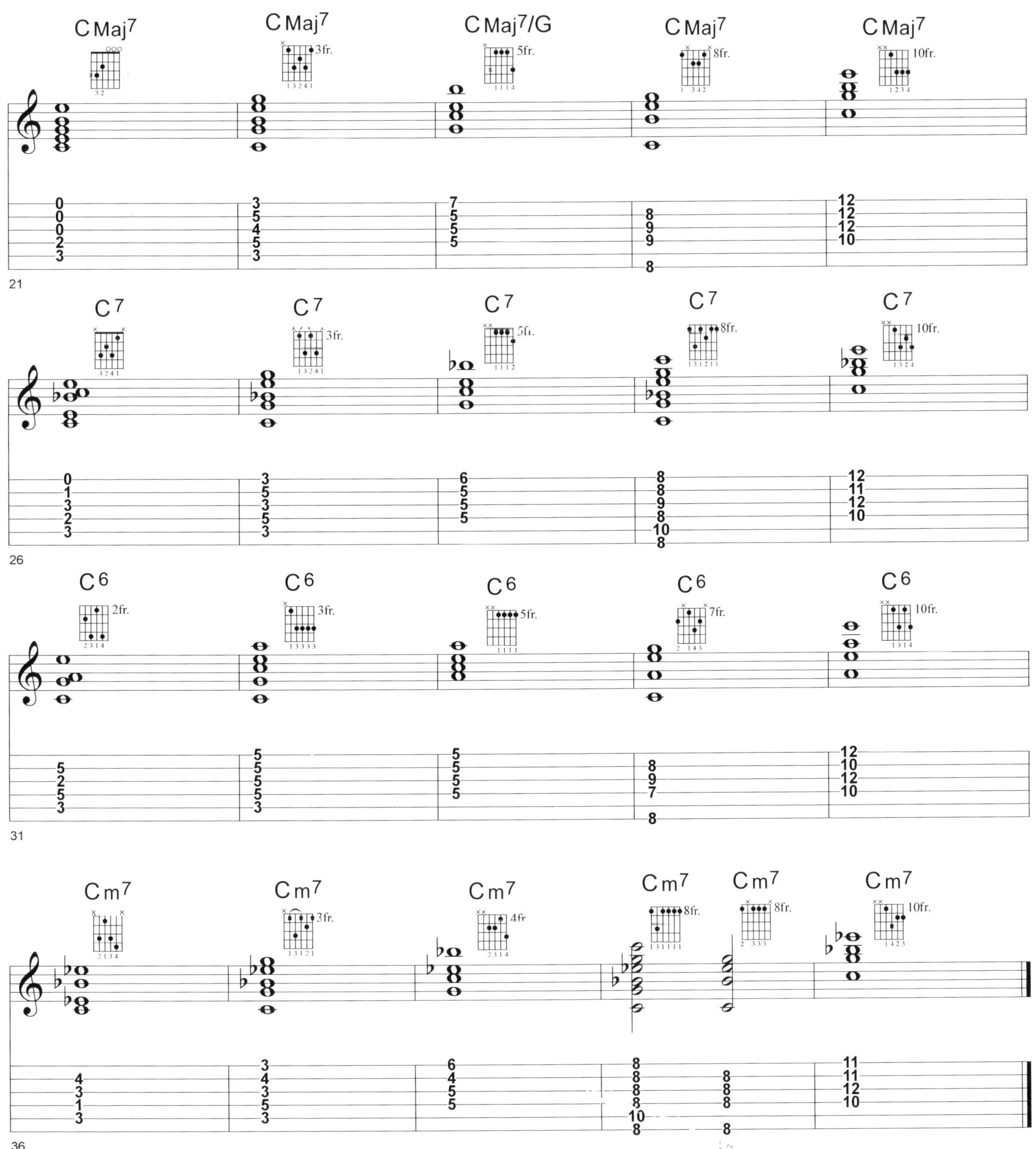
C Maj7
C Maj7
C Maj7/G
C Maj7
C Maj7
21
C 7
C 7
C 7
C 7
C 7
26
C 6
C 6
C 6
C 6
C 6
31
C m7
C m7
C m7
C m7
C m7
C m7
36

Diatonic Major and Minor Scales
Modified Segovia Patterns

Prior to the 20th century, the guitar was considered an instrument fit for parlors, churches and intimate recital halls; in the early 20th century, Andrés Segovia brought the guitar to larger concert halls where it became accepted as a serious instrument. Guitarist and musicologist, Rico Stover estimated that Segovia gave over 5,000 guitar concerts in his long career.

Segovia also expanded the repertoire of the instrument by commissioning works by non-guitarists such as Mario Castelnuovo-Tedesco, Manuel de Falla, Manuel María Ponce, Joaquín Rodrigo, Alexandre Tansman, Joaquín Turina, and many more. Segovia's efforts inspired his students— Christopher Parkening, John Williams, George Sakalleriou, and others—to further commission major works for the guitar. Other artists who came to prominence without Segovia's assistance—Julian Bream, The Assad Duo and David Russell—continued to expand the guitar repertoire with either their own transcriptions or original works.

Later in the 20th century, an exponential expansion of the classic guitar repertoire occurred due to the work of guitarist-composers who did not rely on autodidactic means of composition, but rather composed with informed craftsmanship garnered at universities and conservatories. Many of these composers, such as Sergio Assad, Dušan Bogdanović, Leo Brower, Roland Dyens, Benjamin Verdery, and Andrew York— to name a few— also perform or performed their own works. Classical composers have also been known to collaborate with flamenco artists to produce flamenco guitar concertos; such collaborators include Joaquin Rodrigo with Paco de Lucía, Manuel Barrueco with Manolo Sanlúcar, and Leo Brower with Vicente Amigo.

Published in the early 20th century, Segovia's "Diatonic Major and Minor Scales" became the standard way for classical guitarists to practice scales worldwide. *The Flamenco/Classical Guitar Tradition* uses some of Segovia's concepts but simplifies them, making the patterns easier to remember and play in any position.

The "C-A-G-E-D System" also has its own logic and usefulness for playing scales and improvising. It should be memorized and transposed to every position on the guitar fretboard. By learning three concepts—single-string scales, single-position scales, and multiple-position scales—you'll be able to play scales in 1.5 octaves, 2 octaves, and 3 octaves, all with relative ease.

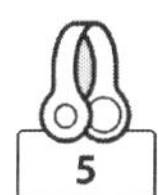

Diatonic Major and Minor Scales

Corey Whitehead

Major Scales in the Circle of Fifths

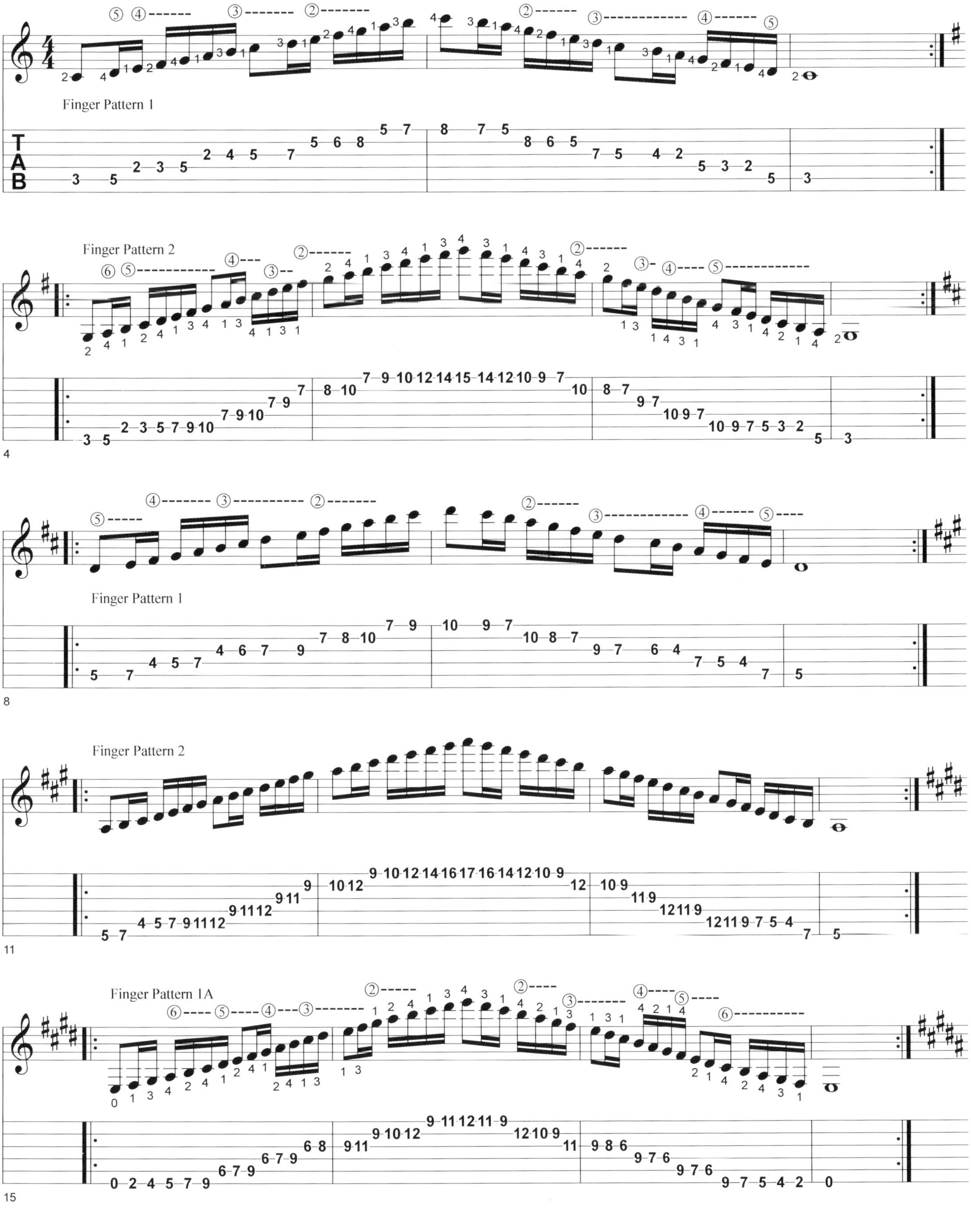

Finger Pattern 1

4 Finger Pattern 2

8 Finger Pattern 1

11 Finger Pattern 2

15 Finger Pattern 1A

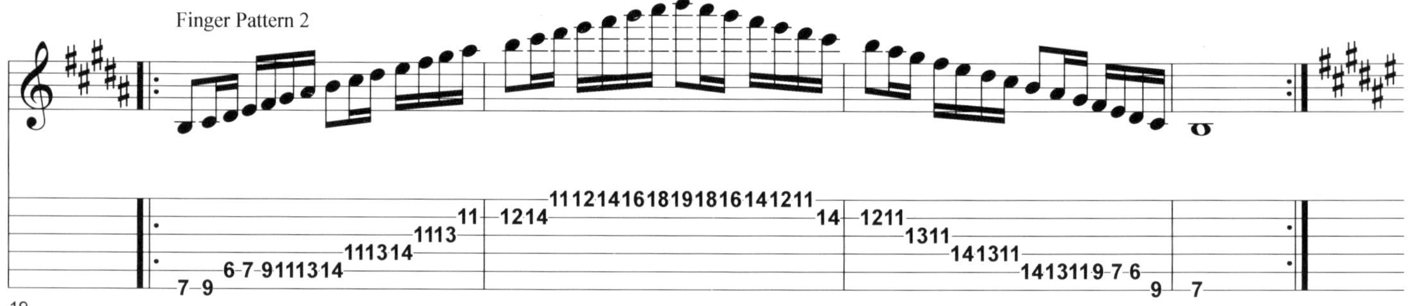
Finger Pattern 2
19

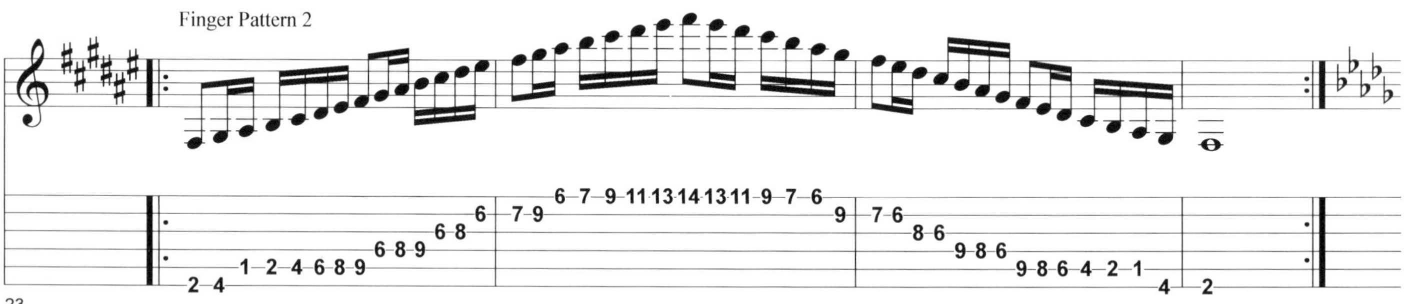
Finger Pattern 2
23

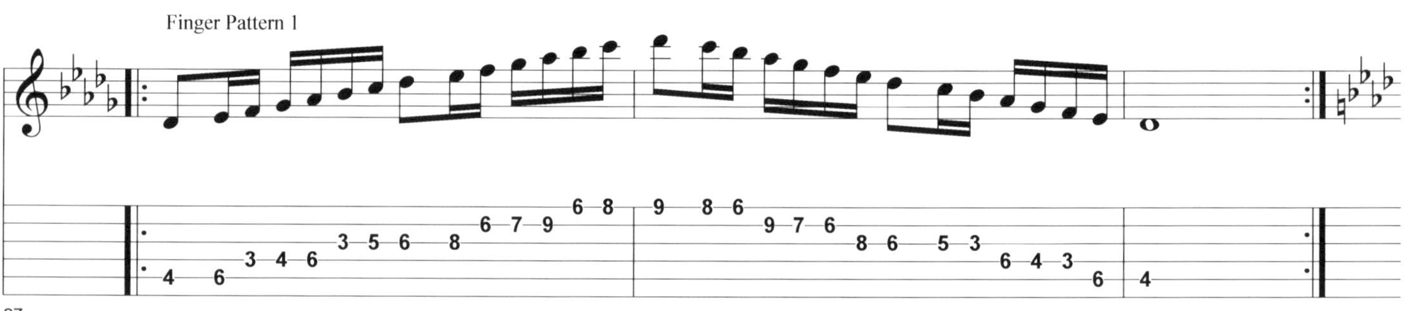
Finger Pattern 1
27

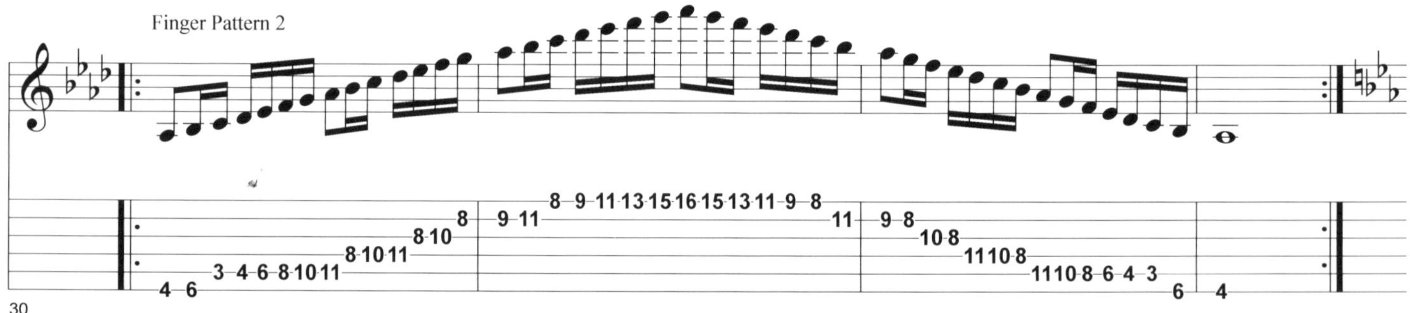
Finger Pattern 2
30

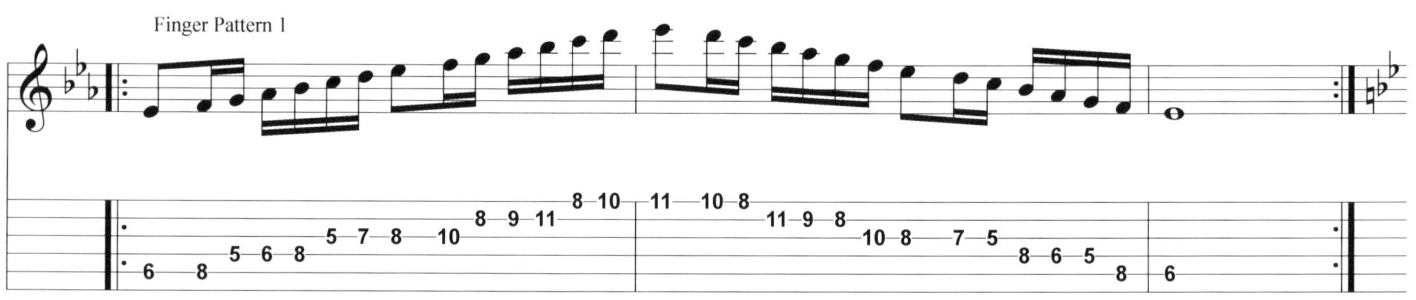
Finger Pattern 1
34

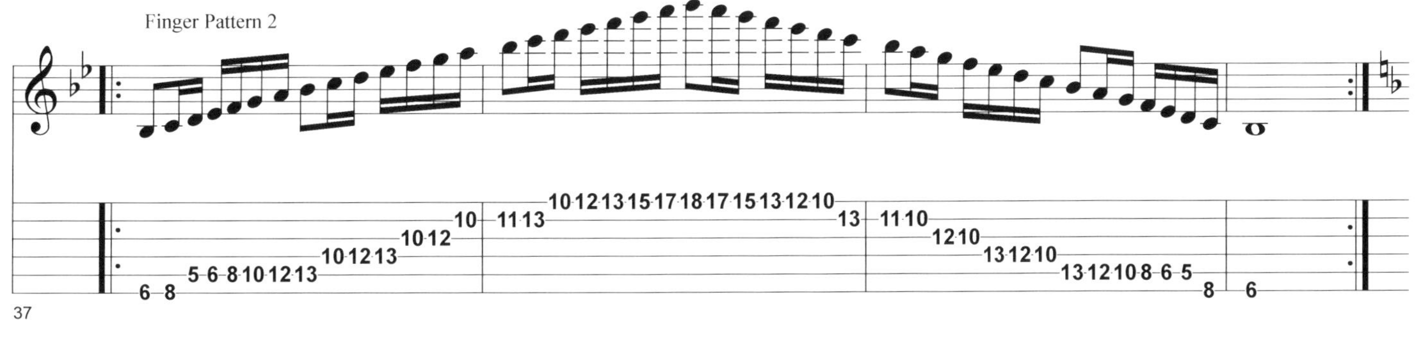

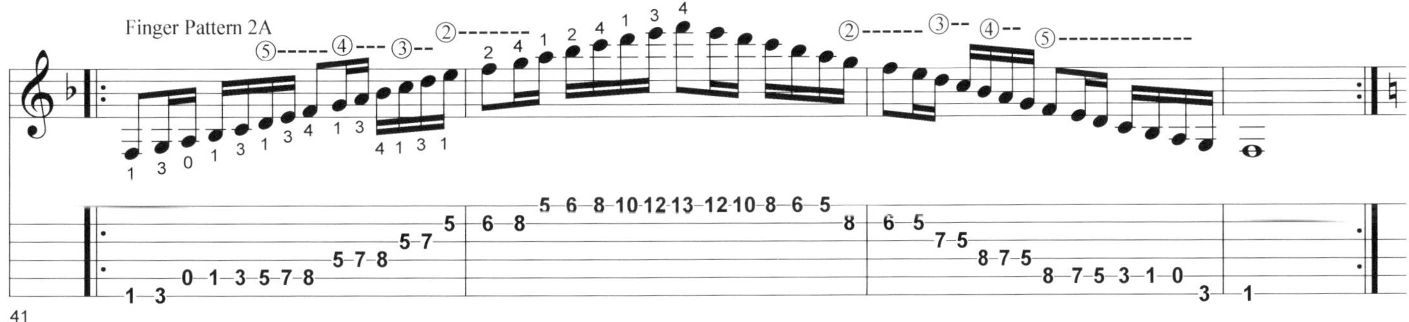

Minor Scales in the Circle of Fifths

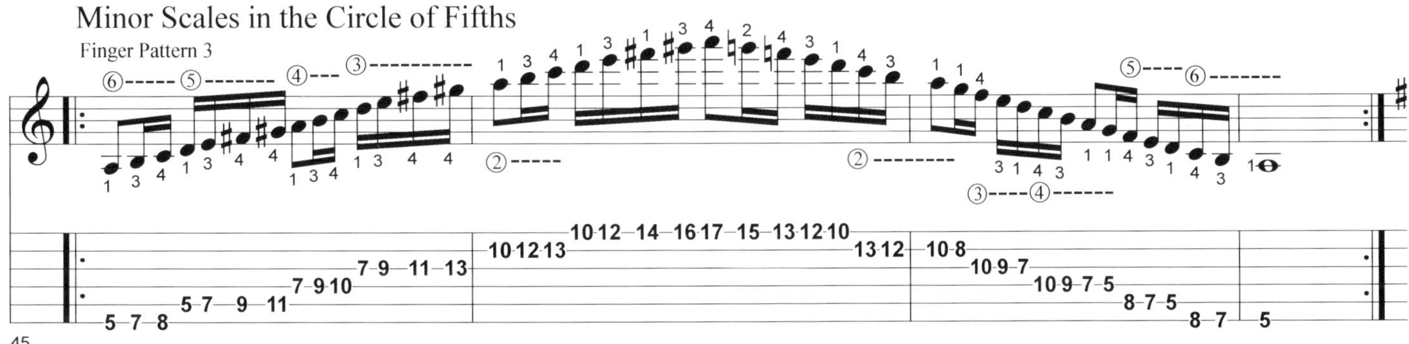

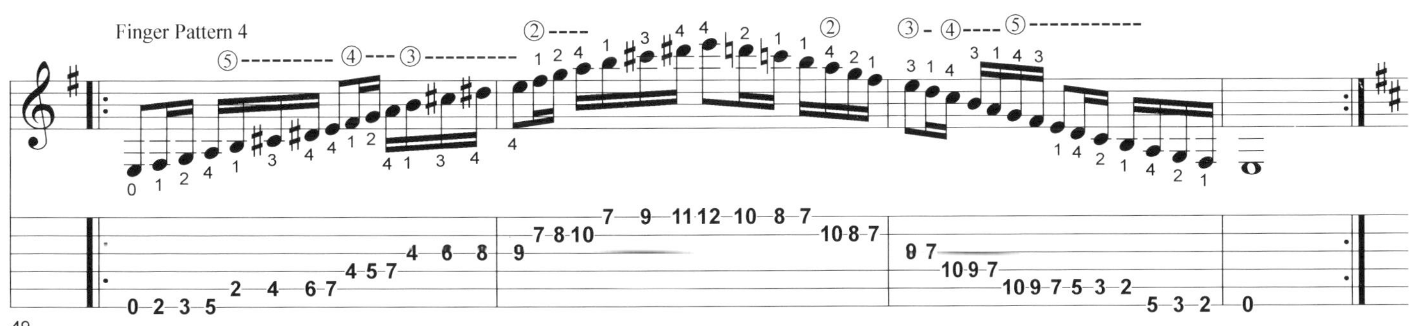

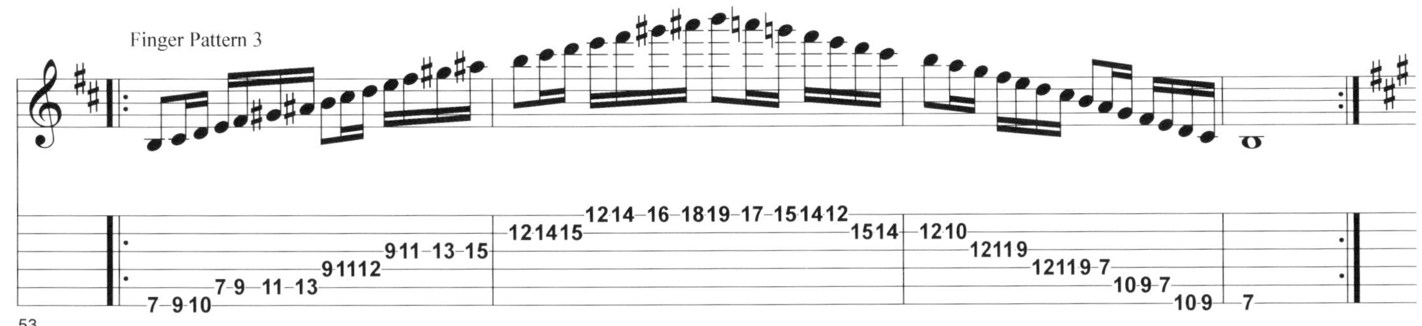

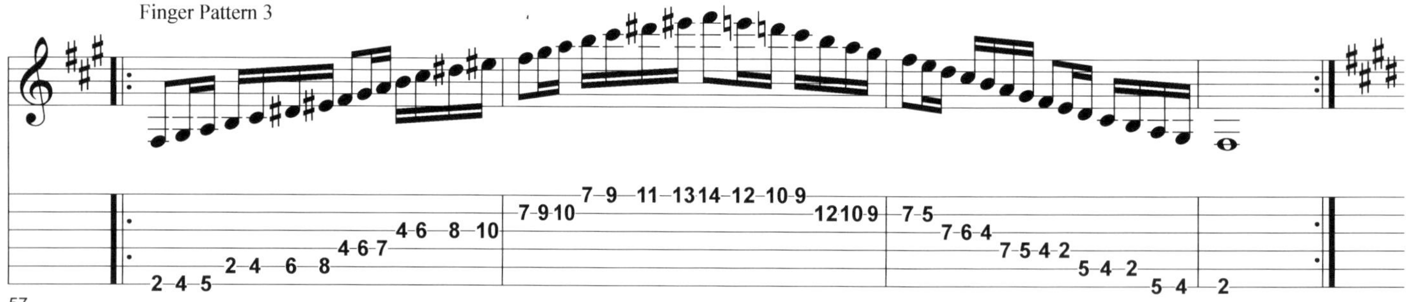
Finger Pattern 3
57

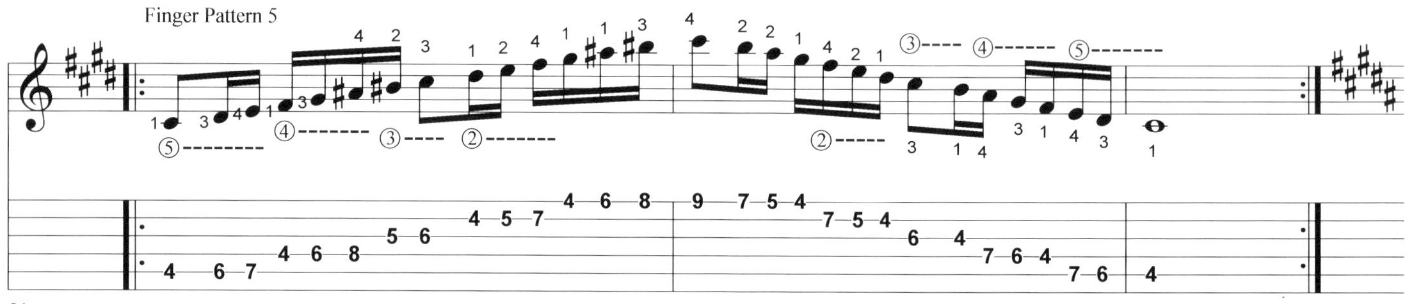
Finger Pattern 5
61

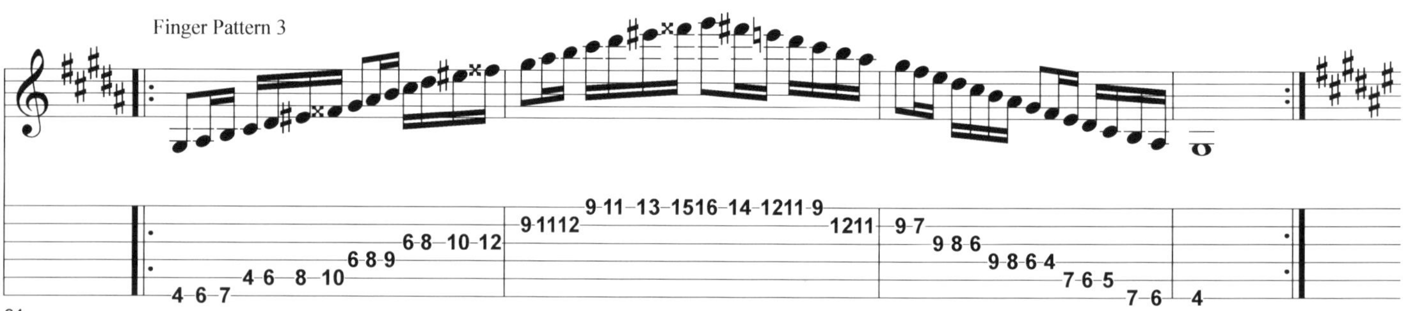
Finger Pattern 3
64

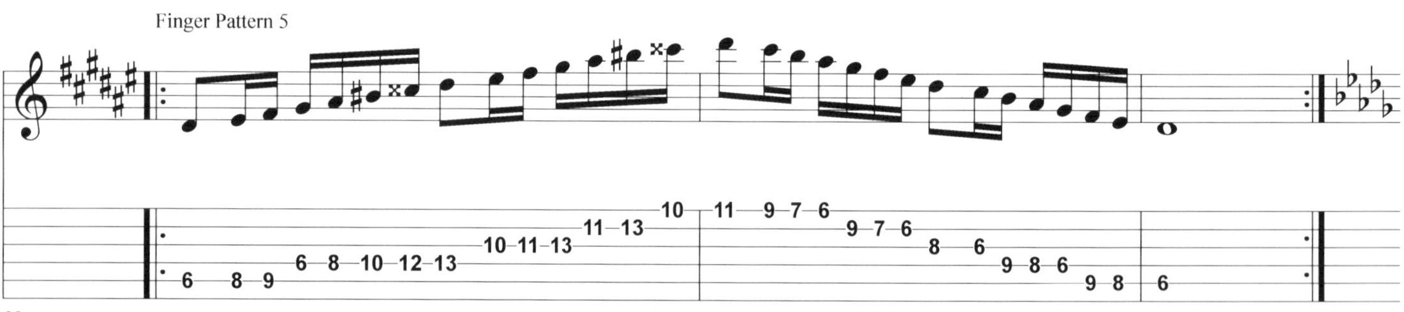
Finger Pattern 5
68

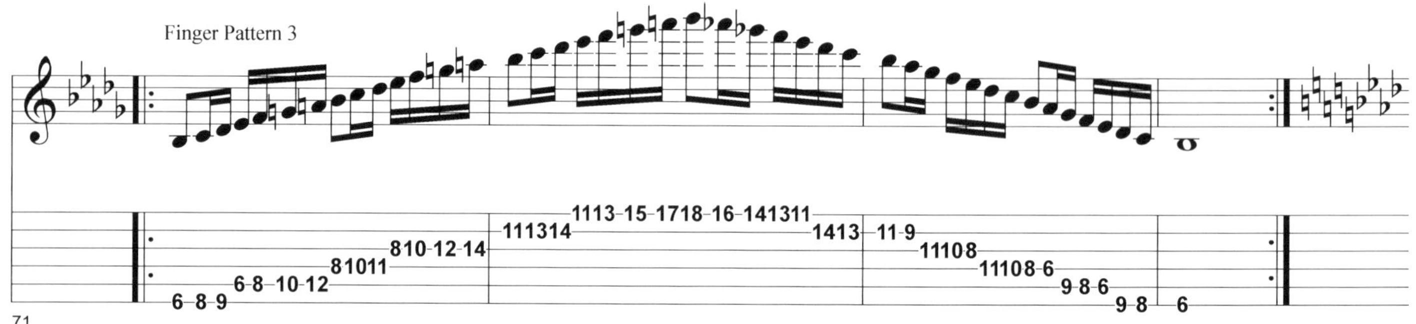
Finger Pattern 3
71

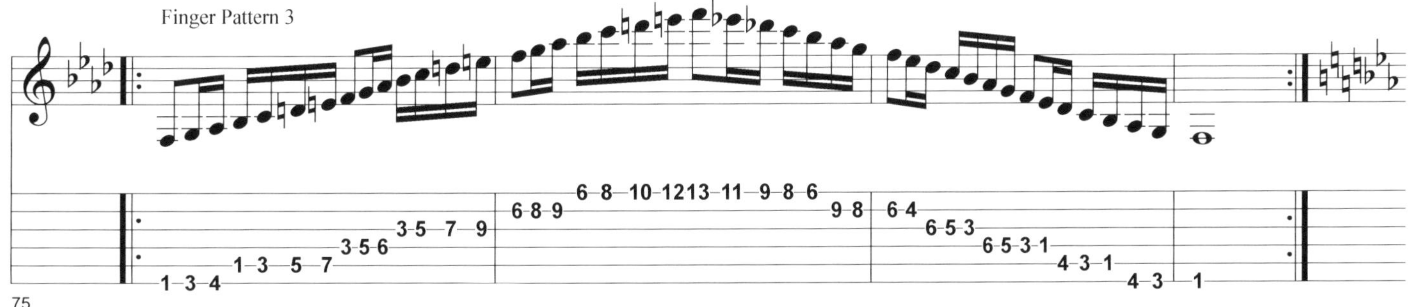
Finger Pattern 3
75

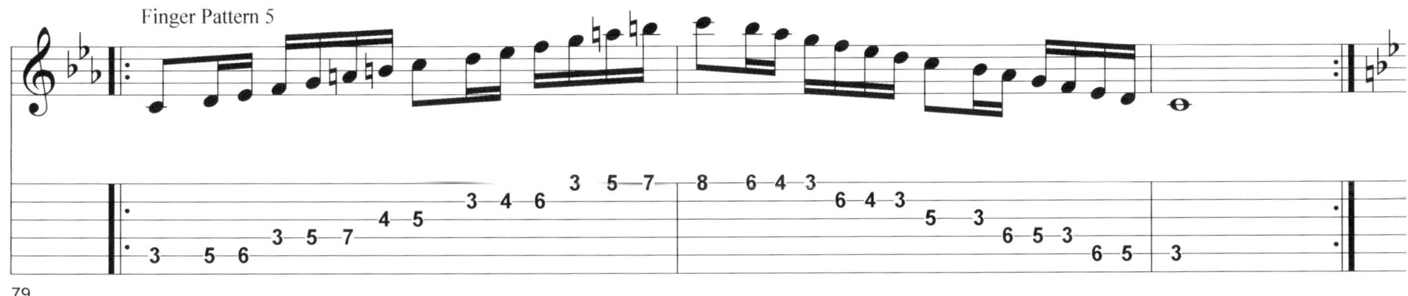
Finger Pattern 5
79

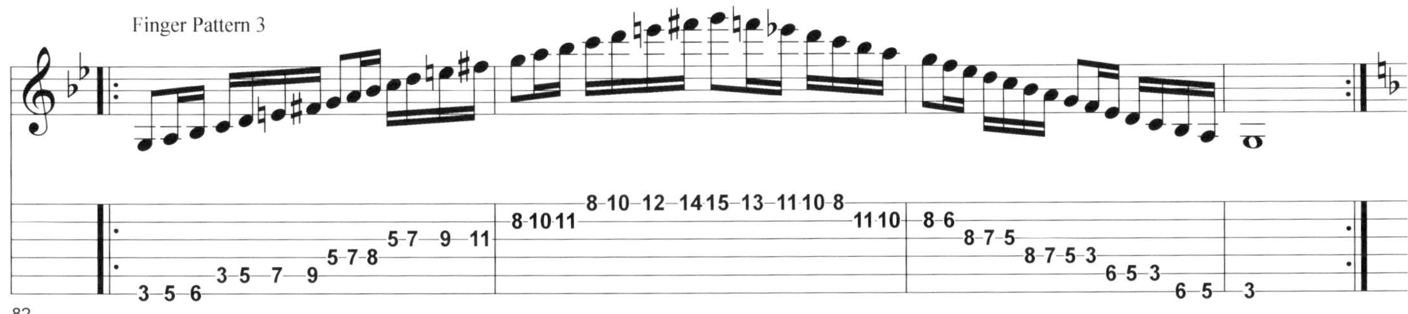
Finger Pattern 3
82

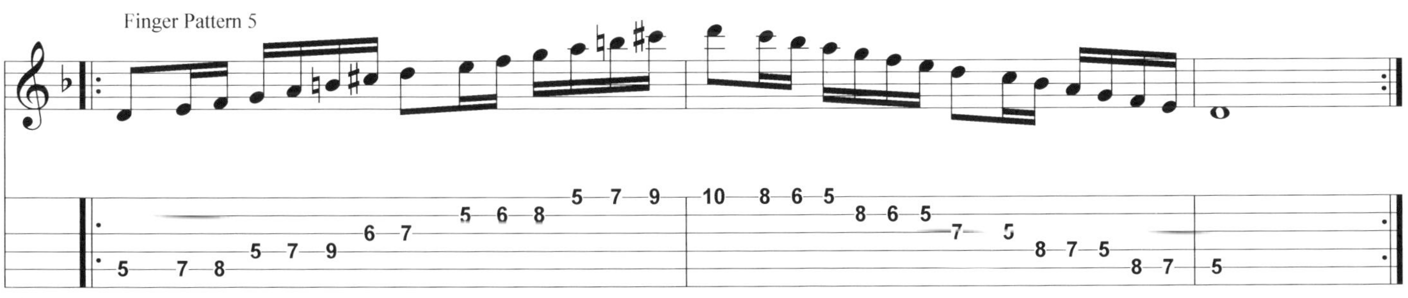
Finger Pattern 5
86

Scales and the CAGED System

Each of the CAGED system chord shapes lie in a "position" which relates to the lowest fret of that particular chord shape; zero (0) would be open position, and 3rd fret would be third position and so on.

Each of the five positions of the CAGED chord system also has a related scale pattern as shown in the following examples.

Memorize each of these scale patterns and transpose them to every fret, to produce each of the 12 major scales. You can play the open notes one fret higher for example, playing every note that was once open (0) at the first fret (1), and so on.

Practice transposing the scales up a perfect fourth (4th) or five semitones (half-steps), and then go up another fourth, and another, until you reach the starting note again: C, F, B♭, E♭, A♭, D♭, G♭/F♯, B, E, A, D, G, C.

Sometimes it's not possible to move up by an interval of a perfect 4th. In this case, transpose down by a perfect 5th. For example, C **up** to F is a perfect 4th, and C **down** to F is a perfect 5th. Notice that the numeric sum of the inverted intervals is always 9. When inserted, perfect intervals remain perfect. Minor intervals become major and vice versa, and diminished intervals become augmented and vice versa.

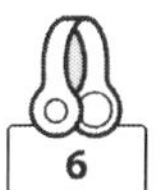

Scales and the CAGED System

Corey E. Whitehead

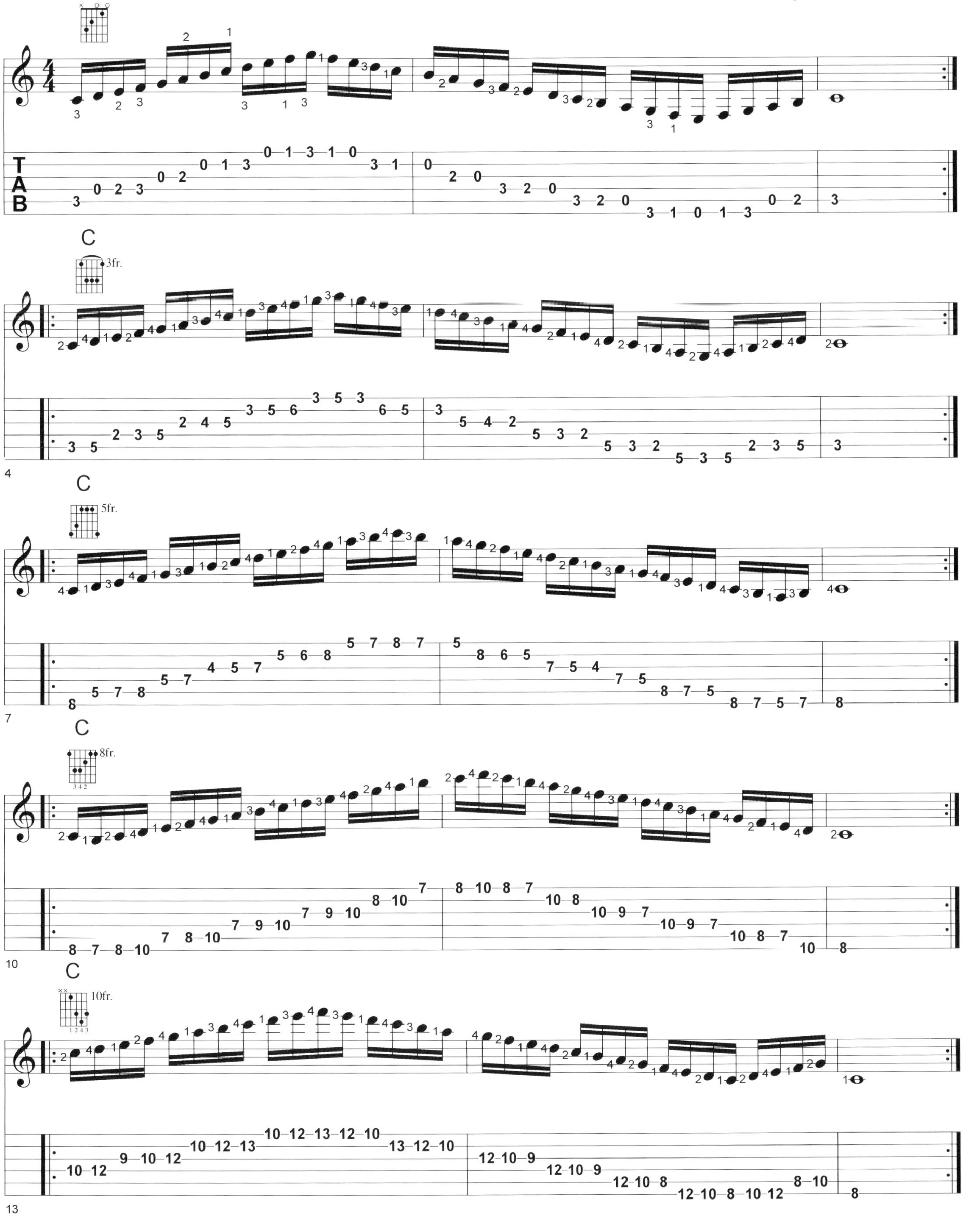

C

C
3fr.

4
C
5fr.

7
C
8fr.

10
C
10fr.

13

CAGED System Modes and Pentatonic Scales

The major (**Ionian**) scale (CDEFGABC) and the natural minor (**Aeolian**) scale (ABCDEFGA) share the same seven notes. Each has a modal name that was created and used by Roman music theorists—up to around 700 A.D.—as well as by teachers and performers. The terms "major" and "minor" being used in reference to scales came about after 1600 and were used by theorists such as Jean-Phillip Rameau who codified the common practices of secular composers of the then new musical genre called **opera**, and those found in the music of Johann Sebastian Bach.

Prior to 1600, scales were referred to by their modal names. **Dorian** (DEFGABCD), **Phrygian** (EFGABCDE), **Lydian** (FGABCDEF), and **Mixolydian** (GABCDEFG) were the primary "Church" modes used for composing music which was primarily sacred, used in music of the Roman Catholic Church. The **Locrian** mode (BCDEFGAB) was not used by the church and was a construct of 20th century music theorists, composers, and jazz musicians. Secular i.e., non-sacred music was also composed using modal scales and accompaniment using chords on lute, vihuela, and guitar prior to 1600. The first publications of such guitar and vihuela music occurred in Spain in 1536 (Milan), 1538 (Narváez), and 1546 (Mudarra).

The Ionian or **major scale** is shown here in the open position and can be played in any of the five "CAGED" positions as shown in the previous example of "Scales and the CAGED System." The related modes: D Dorian, E Phrygian, F Lydian, G Mixolydian, A Aeolian, and B Locrian may also be played in each position just as the Major or Ionian scale. Triads are produced by playing the 1st, 3rd, and 5th notes of each mode.

Next to each mode is the corresponding pentatonic scale produced by elimination of two notes of the diatonic (seven tone) mode. **Eliminating the fourth and seventh tones of the "major modes" will produce the major pentatonic scale.** Major triads are produced by sounding the root, third and fifth of the following modes: Ionian (C-E-G), Lydian (F-A-C), and Mixolydian (G-B-D). **The "blue note" is represented by the lowered third or raised second scale tone and is added to the major pentatonic scale examples.**

Minor triads are produced by the following modes: Dorian (D-F-A), Phrygian (E-G-B), and Aeolian (A-C-E). **These "minor modes" produce a minor pentatonic scale by elimination of the 2nd and 6th tones of the scale. The "blue note" is represented by the lowered fifth or raised fourth scale tone and is added to the minor pentatonic scale example.**

The diminished triad (B-D-F) is produced by the Locrian mode. **The elimination of the 2nd and 6th notes of the Locrian mode produces a minor pentatonic scale with a lowered fifth replacing the perfect fifth. Starting on the fourth note of this scale produces the Japanese mode called "Kumoi."**

The modal scale names we use today were defined by the Romans, who actually misunderstood the Greeks whom they copied, and incorrectly assigned the names we know today. The Greeks conceived the scales as **descending** in nature. The Greek scale from E to E is played in descending order as follows: EDCBAGFE and is called the Doric Scale.

Flamenco musicians refer to the E to E Phrygian scale as the **Greek Doric** scale, and also add two notes that are enharmonic, i.e., sharing the same pitch. The G-sharp (G♯) is used as an alternative to the G at the end of a phrase where the melody is accompanied by an E Major triad; this usually occurs in the fourth measure of a four-measure phrase, or where the melody or accompaniment resolve from A to G-sharp. When used melodically in the first three measures of a phrase, the same pitch is spelled as an A-flat (A♭) and resolves to G. As G♯ and A♭ are identical pitches named differently according to how they are used, they are said to be **enharmonic**.

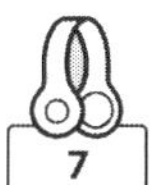

CAGED System Modes and Pentatonic Scales

C

Corey E. Whitehead

Omit 4, Omit 7, Add (♮2/♭3)

Ionian Mode (C Ionian/Major)

C Major pentatonic "blues" (add ♮2/♭3)

Dm

Omit 2, Omit 6, Add (♮4/♭5)

Dorian Mode ("D" Dorian)

D minor pentatonic "blues" (add ♮4/♭5)

Em

Omit 2, Omit 6, Add (♮4/♭5)

Phrygian Mode (E Phrygian)

E minor pentatonic "blues" (add ♮4/♭5)

E

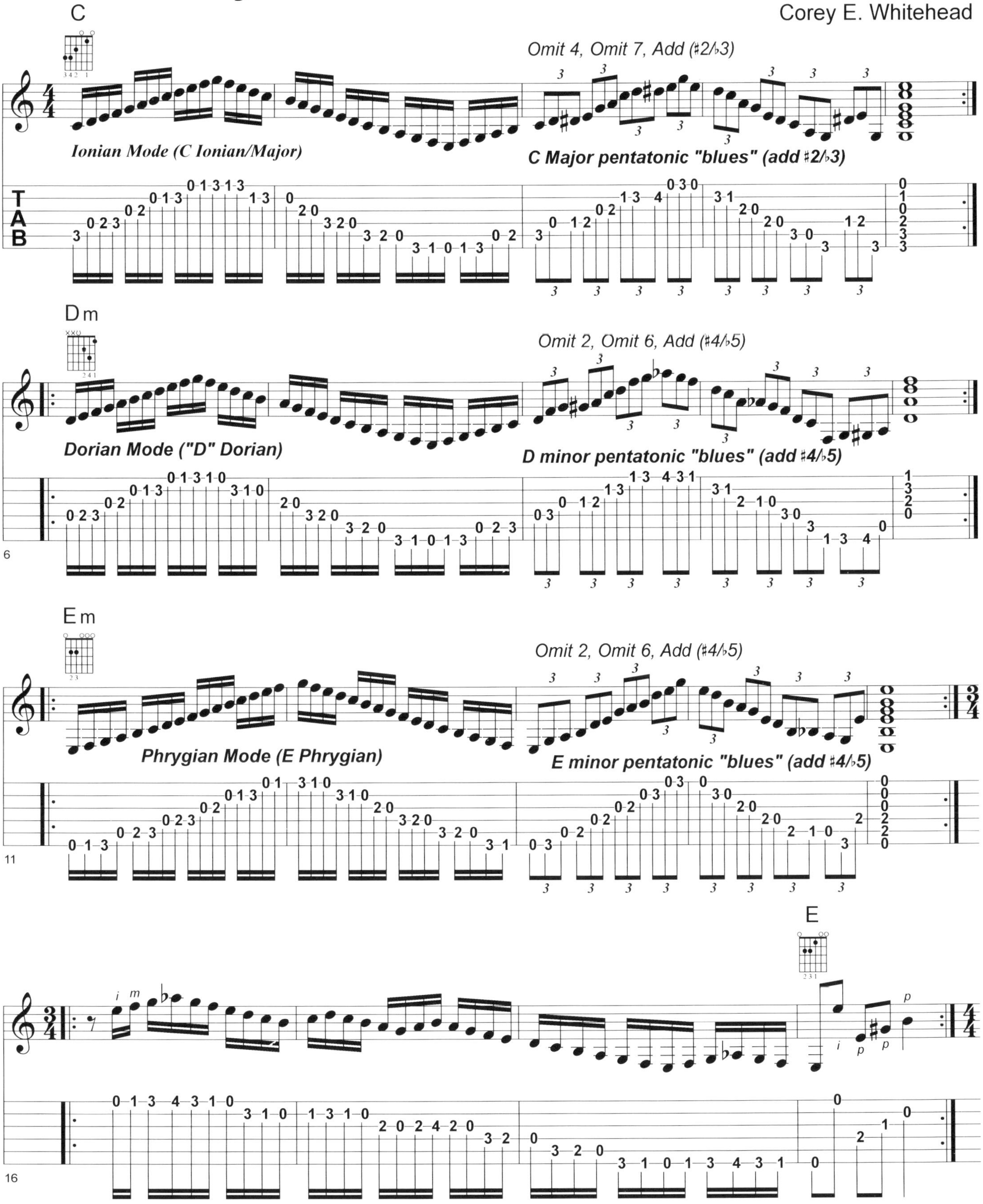

E Dorico Griego (add ♮4/♭3) "8-Tone Spanish" (E Phrygian add ♭4 on melody and ♮3 on harmony)

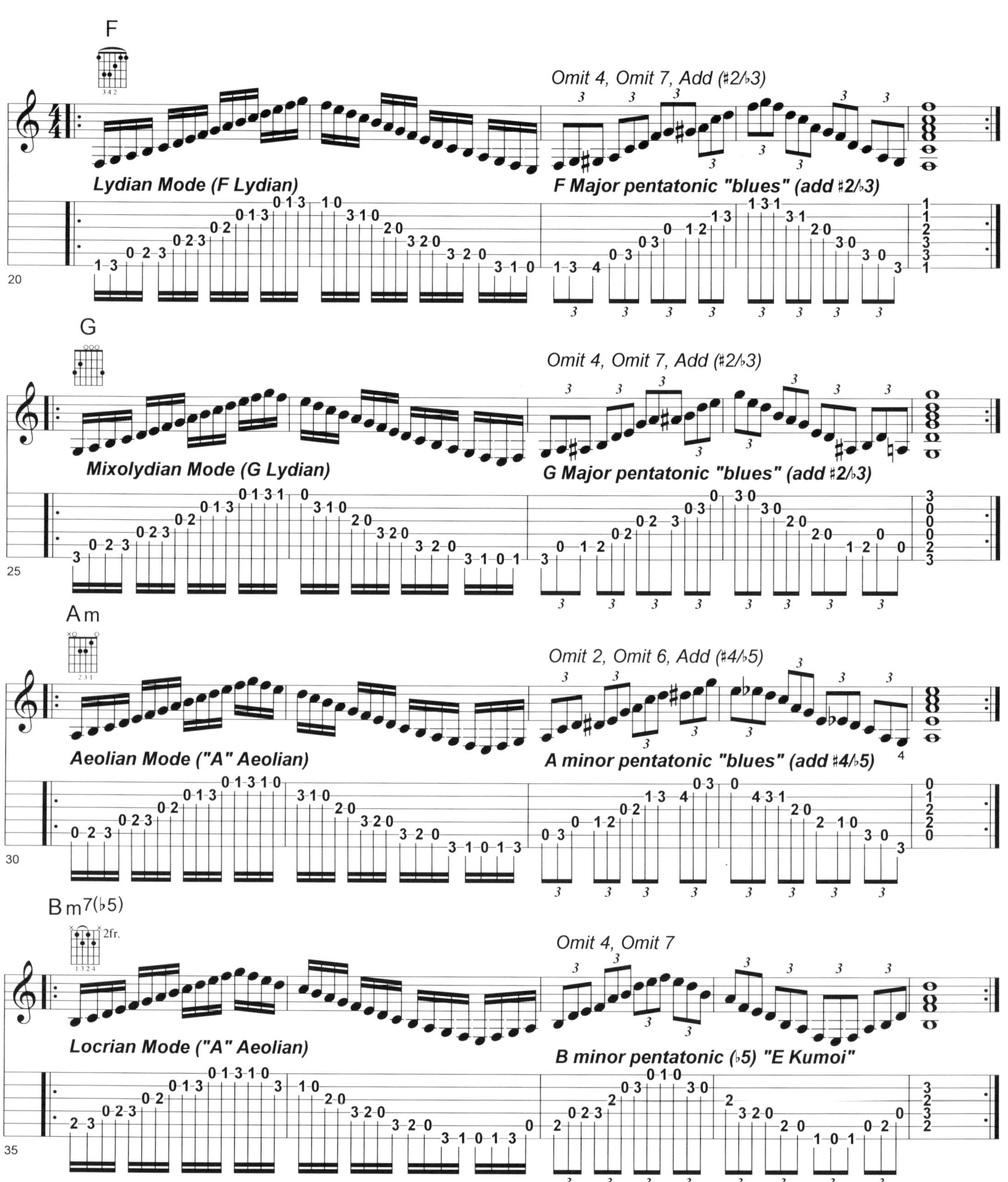

Homework: Find these seven modes and pentatonic scales in each of the five "CAGED" positions.
Omitting two notes from a seven-tone (diatonic) mode produces pentatonic scales.
Omit the 4th and 7th notes from the modes that produce major chords (Ionian, Lydian, and Mixolydian).
Omit the 2nd and 6th notes from remaining modes.

Seventh Chords with Inversions

The following examples illustrate the G major 7th chord (Gmaj7: G-B-D-F♯), and also the chords G7 (G-B-D-F), Gm7 (G-B♭-D-F), Gm7♭5 (G-B♭-D♭-F) and Gdim7 (G-B♭-D♭-F♭).

1) The G Major triad (G) consists of the pitches G-B-D. The seventh chord adds the seventh note above "G," which is "F-sharp" (F♯) or F-natural (F). The pitch "G" ascending to the pitch "F-sharp" creates an interval called a major seventh. The pitch "G" ascending to the pitch "F-natural" creates an interval called a minor seventh.

2) The major triad plus the major seventh above creates a "Major 7th" chord (G-B-D-F♯).

3) The minor triad plus the minor seventh above creates a "minor 7th" chord (G-B♭-D-F).

4) Lowering the seventh of a "Major 7th" (G-B-D-F♯) chord results in a dominant 7th or "7th" chord (G-B-D-F).

5) Lowering the third of a "7th" chord (G-B-D-F) results in a "minor 7th" chord (G-B♭-D-F).

6) Lowering the fifth of a "minor 7th" chord (G-B♭-D-F) result in a "min7♭5" or half-diminished chord (G-B♭-D♭-F)

7) Lowering the seventh of a "min7♭5" chord (G-B♭-D♭-F) results in a "fully diminished 7th" chord (G-B♭-D♭-F♭).

Each of the chords are shown in four positions, first using the 6th string for the lowest note of each chord "voicing" with the 2nd, 3rd and 4th strings. The four voicings are root position (G bass), first inversion (B bass), second inversion (D bass), and third inversion (F-sharp bass).

The next set of voicings uses the 5th string bass with the 2nd, 3rd and 4th strings.

The final set of voicings uses the 4th string bass with the 1st, 2nd, and 3rd strings.

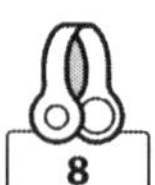

Seventh Chords with Inversions

Corey E. Whitehead

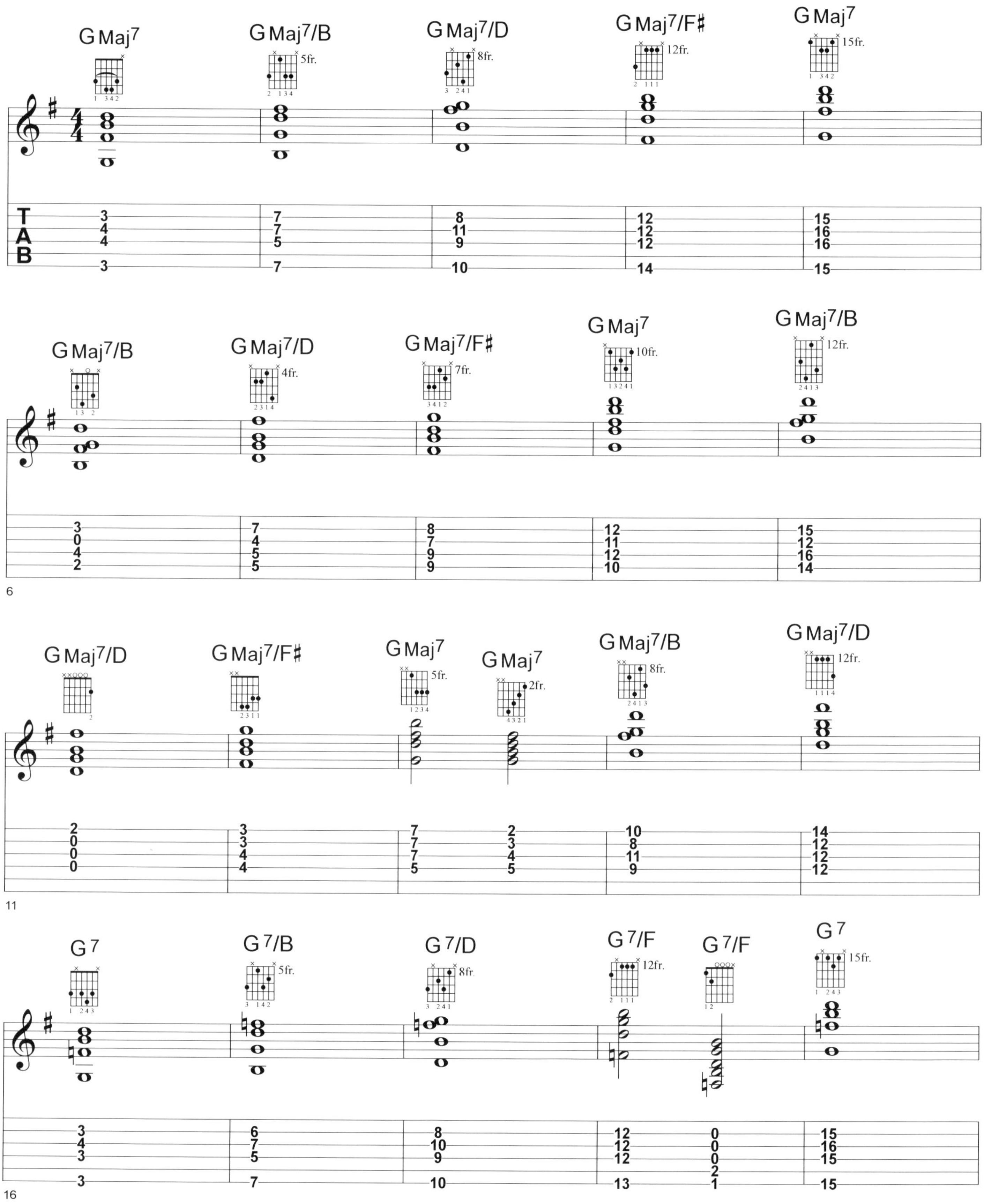

G Maj7 — G Maj7/B — G Maj7/D — G Maj7/F♯ — G Maj7

G Maj7/B — G Maj7/D — G Maj7/F♯ — G Maj7 — G Maj7/B

G Maj7/D — G Maj7/F♯ — G Maj7 — G Maj7 — G Maj7/B — G Maj7/D

G7 — G7/B — G7/D — G7/F — G7/F — G7

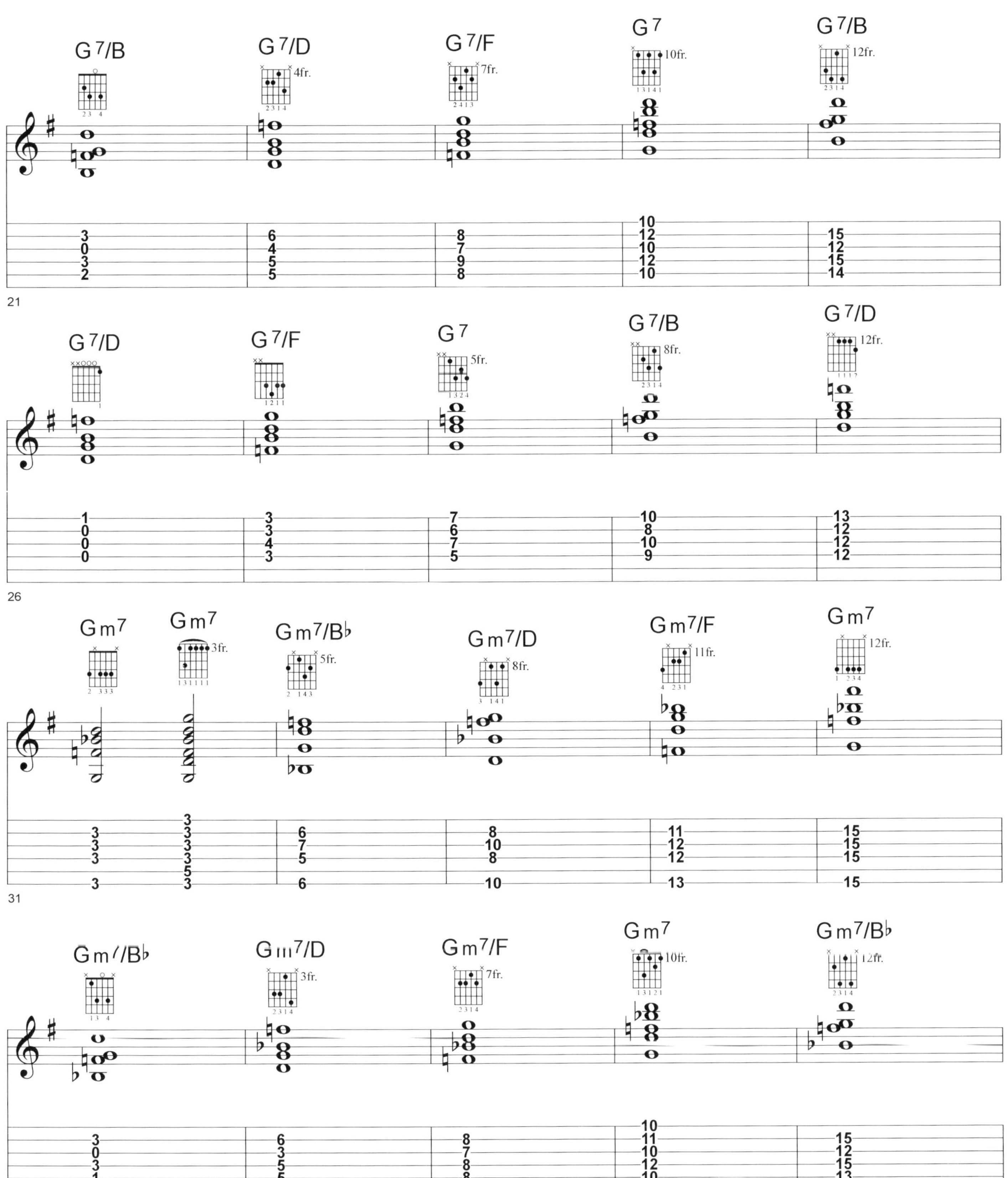
G7/B
G7/D
4fr.
G7/F
7fr.
G7
10fr.
G7/B
12fr.
21
G7/D
G7/F
G7
5fr.
G7/B
8fr.
G7/D
12fr.
26
Gm7
Gm7
3fr.
Gm7/B♭
5fr.
Gm7/D
8fr.
Gm7/F
11fr.
Gm7
12fr.
31
Gm7/B♭
Gm7/D
3fr.
Gm7/F
7fr.
Gm7
10fr.
Gm7/B♭
12fr.
36

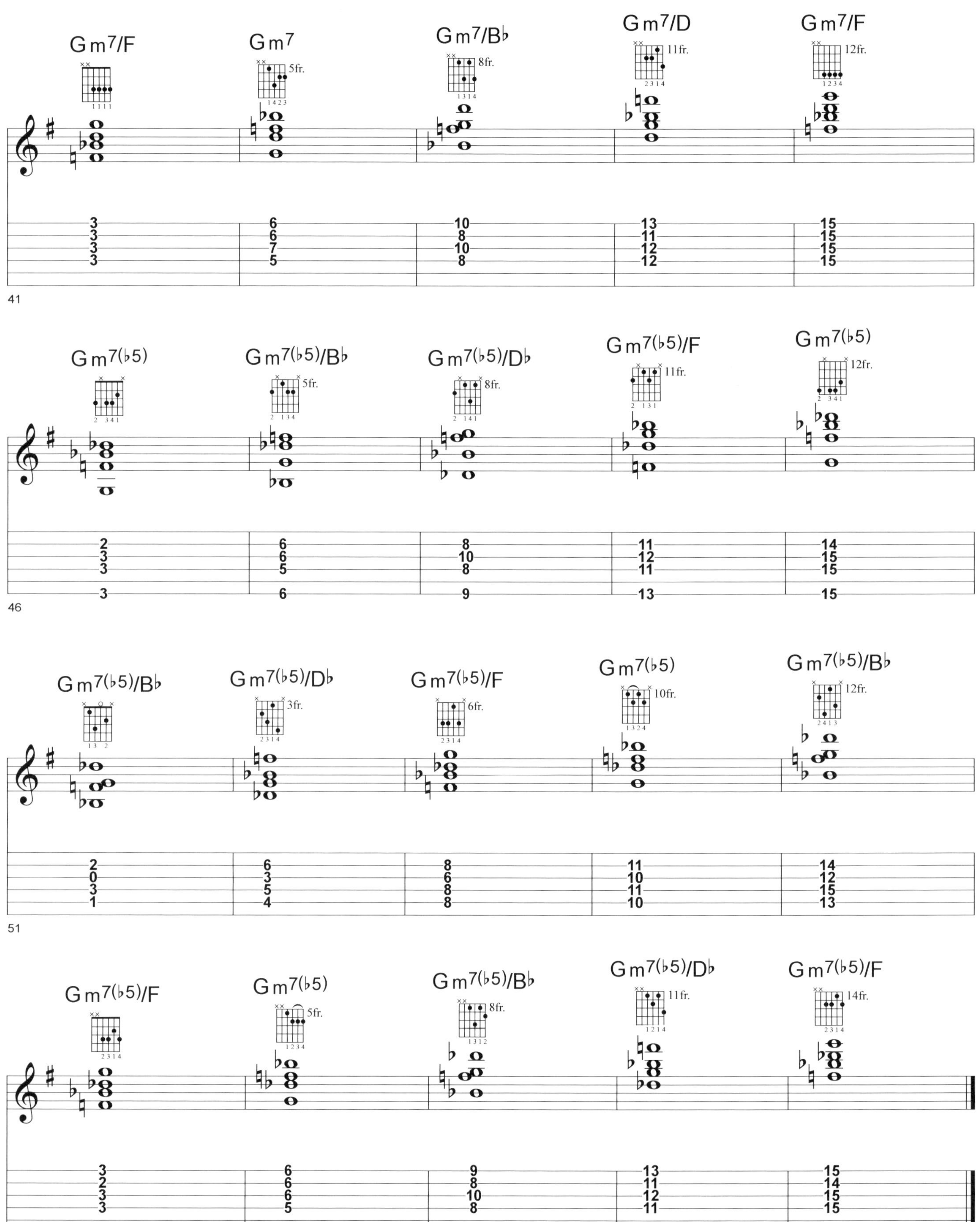
Gm7/F
Gm7
5fr.
Gm7/B♭
8fr.
Gm7/D
11fr.
Gm7/F
12fr.
41
Gm7(♭5)
Gm7(♭5)/B♭
5fr.
Gm7(♭5)/D♭
8fr.
Gm7(♭5)/F
11fr.
Gm7(♭5)
12fr.
46
Gm7(♭5)/B♭
Gm7(♭5)/D♭
3fr.
Gm7(♭5)/F
6fr.
Gm7(♭5)
10fr.
Gm7(♭5)/B♭
12fr.
51
Gm7(♭5)/F
Gm7(♭5)
5fr.
Gm7(♭5)/B♭
8fr.
Gm7(♭5)/D♭
11fr.
Gm7(♭5)/F
14fr.
56

Sixth Chords with Inversions

The following examples illustrate the spelling of seventh chords upon a different note of the chord. Using the same notes as the Gmaj7 chord, the Bm(♭6) chord is spelled (B-D-F♯-G), and in the same way, other chords are produced: G7 becomes Bdim(♭6) (B-D-F-G), Gm7 becomes B♭6 (B♭-D-F-G), and Gm7(♭5) becomes B♭m6 (B♭-D♭-F-G).

1) Gmaj7 (G-B-D-F♯) re-spelled as Bm(♭6): The B minor triad (Bm) consists of the pitches (B-D-F♯). The sixth chord adds the sixth note above "B," which is "G." The pitch "B" ascending to the pitch "G" creates an interval called a minor sixth. All of these elements are contained within the Gmaj7 chord (G-B-D-F♯) if we re-spell the chord as (B-D-F♯-G).

2) The pitch "B-flat" ascending to the pitch "G" creates an interval called a **major sixth**. The "6" refers to the major sixth interval and (♭6) refers to the minor sixth interval. The Arabic numerals that are a part of the chord names refer to the numeric positions of the scale tones as they relate to the major scale. For example, in the G Major scale, G is 1, A is 2, B is 3, C is 4, D is 5, E is 6, F-sharp (F♯) is 7, and the repetition of G an octave higher is 8. The A that follows would be 9, and so on. Any alterations to these notes by use of an accidental (sharp, flat, or natural) would affect the number accordingly. For example, an interval of G ascending to F-natural would be called a flat-7th (♭7). If one were to descend from G (downward in pitch) to F-sharp, the interval of seven letters becomes an interval of two letters. (Always count the starting note as number 1.)

3) The Major 7th inverts to a Minor 2nd, and the Minor 7th inverts to a Major 2nd.

4) Major intervals invert to minor intervals and vice versa. Augmented inverts to diminished and vice versa. Perfect inverts to Perfect.

5) Unison (1) inverts to Octave (8), Second (2) inverts to Seventh (7), Third (3) inverts to Sixth (6), Perfect Fourth (4) inverts to Perfect Fifth (5), Perfect Fifth (5) inverts to Perfect Fourth (4), Sixth (6) inverts to Third (3), Seventh (7) inverts to Second (2), and Octave (8) inverts to Unison (1). Again, note that the sum of the original interval number and the inverted interval number is always 9.

6) G7 (G-B-D-F) re-spelled as Bdim(♭6) (B-D-F-G): The diminished triad is contained within the 7th chord as the 3rd, 5th and 7th of the G7 chord are each a minor 3rd apart. The diminished triad consists of two minor thirds (B-D and D-F) or (B-D-F). The ascending interval B to G is a minor sixth consisting of nine semitones (half-steps). Assembling these four notes (B-D-F-G) together produces a Bdim(♭6) chord.

7) Gm7 (G-B♭-D-F) re-spelled as B♭6 (B♭-D-F-G): (B♭-D-F) is a major triad as the lower notes (B♭-D) are a major third apart and the upper notes (D-F) are a minor third apart. The notes B♭ to G form an ascending major 6th interval.

8) Gm7(♭5) re-spelled as B♭m6 (B♭-D♭-F-G): Lowering the third of the chord above, or re-spelling the Gm7(♭5) chord, the B♭m6 chord is produced.

Each of the chords are shown in four positions, first using the 6th string for the lowest note of each **chord voicing** with the 2nd, 3rd and 4th strings. The four voicings appear in root position (G bass), first inversion (B bass), second inversion (D bass), and third inversion (F-sharp bass).

The next set of voicings uses the 5th-string bass with the 2nd, 3rd and 4th strings.

The final set of voicings uses the 4th-string bass with the 1st, 2nd, and 3rd strings.

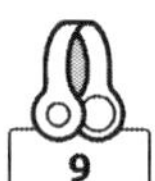

Sixth Chords with Inversions

Corey E. Whitehead

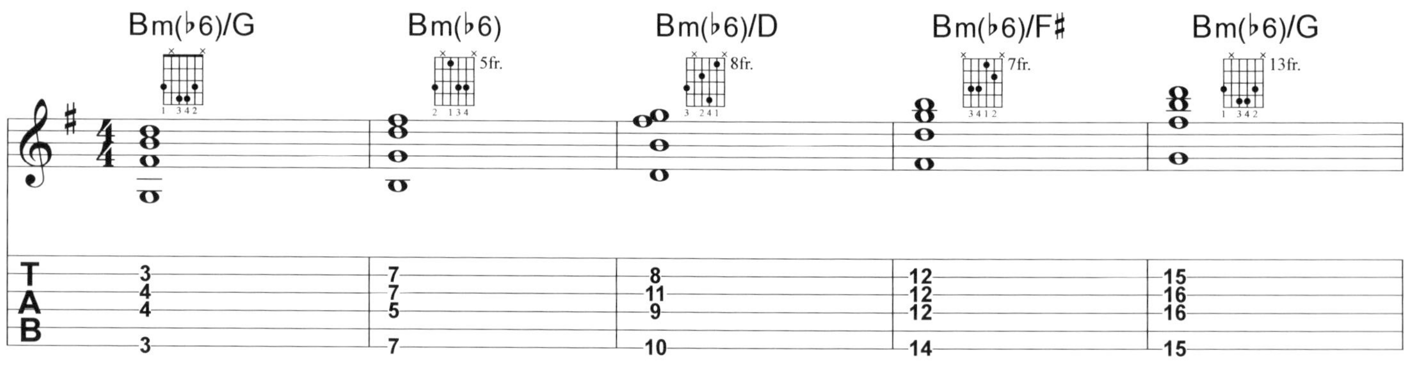

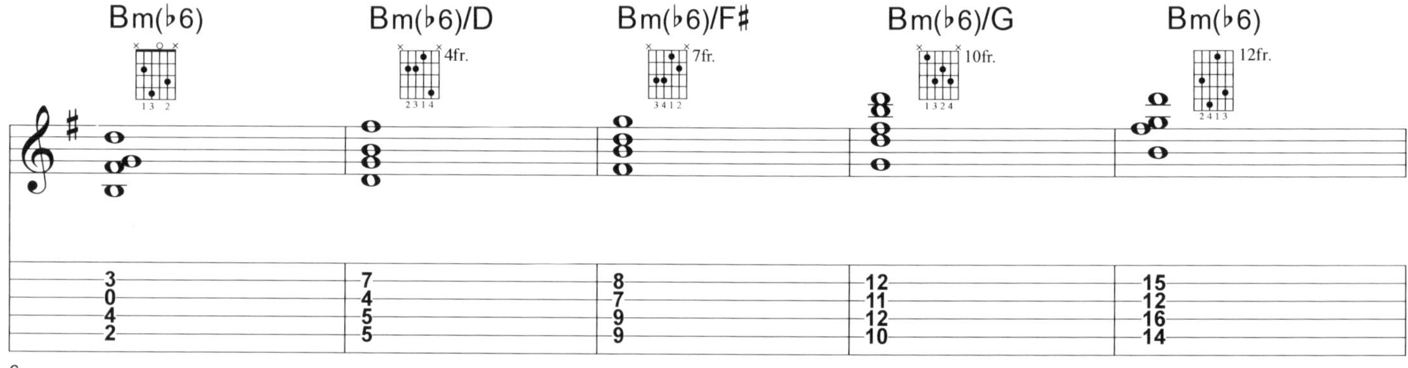

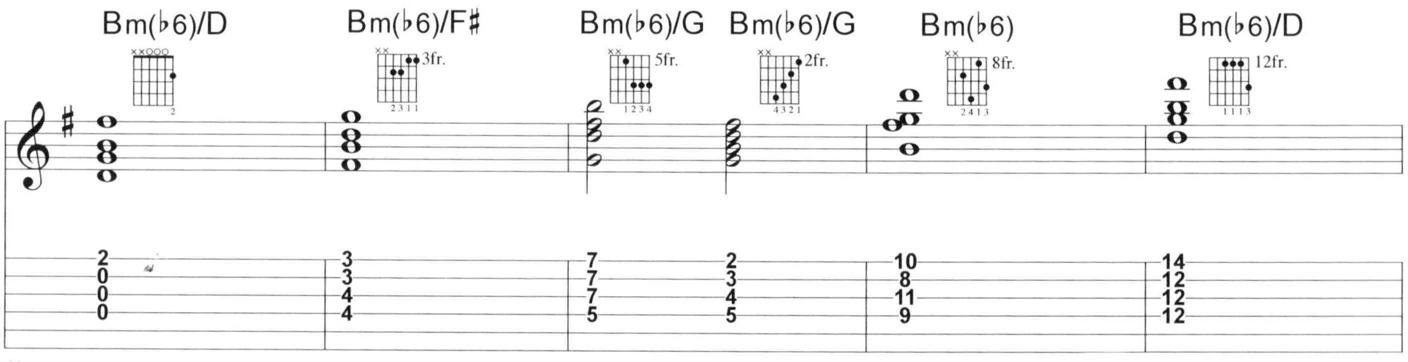

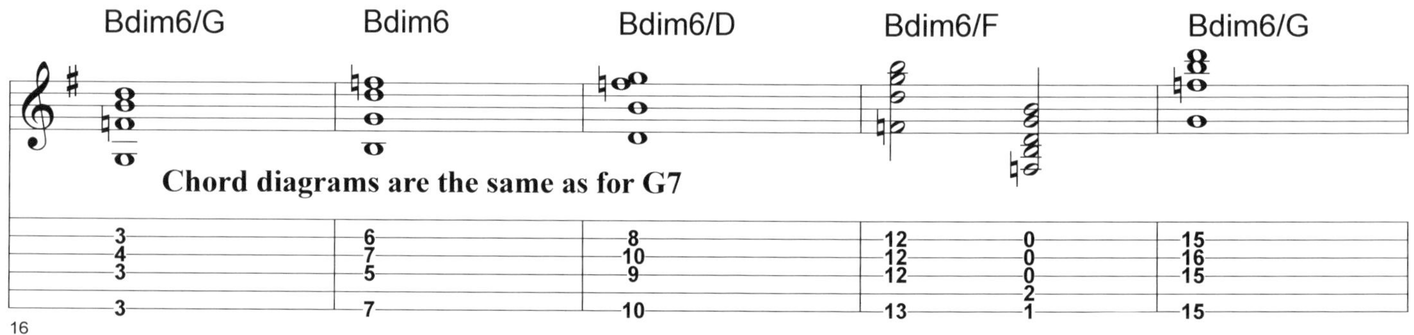

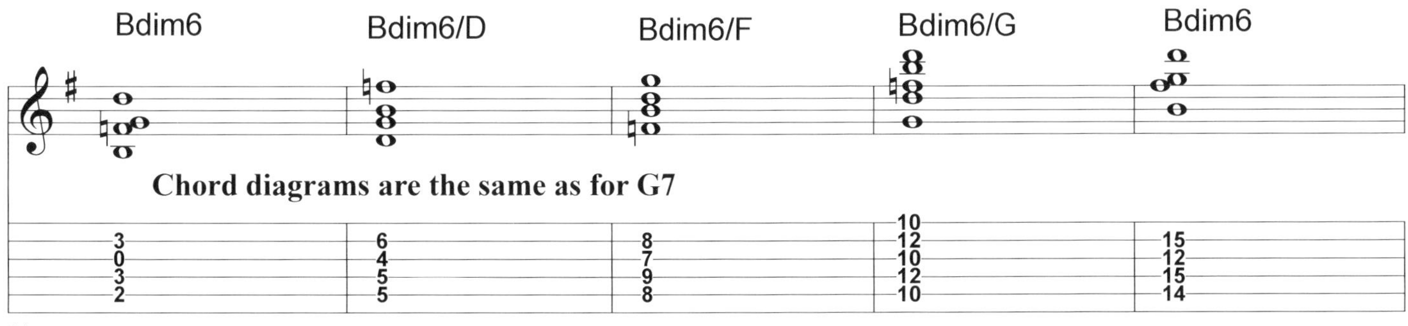

Bdim6/D Bdim6/F Bdim6/G Bdim6 Bdim6/D

26 Chord diagrams are the same as for G7

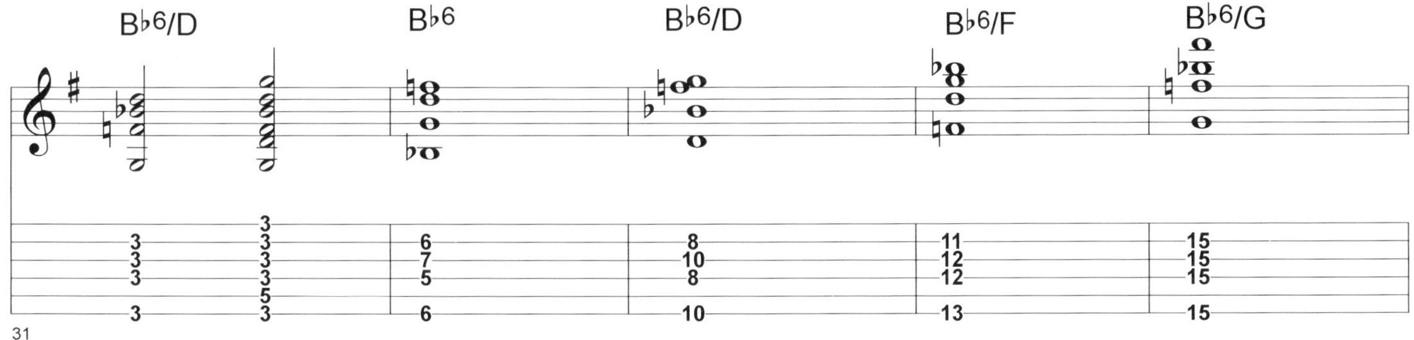

Chord diagrams are the same as for Gm7

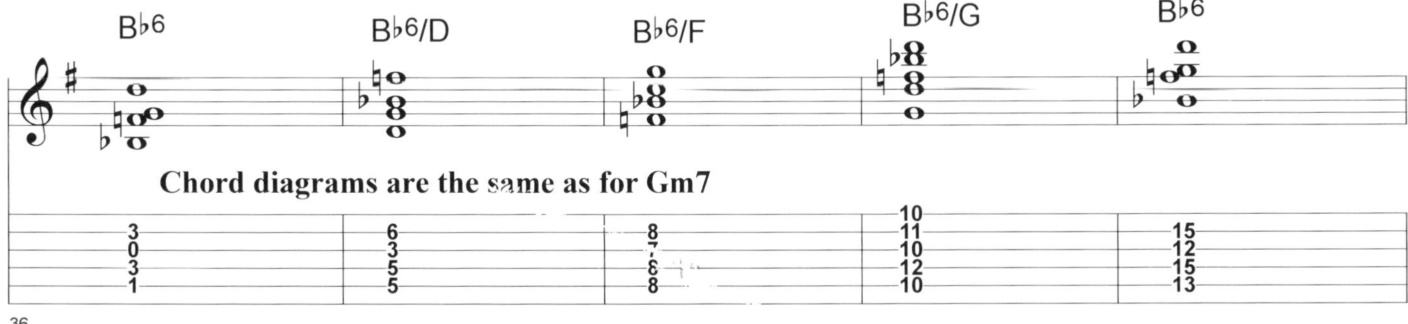

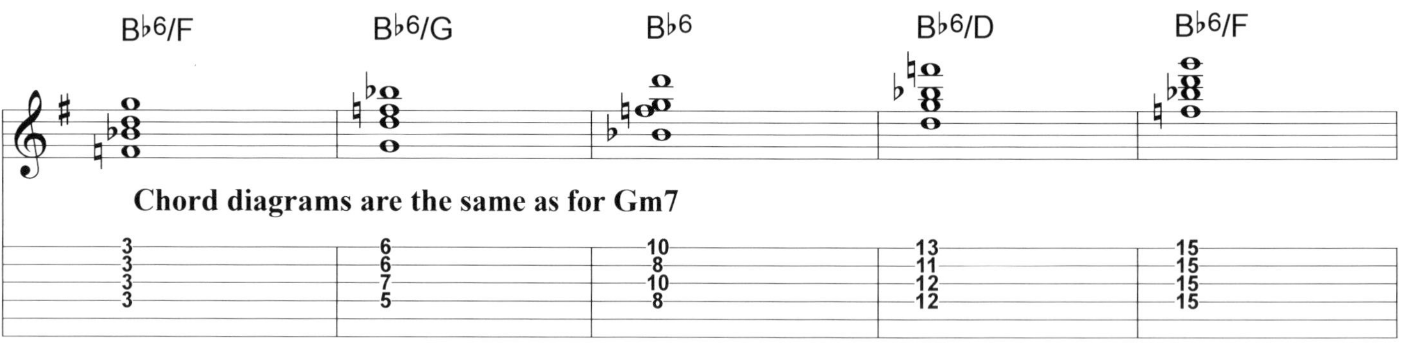
B♭6/F
B♭6/G
B♭6
B♭6/D
B♭6/F
Chord diagrams are the same as for Gm7
41

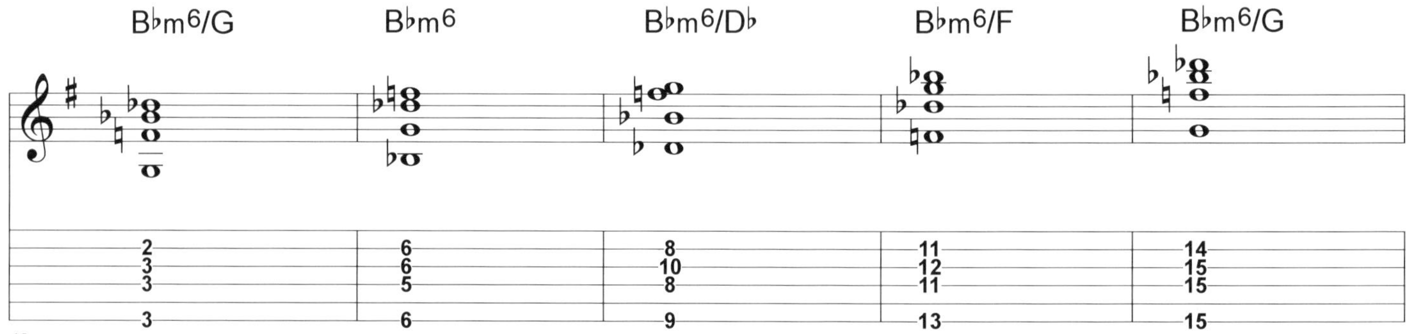
B♭m6/G
B♭m6
B♭m6/D♭
B♭m6/F
B♭m6/G
46
Chord diagrams are the same as for Gm7♭5

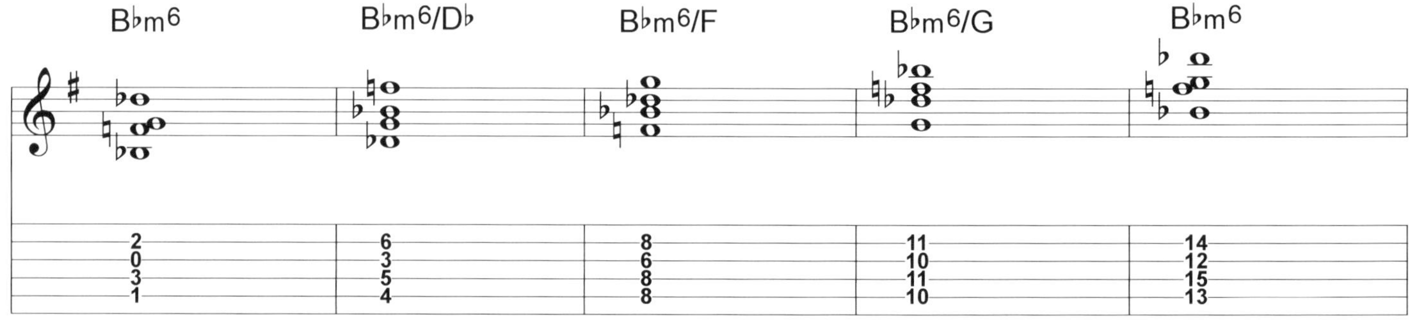
B♭m6
B♭m6/D♭
B♭m6/F
B♭m6/G
B♭m6
51
Chord diagrams are the same as for Gm7♭5

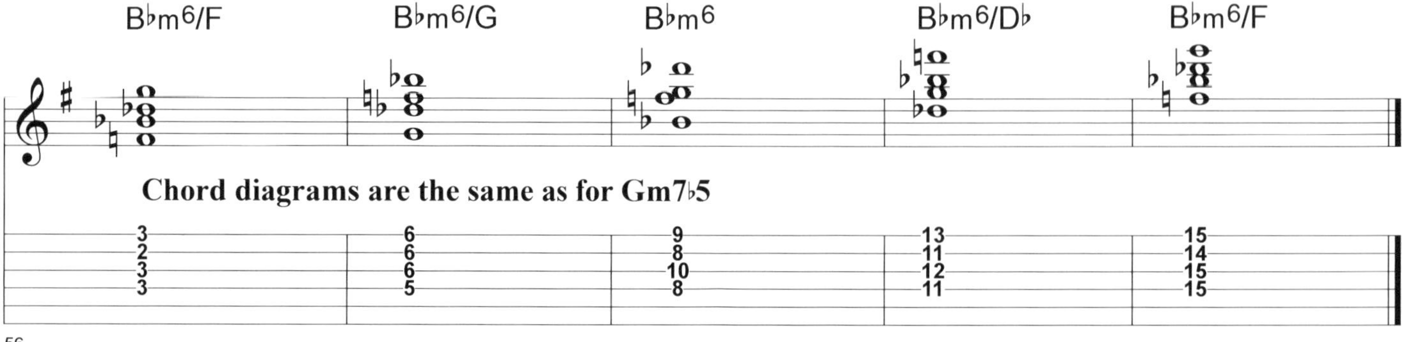
B♭m6/F
B♭m6/G
B♭m6
B♭m6/D♭
B♭m6/F
Chord diagrams are the same as for Gm7♭5
56

The Andalucian Cadence
Seven Tonal Centers

The so-called **Andalucian Cadence** is the framework for all profound or deep-song forms of flamenco referred to as *cante jondo.* The harmony results from the accompaniment of the melodic figure that descends from the fourth note of the Greek Doric scale (*Dorico Griego)*: A-G-F-E. The chords that accompany this melodic figure are: (Am), (G Major), (F Major), and (E Major). In pop-chord notation symbols the same progression would be noted as: Am-G-F-E.

The various *palos* or forms of *cante jondo* flamenco are associated with certain tonal centers. The four primary *palos* or forms are: ***Soleá*** in E and A, ***Tango*** in E and A, ***Siguiriyas*** in E and A, ***Fandangos*** in E and A. **Sub-forms of Fandango:** *Tarantas* in F-sharp (F♯), *Rondeñas* in C-sharp (C♯), *Granaínas* in B, and *Mineras* in G-sharp (G♯). Modern flamenco artists also use D-sharp (D♯) for these sub-forms of *Fandangos*. In addition, modern players use all seven tonal centers for their compositions, solos and improvisations in *Bulerías, Soleares, Tangos, Fandangos and Siguiriyas,* therefore expanding the harmonic territory for the composer or soloist, and allowing for accompaniment of *cante* (song) in any tonal center without a *cejilla* (capo).

The Andalusian Cadence has been transposed to each of the seven tonal centers, with alternative chord voicings, and "passing chords" which are usually a 7th chord a fourth below the goal, or an altered 7th chord a minor second away, referred to as a **flat-five** or **tritone substitution**. Change the root note of a 7th chord by moving it three whole-steps (tri-tone) and the result is a 7th chord with a flat-5th (♭5), with the root being a half-step (semitone) away from the goal chord. Example: D7 (D-F♯-A-C) becomes A♭7(♭5) (A♭-G♭-C-E♭♭), each chord resolving to G or G7.

Using passing 7th chords a fourth below the goal chord, or 7(♭5) chords a semitone above the goal chord expands the standard cadence of four chords, as is common practice in country, bluegrass, blues and jazz.

Usually, singers prefer the traditional key centers associated with each *palo* and guitarists move the capo up or down the neck accordingly to match the singer's range.

Guitarists should first study the traditional examples of the great masters of the early and mid-20th century (Ramón and Carlos Montoya, Sabicas, Juan Serrano, Niño Ricardo, Enrique Melchor), and then graduate to the more advanced harmonic language of Manolo Sanlúcar, Paco de Lucía, Victor Monge Serranito, Rafael Riqueni, Gerardo Núñez, Manolo Franco, José Antonio Rodríguez, Paco Serrano, and Vicente Amigo.

Andalucian Cadence

Corey E. Whitehead

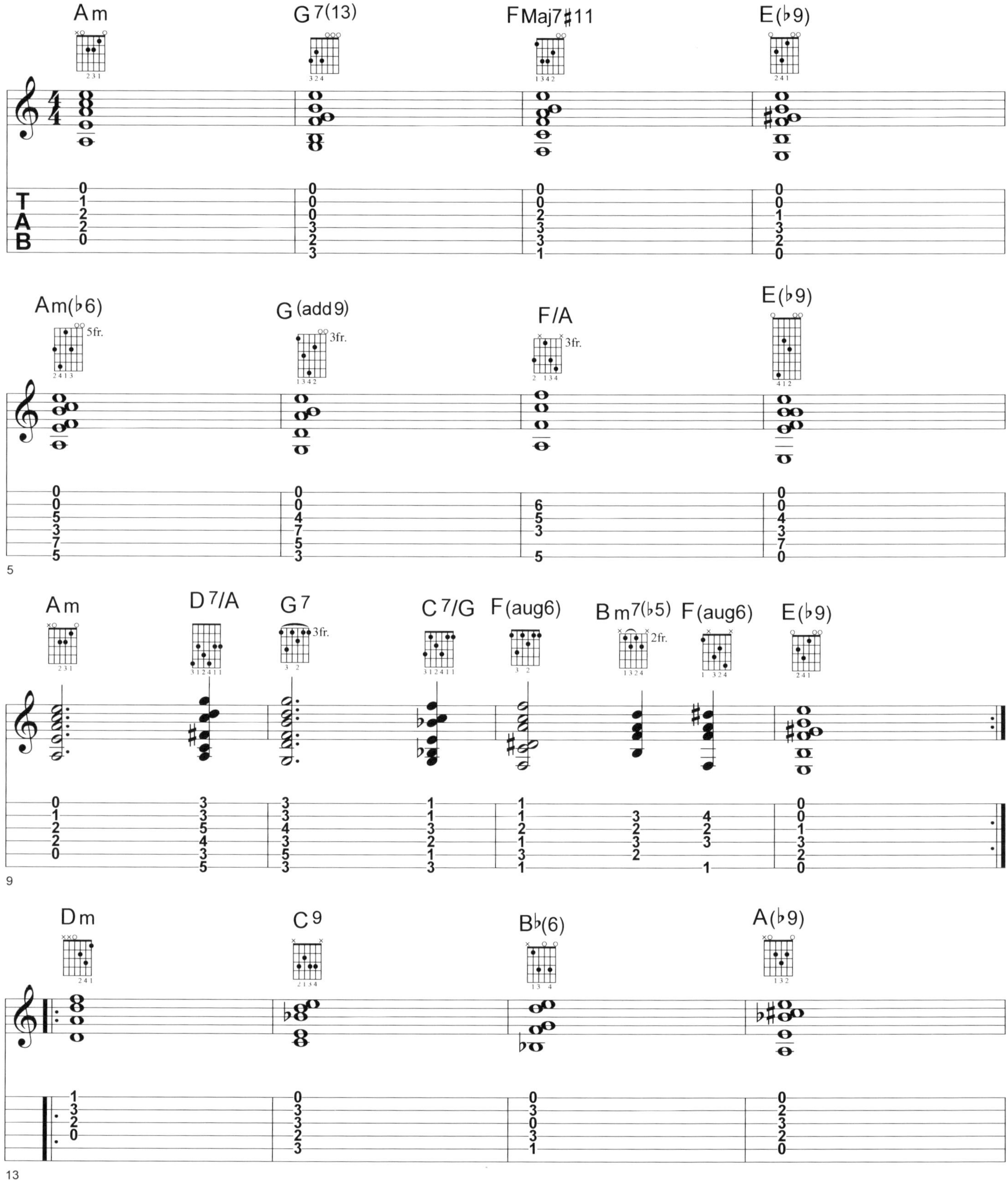

Am G7(13) FMaj7♯11 E(♭9)

Am(♭6) G(add9) F/A E(♭9)

5

Am D7/A G7 C7/G F(aug6) Bm7(♭5) F(aug6) E(♭9)

9

Dm C9 B♭(6) A(♭9)

13

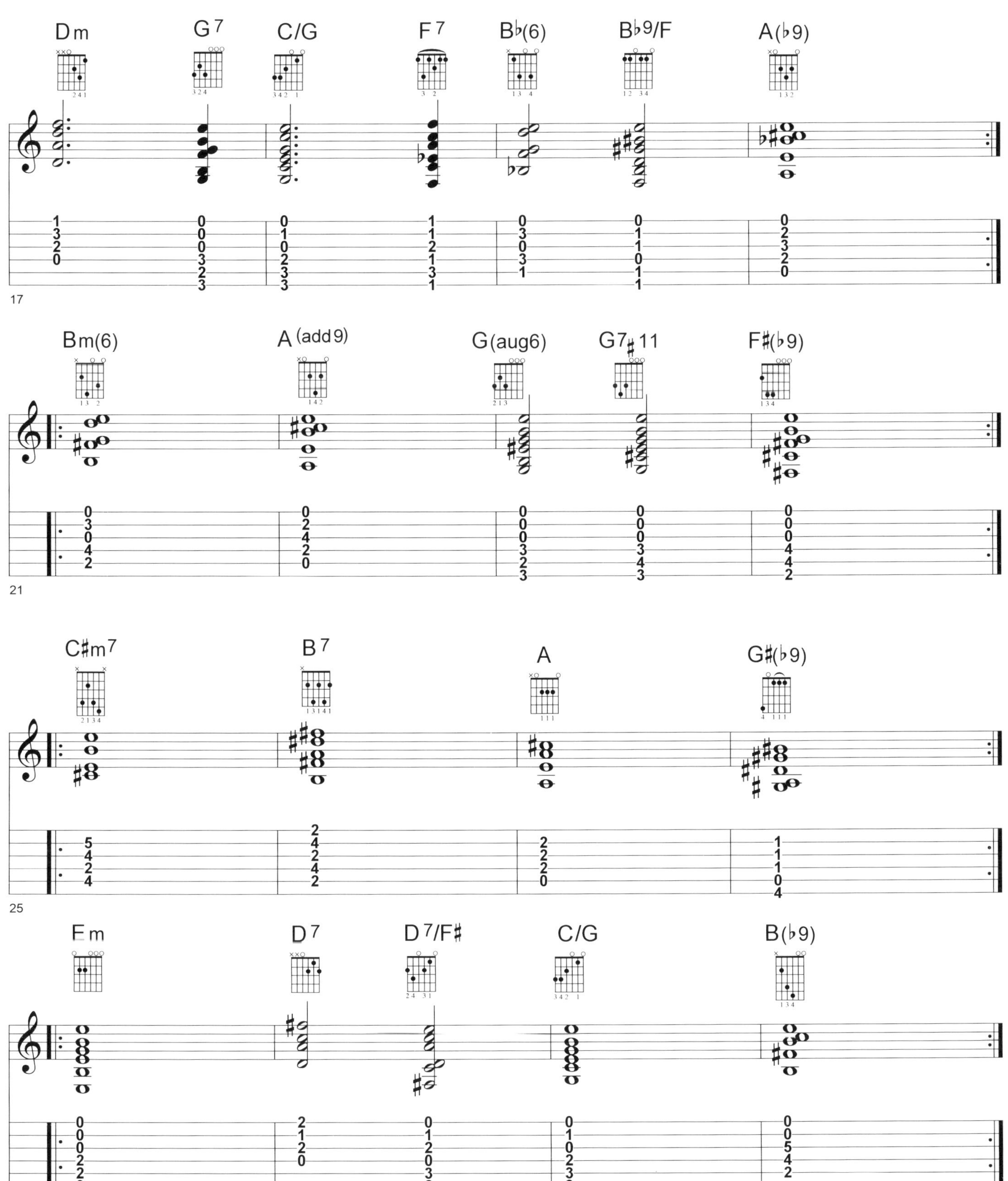
Dm
G7
C/G
F7
B♭(6)
B♭9/F
A(♭9)
17
Bm(6)
A (add 9)
G(aug6)
G7♯11
F♯(♭9)
21
C♯m7
B7
A
G♯(♭9)
25
Em
D7
D7/F♯
C/G
B(♭9)
29

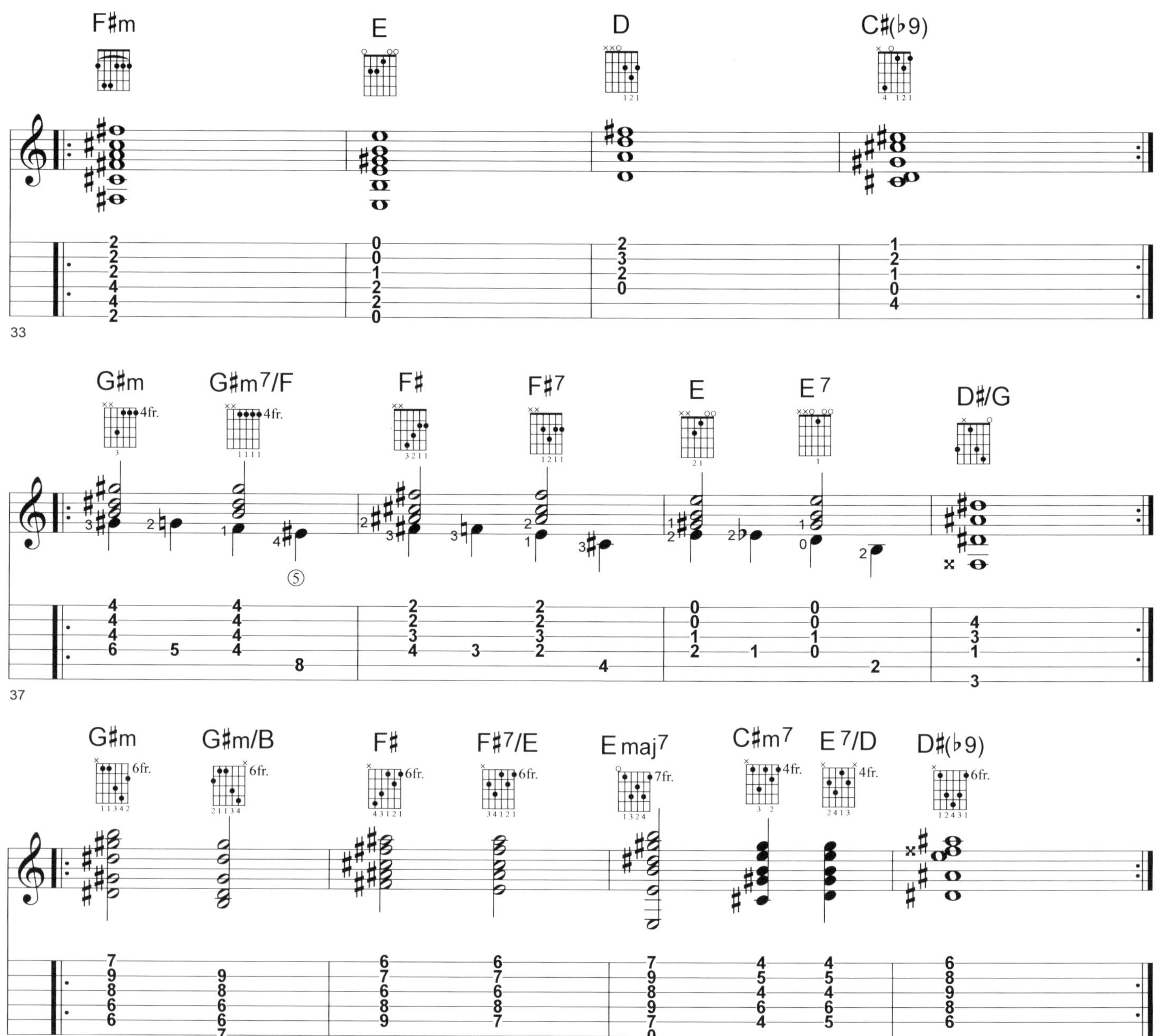
F♯m
E
D
C♯(♭9)
33
G♯m
G♯m7/F
F♯
F♯7
E
E7
D♯/G
4fr.
37
G♯m
G♯m/B
F♯
F♯7/E
E maj7
C♯m7
E7/D
D♯(♭9)
6fr.
7fr.
41

Unit I, Part II

Introductory Classical Guitar Repertoire

Unit I, Part II
Introductory Classical Guitar Repertoire

The so-called Classical period of music is generally defined as from the birth of the *"Gallant"* and *"Rococo"* in 1730, to the end of the early period of Beethoven in 1810. The "Romantic" period began in 1810 with the mature works of Beethoven and continued to 1900 with the works of Brahms, Bruckner, Mahler, and Strauss. In the classical guitar repertoire, there is some overlap of Classical period mannerism into the 1830s. The repertoire chosen for this book is from the Romantic Era, the earliest work being a mature work of Dionisio Aguado (1784-1849). Aguado, a Spaniard who first used fingernails on the right hand to produce tone and more volume, was immersed in the *coplas* (light-hearted popular song verses) of the *Fandango de Huelva*. In contrast, the *gitanos* and *gitanas* performed *Fandangos* with great affectation of pain, grief and loss (*Fandango Grande)*. Aguado, born in Madrid, was a pupil of Miguel García "Padre Basilio" of the convent of San Basilio in Madrid and organist of the *Monasterio de El Escorial*. Like Fernando Sor, Aguado followed Federico Moretti and his teacher Miguel García (1790-unkown) in the standard use of a five-line musical staff with a treble clef rather than the six-line tablature with numbers representing the frets and the lines representing the strings. One may read more in depth on this subject in the article by Franco Poselli, *"L'enigmatica figura di Padre Basilio"* in Guitar and Lute, Vol. 1, No. 2, April 1973, p. 27-29.

The remaining works are from the mid-late 19th century that represent "*palos*" of flamenco and of the popular song verses called "coplas". The music of Tomás Damas, Julian Arcas, and Francisco Tárrega, are a representation of the sounds of the *palos* of flamenco. José Patiño influenced *gitanos* such as Francisco Sánchez Cantero "Paco El Barbero," who was one of the leading accompanists in the provinces of Sevilla and Cádiz in the mid-18th century. Since he was known to have influenced Cantero, he surely had some influence on solo flamenco interludes known as *falsetas,* and on the solo literature that followed in the latter half of the 20th century. Javier Molina influenced Antonio Serrano, Isidro Muñoz, Esteban de Sanlúcar, Carlos Montoya, Juan Morao, Agustín Castellón "Sabicas," Juan Serrano, Manolo Sanlúcar, and Paco de Lucía, who were all foundational in the formation of flamenco guitar in the 20th century.

Performance Notes

"Malagueña fácil" by Francisco Tárrega (1852-1909) *is from the province of Málaga and is a regional sub-form of the Fandango de Huelva:*

1) Play *apoyando* (rest-stroke) with the thumb in the bass.
2) Play *tirando* (free stroke) on the chords.
3) The long melodic passages in measure 22 and onward may be played entirely with the right-hand thumb *(pulgar),* or with alternation of right-hand fingers i-m *(picado).*
4) Wherever accompanied melodic notes occur above a bass note or chord, one may play *picado,* using rest strokes whenever possible.

"Rondeña nueva" by Tomás Damas (1817-ca.1880)

1) This solo work by Spanish guitarist, conductor, and composer, Tomás Damas (1817-1880), is new in that the *Rondeña* is an accompanied song which is a regional variation of one of the four main forms of flamenco, the *Fandango*. It is written that Damas was a pupil of Francisco Tárrega, although it seems illogical that Damas would have been a pupil of someone 35 years his junior as Tárrega was born in 1852. It is more logical that Damas was a contemporary of Julian Arcas (1832-1882), and that they knew one another. According to Rafael Antón Palacios' recent article posted at JSTOR (www.jstor.org/stable/266), Damas was a student at Madrid's *Maria Cristina Royal Conservatory of Music* and was already one of the leading guitarists of his generation when Arcas came onto the scene. As Palacios writes in his article *"El guitarrista Tomás Damas (1817-ca.1880), Revision biográfica y catálogo compositivo."* Revista de Musicologia. January, 2019. This article also corrects the previous known dates of birth and death of Damas, placing his life and career earlier in the history of the Spanish guitar than Arcas and Tárrega.
2) Typically, the *Rondeña* uses a key signature of three sharps, with the rhythmic sections of the guitar interludes *(compás)* being in the tonality C-sharp (C♯) Greek Doric (Dórico Griego) also known as C♯ Phrygian, and the *coplas* (lyric verses) being in the tonality of the relative "major" or Ionian mode, A Major.
3) Instead, this work uses a key signature with two sharps, (D Major) and centers the tonality on F-sharp (F♯) Greek Doric (Dórico Griego) also known as F♯ Phrygian, for the rhythm *(compás)* and for the *falsetas* (solo guitar variations on the theme). The *coplas* (lyric verses) are in the tonality of the relative "major" or Ionian mode, D Major.
4) The three *coplas* are preceded by an introduction in the F♯ Doric tonality, creating a sort of *Rondo* form, as the guitar solos are similar each time, like a refrain, and the *coplas* are varied each time.
5) This work is an introduction to the way a guitarist accompanies *coplas* and interjects *falsteas* or rhythmic variations *(compás).*

6) This work uses the fretboard up to the 7th position (CVII) and makes use of **accidentals**, sharps and flats not indicated in the key signature that only apply in the measure in which they are written.

"Jota Aragonesa" by Julian Arcas (1832-1882)

Spanish guitarist Santiago de Murcia (1673-1739) wrote a work entitled *Jota* for five-course Baroque guitar. Although this dance originated in Aragon, in the North of Spain, and was disseminated to Castile, The Phillipines, and Alta California, it also influenced the music of Cádiz, namely the *Alegrías.* Other composers who wrote in this form include Manuel de Falla, Pablo de Sarasate, Francisco Tárrega, Maurice Ravel, Issac Albéniz, Camile Saint-Saëns, Franz Liszt, Mikhail Glinka, Georges Bizet, Louis Gottschalk, Alfred Reed, Frederick Loewe, and Raoul Laparra. Recommended reading on the latter subject includes Mende Grey, Vykki (2016). *Dance Tunes from Mexican and Spanish California.* San Diego, CA: Los Californios, and, Back, Douglas (2003). *Hispanic-American Guitar.* Mel-Bay. p. 9.

1) The five-course guitar has five doubled strings (courses) and a single high string *(chantarelle)* is often played in modern historic ensembles with lute, drums, viola de gamba, viols, and other period instruments of the Spanish Baroque, just as it was used prior to the advent of the modern fan-braced Spanish guitar of Louis Panormo and Antonio de Torres.
2) This work is in the key of A Major (three sharps) and is written in ¾ meter, although the rhythmic phraseology is similar to that of the *Alegrías.* The *Alegrías* shares the same rhythm as the *Soleá,* with less weight, and a faster tempo. This musical form is explained in detail metrically and harmonically in Unit III. For now, remember that each phrase is felt, and not counted, but at first, count the first beat of measure one as "1" and continue to "10" which falls on the first beat of the fourth measure. The final "1-2" fall on the final two beats of measure 4. Although the phrase is four measures (12 beats) long, the phrase ends on beat 10 followed by a count of 1-2. This is similar to lute music of the Renaissance, having a chordal ending that begins on the first beat of a final measure, and continues to the end of that final measure. The barlines as they are written, somewhat confusingly, follow the chord progression, and not the actual meter.
3) The actual first beat of the meter as it is felt by the dancers is on the "2" of the "1-2." Ex. **2** 1 2 **3** 4 5 **6** 7 8 9 **10** 1. This ends up sounding like **1** 2 3 **1** 2 3 **1** 2 **1** 2 **1 2**
4) Use *apoyando* on single-note melodic passages whenever possible.
5) Single notes played by the thumb *(pulgar)* should be played *apoyando* whenever possible.
6) The beats **10**-1-2 often feature a closing harmonic feature called the *cierre* or "closing."
7) In mm. 118-125 one plays like "the imitation of a drum" by hitting the index and middle fingers onto all strings at once in alternation like hitting a drum. The thumb may also be used for this effect. By hitting the strings as one frets the notes of a chord, the strings sound as the guitar also sounds like a drum being hit.
8) In mm. 126-133, play by strumming with the flesh of the thumb only, avoid the fingernail.
9) The indications for natural open-string harmonics beings at m. 134. The string is indicated by a note with a custom diamond head, in this case open A, 5th string. And then the fret at which one finds the harmonic by touching without pressure is indicated by the Arabic numeral "5" in *italics.*

"Murcianas" by Julian Arcas (1832-1882)

1) The *Muricianas* are an accompanied song from the province or region of Murcia, which is a regional variation of one of the four main forms of flamenco, the *Fandango*. Murcia was once considered to be a part of Andalucía. Like the *Rondeñas* previously described, the *Muricianas* feature a song or *cante* that is based upon the *Fandango*. The *Fandango* is one of the four primary forms of flamenco, related to the *Soleá*, the mother of all flamenco forms, and the *Verdial*, or *Verdiales*, which have a history related to the *Rocio,* a religious pilgrimage to the Doñana de Heulva/Cádiz, going back more than 2000 years, to the times of the Tartessos.
2) The tonality is B *Dórico* (Phrygian) and shares the same key signature as G Major/E Minor (one sharp).
3) The *falstetas* are in the tonality of B *Dórico* (Phrygian), and the *copla* which ends each section of the work, at first is called *Canto (m.76-94),* is in G Major until the final phrase where the *cante/copla* or in this case *canto,* modulates to tonicize the third note of the scale, B (m.94). This gives the work a feeling of ending with the Andalucian cadence, which it does, just as does the *Fandango.*
4) The original publisher of this work used a different method of notation for the harmonics, for example in m. 25, the first two notes are indicated just as the publisher noted, although it is confusing, here is some assistance: 6th string/7th fret, and 2nd string/7th fret, 1st string/7th fret. Another *copla* occurs from mm.108-132, and yet another from mm. 202-227.
5) The *Fandango* and its related forms often have a 12-beat phrase with a rhythmic pattern of four measures of ¾ time counted or felt as follows: **1** 2 3 1 **2** (3), **1** 2 3 1 **2** (3)
6) Use rest strokes on single-note melodic passages whenever possible.
7) When playing with the thumb, use rest stroke whenever possible.

Malagueña fácil

Francisco Tárrega
Edited by Corey E. Whitehead

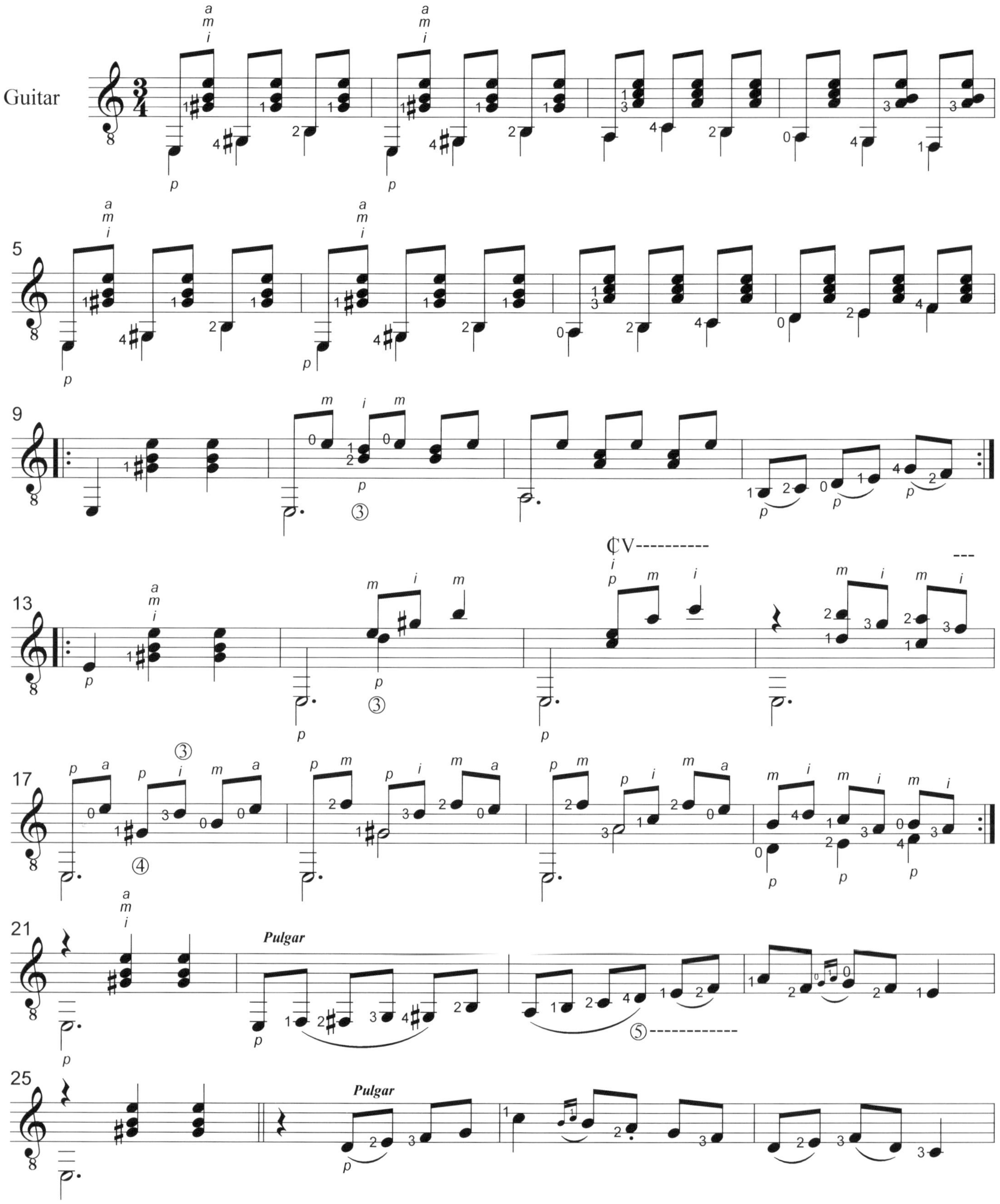

Guitar

Pulgar

Pulgar

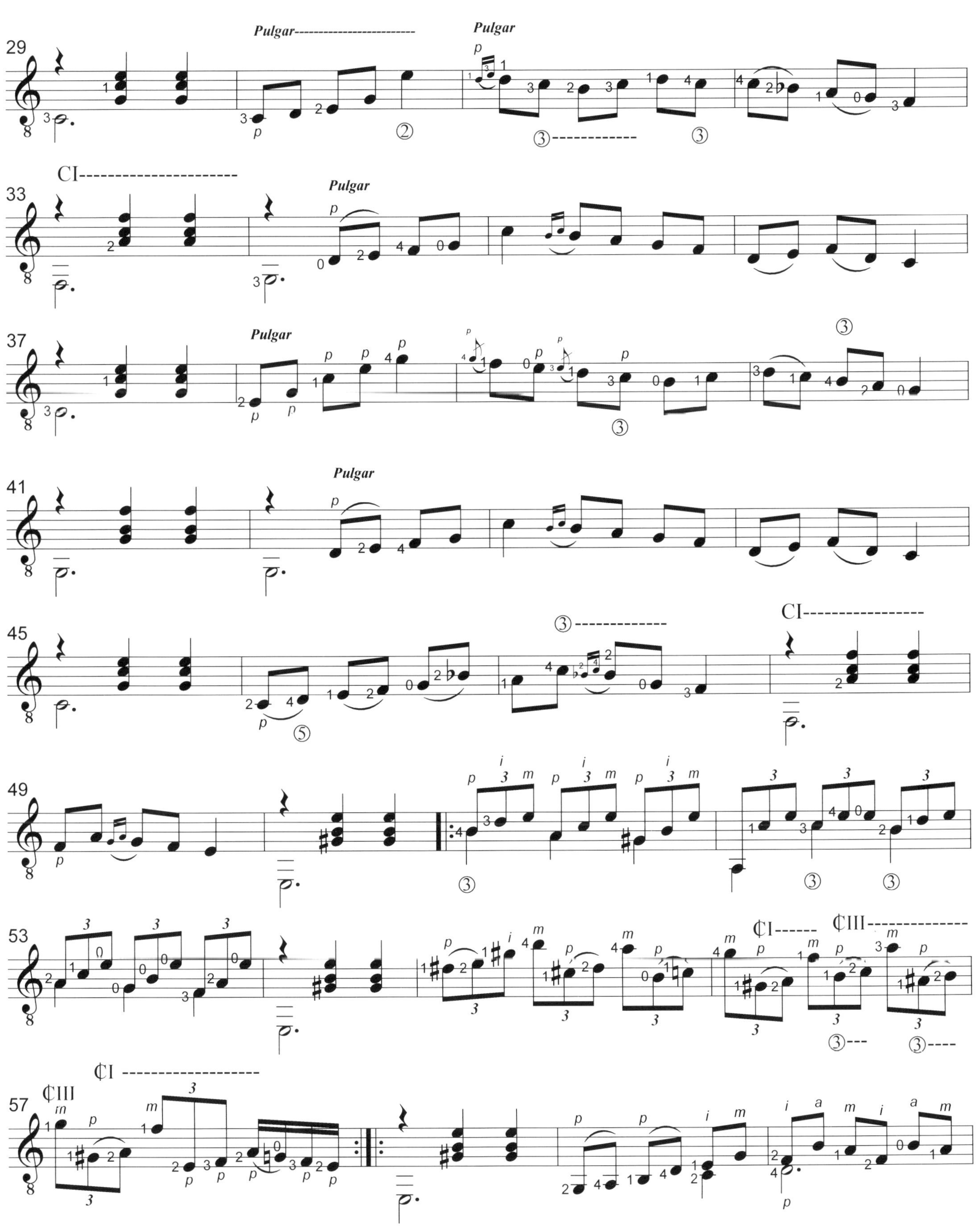
Pulgar
Pulgar
CI
Pulgar
Pulgar
Pulgar
CI
ȼI
ȼIII
ȼI
ȼIII

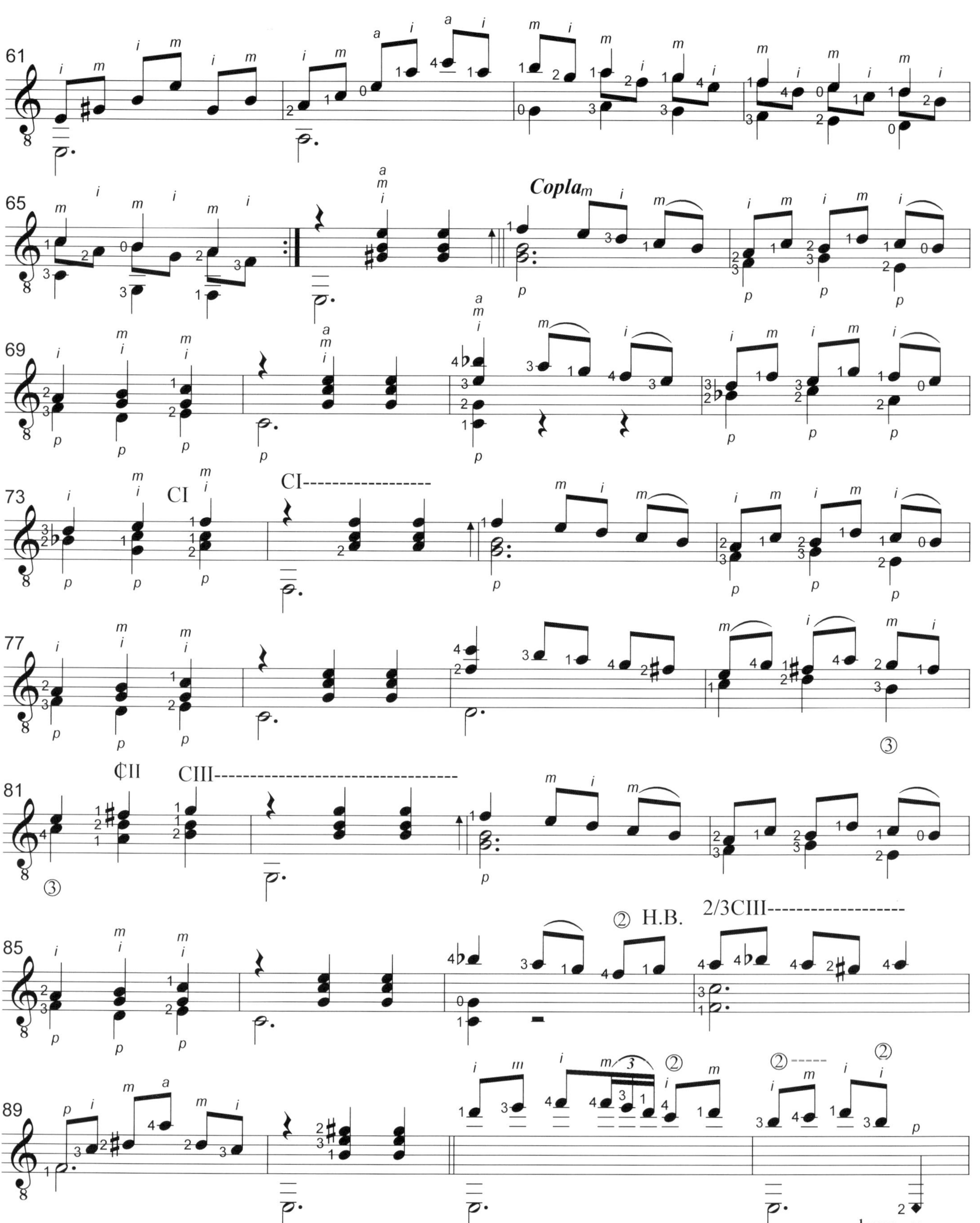
61
65
Copla
69
73
CI
CI
77
81
CII
CIII
85
H.B.
2/3CIII
89
harm. 12

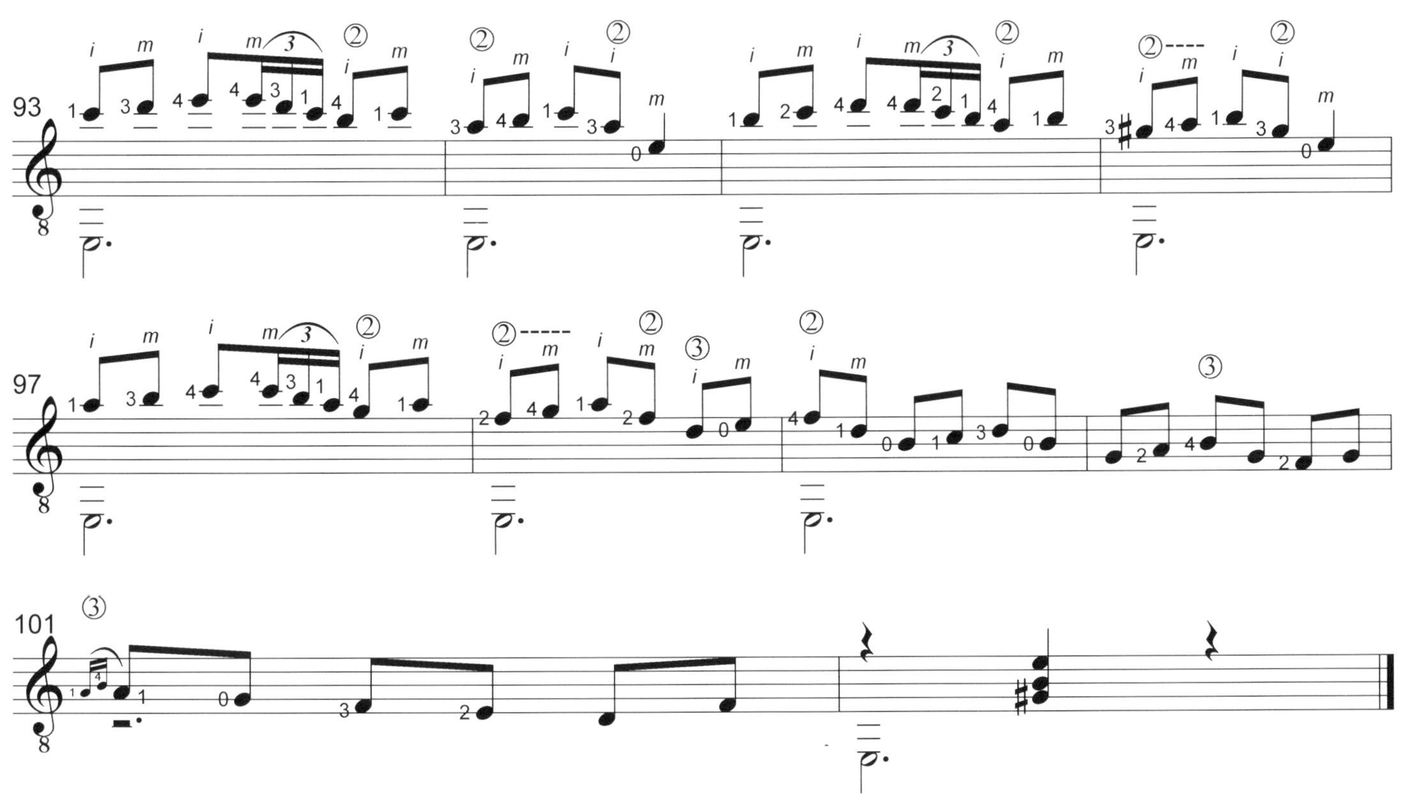
93
97
101

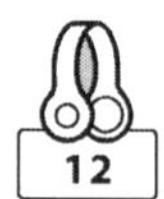

Rondeña nueva

Tomás Damas
Edited by Corey E. Whitehead

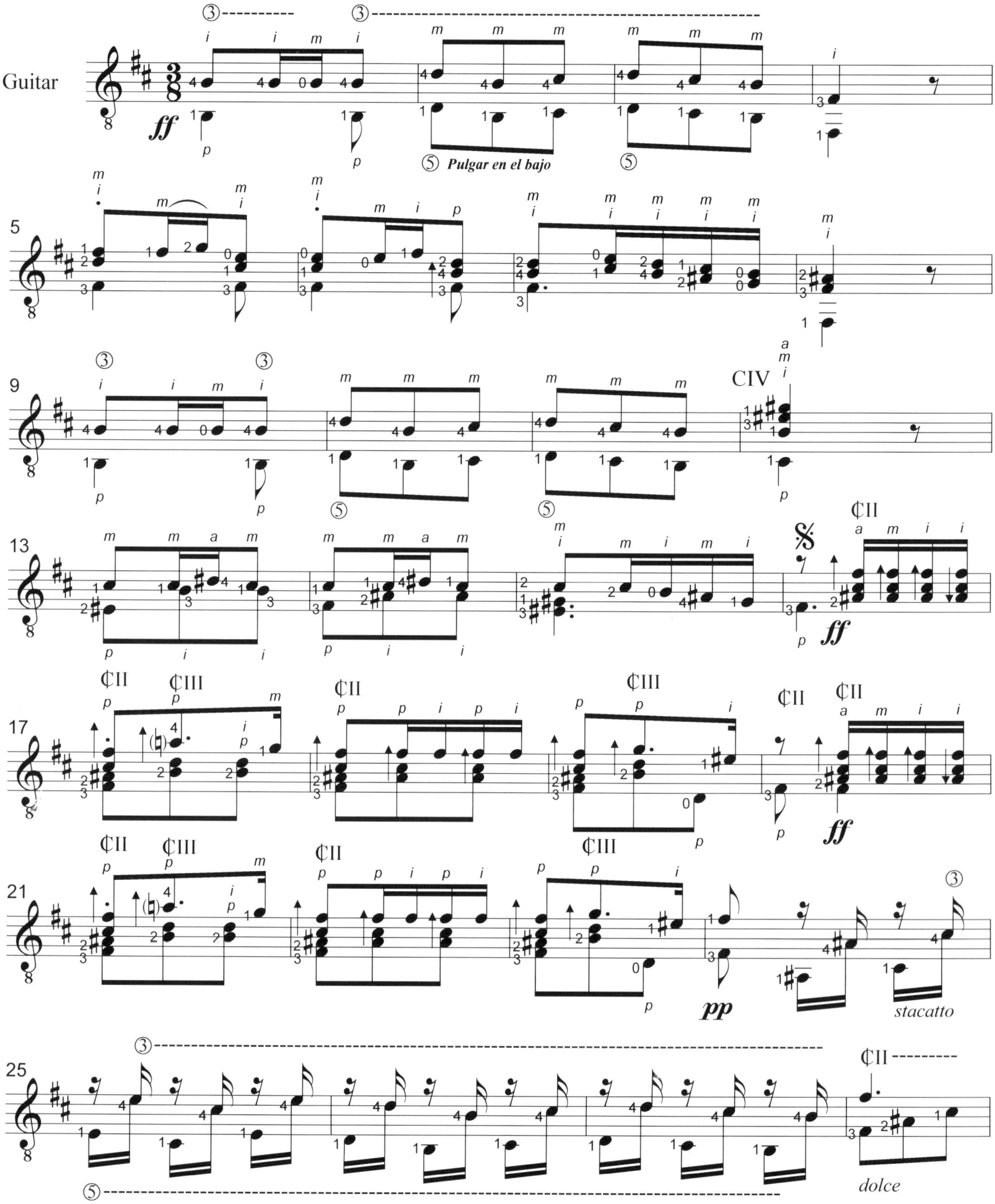

Guitar

Pulgar en el bajo

CIV

stacatto

dolce

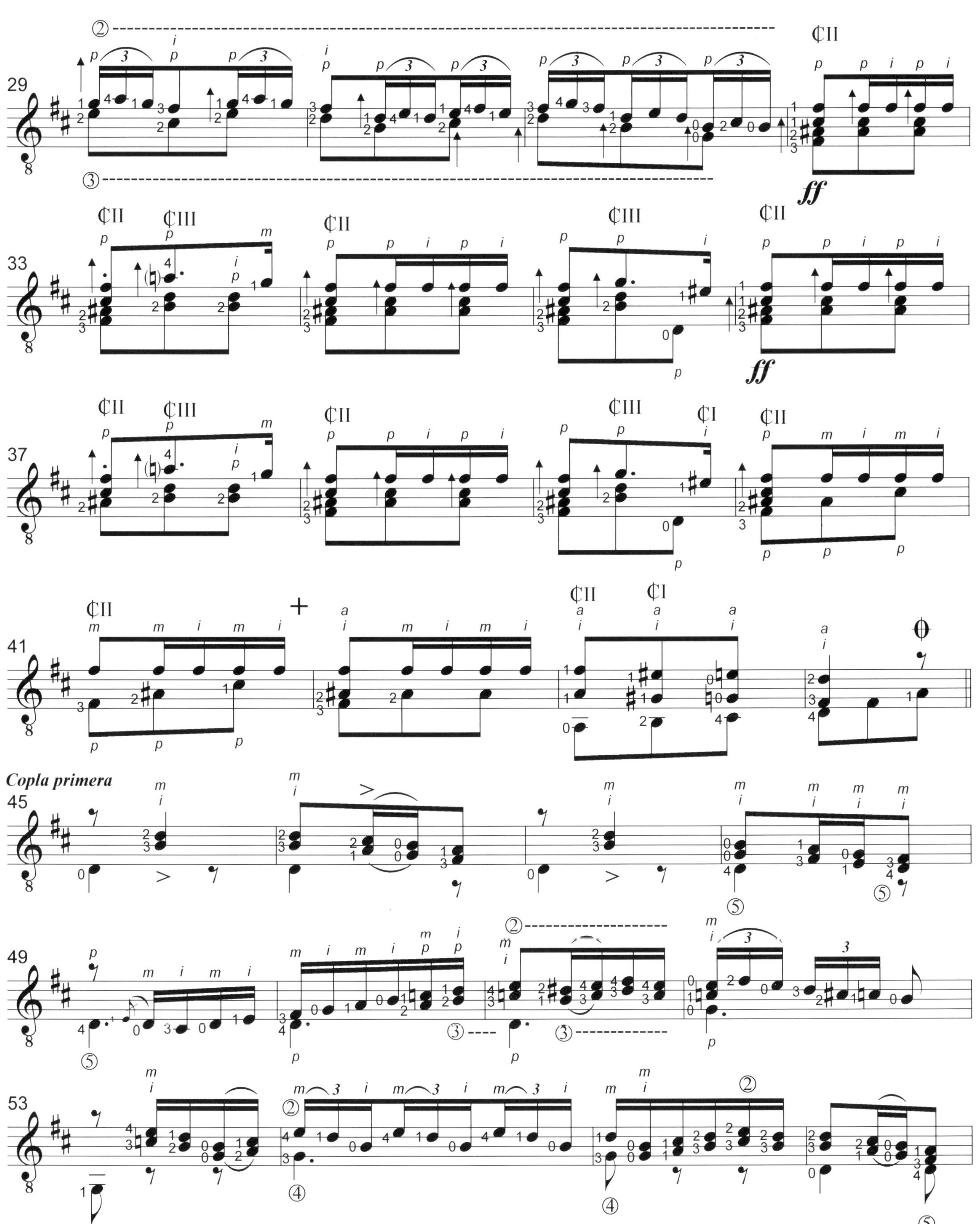
Copla primera

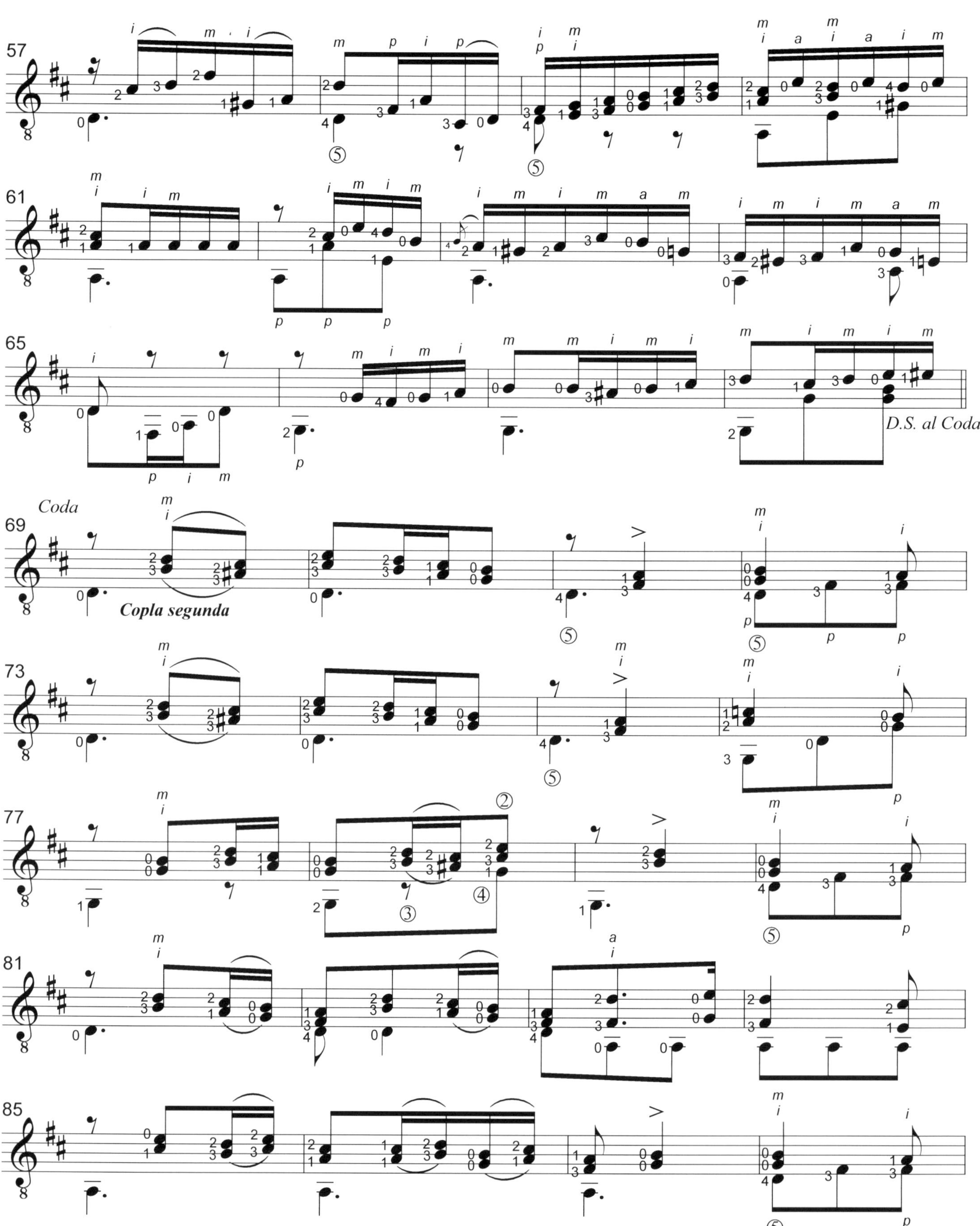

D.S. al Coda
Coda
Copla segunda

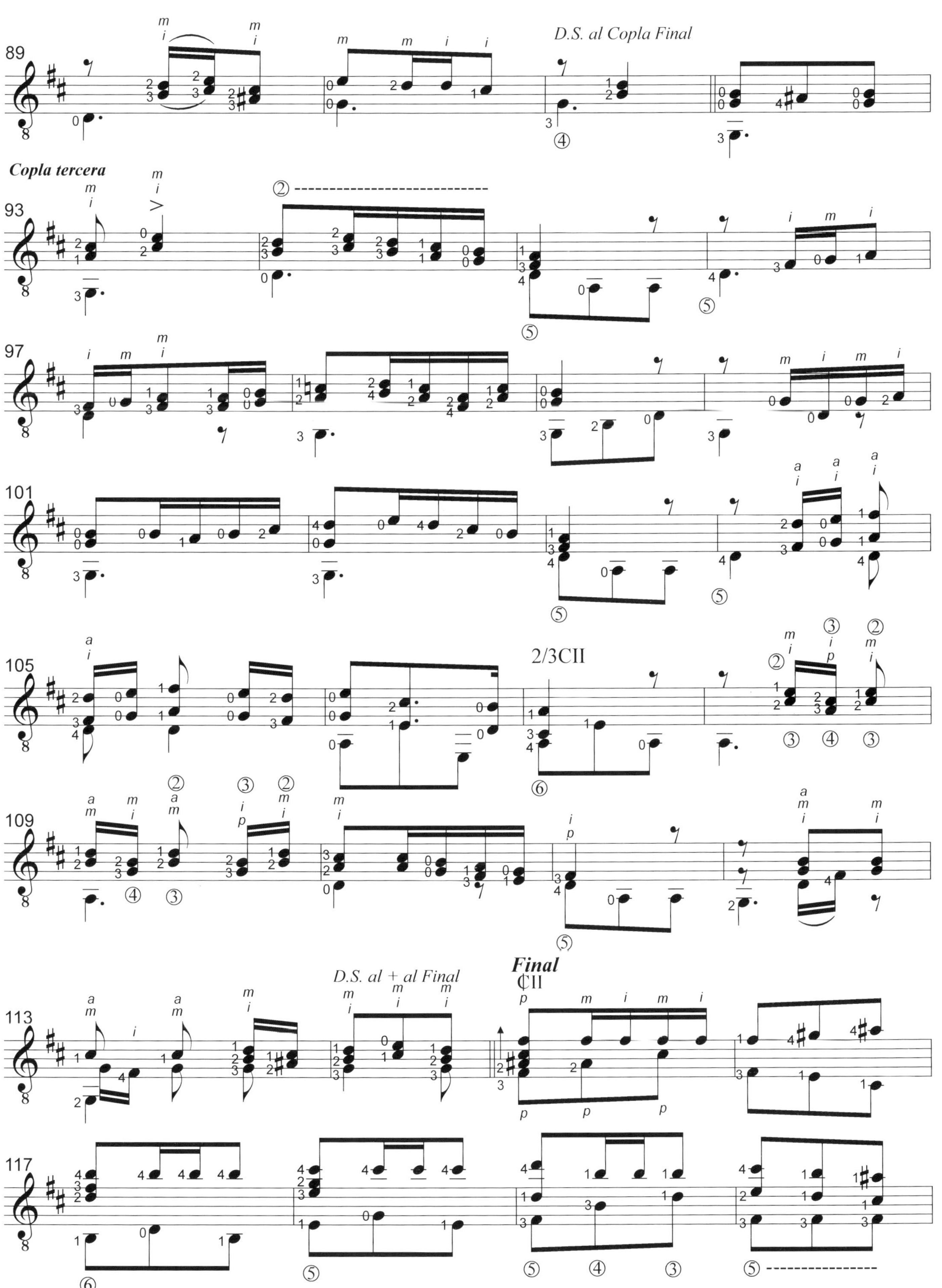
D.S. al Copla Final
Copla tercera
2/3CII
D.S. al + al Final
Final
CII

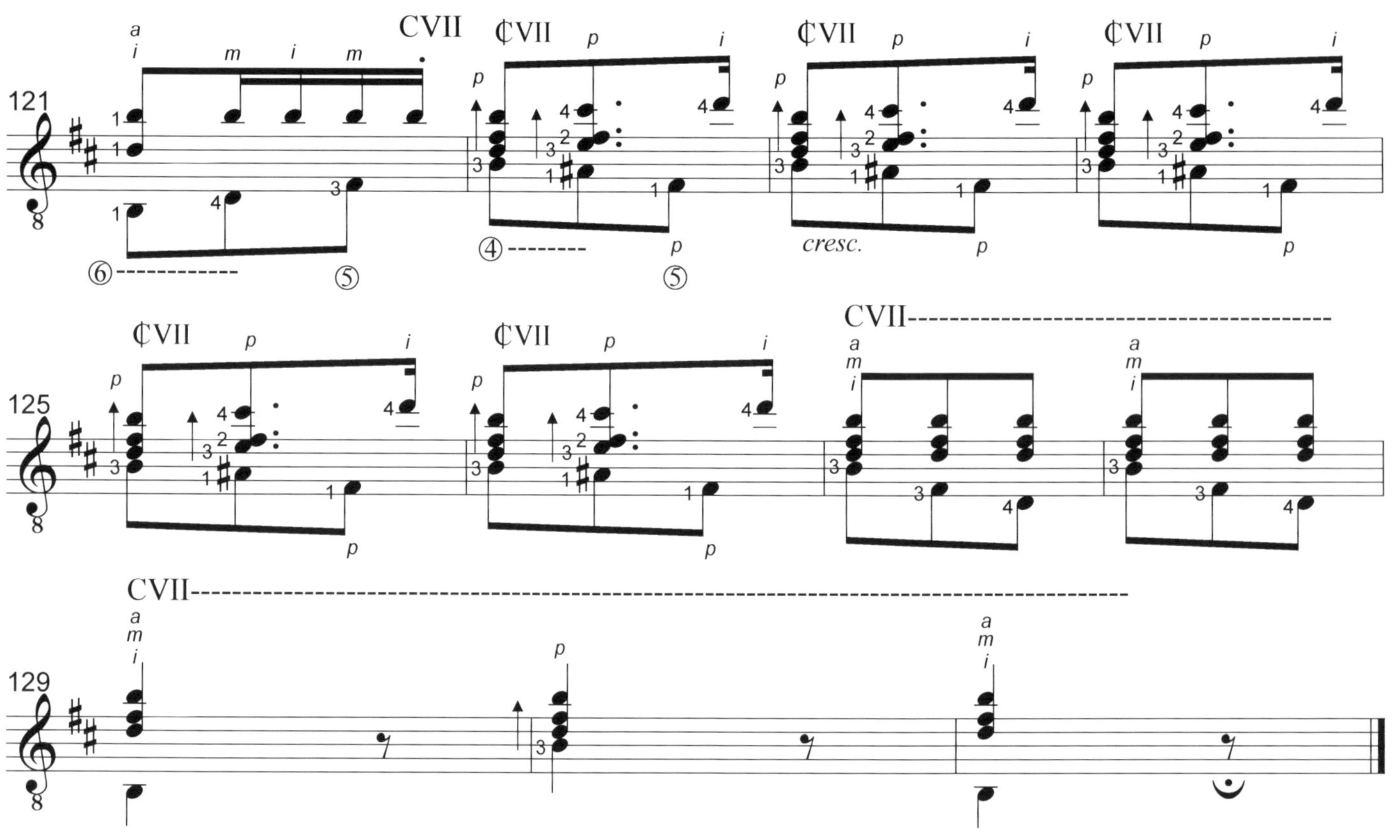
CVII
ȻVII
ȻVII
ȻVII
cresc.
ȻVII
ȻVII
CVII
CVII

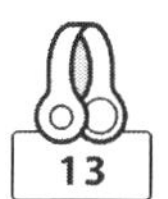

Jota Aragonesa

Julian Arcas

"a mi amigo D. Magin Alegre"

Edited by Corey E. Whitehead

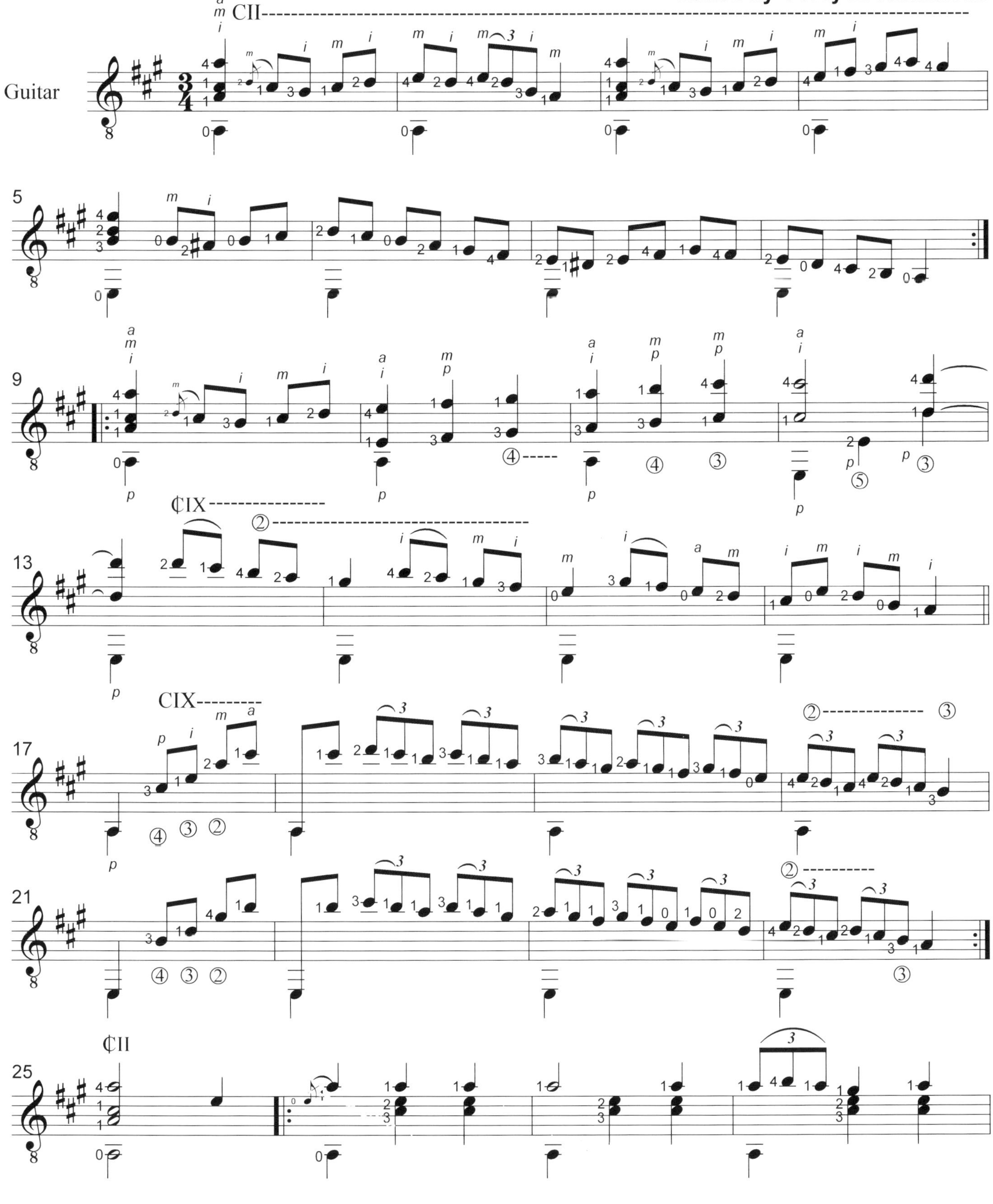

Guitar

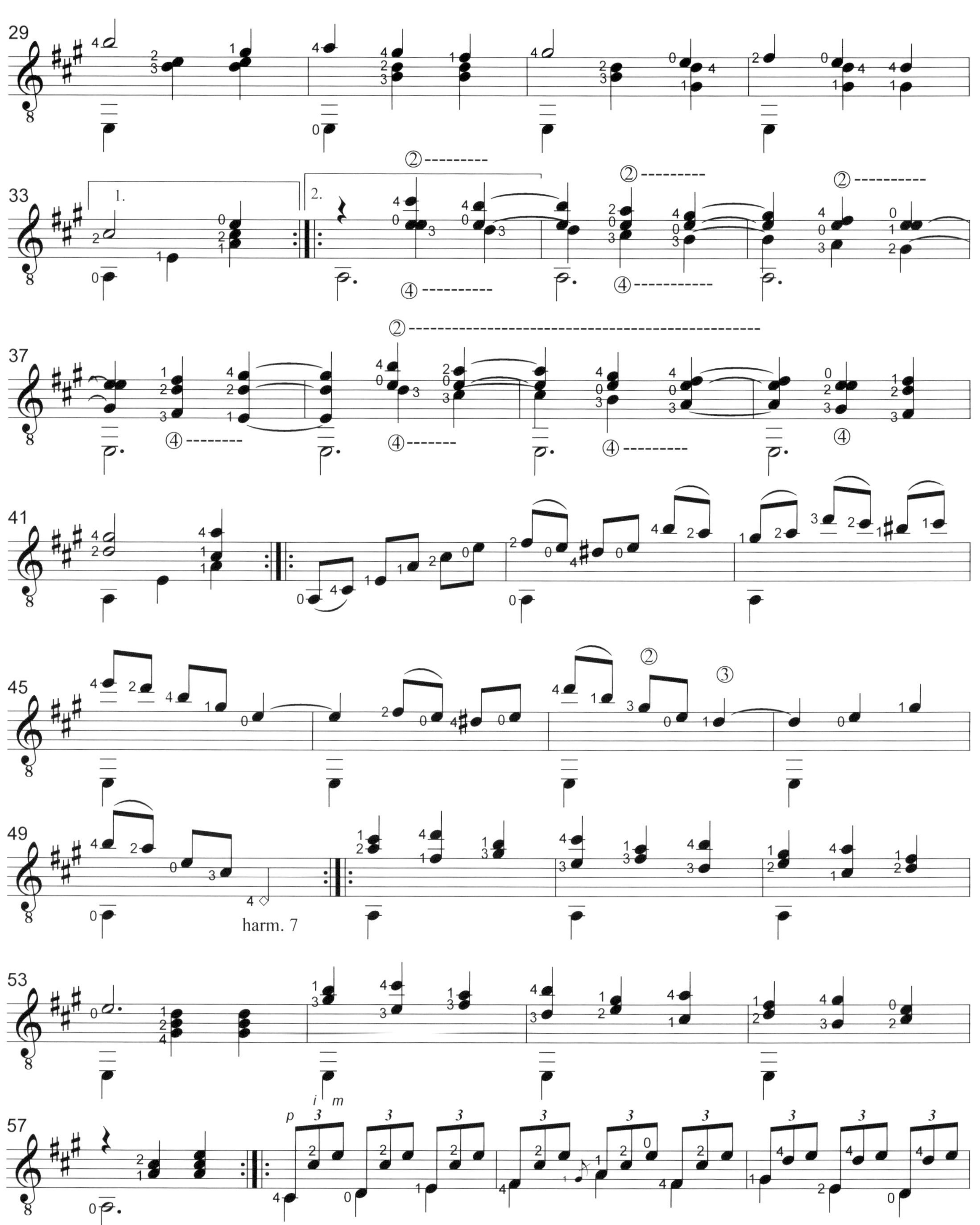
1.
2.
harm. 7

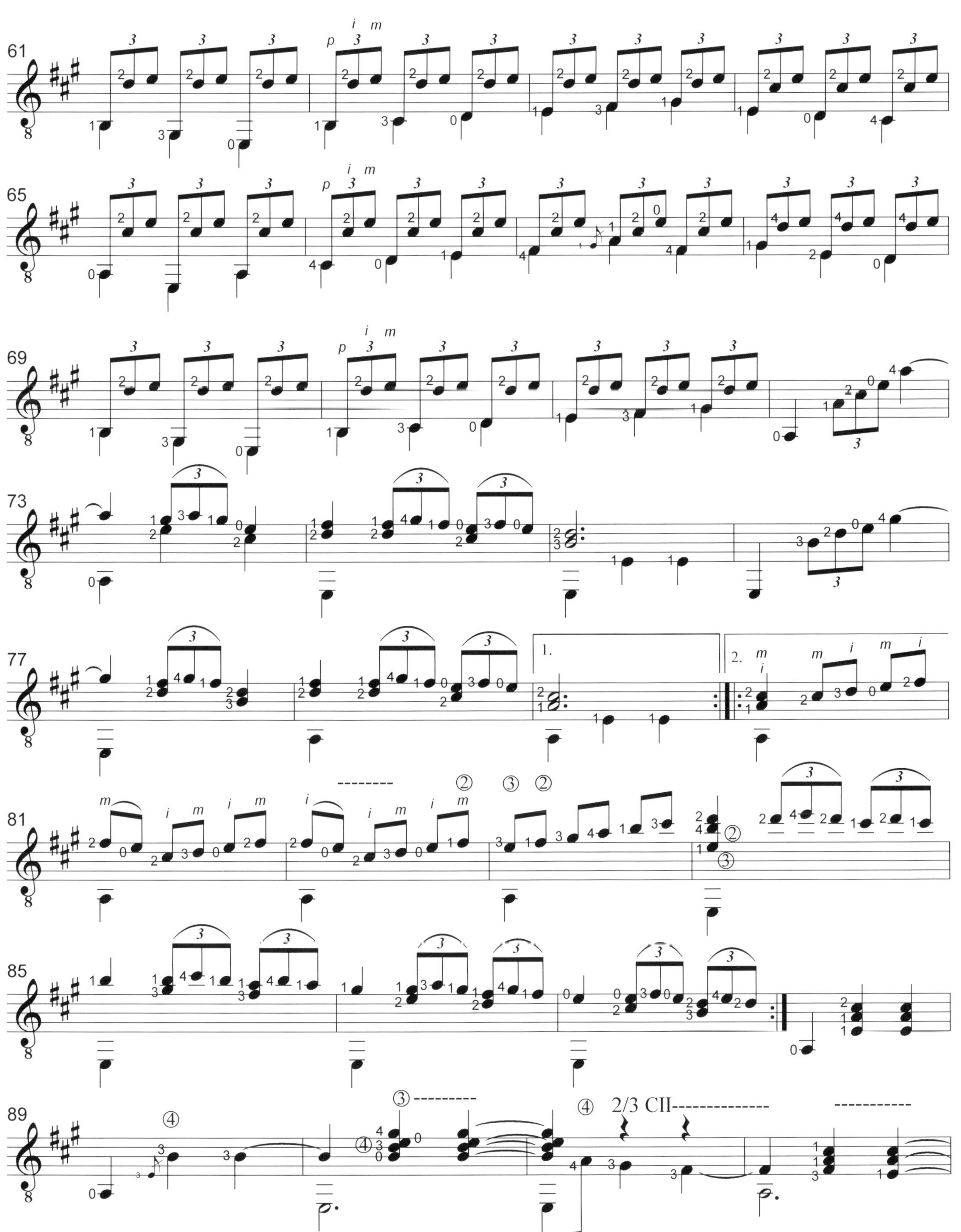

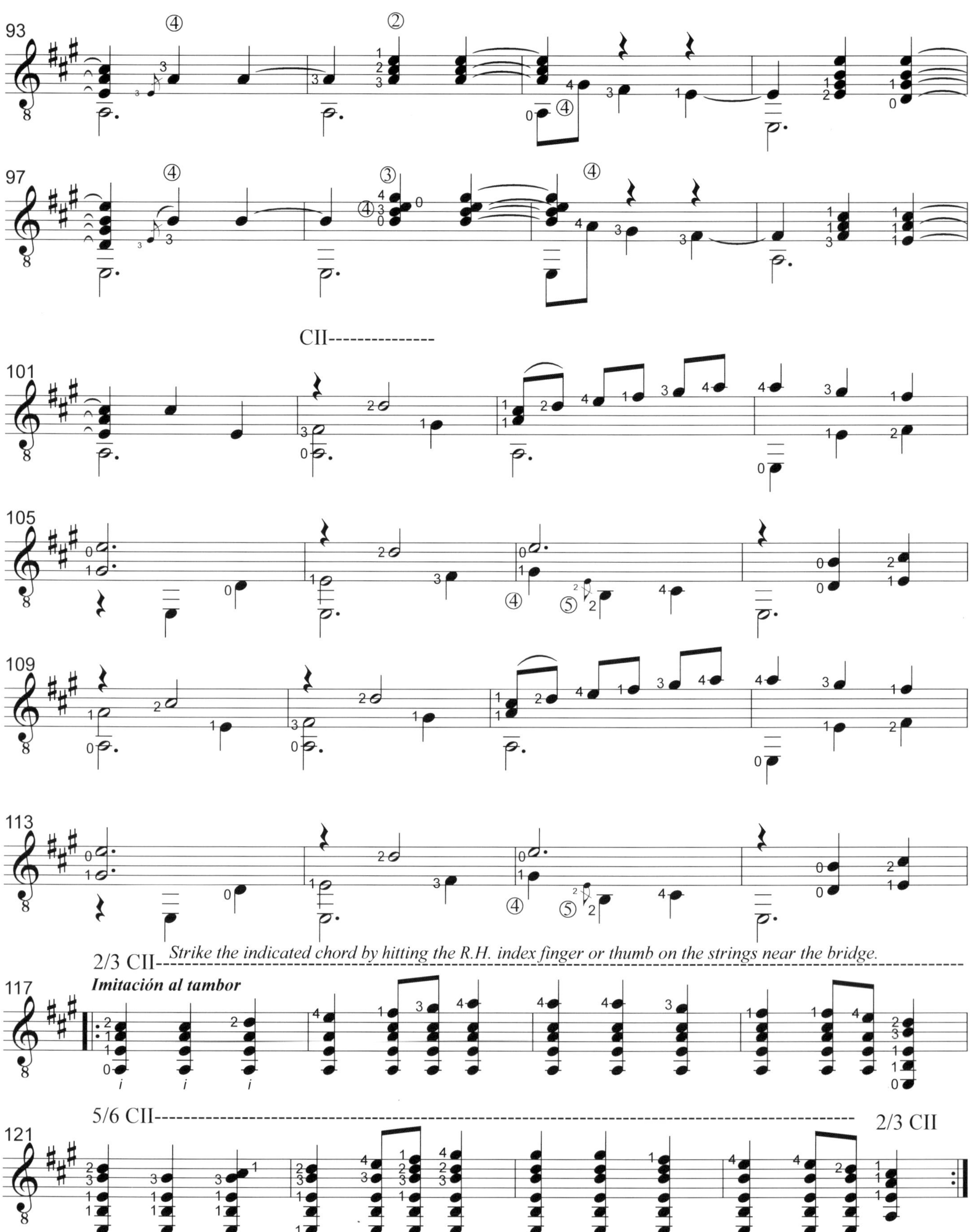
CII
2/3 CII
Strike the indicated chord by hitting the R.H. index finger or thumb on the strings near the bridge.
Imitación al tambor
5/6 CII
2/3 CII

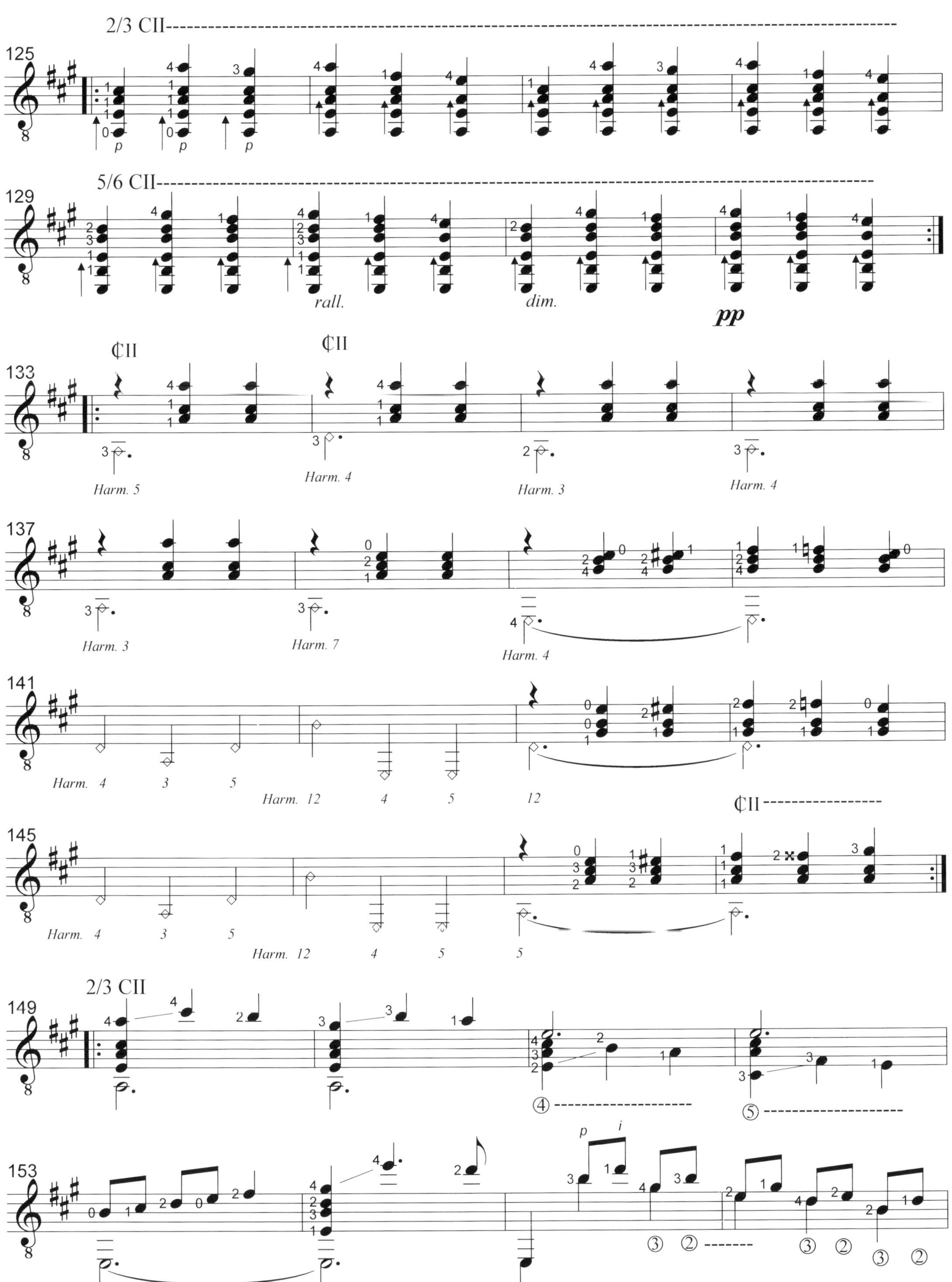
2/3 CII
125
p
p
p
5/6 CII
129
rall.
dim.
pp
ȼII
133
ȼII
Harm. 5
Harm. 4
Harm. 3
Harm. 4
137
Harm. 3
Harm. 7
Harm. 4
141
Harm. 4 3 5
Harm. 12 4 5 12
ȼII
145
Harm. 4 3 5
Harm. 12 4 5 5
2/3 CII
149
④
⑤
153
p i
③ ②
③ ②
③ ②

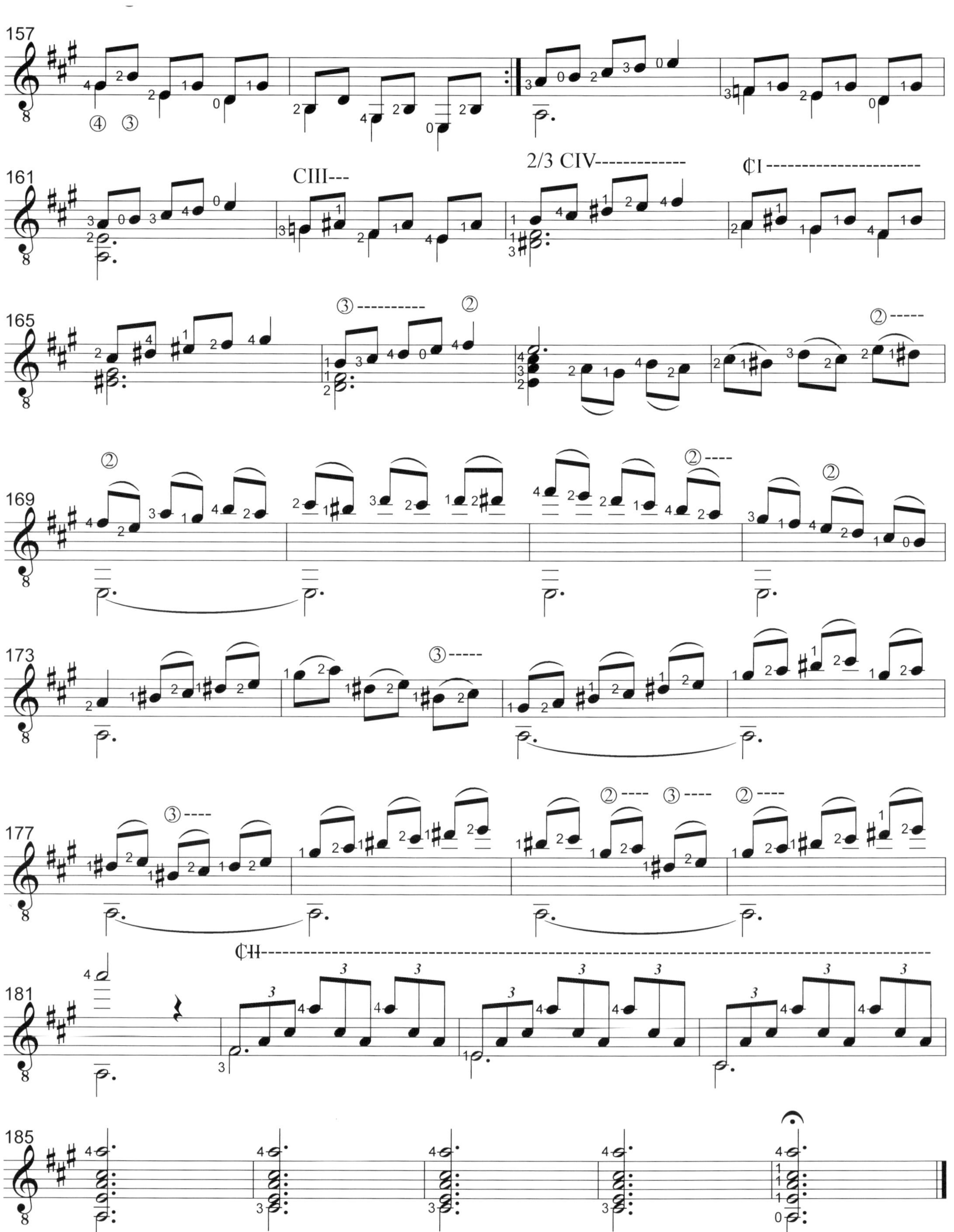
157
161
CIII---
2/3 CIV-------------
₵I ----------------------
165
169
173
177
181
₵II
185

Murcianas

Julian Arcas

Edited by Corey E. Whitehead

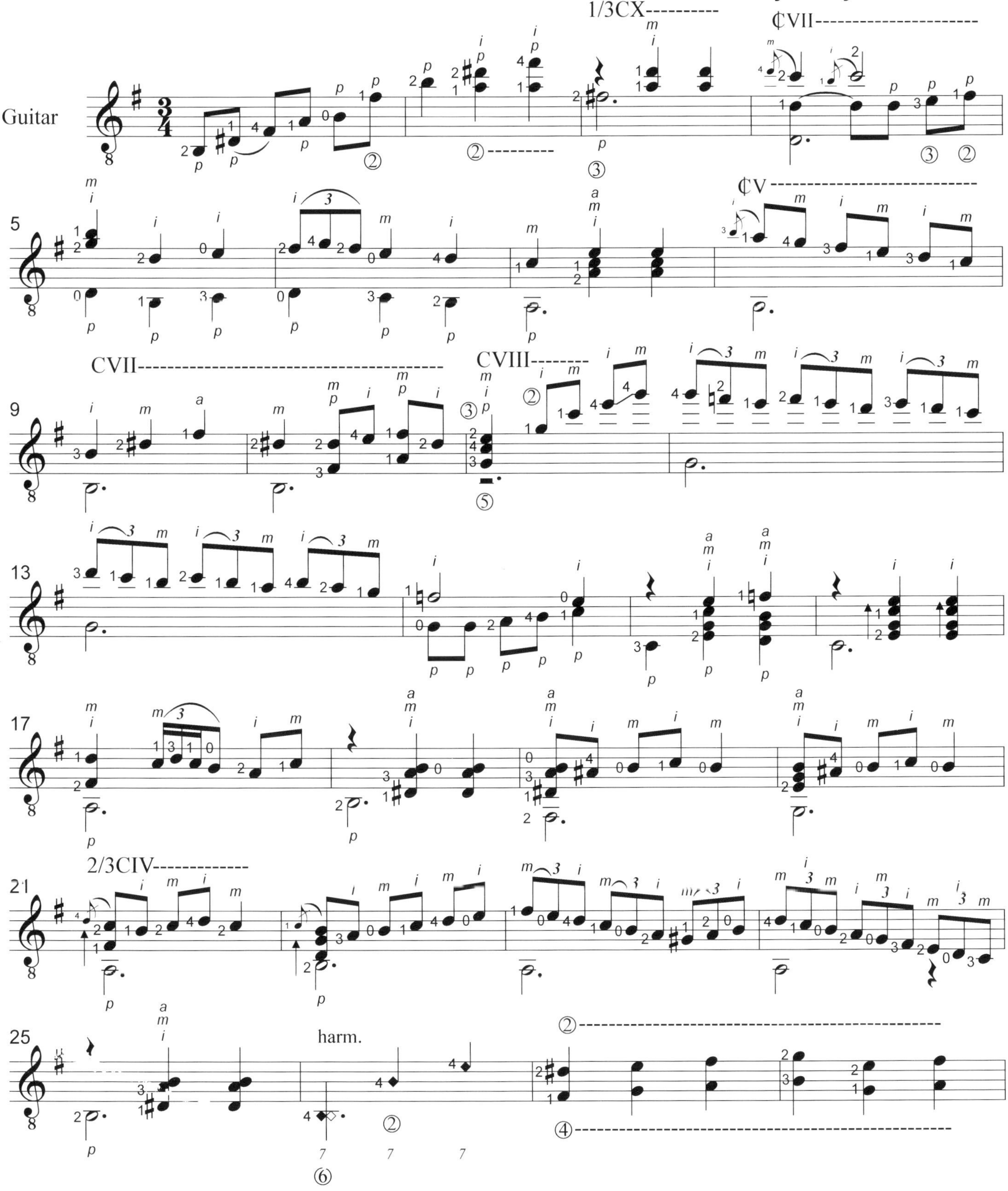

Guitar

harm.

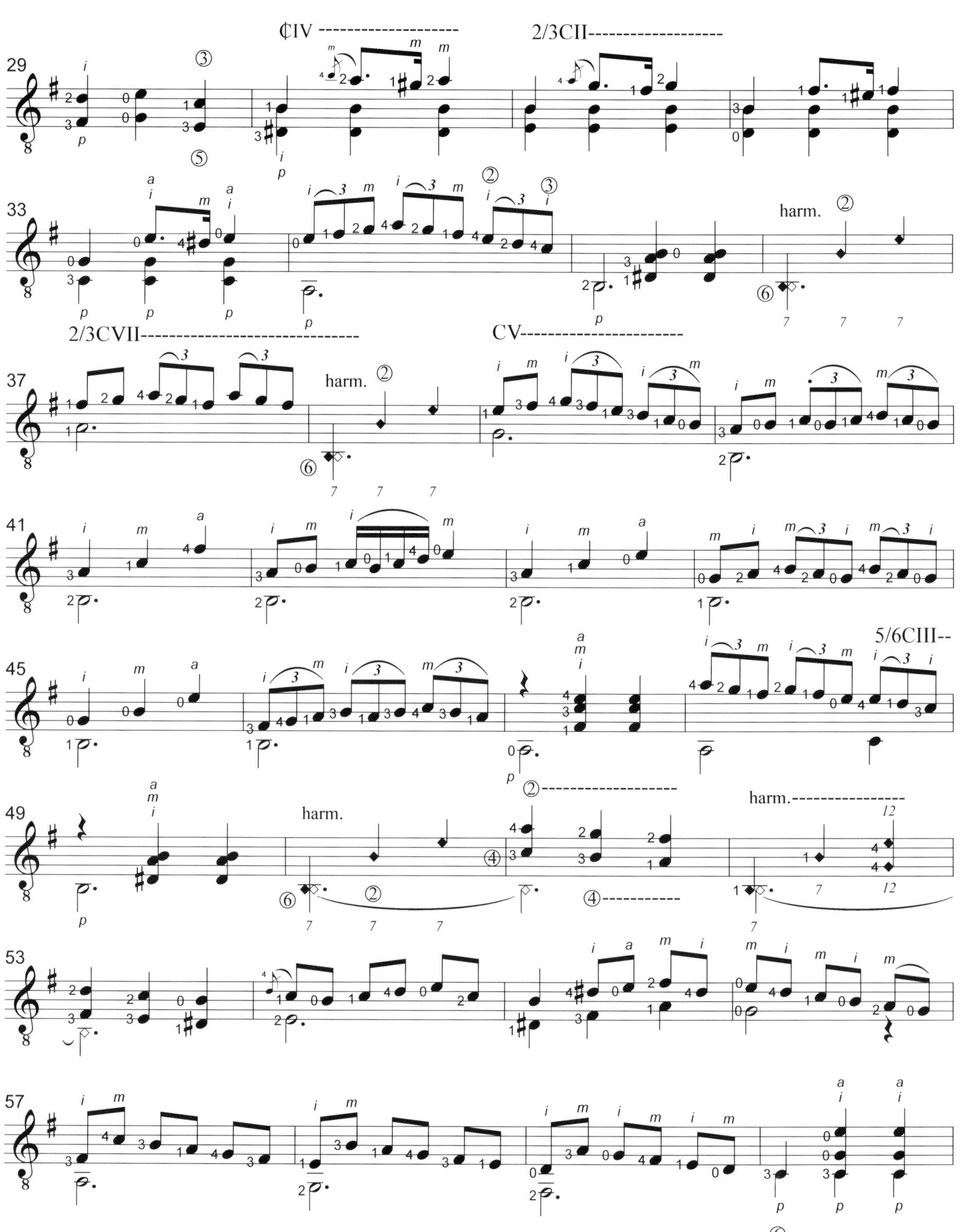
ȻIV
2/3CII
harm.
2/3CVII
harm.
CV
5/6CIII
harm.
harm.

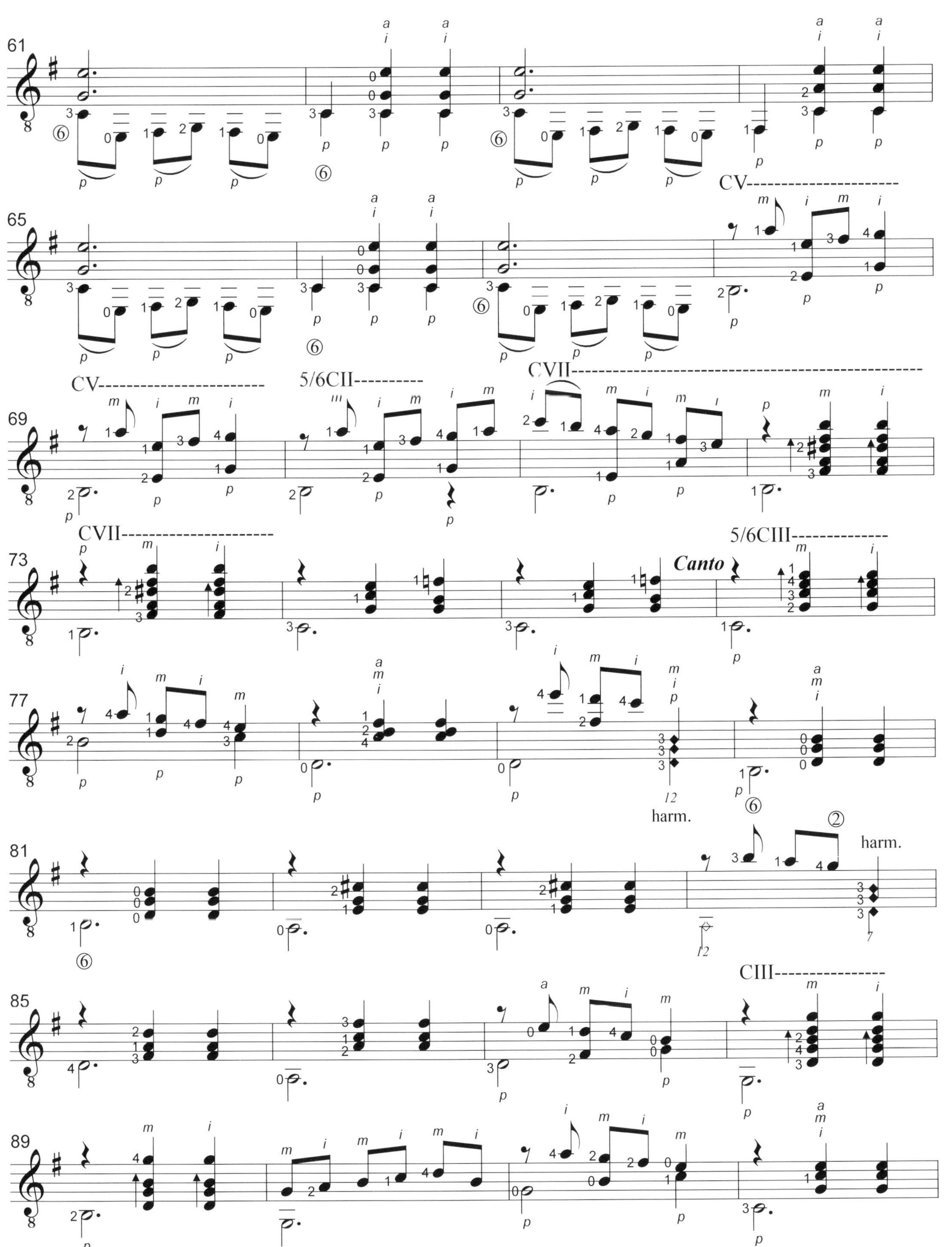
CV
CV
5/6CII
CVII
CVII
Canto
5/6CIII
harm.
harm.
CIII

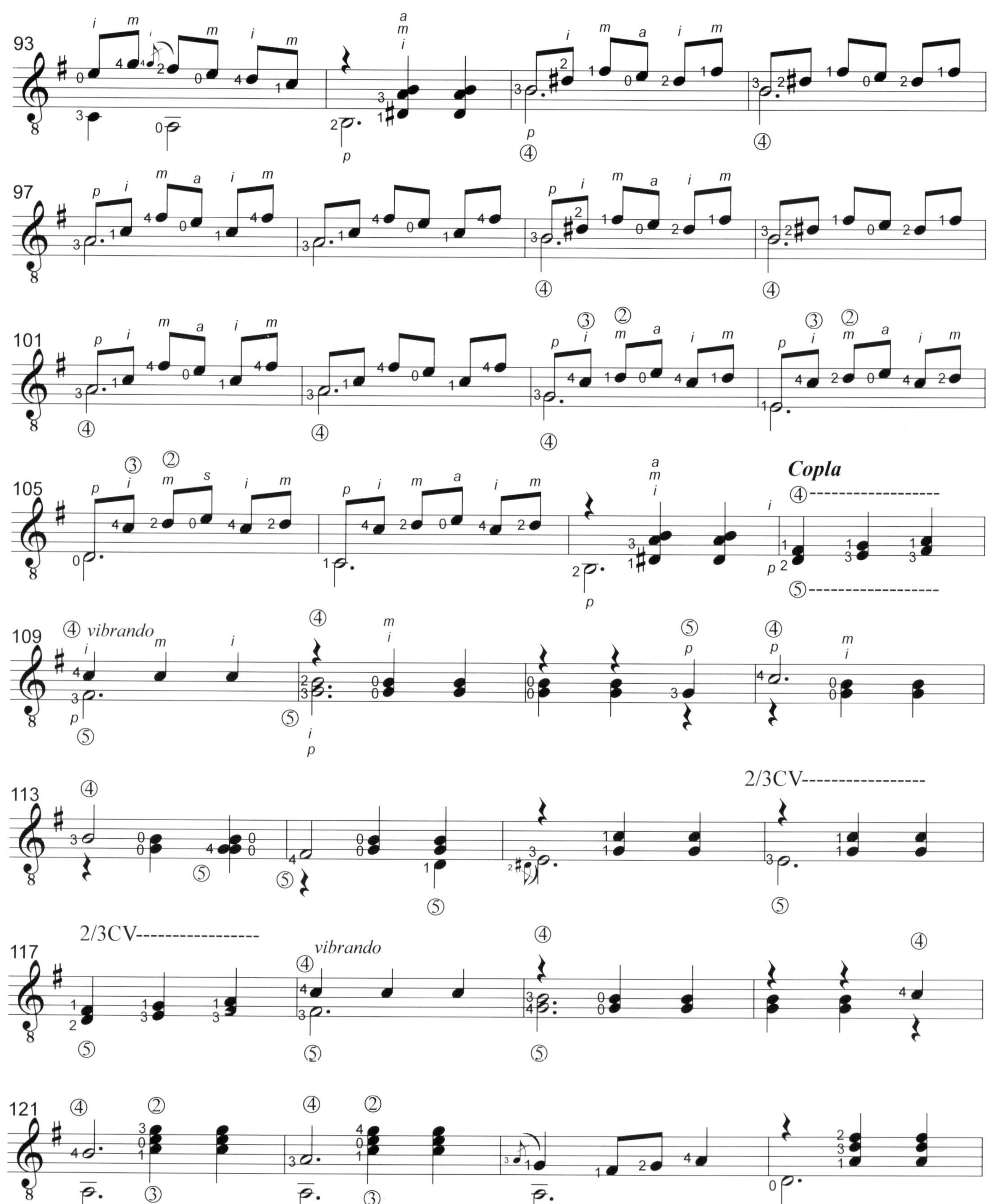
Copla
vibrando
2/3CV
vibrando

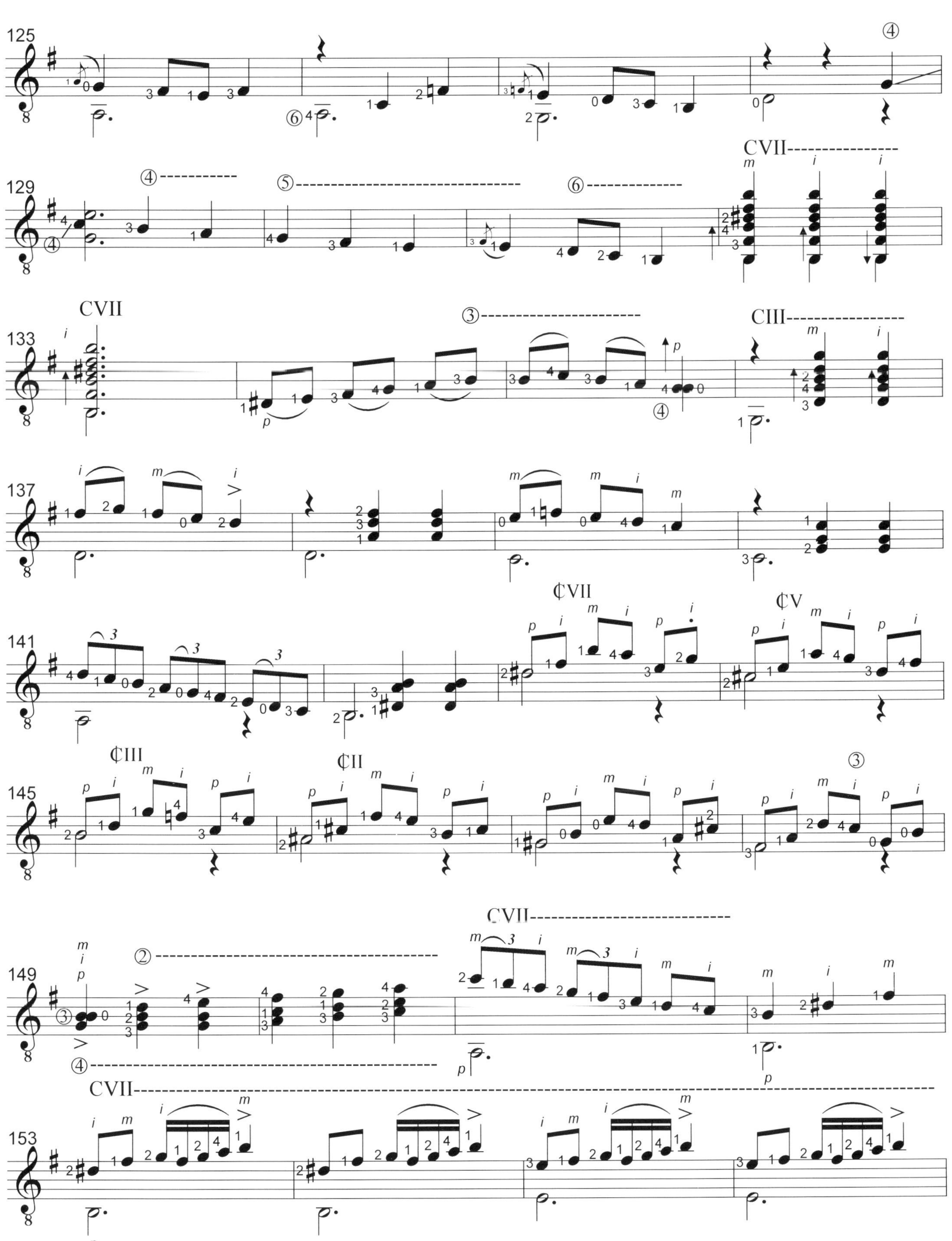

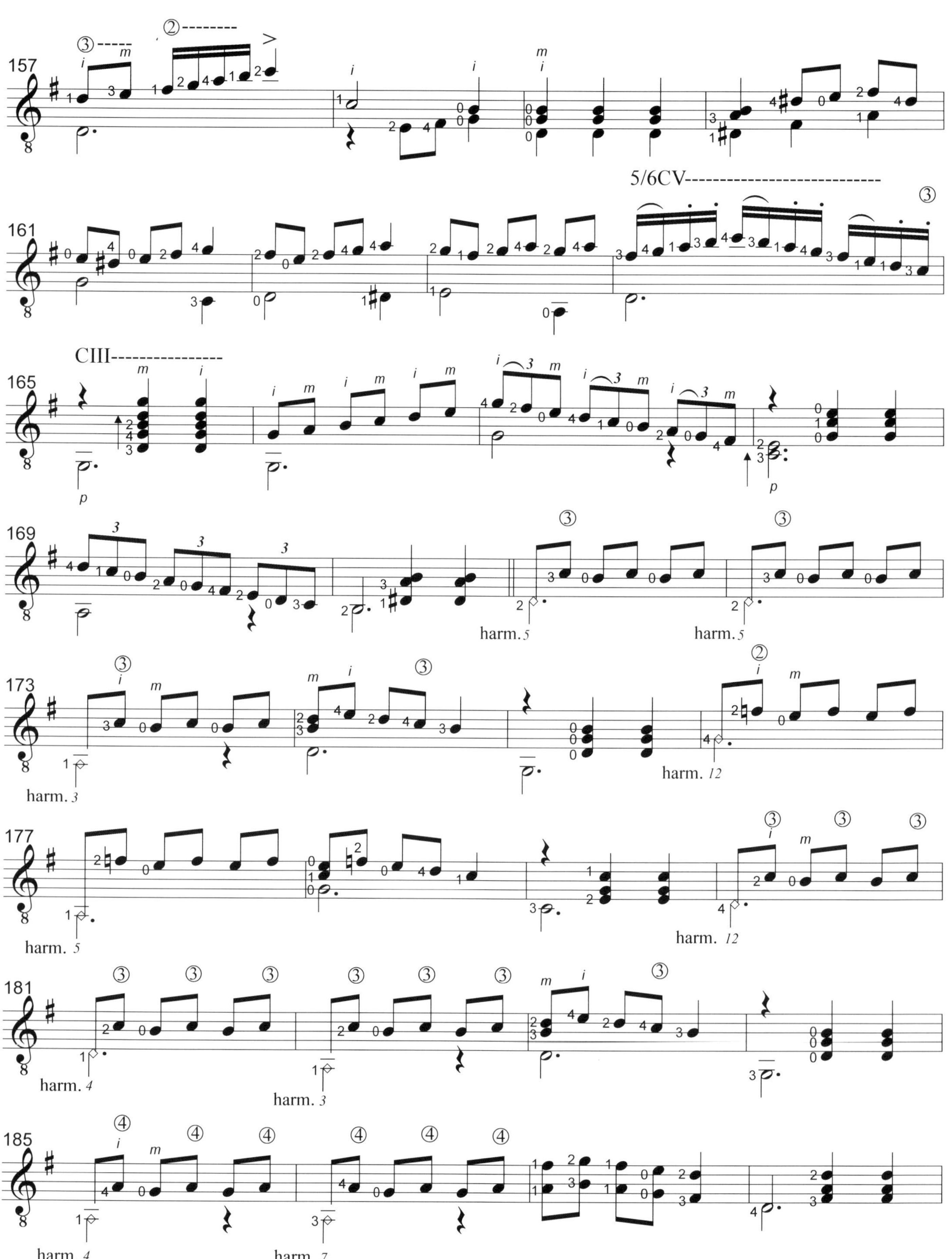
157
5/6CV
161
CIII
165
169
harm. 5
harm. 5
173
harm. 3
harm. 12
177
harm. 5
harm. 12
181
harm. 4
harm. 3
185
harm. 4
harm. 7

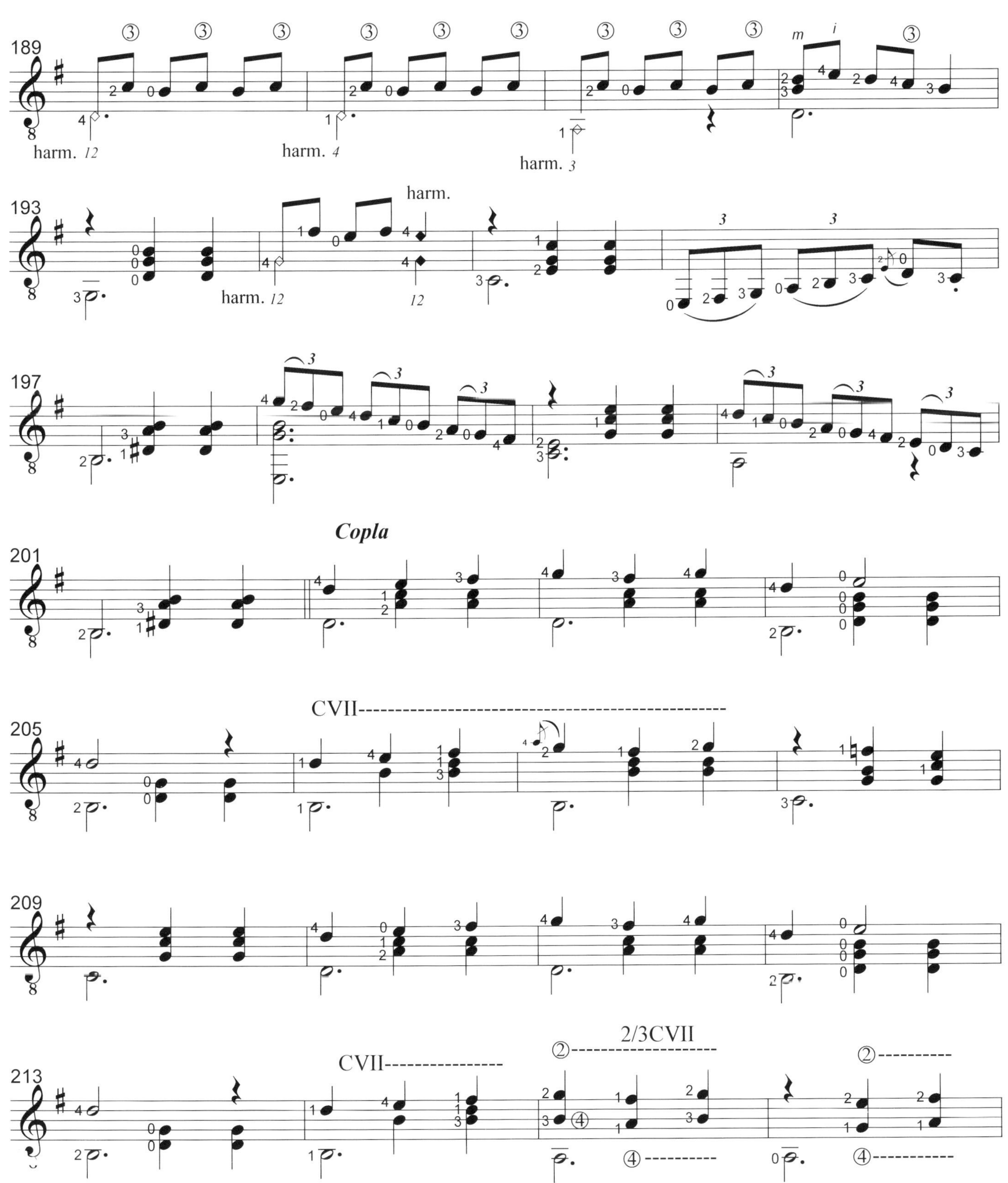
harm. 12
harm. 4
harm. 3
harm.
harm. 12
12
Copla
CVII
2/3CVII

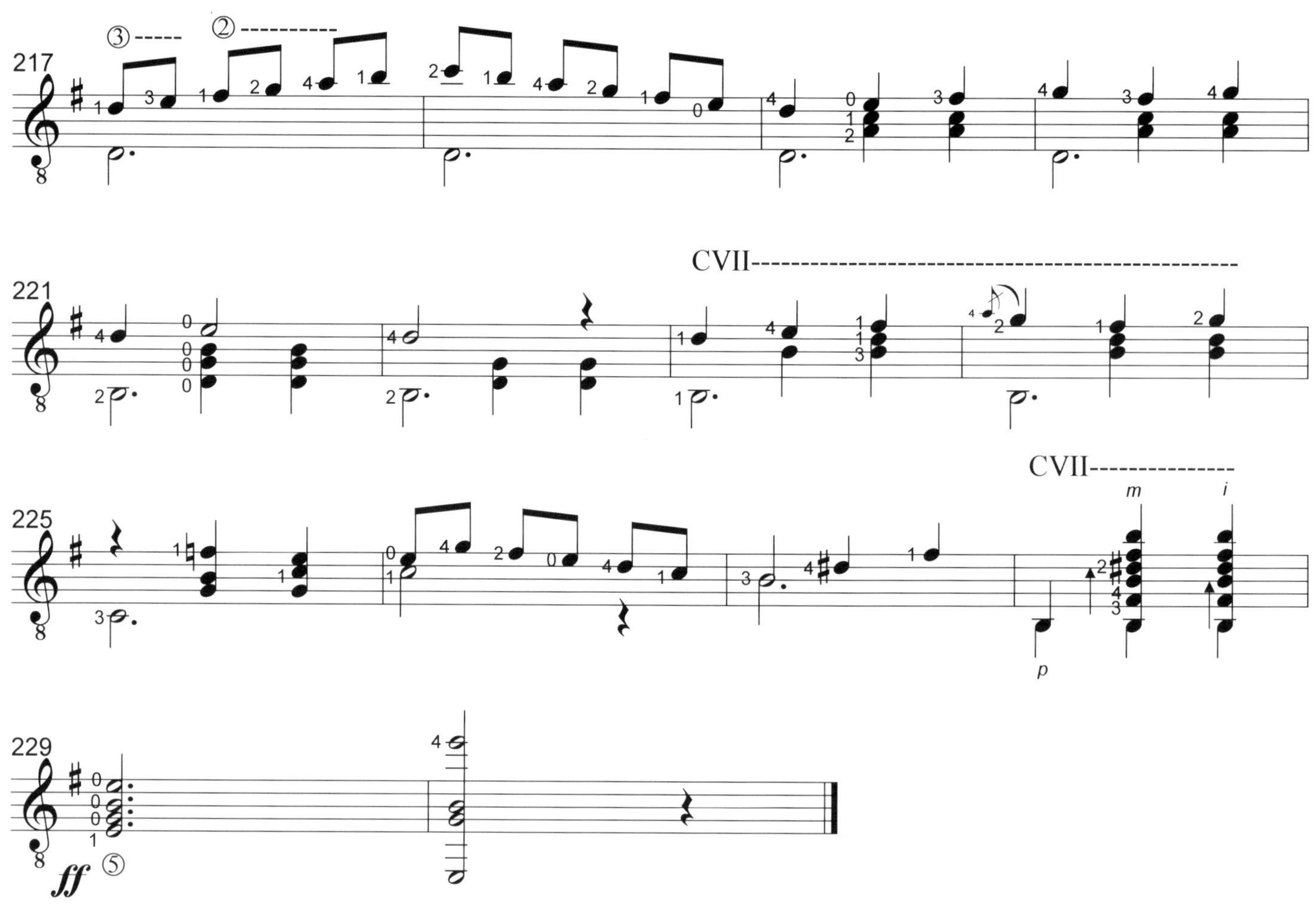
217
221
CVII
225
CVII
m
i
p
229
ff

Unit I, Part III

The Four Primary Palos of Flamenco: Soleá, Fandango, Siguiriyas, Tango

Unit I, Part III
The Four Primary *Palos* of Flamenco
Soleá, Fandango, Siguiriyas, Tango

The four primary forms of flamenco are the *Soleá, Fandango, Siguiriyas, and Tango*.

Flamenco first began with *cante jondo,* singers with percussionists and dancers accompanying them. The older forms of flamenco include the unaccompanied *sub-palos* related to ***Siguiriyas*** such as *Trilla, Tona (Tonada), Martinete,* and *Carcelera;* all share the same metric scheme, and do not use guitar accompaniment to this day.

The mother of all of the flamenco forms is the ***Soleá***. The other forms branch out from this root. The *Fandango de Huelva* and *Verdial* are similar, as are the *Verdial* and the *Soleá*. The *Soleá* has several regional variations and many *sub-forms,* such as *Alegrías, Caracoles, Bulerías, Bulerías por soleá, Caña, Polo, Jaberas, Romeras, Alboreas,* and more. Flamencologist and musician Pedro Camacho has been quoted widely saying that, "There is no *cante,* be it *Malagueña, Taranta, Alegría, Saeta, Siguiriya, Fandango,* or *Serrana* that does not have some of the blood of the *Soleares* running through its veins." (Serrano, Juan, and José Elgorriaga. *"Flamenco, Body and Soul."* The Press at California State University, Fresno. 1990. pp.77-78.)

The *Fandangos de Huelva* are rhythmic and popular in nature; however the *Fandango Grande* has an internal rhythm that is not overt, but is omni-present. Such are the related *sub-palos* of the ***Fandango Grande***: *Malagueña, Granaína, Rondeña, Cartenegera, Tarantas, Mineras, Serranas,* and *Livianas.*

The *Fandangos* and the *Verdial* have obvious similarities and a parallel existence as they are related to the ancient religious pilgrimage to the *Doñana* known as the *Rocío.*

The ***Tangos*** exist on their own, standing as the only *palo* that uses an eight-beat phrase, written in two measures of 4/4 or common time. All of the *palos* previously mentioned use a twelve-beat phrase. *Tangos* borrowed the dark and forlorn *sonidos negros* of *Siguiriyas,* as singer Manuel Torre called them. The *Tangos* are related to an older form called *Tientos,* which is in the same meter, but slower, and with a juxtaposition of rhythmic divisions of 2 and 3, in a *hemiola. Tangos* also have *sub-palos* such as the *Tanguillo, and Zarabanda.* Written in tablature, *Tientos* appear in the early 16th century in the first printed books of Spanish music. Since these early books of Milan, Mudarra, and Narváez are part of the standard repertoire of classical guitarists, it is notable that one of the foundational forms of flamenco, the *Tientos*, are common. This further illustrates the connection between flamenco and classical guitar dating back to 1536.

"Soleá" by Julian Arcas (1832-1882)

1) The *Soleá* refers to a singular lyric (*coplas en tercio, three-part couplets or verses)* of the *palo. Soleares* refers to several *coplas* or *tercios.*
2) The song form of *Soleá* is dictated by the singer as follows: ***Temple*** *(The singer begins with "Ay!" as the guitarist plays an andalusian cadence: iv-♭III-♭II-I).* ***Planteo*** *(The theme of 'cante' is stated).* ***Tercio Grande*** *(The primary three-line couplet or verse of the cante).* ***Alivio*** *('Relief' in the resolution of the tension).* ***Valiente or Peleon*** *('Daring' or 'fiesty', sometimes called the "macho" verse; the guitarist plays V7/iv-iv, V7/iv-iv, ♭III, ♭II, I).* ***Remate*** *(The cantaor finishes by singing a personalized variation on the andalusian cadence).*
3) More detail on the subject may be found in: Juan Serrano and José Elgorriaga, *Flamenco, Body and Soul,* The Press at California State University, Fresno 1990.
4) *Siguiriyas* was originally only a song, which was later developed into a dance. The *Soleá* was once a popular dance that developed into a *cante* which was first interpreted by the mistress of the singer *El Filo (Demofilo),* in the early 19th century. (Serrano/Elgorriaga, p.78).
5) The *Soleá* consists of three or four verses of eight syllables each.
6) The *Soleá* is typically played in E (Mi) *por arriba.* In Utrera, and often in Jerez de la Frontera, the *Soleá* is played *por medio* in A (La), and with a faster tempo.

7) Julian Arcas used the *por medio* key of A (La) and uses a *scordatura* or alternate-tuning for the 6th string, which is down a whole-tone to "D."
8) Study of the basic form of the *Soleá* is recommended to understand the "pillars and canons" of this *palo.*
9) Single melodic notes should be played rest stroke when possible, as should bass notes.
10) Listen to various singers performing *Soleá,* and then play this work discerning which sections are *"cante,"* which are solo guitar *falsetas,* and which are *compás.*

"Seguidillas Gitanas" by Tomás Damas (1817-ca.1880)

1) *Siguiriyas,* is a different *palo* than *Seguidillas* with a phonetic alternative spelling from archaic Spanish. These two forms are only associated by this phonetic similarity. The meter and rhythm of the *Seguidilla* is similar to the *Sevillanas.*
2) *Seguidilla* is the diminutive form of the word *seguida,* which means "sequence" and most often refers to a Castilian (Castile is a Northern Spanish province of Spain) folksong and dance form in a brisk ¾ meter, and was for two dancers. The song and dance began on an *anacrusis* or pick-upbeat or beats. The meter, tempo, and *anacrusis* are therefore interestingly similar to the popular song and dance called *Sevillanas.*
3) The term *seguidilla* also may refer to the lyric stanza form with four to seven assonant (consonant vowels and consonants) lines in a rhythm that fits the words into the meter.
4) The light-hearted *seguidillas* are of two types: from *La Mancha (Seguidilla Manchega, Sevillana Gallego),* or from *Andalusia (Sevillanas de Sevilla)* and *Murciana (Murcia).* The latter are often referred to as a regional sub-form of the *Fandango Grande.*
5) The *Siguiriyas* as interpreted by *cantaors* (flamenco singers) is with *sonidos negros* of the guitar and voice, and is *cante jondo.* The beat pattern begins on the second (2nd) beat of a ¾ measure (in 8th notes) to a complete measure of 6/8, terminating on the first beat of the next measure (3/4): **1** 2 **1** 2 | **1** 2 3 **1** 2 3 | **1** 2
6) Tomás Damas' interpretation of this *palo* within a solo guitar work does exhibit elements of song and accompaniment. Of course, the song is without words when played as a solo. This is not uncommon for Spanish guitarists to harmonize a commonly known melody, and play it as a solo, just as jazz musicians.
7) The *Seguidillas Gitanas* uses the same key signature and tonality (F-sharp Dorico/Phrygian) as used previously in *Rondeña Nueva.* The guitar is tuned to "Drop-D" just as Julian Arcas tuned the guitar for his *Soleá.*
8) The diminutive note heads in m.6 and m.11 are called "grace notes." The small grace note is played simultaneously with the large bass note. The subsequent melodic note (above the bass, following the grace note) immediately follows the grace note. In other words, play the bass and grace note together, and pull-off quickly from the grace note to the large melodic note.
9) The ***tr*** symbol in measure 19 above the F-sharp indicates a *trill.* The *trill* is a rapid hammer-on and pull-off on the notes F♯-G-F♯. The first note (F♯) is articulated (picked) by the right hand as the left-hand index finger (1) presses F♯, it remains pressed as the middle (2) hammers on to G and then pulls-off to F♯. The bass note is played with the written note of the trill, F♯.

"Coleccion de Tangos" by Julian Arcas (1832-1882)

1) The introduction and first *Tango* are in the appropriate key for *Tangos* (A Dórico/Phrygian) and is in standard tuning.
2) The indications for natural harmonics are the simple and clear indications first used in the sequence of works in this book. The string is indicated by the note head, and the fret is indicated by an Arabic numeral.
3) The second *Tango* in this collection is in the parallel major key, D Major (two sharps).
4) The third *Tango* is in the key of G major, down a fifth from D Major.
5) The fourth *Tango* is in the key of E minor, which is the "relative minor" key of the previous tonality G Major.
6) The final *Tango* is in the festive key of A Major with three sharps.
7) The percussionists and dancers emphasize the eight-beat pattern as follows: **1** 2 **3** 4 | **5** 6 **7** 8, or **1** 2 **3** 4 | **1** 2 **3** 4
8) Guitarists emphasize beats "2" and "4." Jazz and Rock musicians call this the "backbeat." The guitarist is also responsible for playing syncopations, referred to by jazz and rock musicians as "pushing" the beat [early]. This is also called "jumping" the beat by some guitarists in Spain. This means one has license to emphasize beats "2" and "4," and to also emphasize or accent notes in between the beats.

9) The straight line that connects two note heads when combined with a slur indication (curved line) means to create a slur by sliding the finger to the second note of the pair without striking the second note. The sound of the second note is produced by the rapid slide up the string at the moment the second note begins. This technique and sound is called *glissando.* The *glissando* is similar to another technique called *portamento* in that both contain a slide symbol between two notes, sliding the same left-hand finger from the first note to the next. The difference in the *portamento* is that both notes are articulated by a right-hand finger stroke.

"Fandango Variado" Op. 16 by Dionisio Aguado (1784-1849)

1) This work is in the tonality of A Dórico (Phrygian), using the key signature for D minor.
2) These "Fandango variations" are somewhat of a fantasy, juxtaposing sections of *copla* (mm.34-47, 132-144, 198-213) with *falsetas* (guitarist plays variations) and *rítmo en compás* (guitarist plays rhythmic chordal accompaniment).
3) The first three notes are played by plucking the first note with the thumb and then hammering-on and sliding (*glissando*) successively on the 4th string with the 1st finger of the left hand. The two grace notes are played quickly and may fall slightly before the beat. The large note may be placed on the beat. Alternatively, play the first grace note **on** the beat and the subsequent notes slightly **behind** the beat. The former is often the standard, however at times the latter may serve the music better.
4) Measure one (1) through the downbeat of measure eight (8) is played entirely with the thumb.
5) The last beat of measure seven (7) features a *melisma* (melodic flourish) which is called a *turn* in Baroque performance practice. The small grace notes approach a large note head. The large note head is the goal. First play the measure without the grace notes, playing only the large notes. Then add the grace notes, attempting to preserve the rhythm of the large notes.
6) In measures 116-119, make sure to preserve the tempo and rhythm of the large 8th notes. The grace notes are effectively a written ornament.

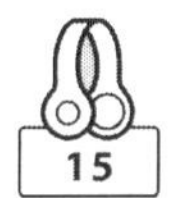

Soleá

Julian Arcas
Edited by Corey E. Whitehead

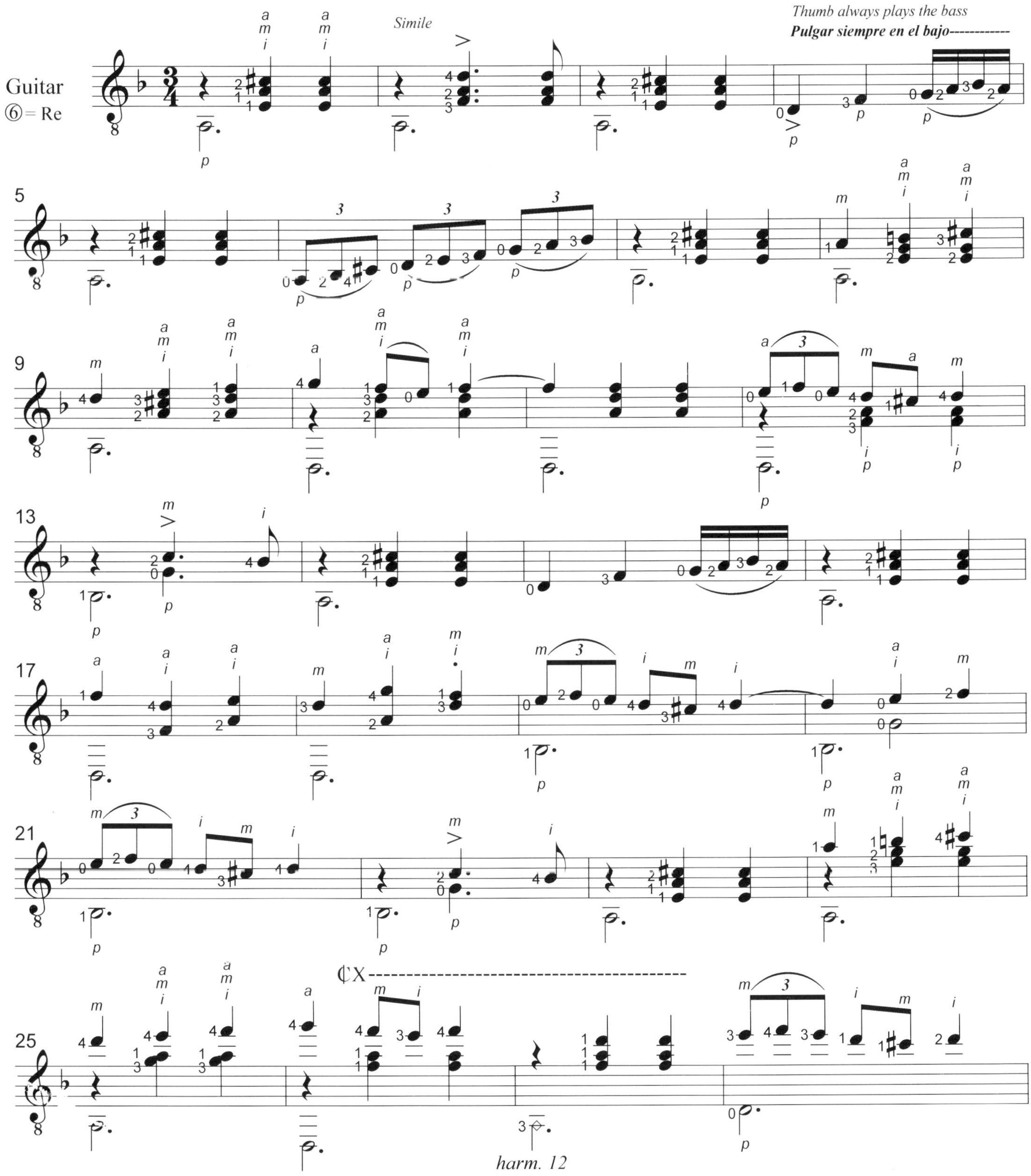

Thumb always plays the bass

Pulgar siempre en el bajo

Guitar

⑥ = Re

Simile

harm. 12

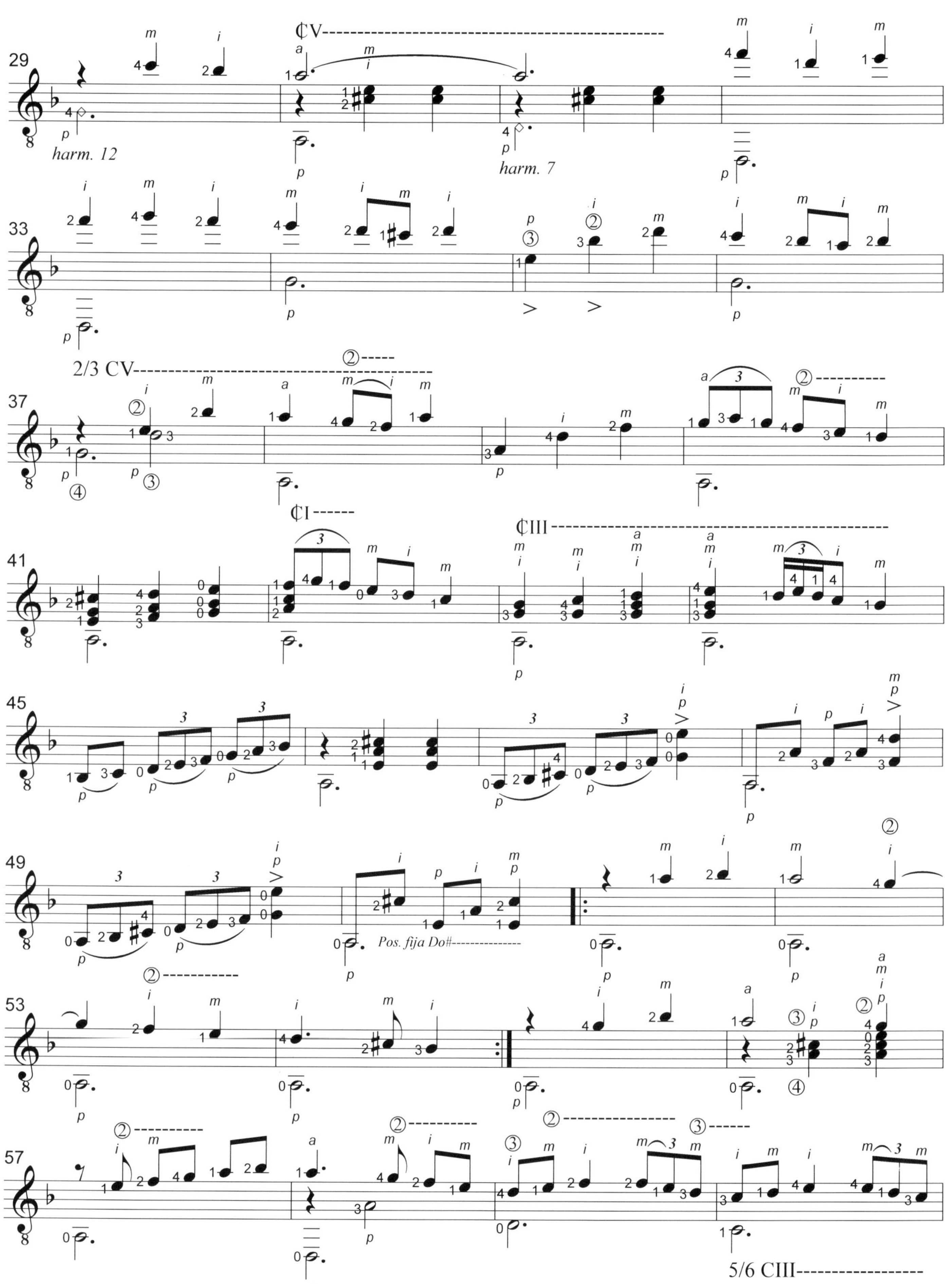
29
harm. 12
CV
harm. 7
33
37
2/3 CV
41
CI
CIII
45
49
Pos. fija Do#
53
57
5/6 CIII

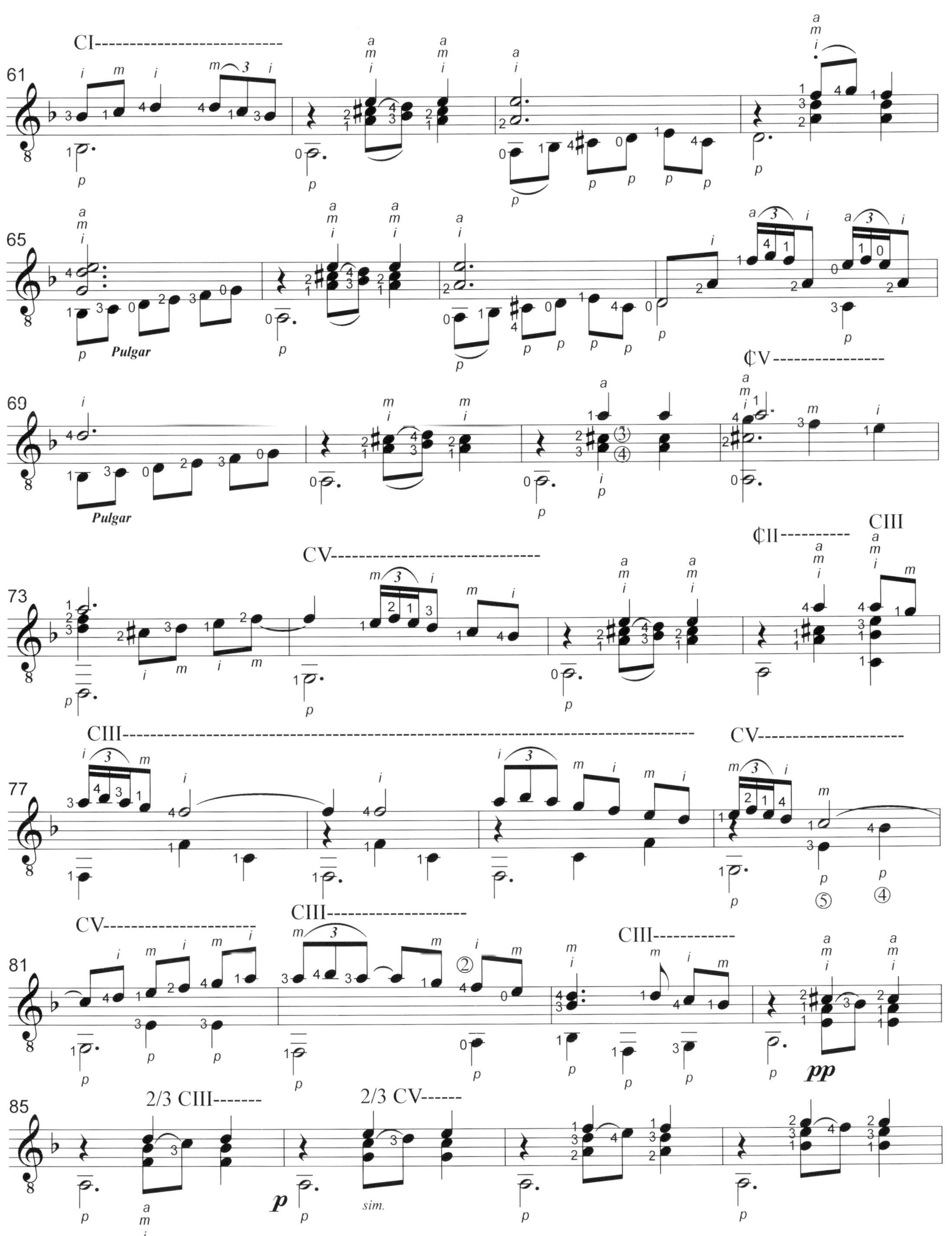
CI
Pulgar
Pulgar
CV
CV
CII
CIII
CIII
CV
CV
CIII
CIII
2/3 CIII
2/3 CV
sim.

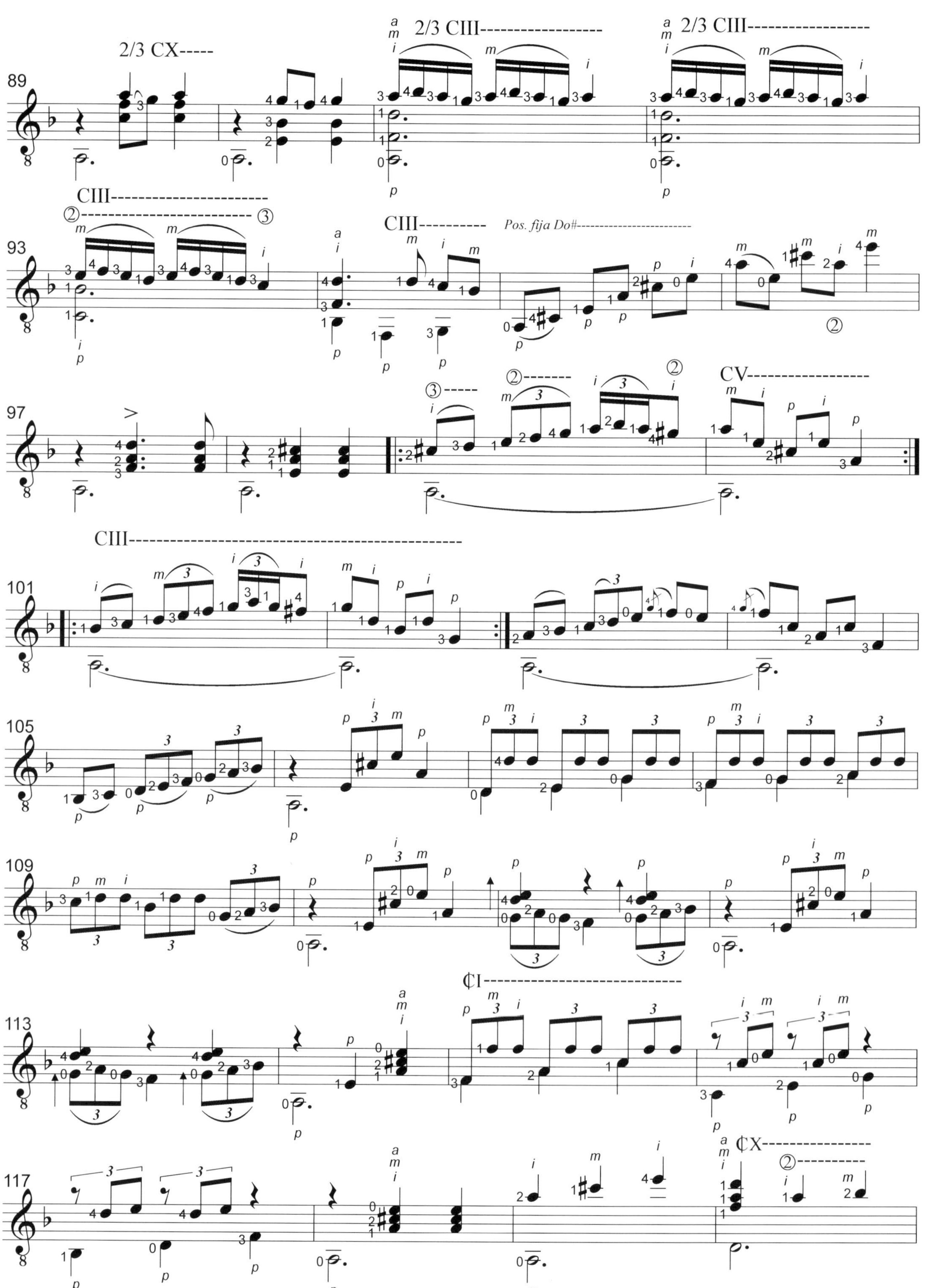
2/3 CX-----
2/3 CIII
2/3 CIII
89
CIII
93
CIII
Pos. fija Do#
97
CV
CIII
101
105
109
ȼI
113
ȼX
117

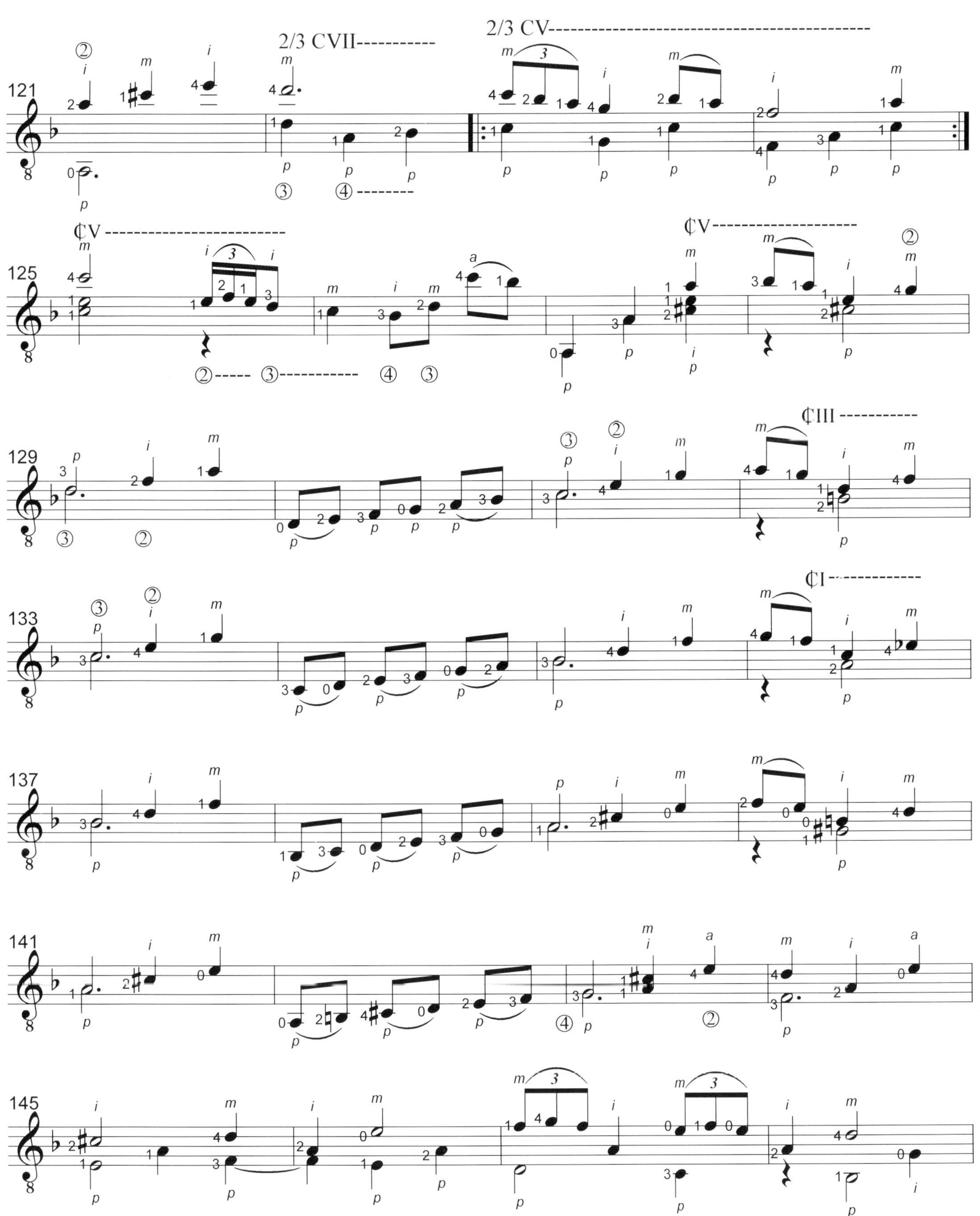
121
2/3 CVII
2/3 CV
125
CV
CV
129
CIII
133
CI
137
141
145

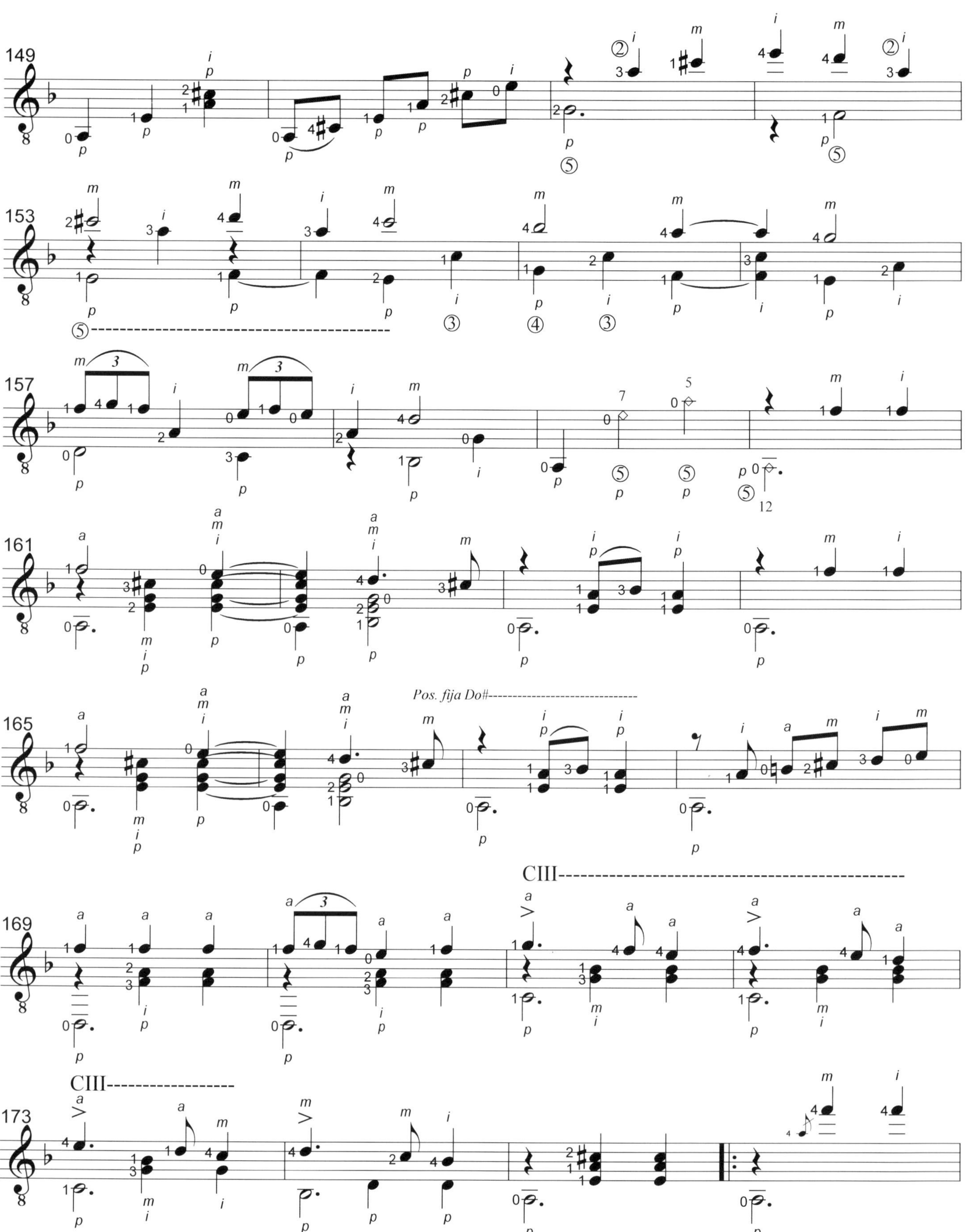
Pos. fija Do#
CIII
CIII

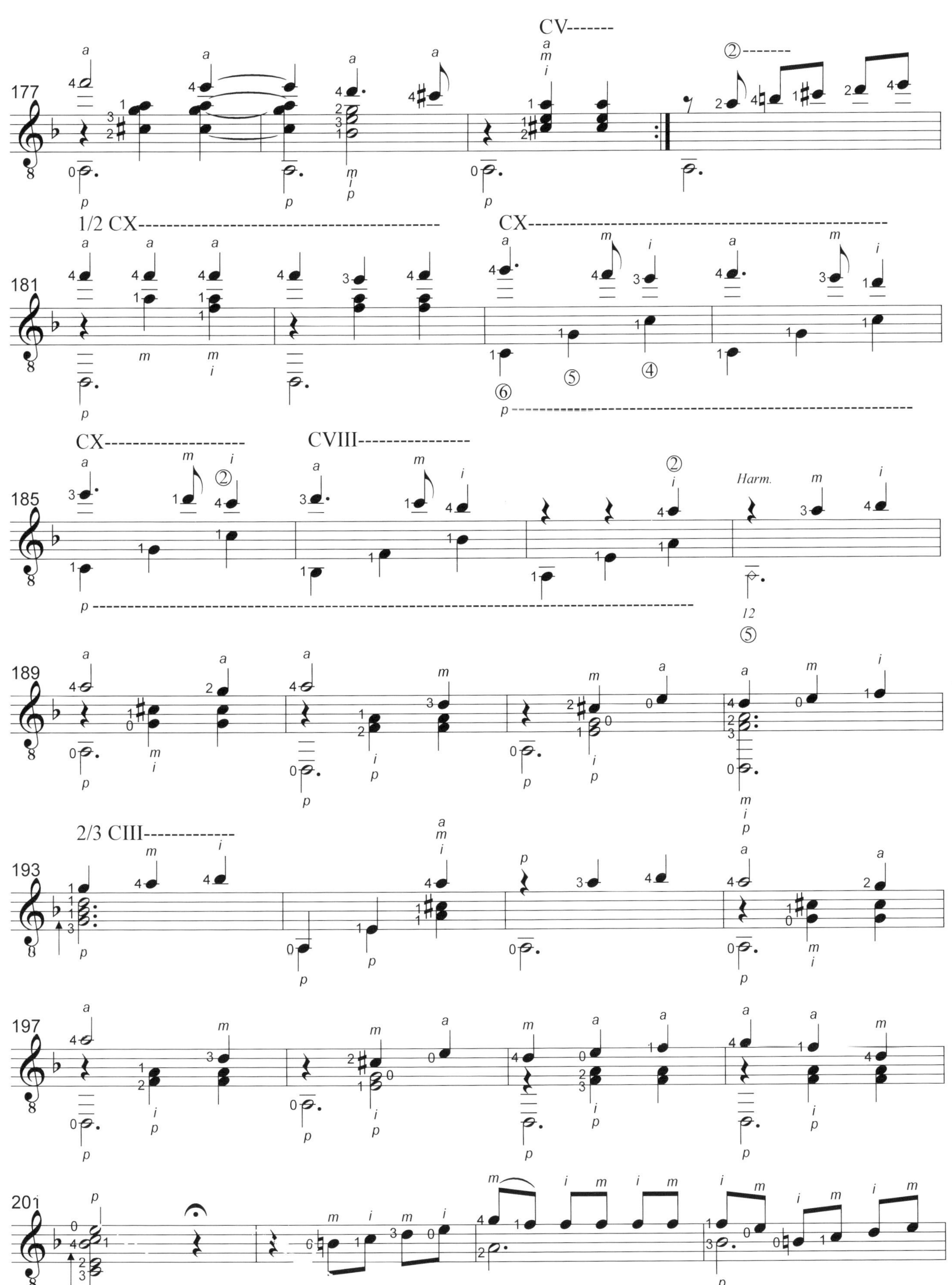
177
CV
181
1/2 CX
CX
185
CX
CVIII
Harm.
189
193
2/3 CIII
197
201

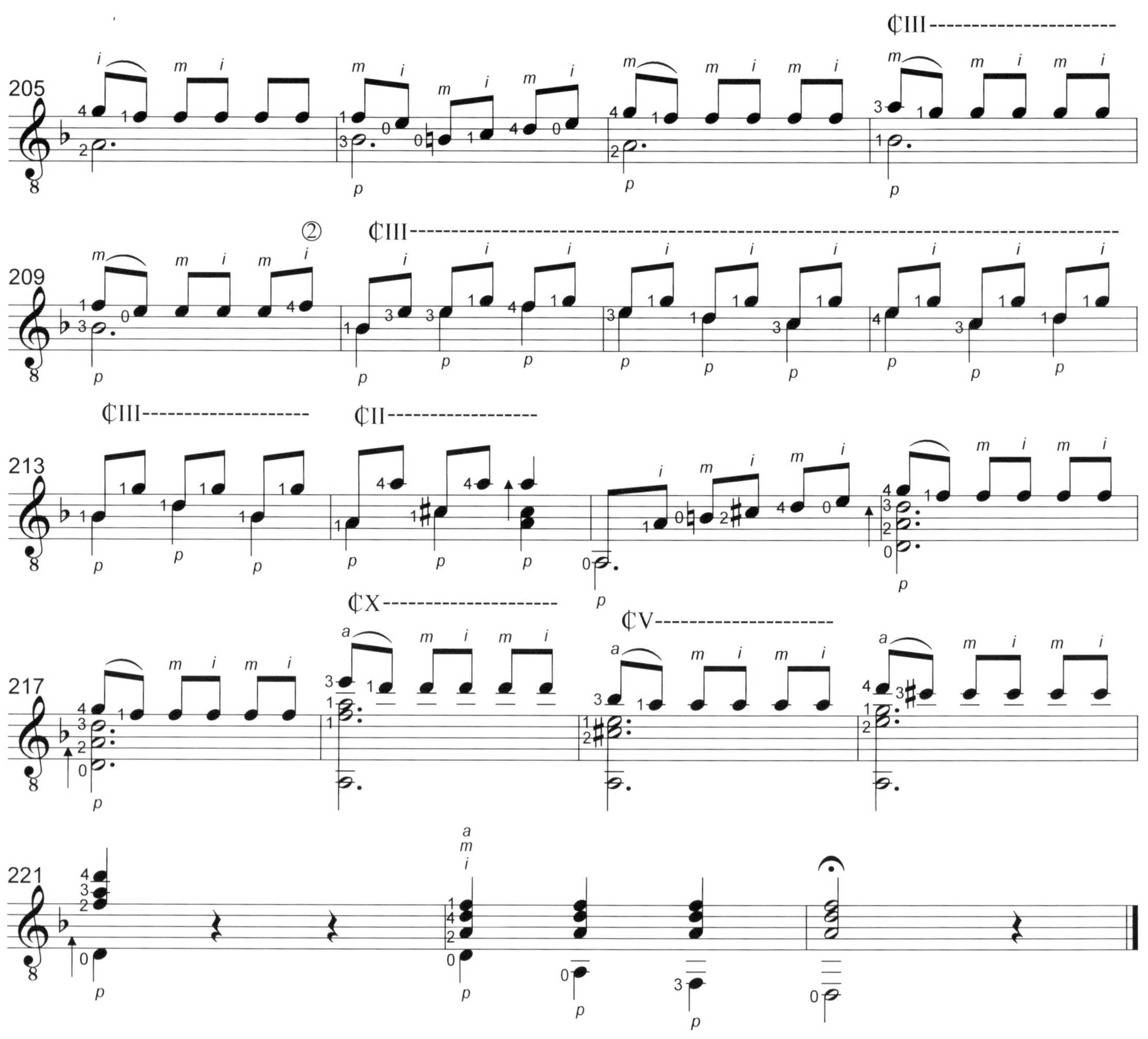

205
CIII
209
CIII
213
CIII
CII
217
CX
CV
221

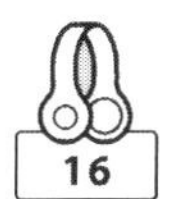

Seguidillas Gitanas

Tomás Damas
Edited by Corey E. Whitehead

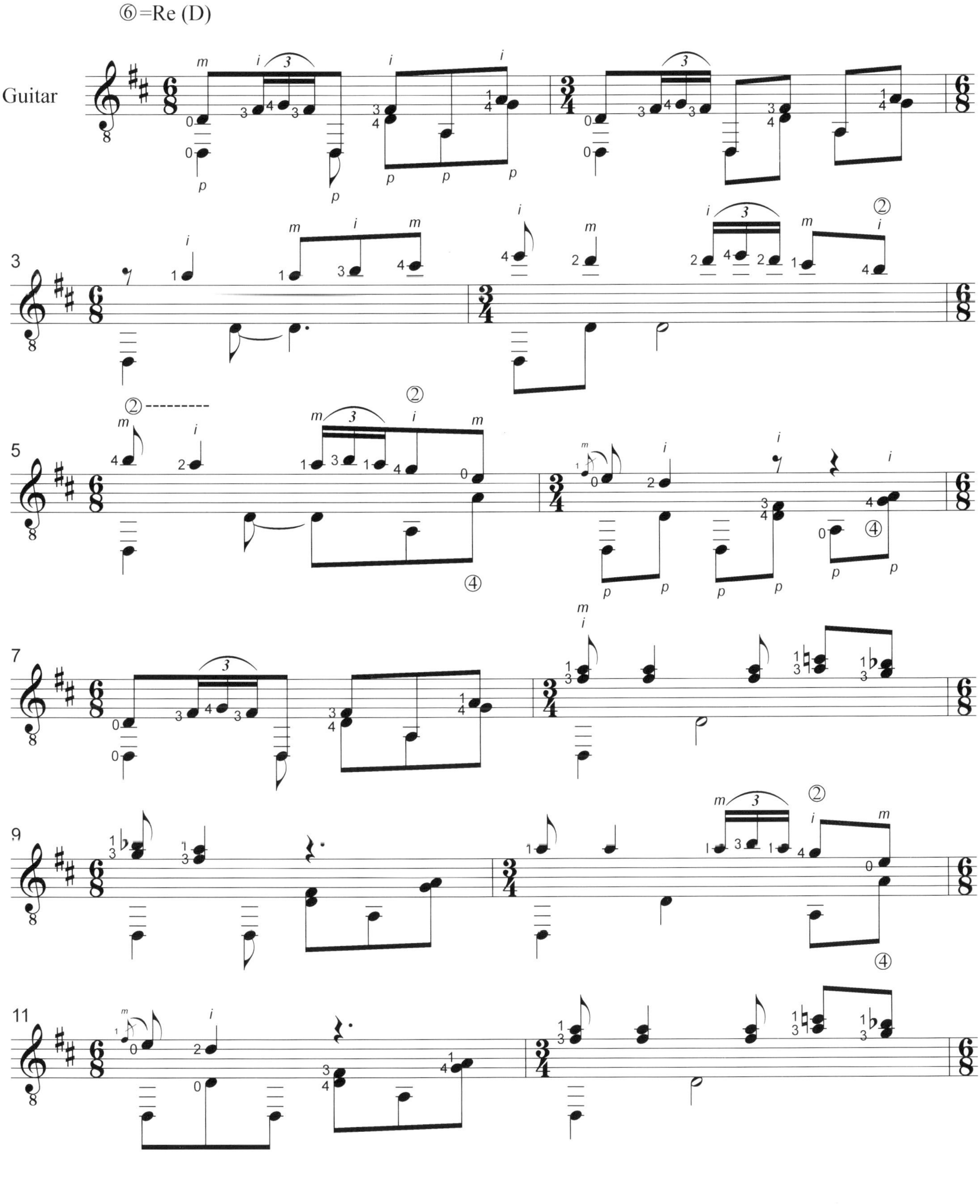

⑥=Re (D)

Guitar

3

5

7

9

11

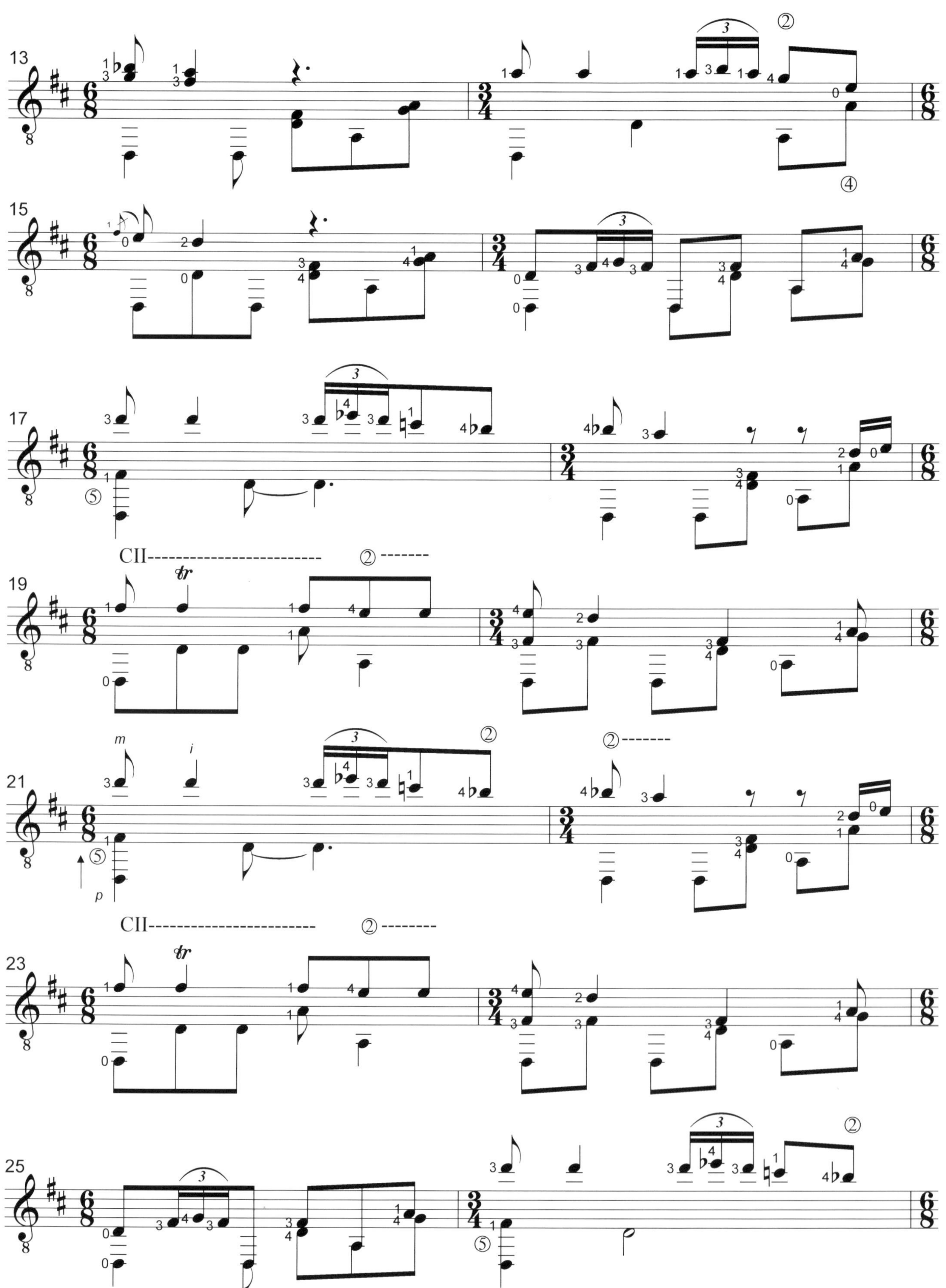

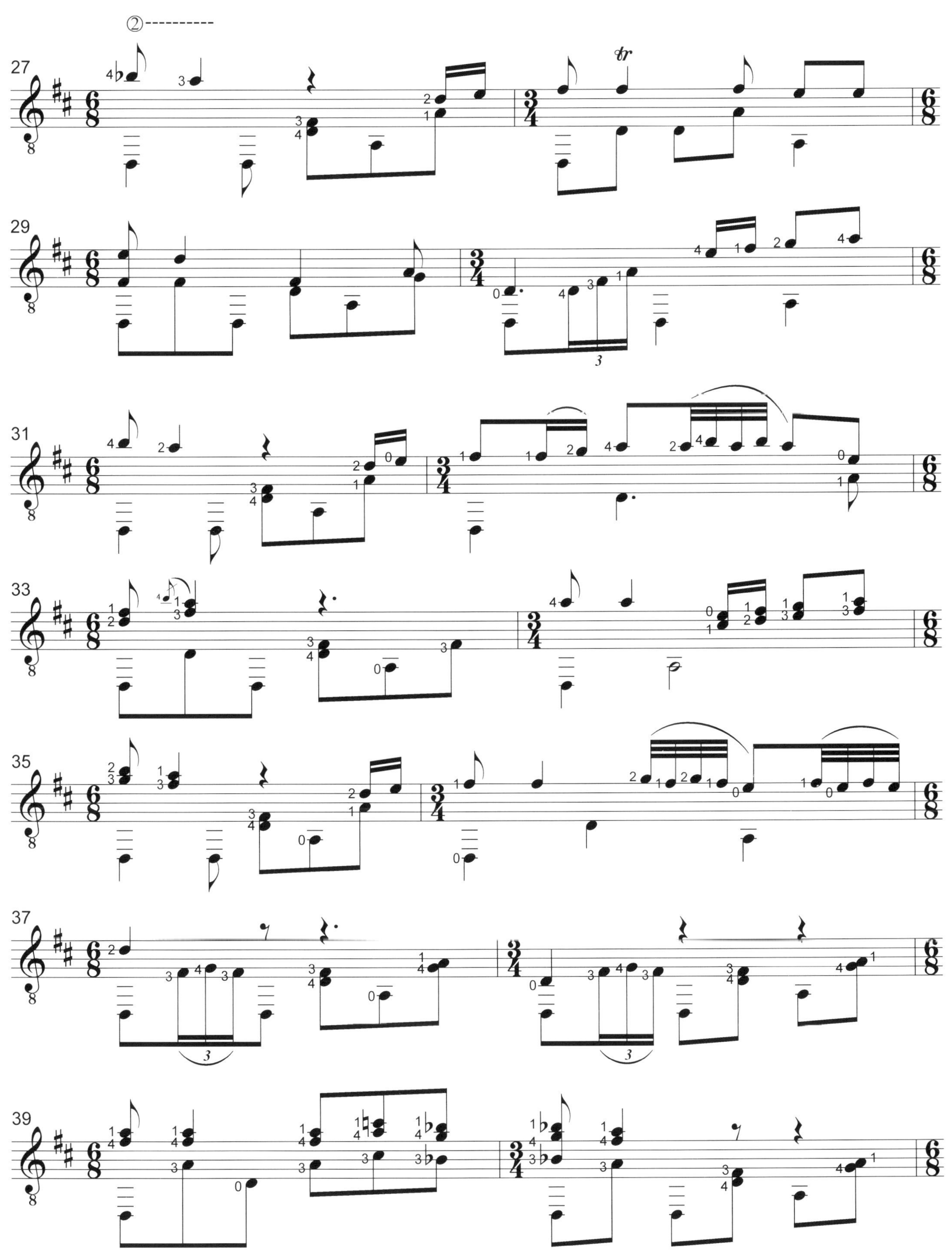

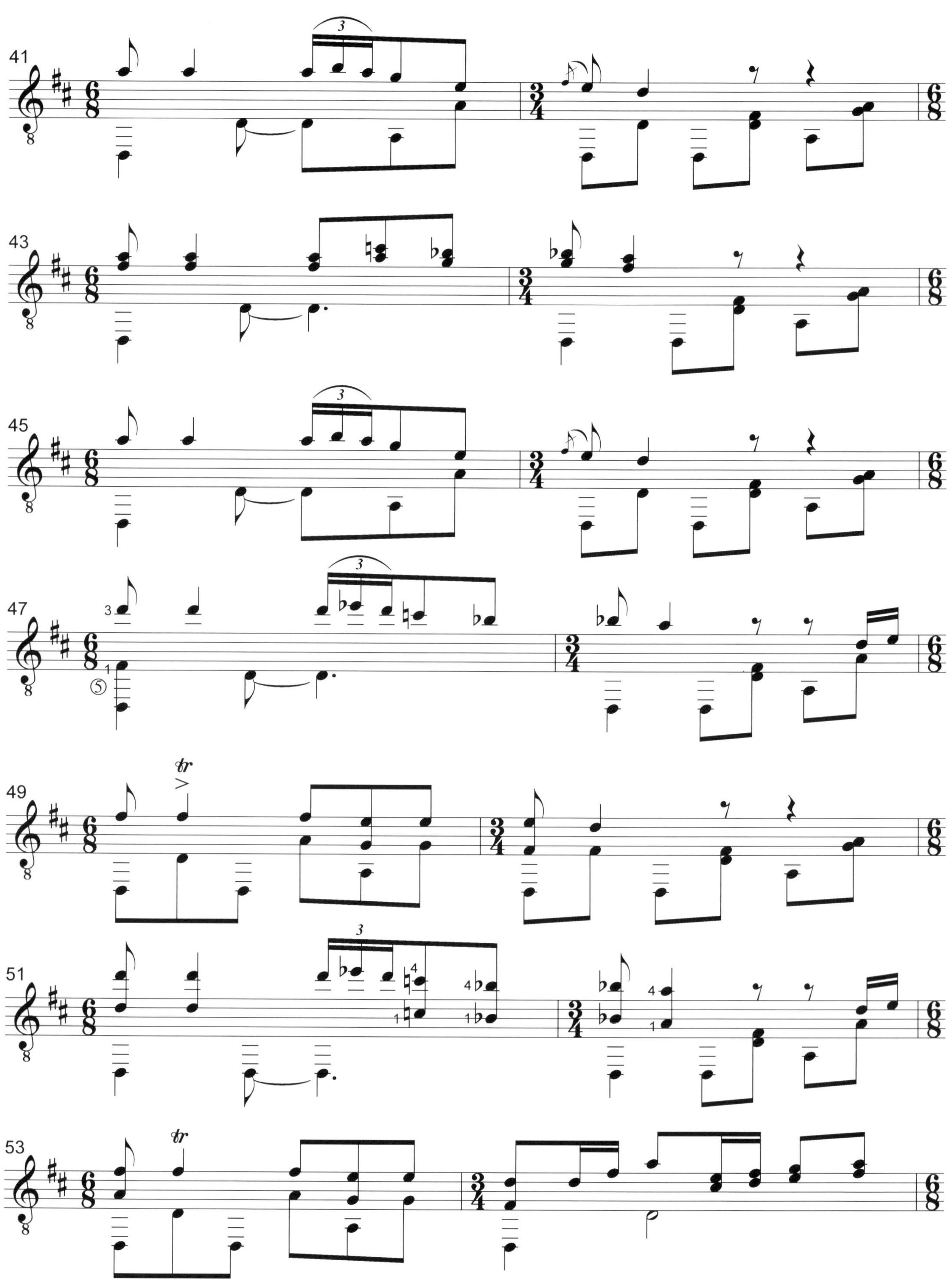
41
43
45
47
49
51
53

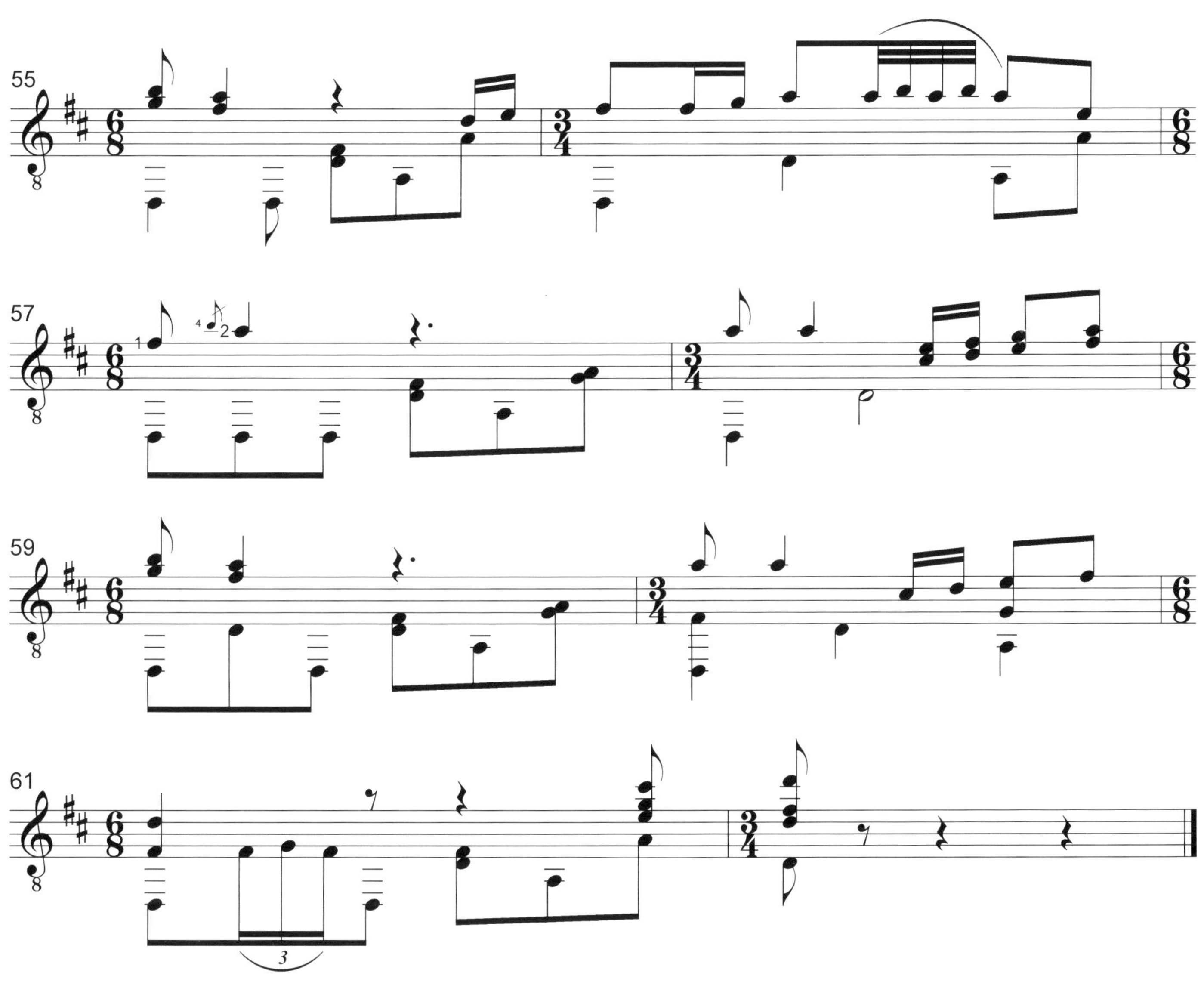

55
57
59
61

Colección de Tangos

Julian Arcas
Edited by Corey E. Whitehead

Introducción

Andante moderato

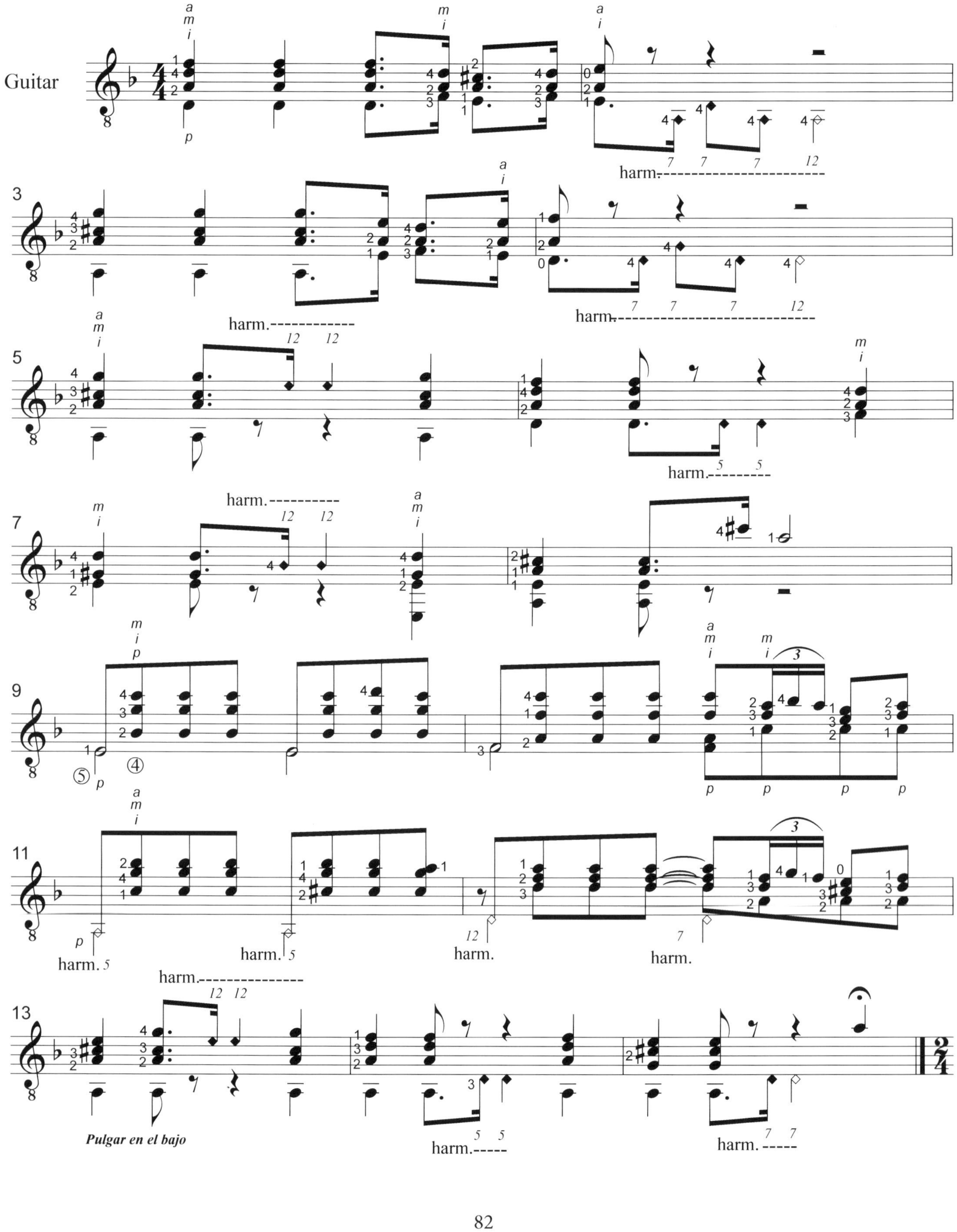

Guitar

harm.

Pulgar en el bajo

Tango Número 1: "Aire de Tango"

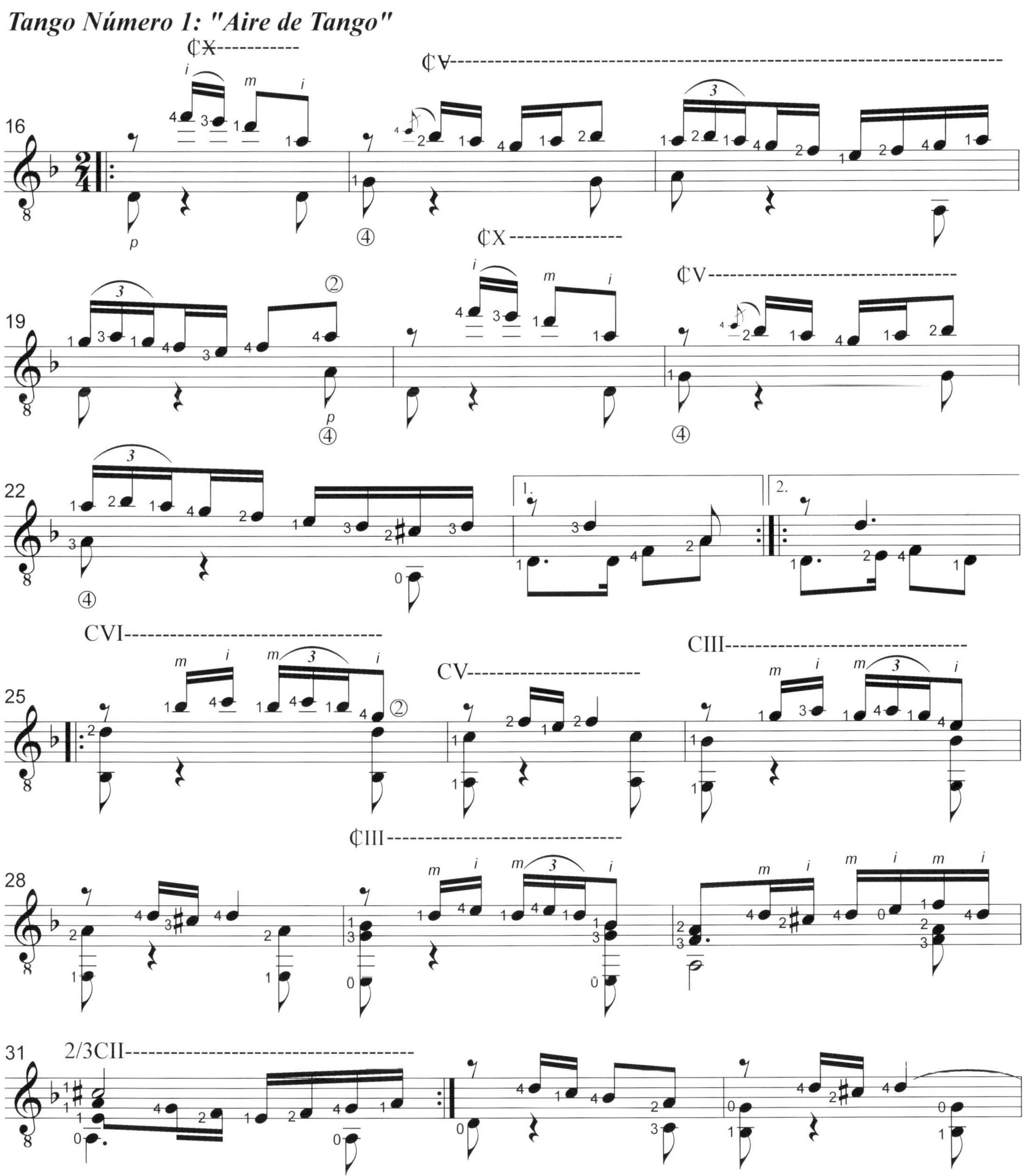

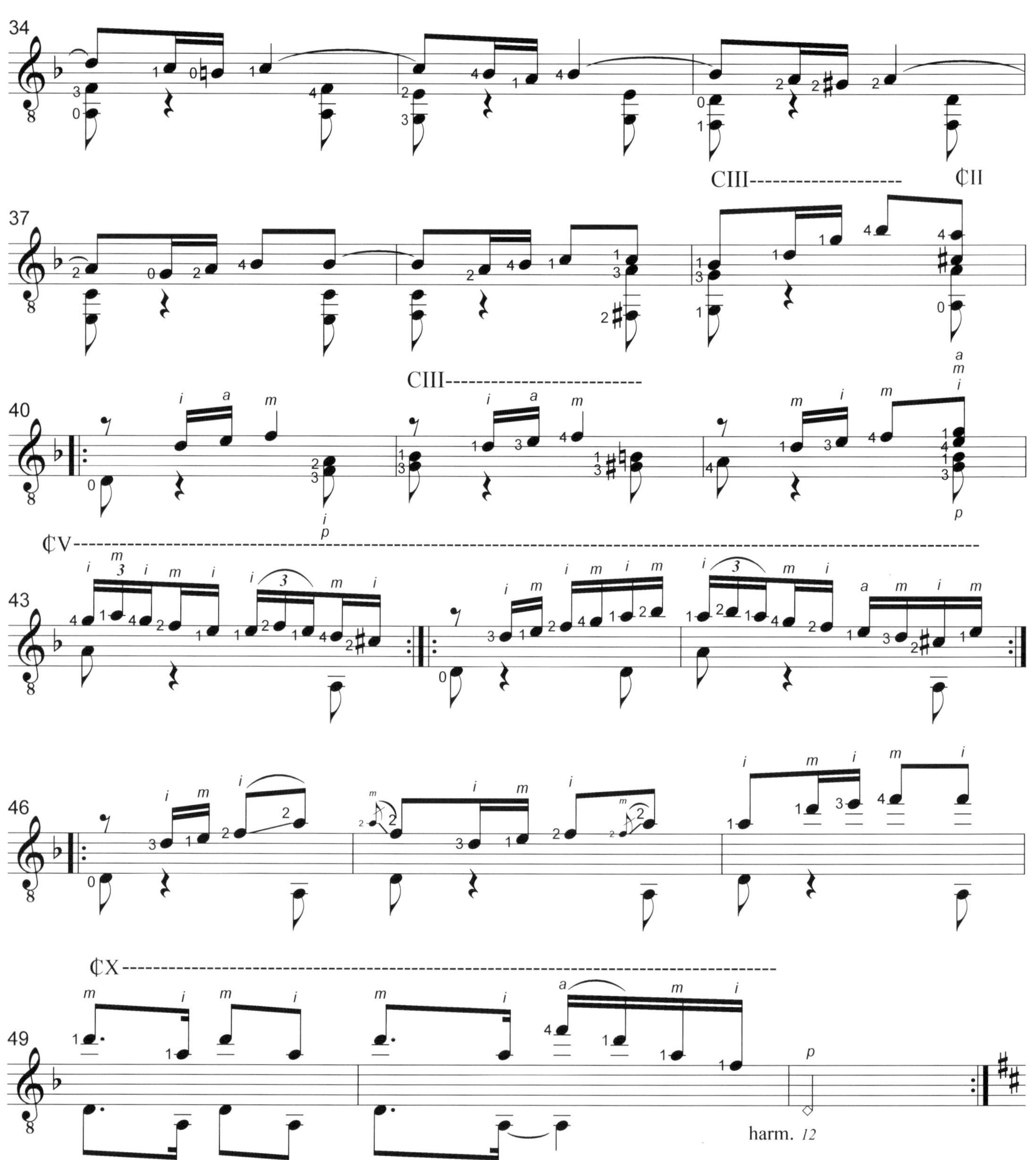
CIII
₵II
CIII
₵V
₵X
harm. 12

Tango Número 2

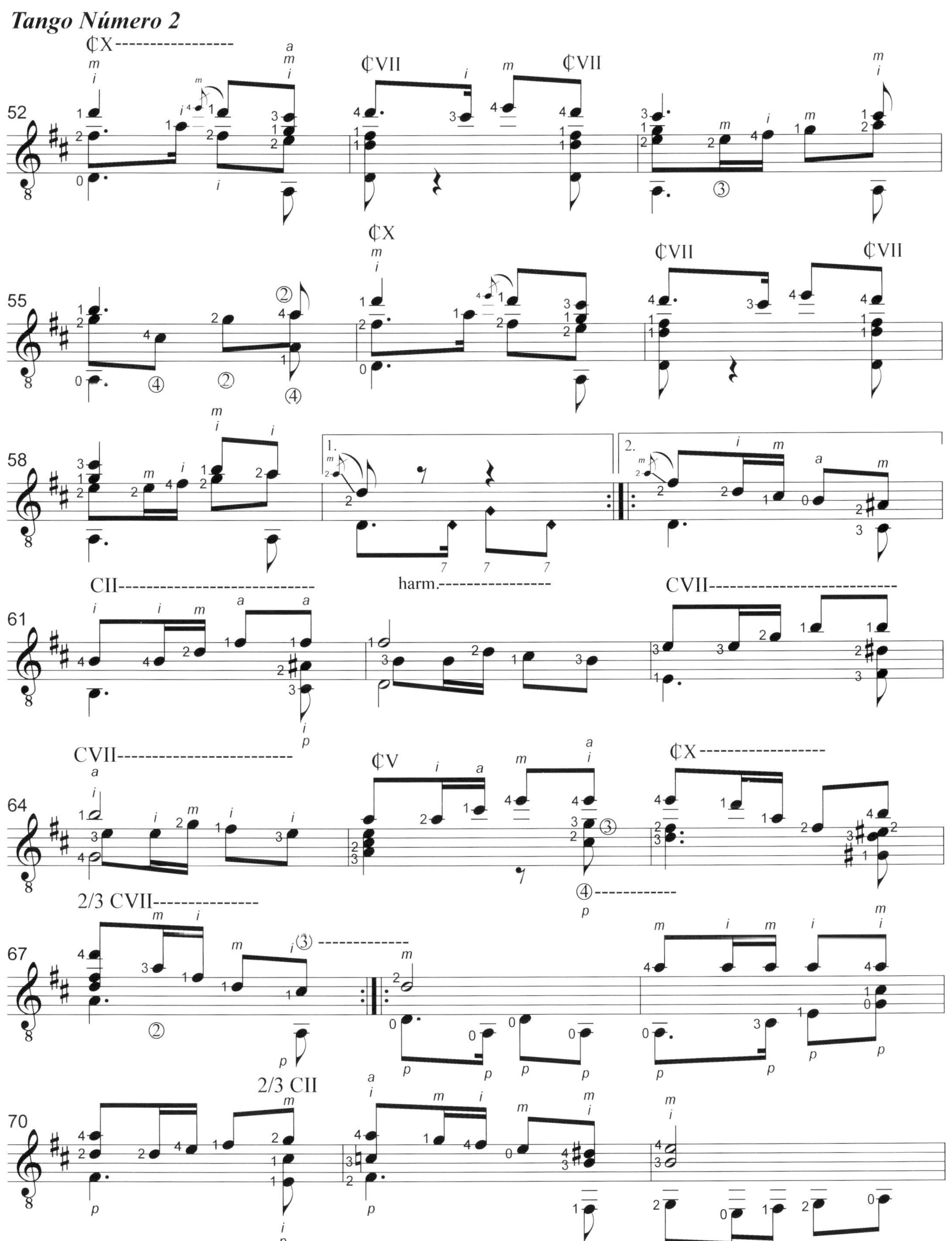

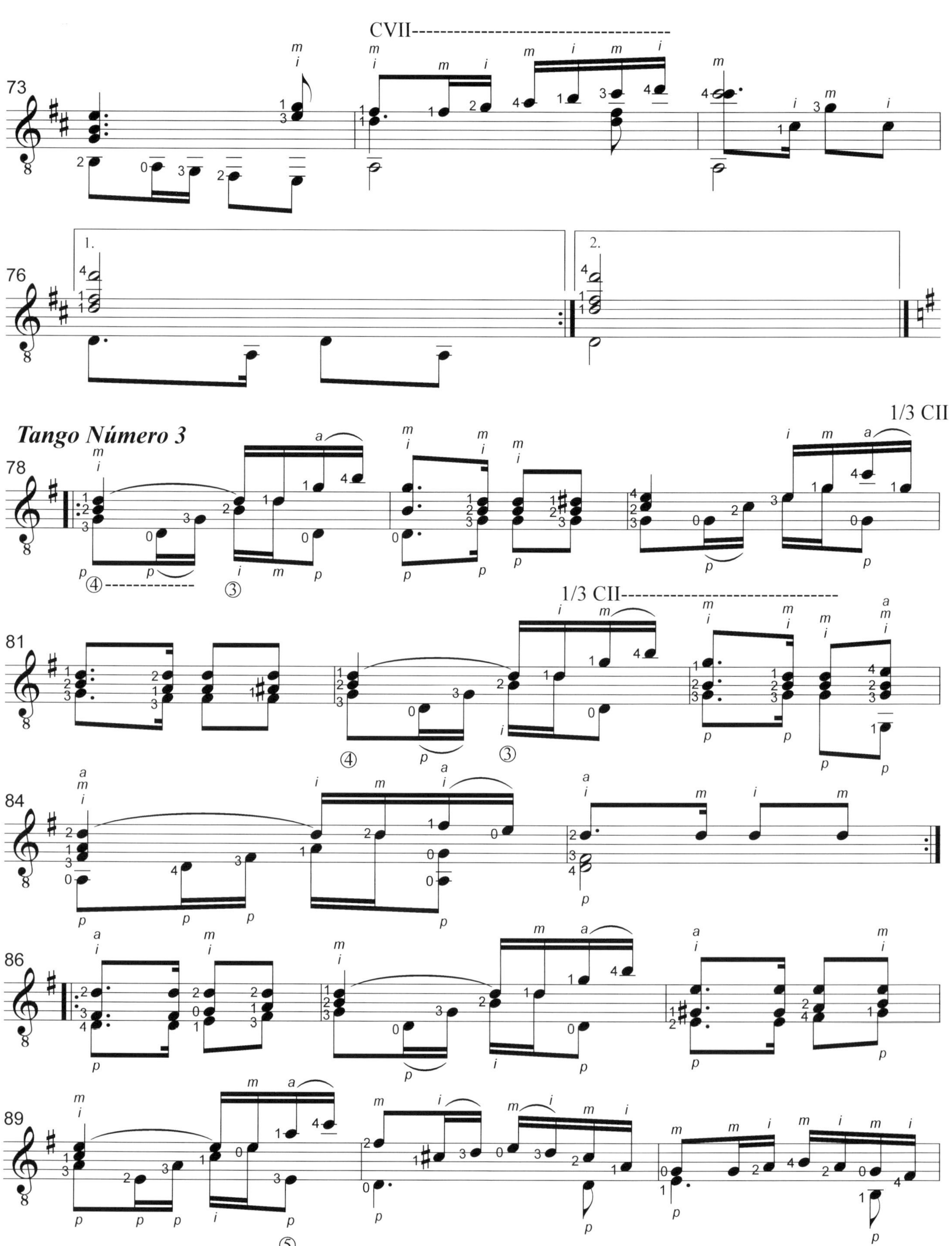
CVII
Tango Número 3
1/3 CII
1/3 CII

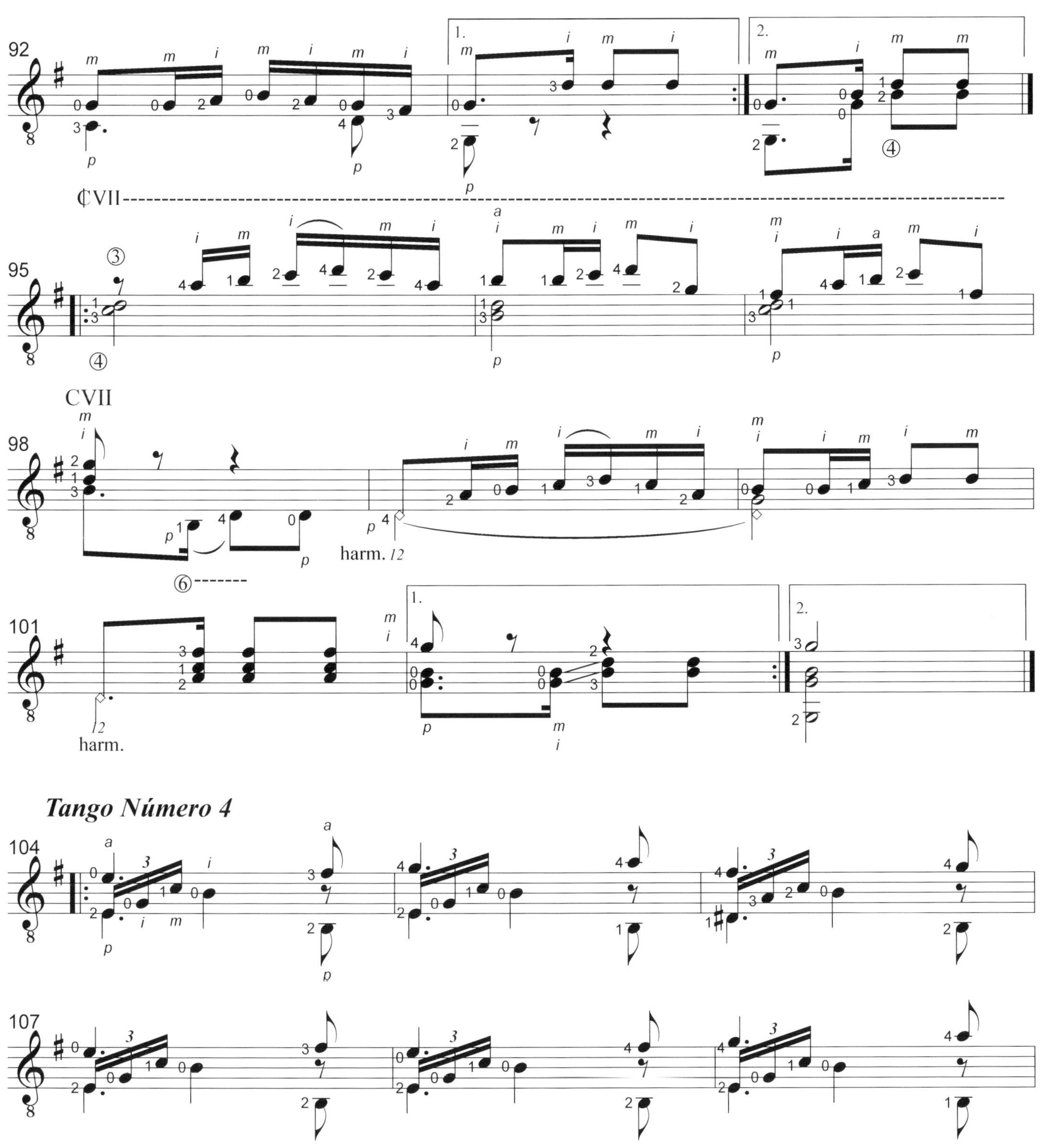
92
¢VII
95
CVII
98
harm. 12
101
harm.
Tango Número 4
104
107

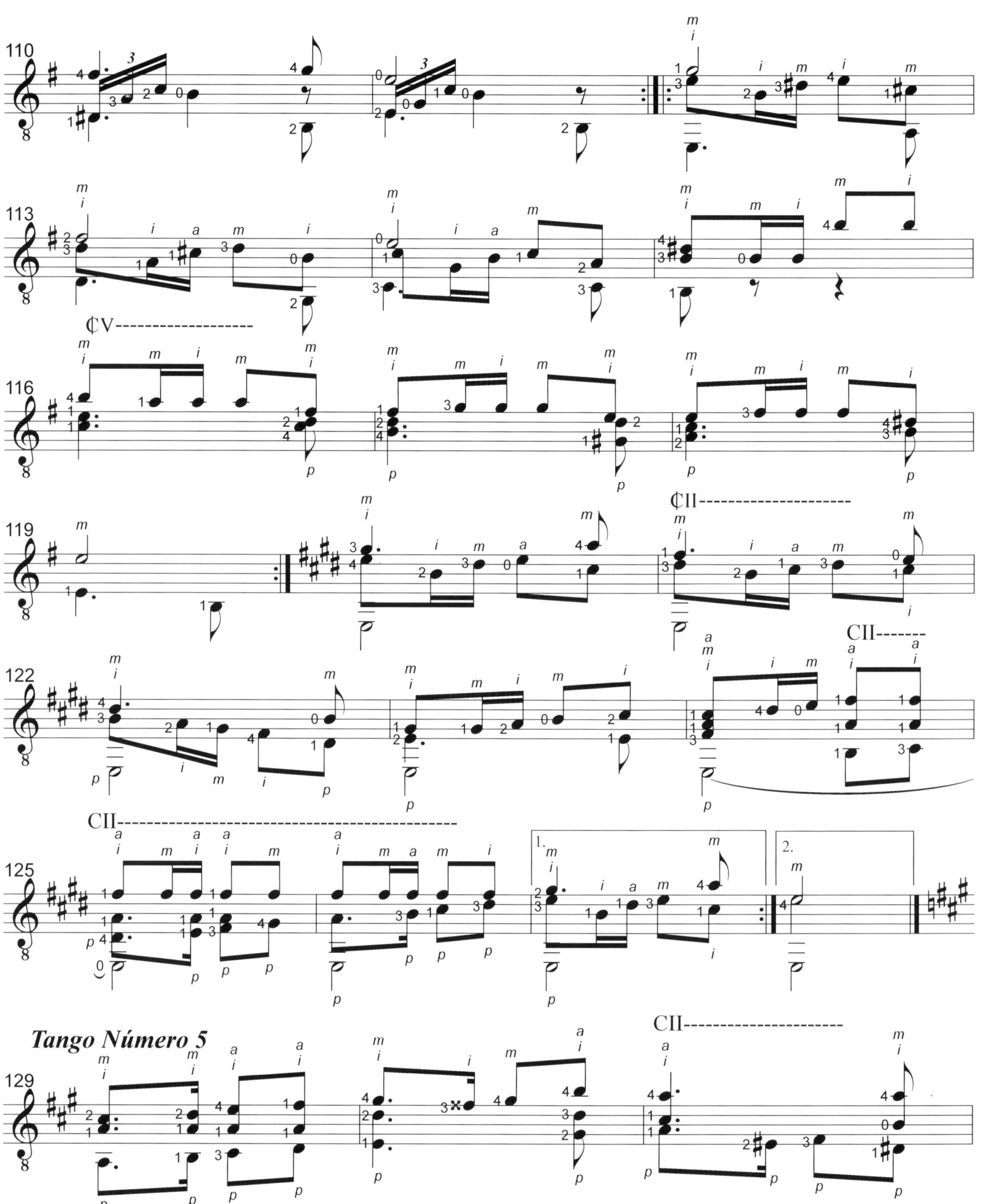
CV
CII
Tango Número 5

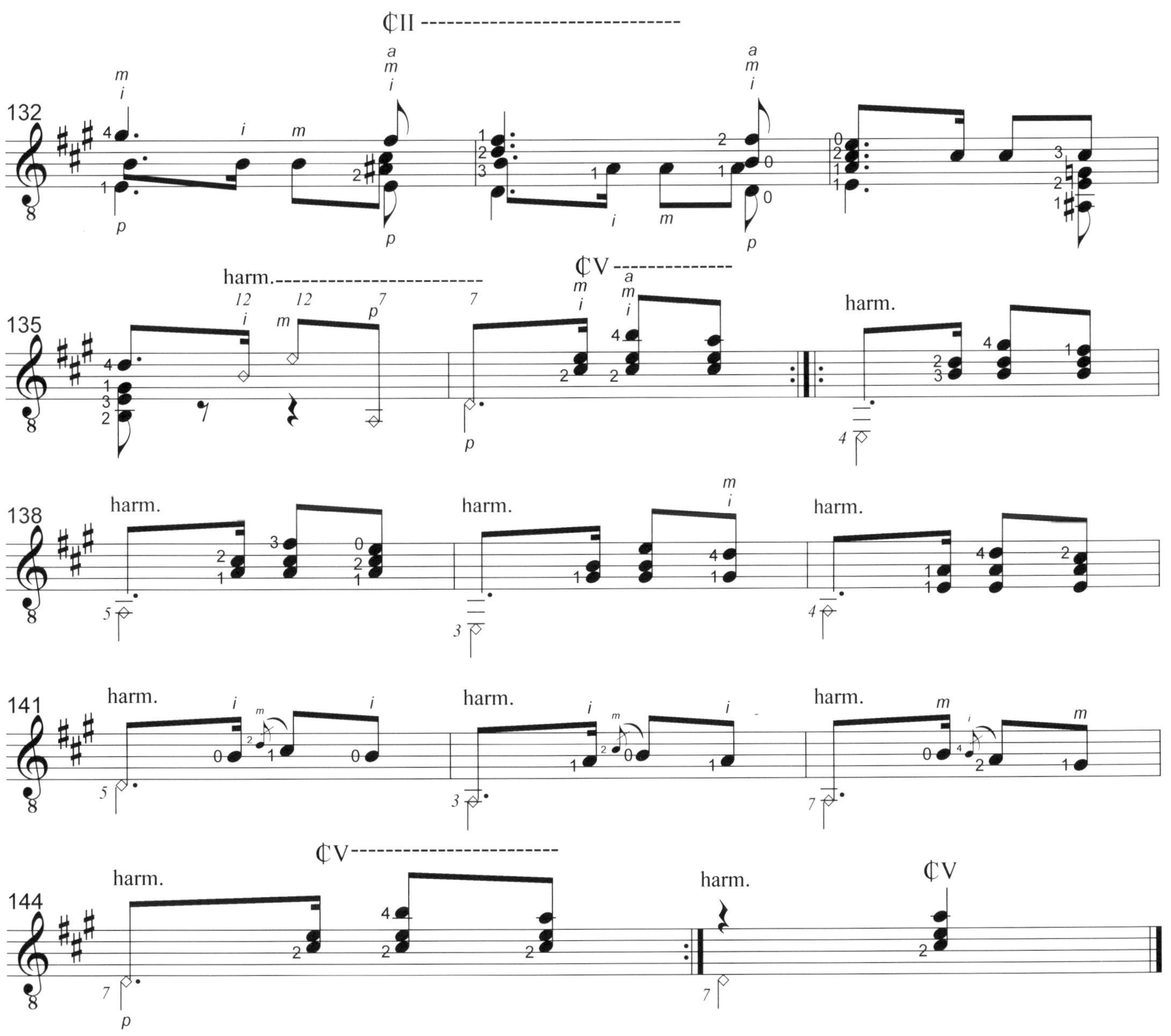

ȻII
132
harm.
ȻV
135
harm.
138
harm.
harm.
harm.
141
harm.
harm.
harm.
ȻV
144
harm.
harm.
ȻV

Fandango Variado Op. 16

Dionisio Aguado
Edited by Corey E. Whitehead

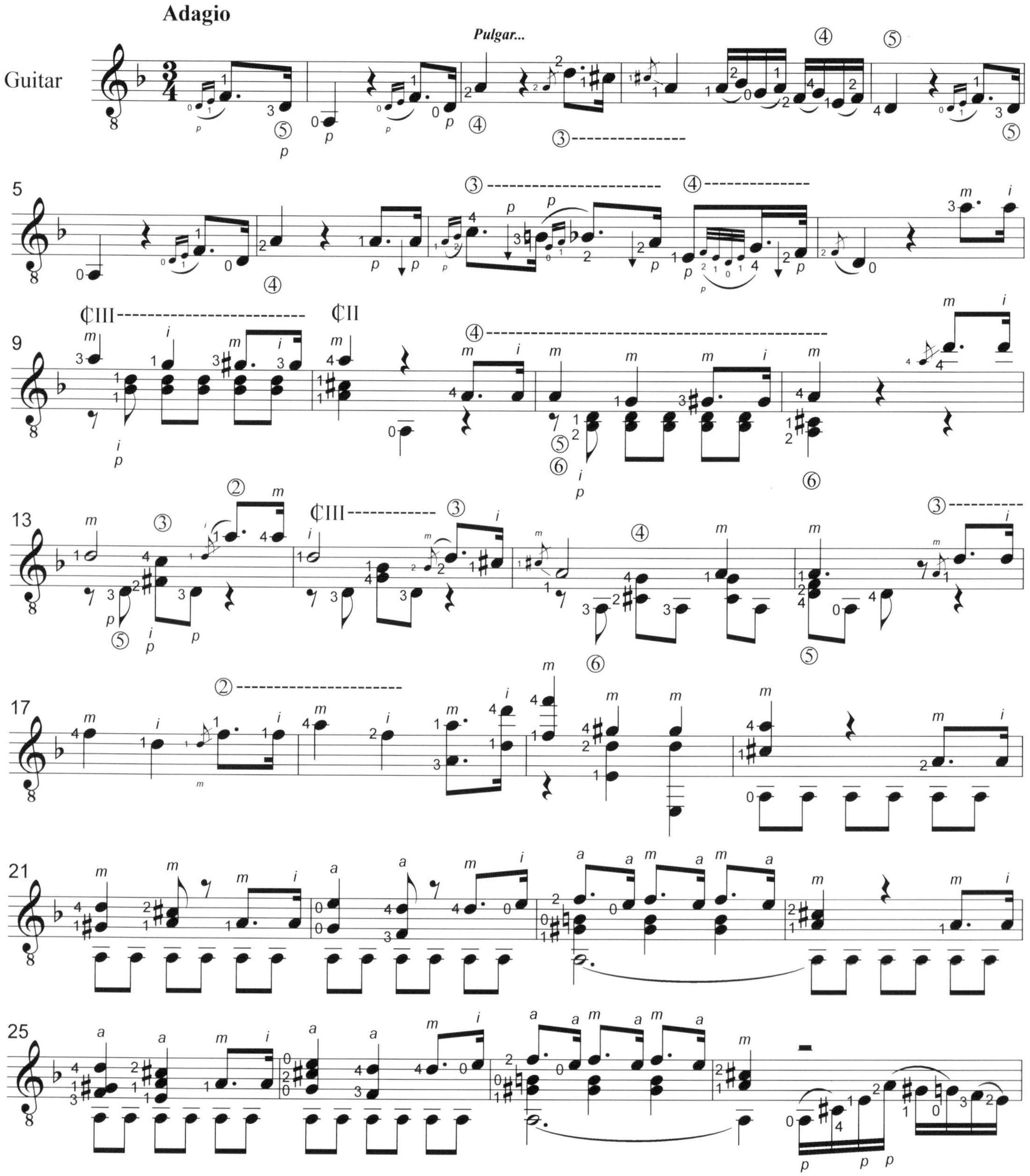

Adagio

Guitar

Pulgar...

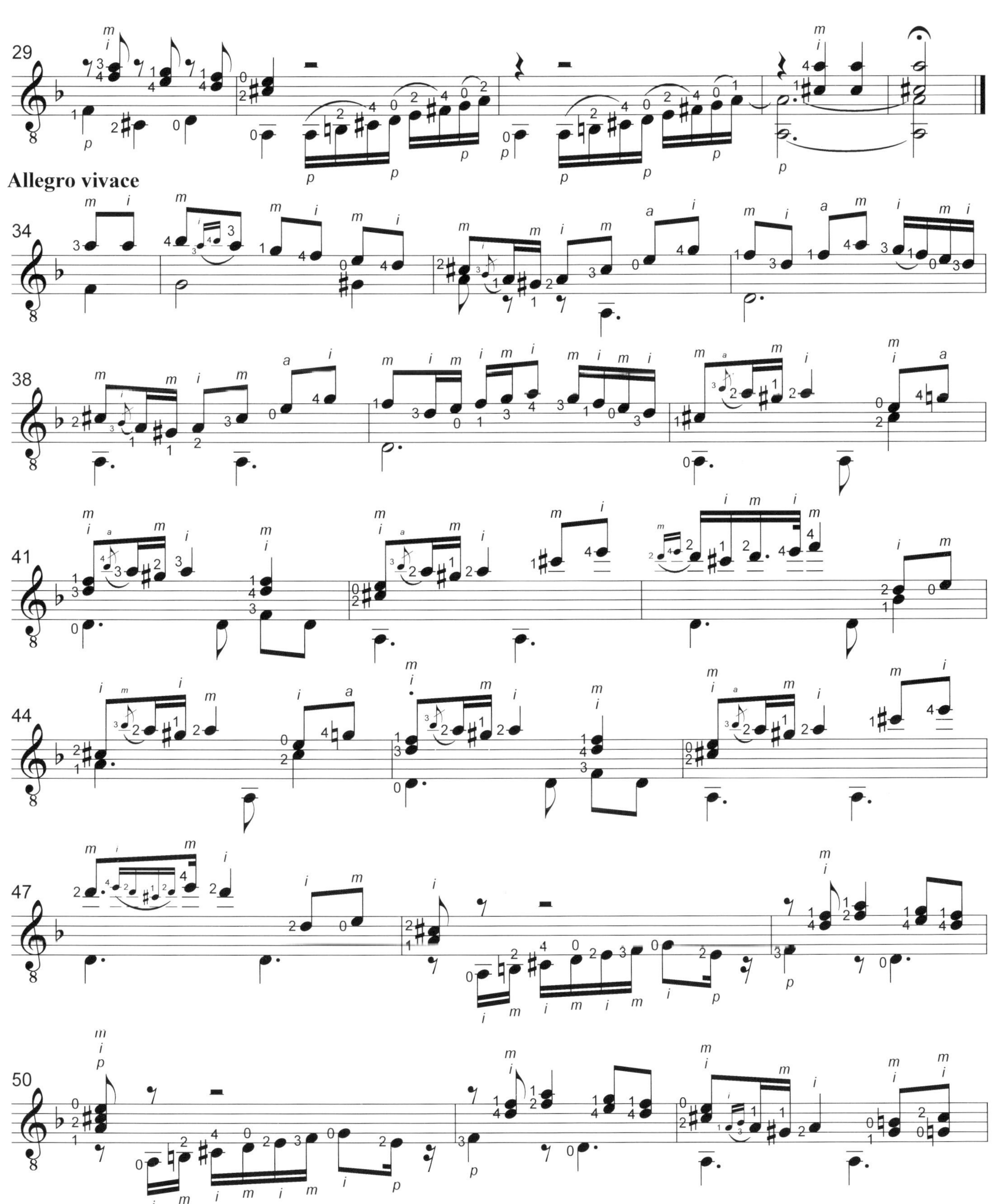
Allegro vivace

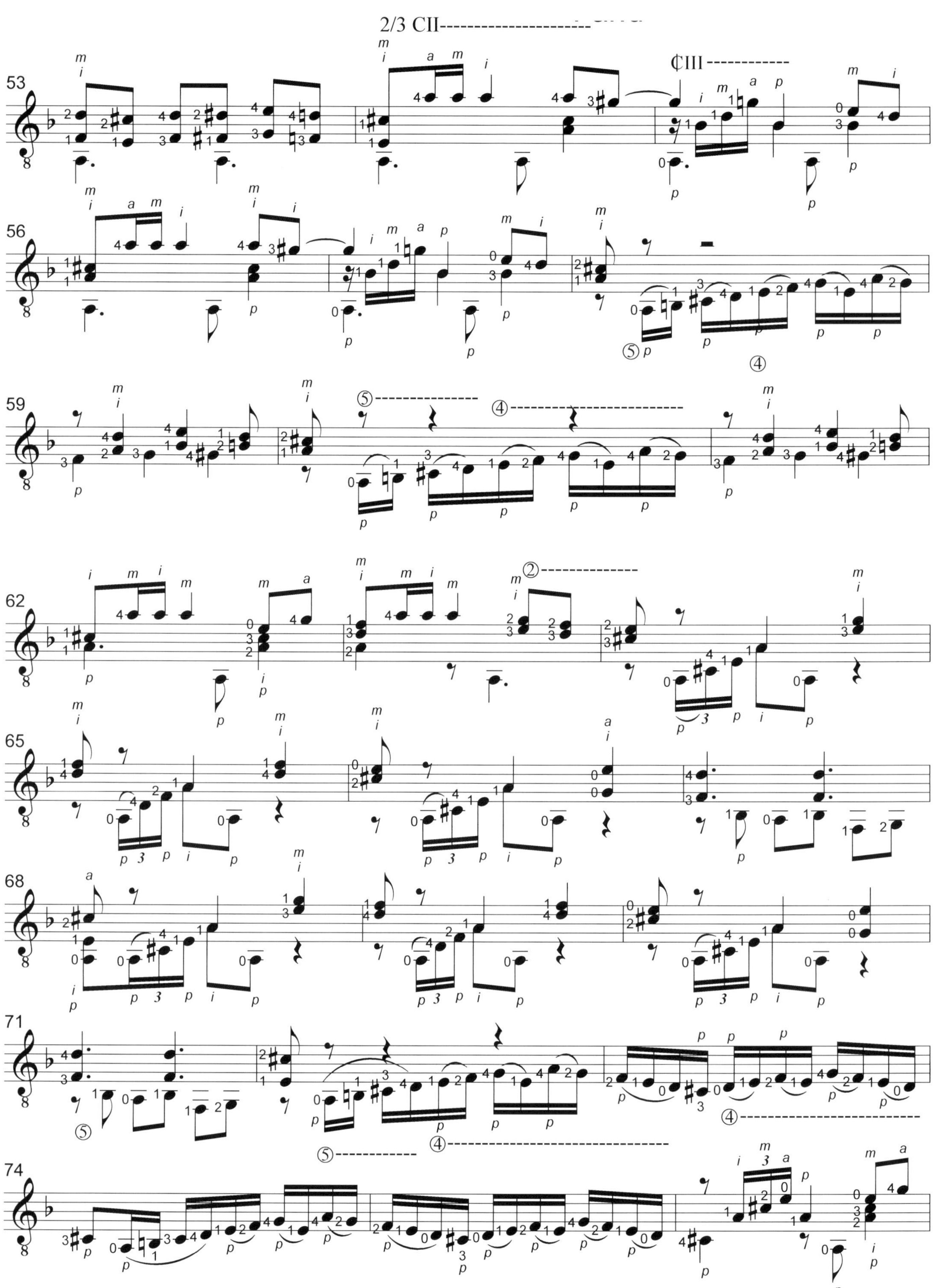
2/3 CII
₵III
53
56
59
62
65
68
71
74

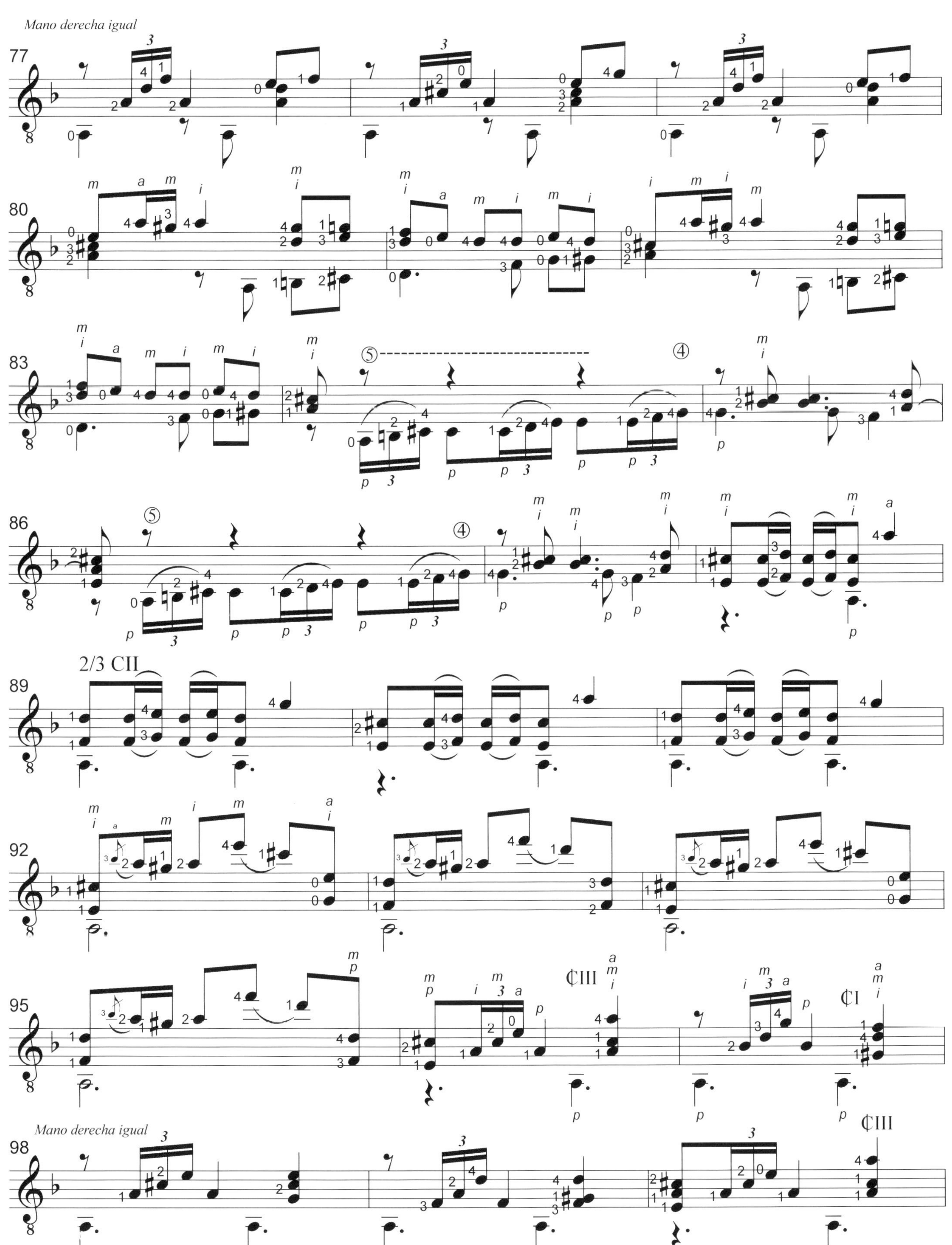
Mano derecha igual
77
80
83
86
89
2/3 CII
92
95
ȻIII
ȻI
Mano derecha igual
98
ȻIII

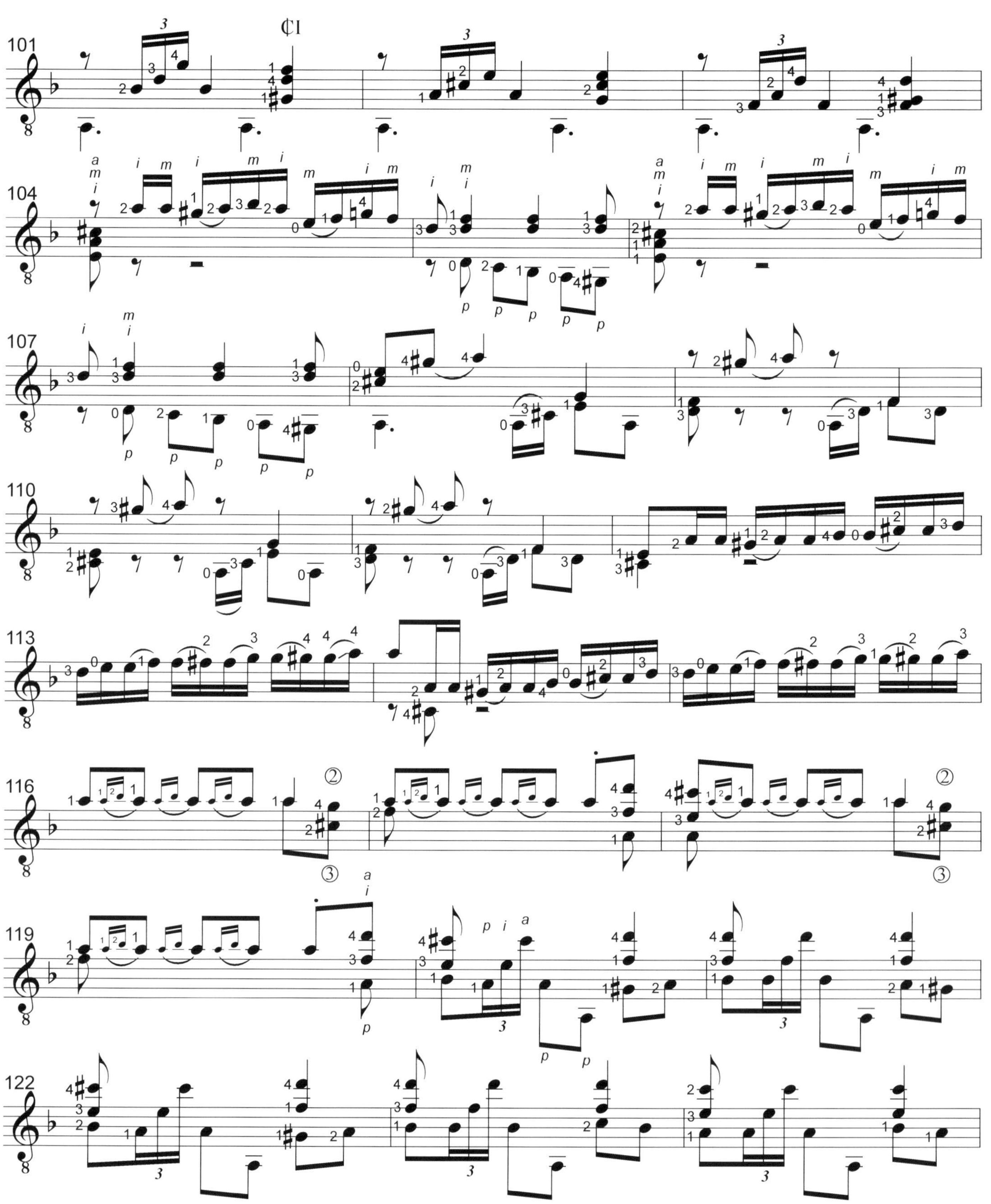

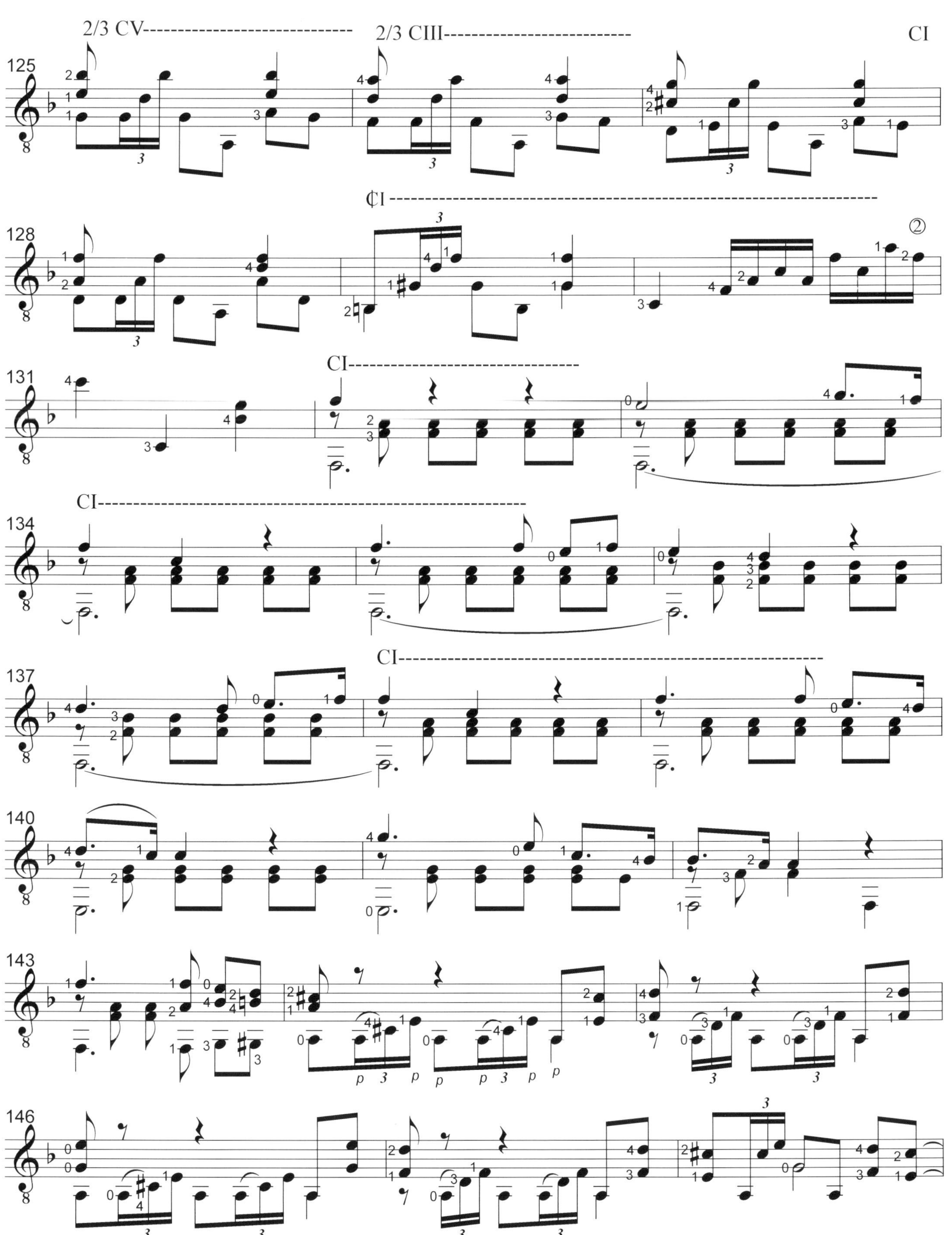
2/3 CV
2/3 CIII
CI
125
128
CI
131
CI
134
CI
137
CI
140
143
146

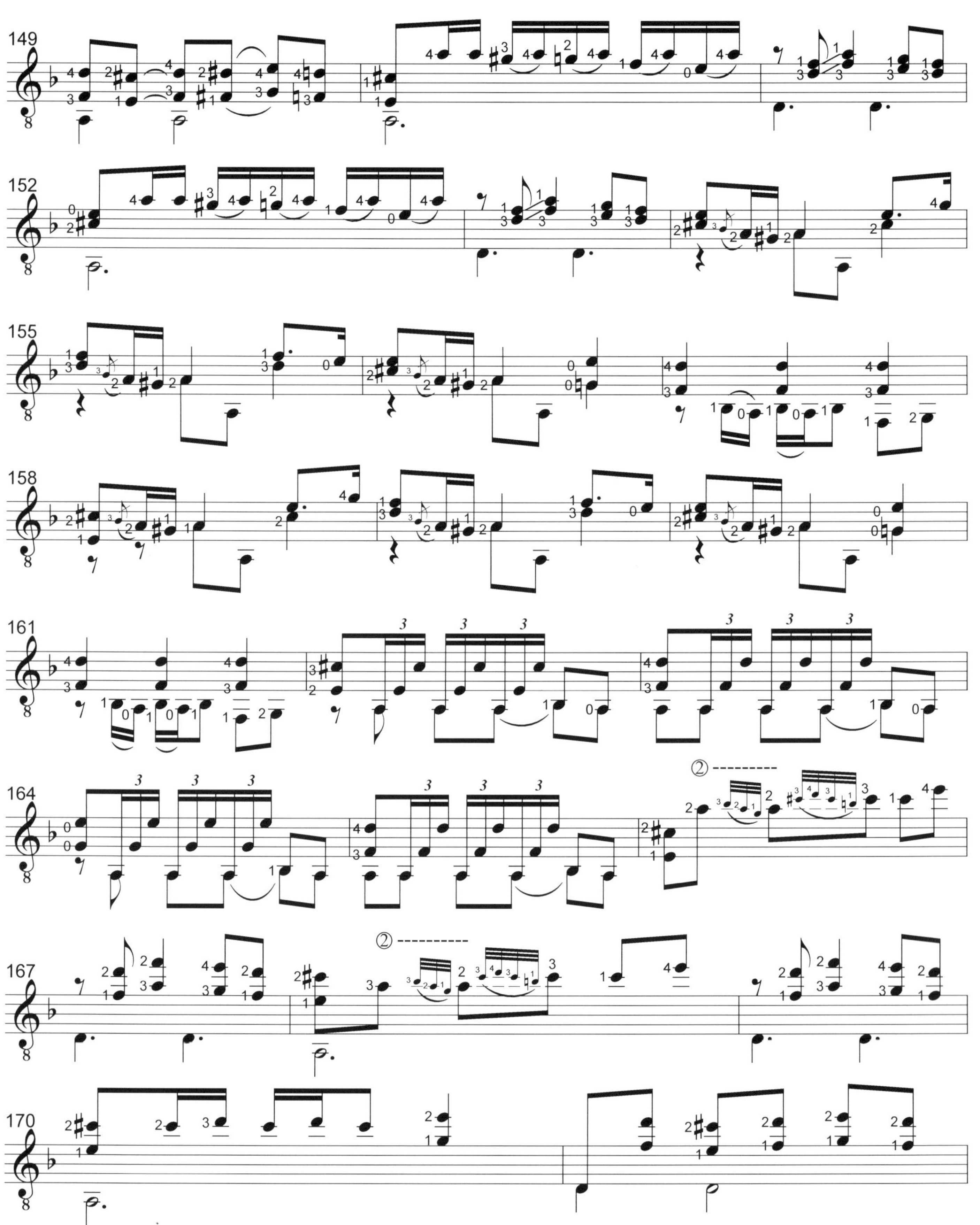
149
152
155
158
161
164
167
170

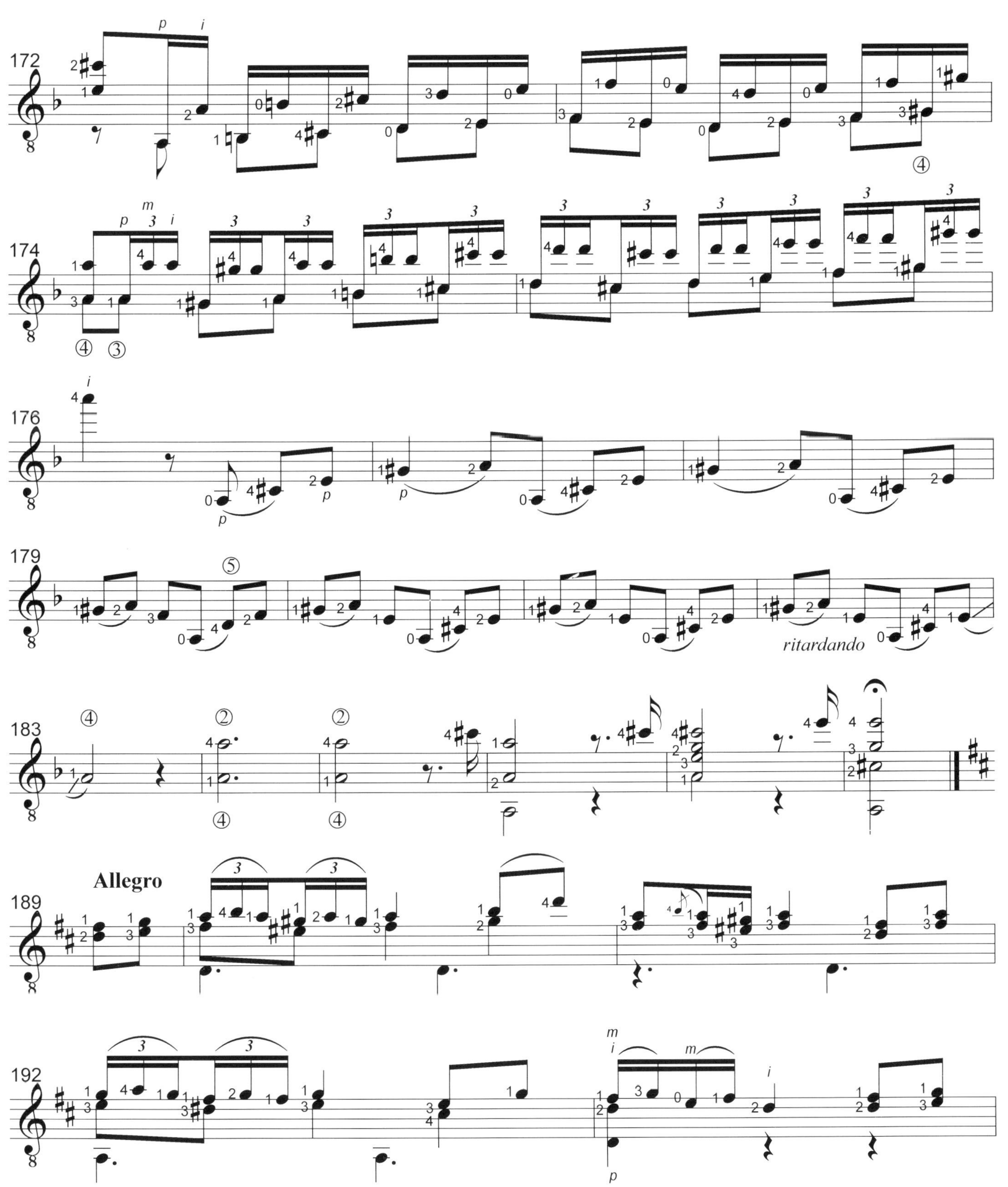
172
174
176
179
ritardando
183
Allegro
189
192

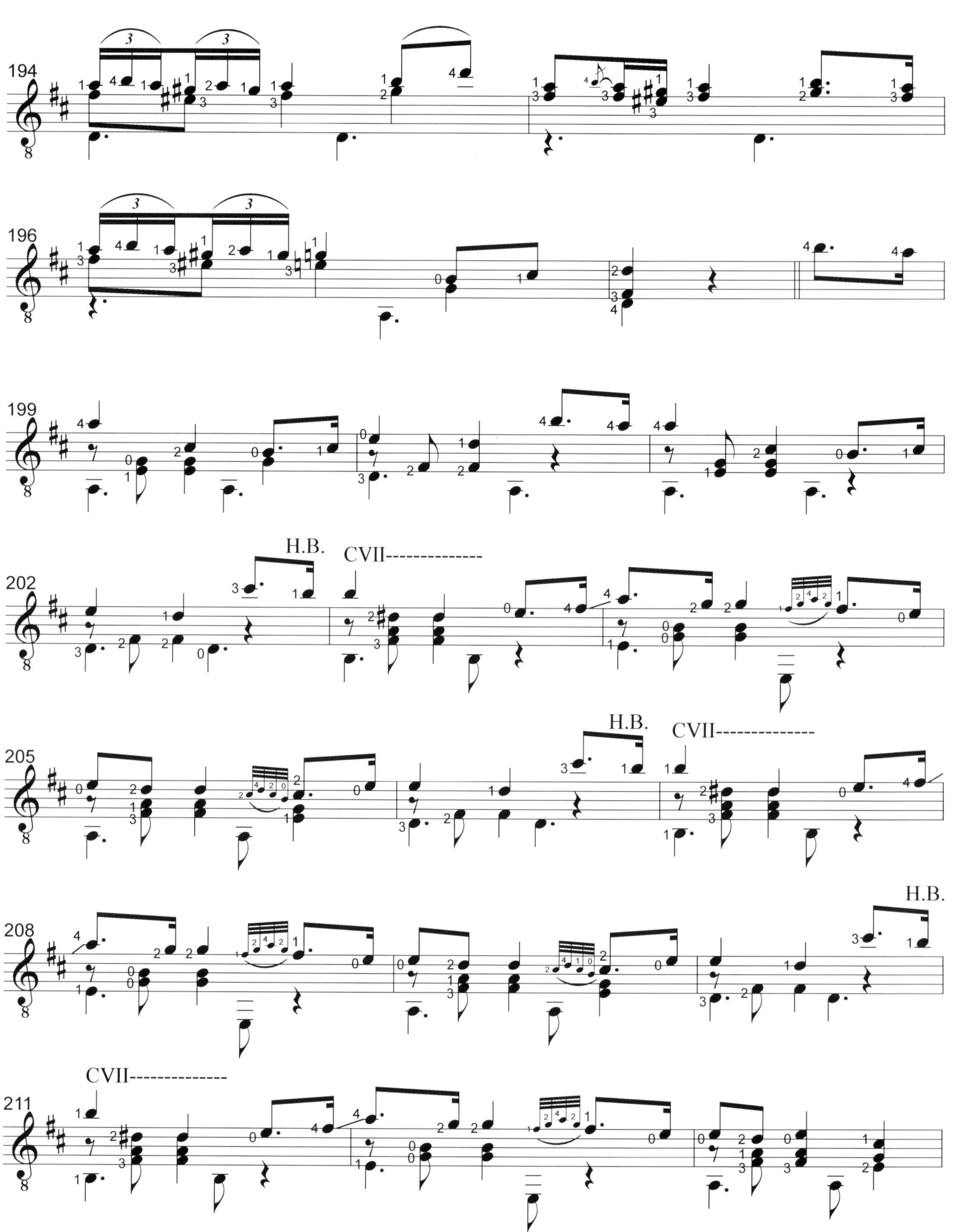
194
196
199
202
H.B.
CVII-------------
205
H.B.
CVII-------------
208
H.B.
211
CVII-------------

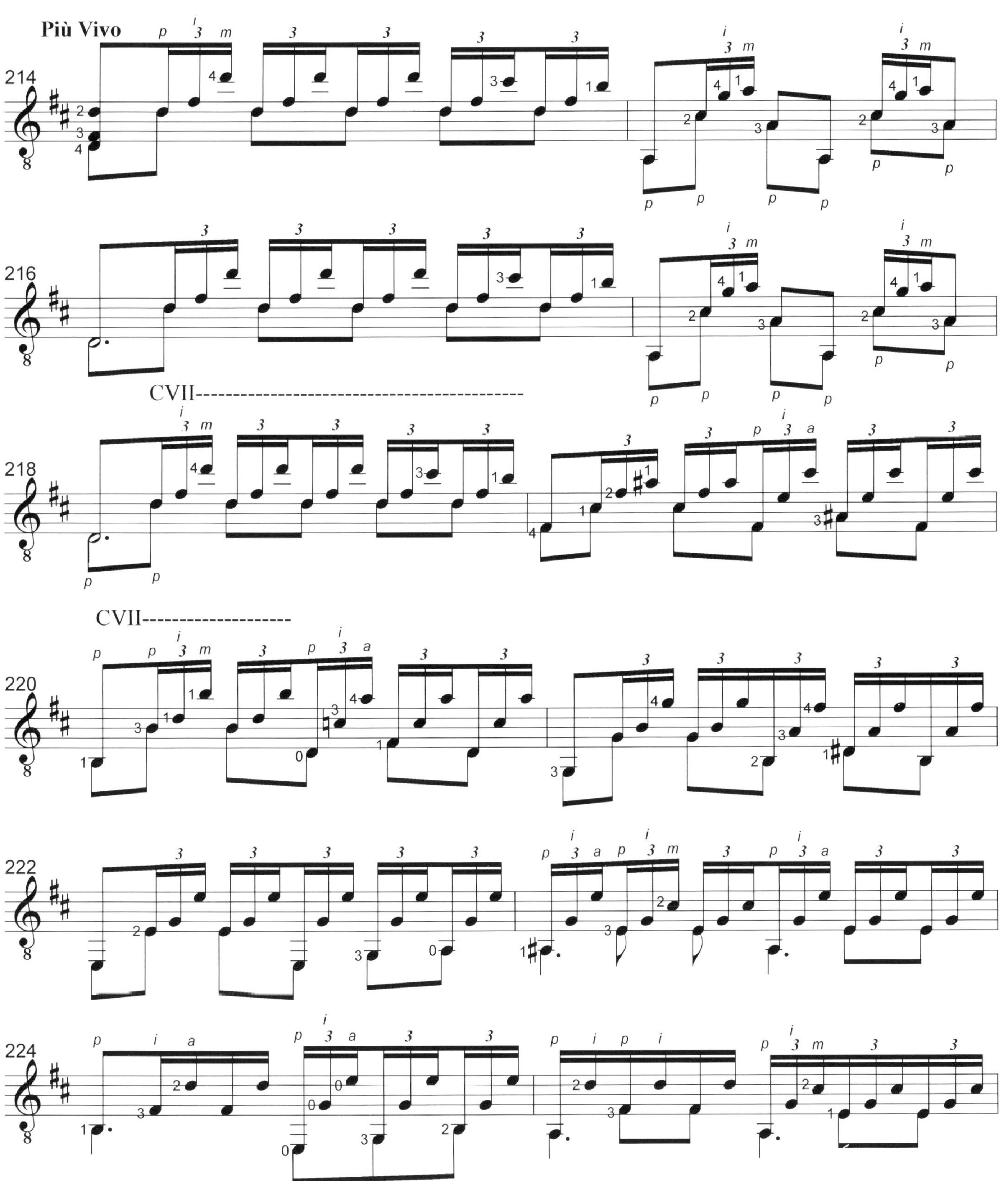
Più Vivo
214
216
CVII
218
CVII
220
222
224

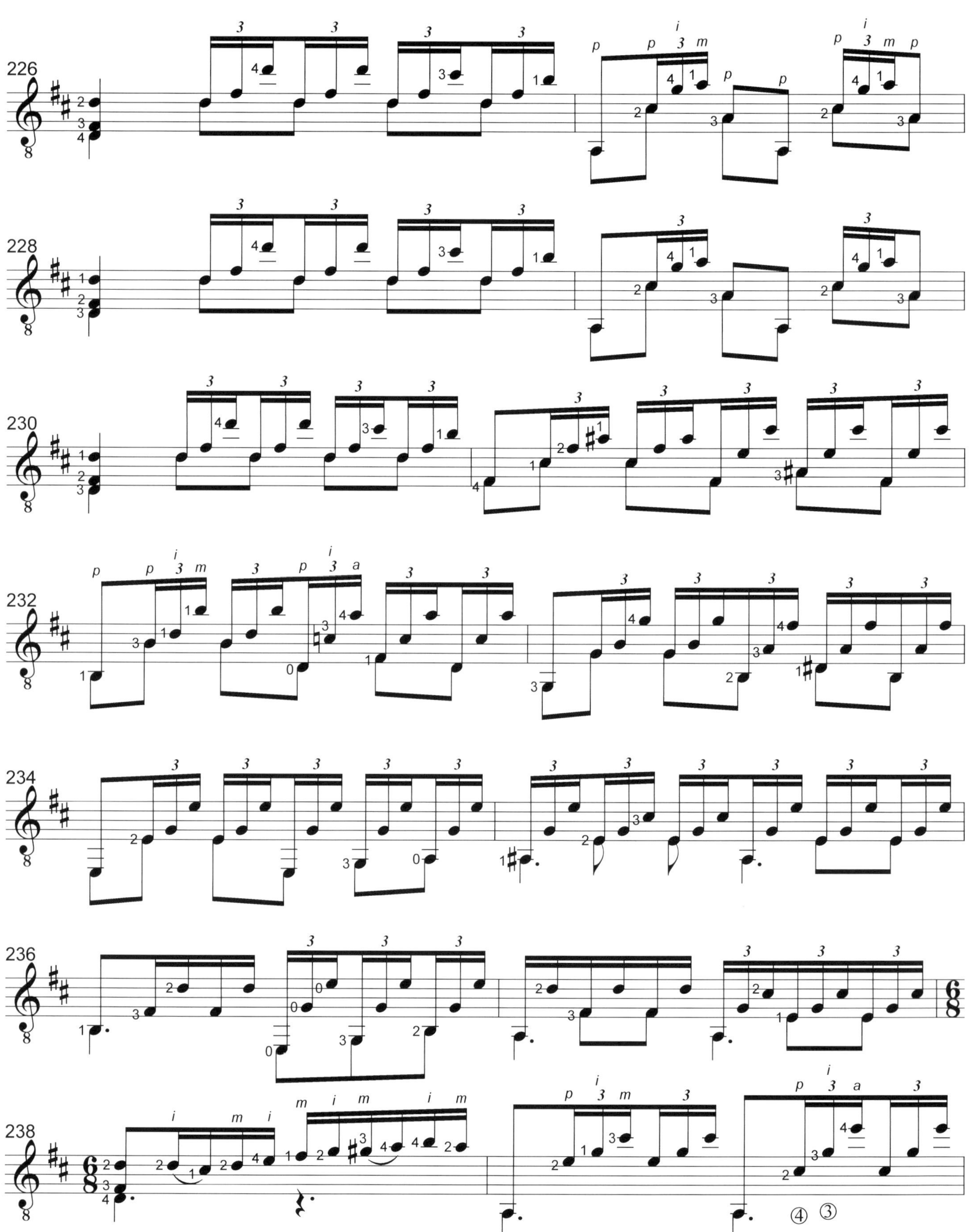
226
228
230
232
234
236
238
④ ③

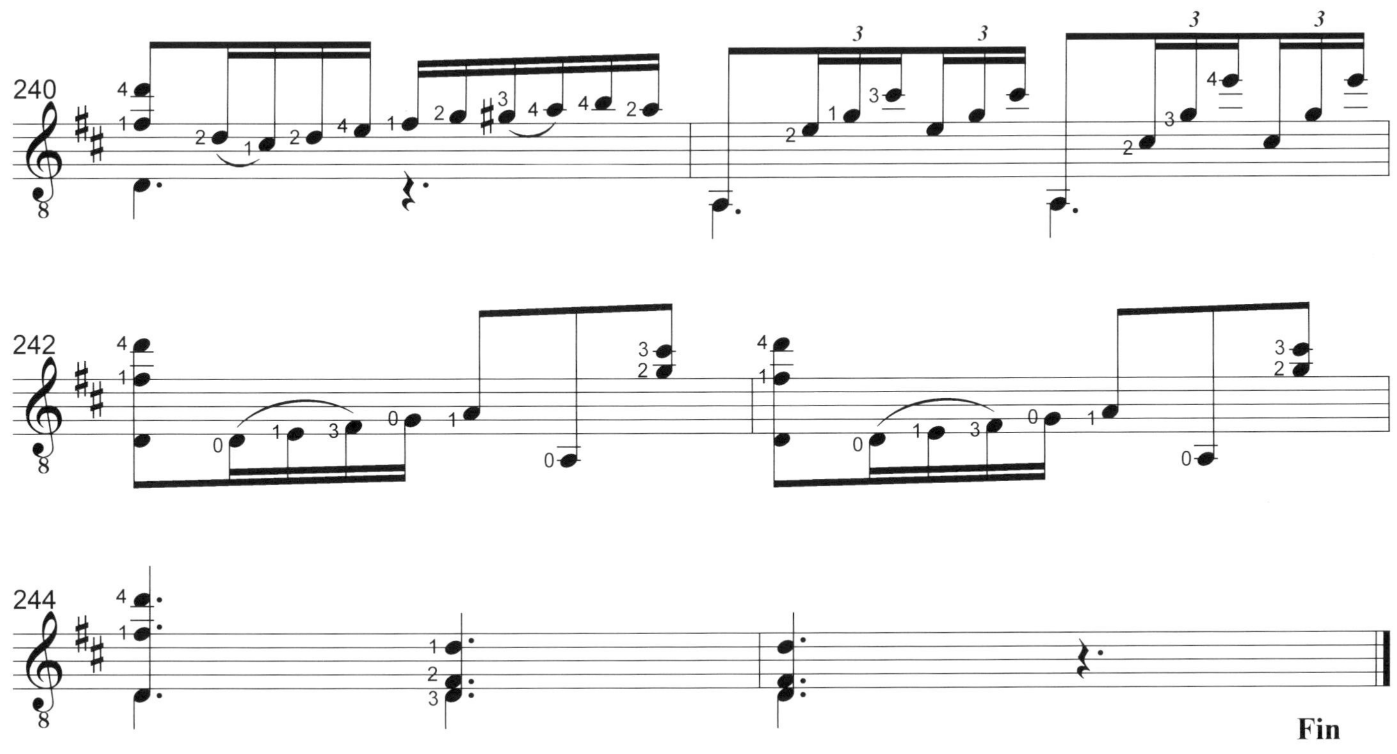
240
242
244
Fin

Unit I, Part IV

"Guitarra aflamencada"

Advanced Classical Guitar Repertoire with Flamenco Form, Rhythm and Melody

Unit I, Part IV: *"Guitarra aflamencada"*

Advanced Classical Guitar Repertoire with Flamenco Form, Rhythm and Melody

"A mi morena" (Malagueña característica) by Tomás Damas

1) Like the other stylized solo classical guitar works that exhibit elements of flamenco form, rhythm, harmony, and melody, this work attempts to capture the essence of a conversation between a singer and a guitarist. The guitarist however is alone, playing both roles, just as a jazz guitarist or pianist interprets a standard tune, flamenco guitarists and even pianists arrange themes for solo or duo. Paco de Lucía did this with famous tunes such as "Pica-Pica" and "El Vito," as well as an album of Latin-American favorites for guitar duo. The early duo and trio records of Paco de Lucía also exhibit this practice of "singing" with the guitar. Today, this is common practice in flamenco groups led by a guitarist; the guitar is the protagonist and does the "singing" primarily, and the singers play a secondary role, playing palmas and singing a popular refrain or chorus, or a single tercio.
2) Imagine the *copla* (verse) of this work having lyrics that begin with *"A mi morena…"*
3) Search for *Malagueña* lyrics that begin with those words.
4) This work begins with 59 measures of solo guitar introduction. This is how a traditional accompanied *Malagueña* begins, with a solo guitar introduction, setting up the first *copla.*
5) The *copla* begins in measure 60, and is indeed accompanied. Just as in a "classical" guitar piece, there is a melody and sparse accompaniment. Sometimes both melody and accompaniment are present, and other times, only one of the two is there. For example, one could play three measures of single-note melody and answer rhythmically and harmonically with a chord strum pattern or arpeggiated chord pattern, or *vice versa.* It is very common to play one measure of melody and one measure of rhythm. Discern which of the notes are melody or rhythm and treat them accordingly. If melody and accompaniment are present, favor the melody.
6) The first *copla* is stated in measures 60-88, and is followed by a characteristic guitar solo variation *(falseta)* that continues from measures 88-128.
7) Measures 129-169 constitute the second *copla.*
8) Another typical guitar solo *falseta* runs from measures 129-213.
9) Measures 214-236 makeup the final *copla* before the final guitar solo, labeled *Coda.*
10) A rule in flamenco *cante jondo* is to end on the E chord, not on Am. This final cadence to Am at the end of the work is not characteristic of flamenco, and frankly could be omitted editorially by the performer as a "personal" choice.

"Los Panaderos" by Julian Arcas (1832-1882)

1) Panaderos are the bread-makers of the province of Cádiz. They are essential to the life of the region, as in each region, bread is baked fresh each day and not intended for use after the second day on the shelf. The bread-makers sing to the rhythm of their bread-making. *"Los Panaderos"* is a theme interpreted by many in the history of flamenco. Others include the famous version by Estebán de Sanlúcar. Isidro Muñoz, the father of Manolo Muñoz Alcón (Manolo Sanlúcar) was a bread maker, **and** a professional flamenco guitarist.
2) Notice the rhythm in measure 8 is exactly the same as the solo piano work by Issac Albéniz entitled *"Cádiz."* This work by Issac Albéniz is a part of *Suite Española* for piano solo and is indeed a *"Panadero."*
3) Notice the *"alzapúa"* or upward stroke of the fingernail of the right-hand thumb to play the off-beat E major chord in measure 8.
4) Strictly execute the accents, especially an accent on beat 2. The second-beat accent in ¾ time is a feature of the Baroque *Sarabande*, and of the popular flamenco *Fandango.*
5) A *copla* begins in measure 23 and continues until measure 31. This is promptly answered by the accompaniment figure stated in measures 8-9.
6) The *anacrusis* (pickup notes) to measure 34 (at the end of measure 33) begins the next statement of the melody, as if a conversation is occurring between the melody and rhythm.
7) A short interjection of the two-measure rhythmic figure follows in measures 41-42.
8) A sort of "closing theme" occurs from measures 43-49, followed by a guitar *falseta* from measures 50-59. A similar structure of form continues through measure 89.
9) Measure 87 to the end follows the same formal structure, the difference being that here, the melody climbs high into the upper positions on the first string for a climactic effect.

"A mi morena" (Malagueña característica)
Copla y acompanimiento por Tomás Damas

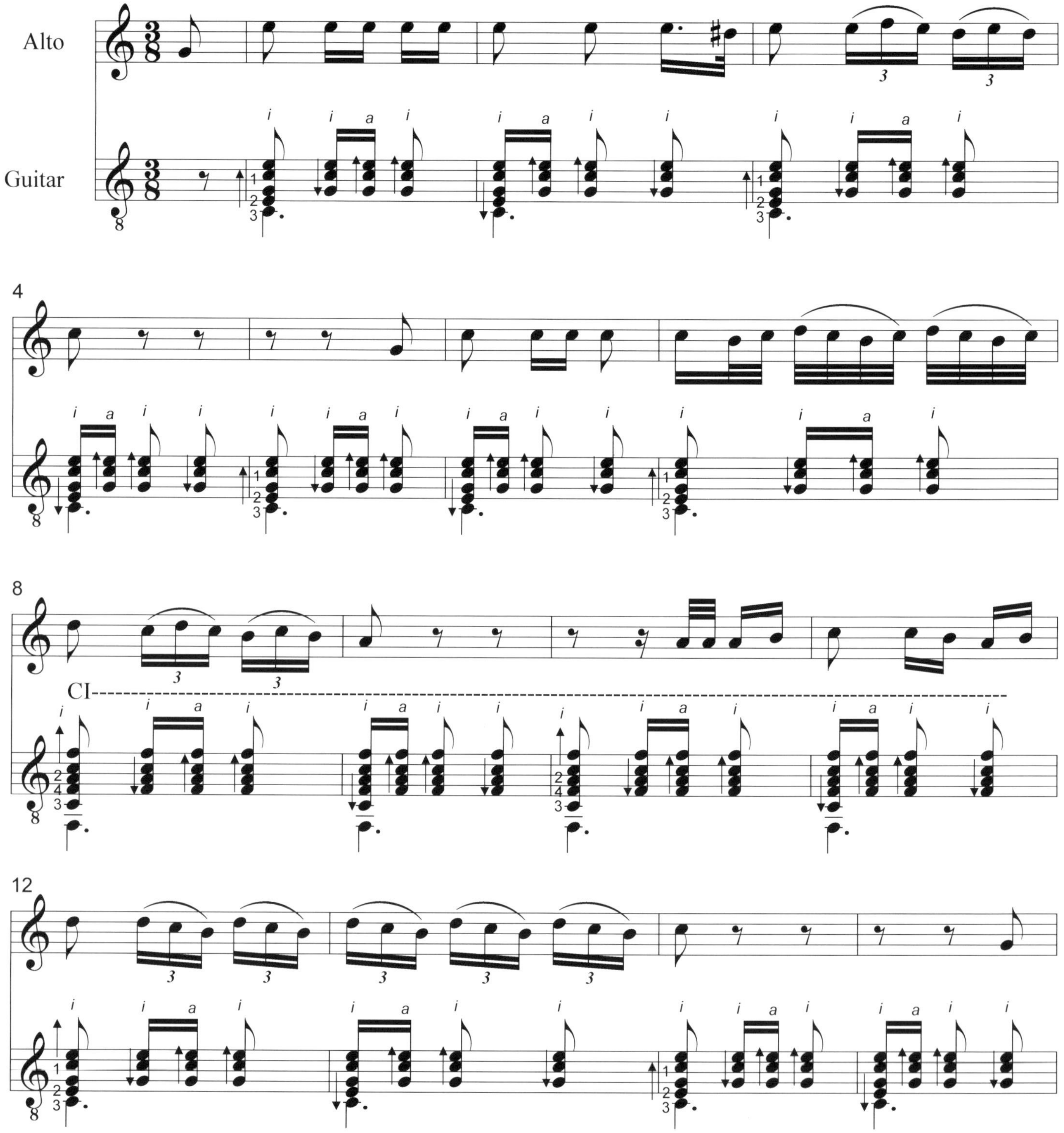

Alto

Guitar

CI

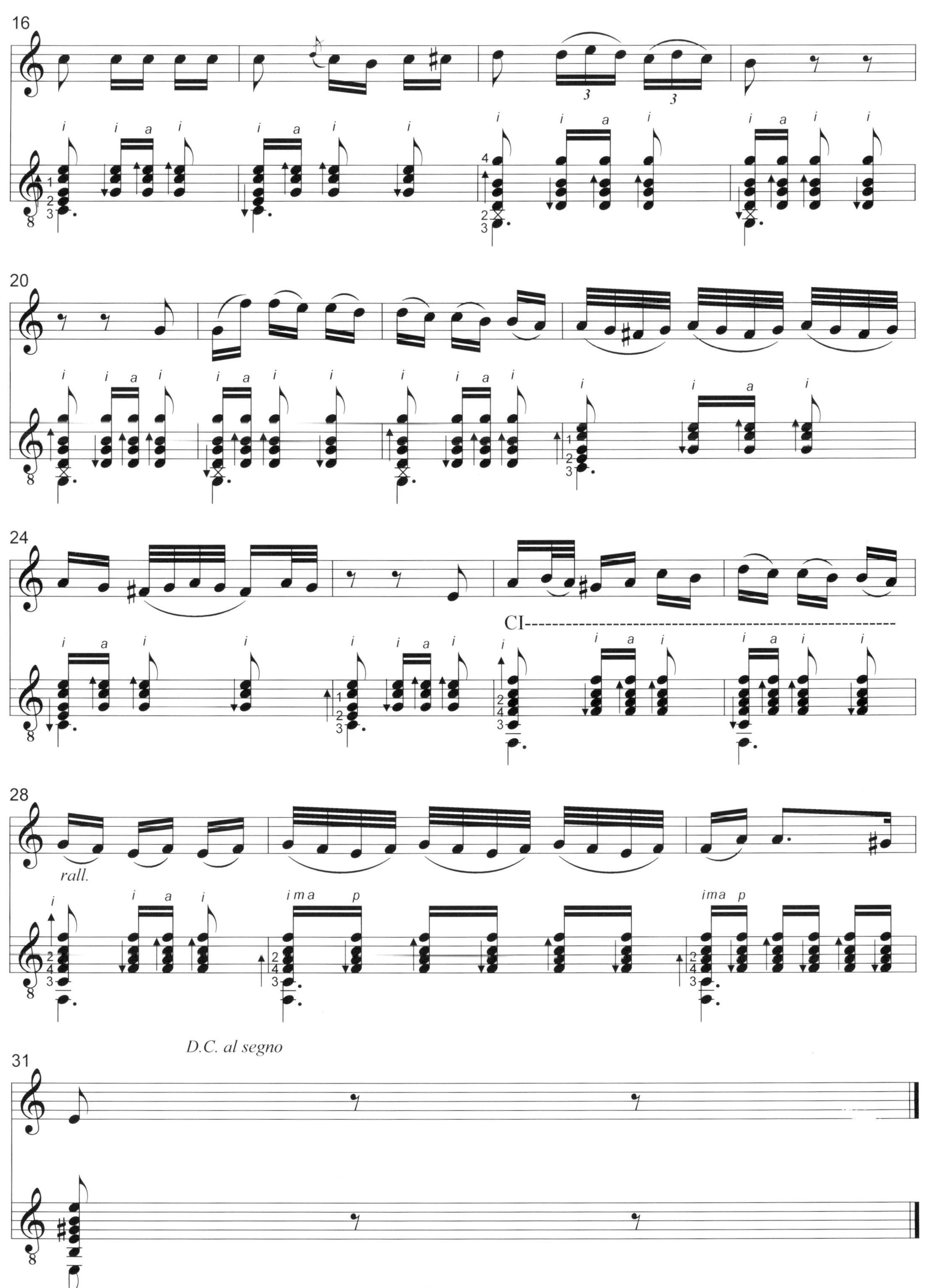
rall.
CI
D.C. al segno

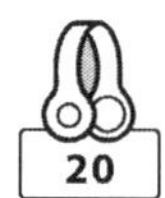

"A mi morena" (Malagueña característica)

Tomás Damas

Edited by Corey E. Whitehead

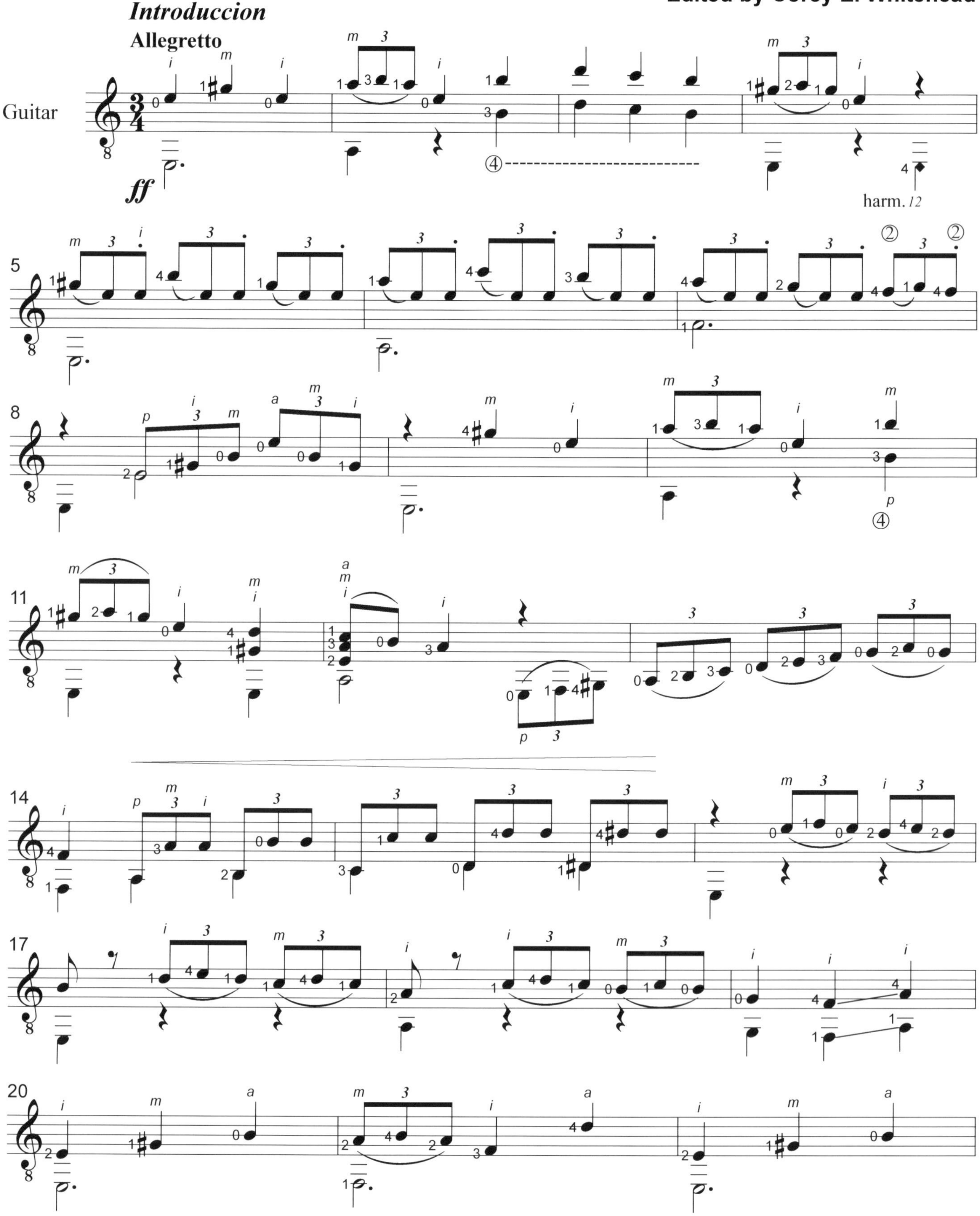

Introduccion

Allegretto

Guitar

ff

harm. *12*

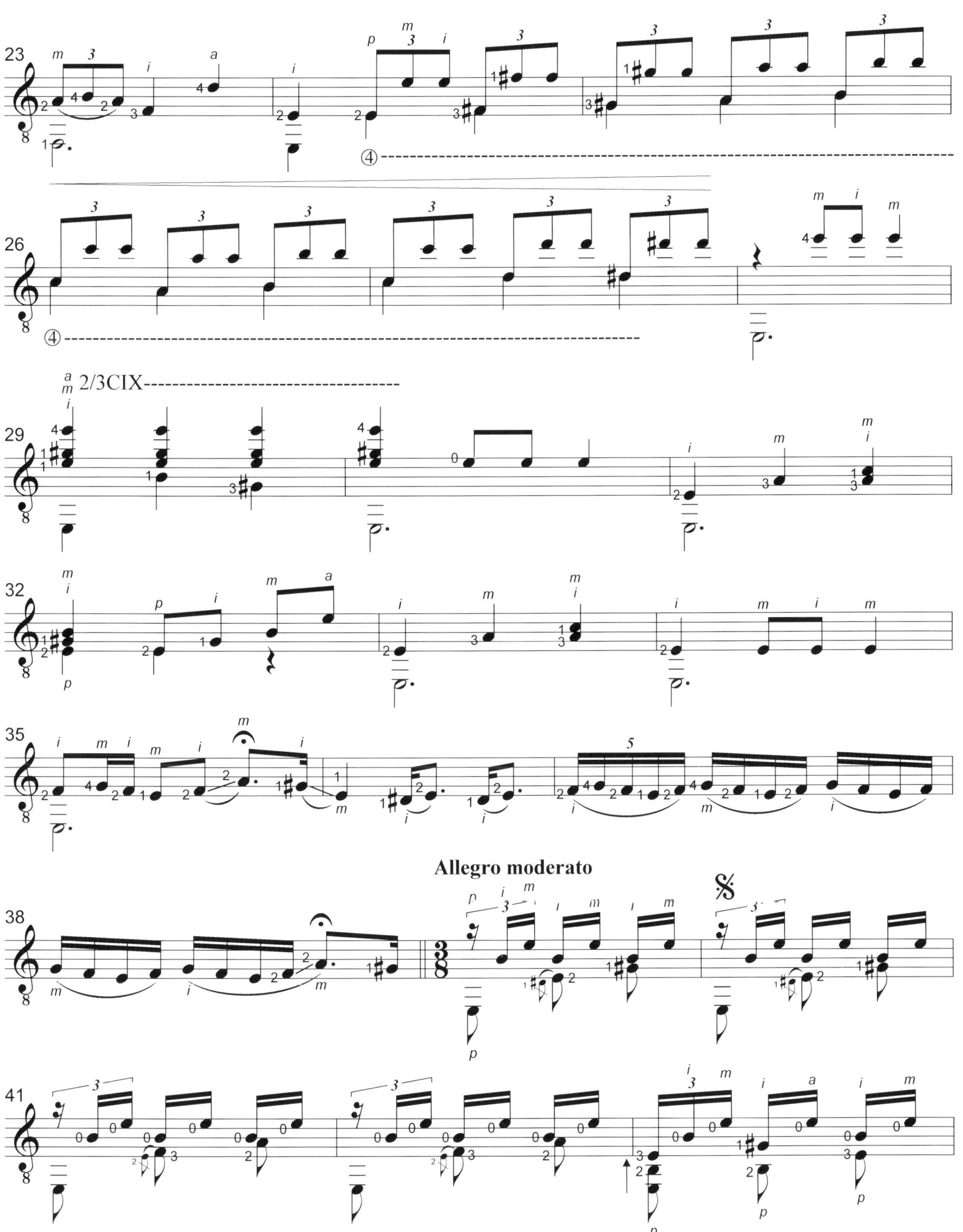
2/3CIX
Allegro moderato

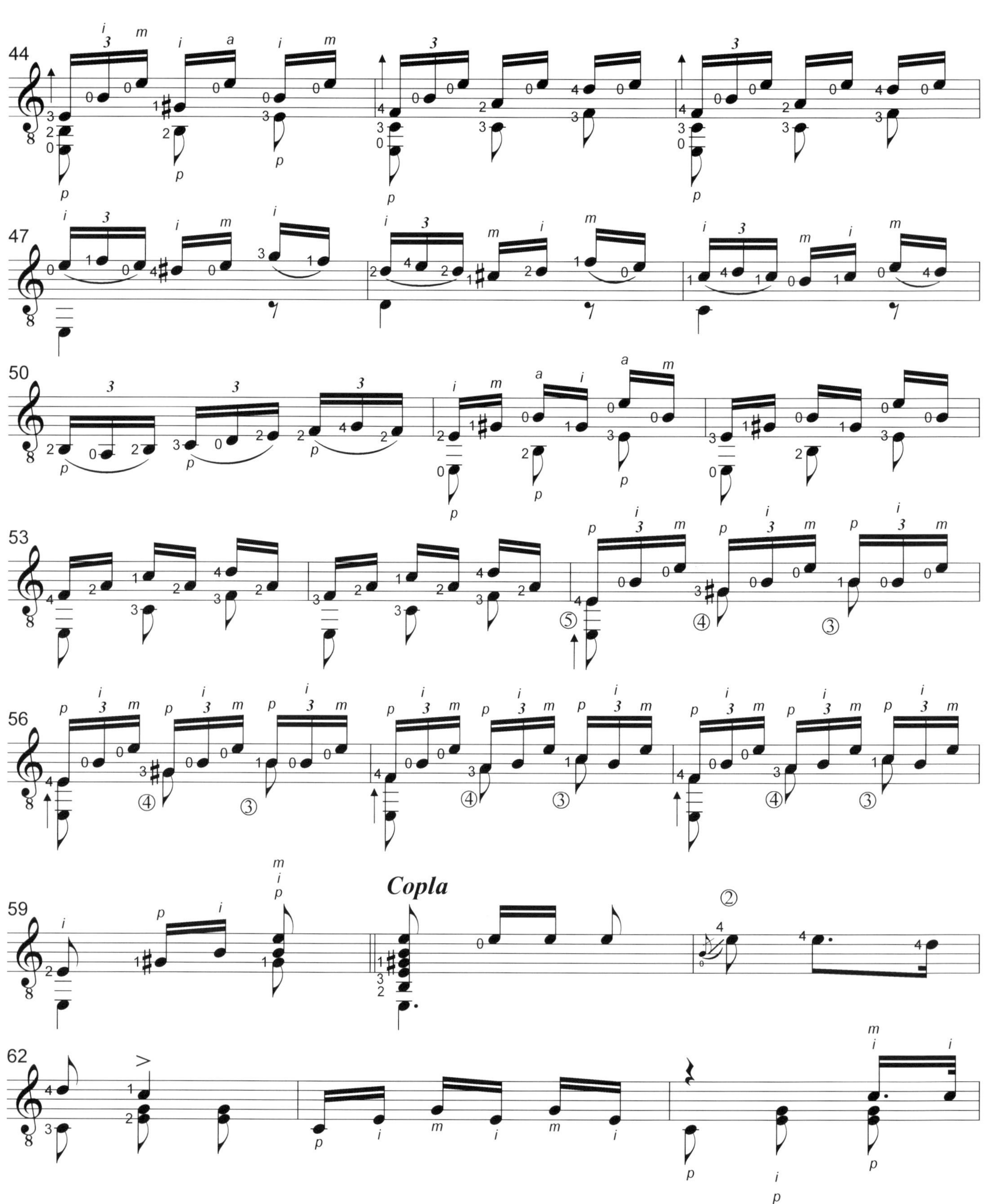
Copla

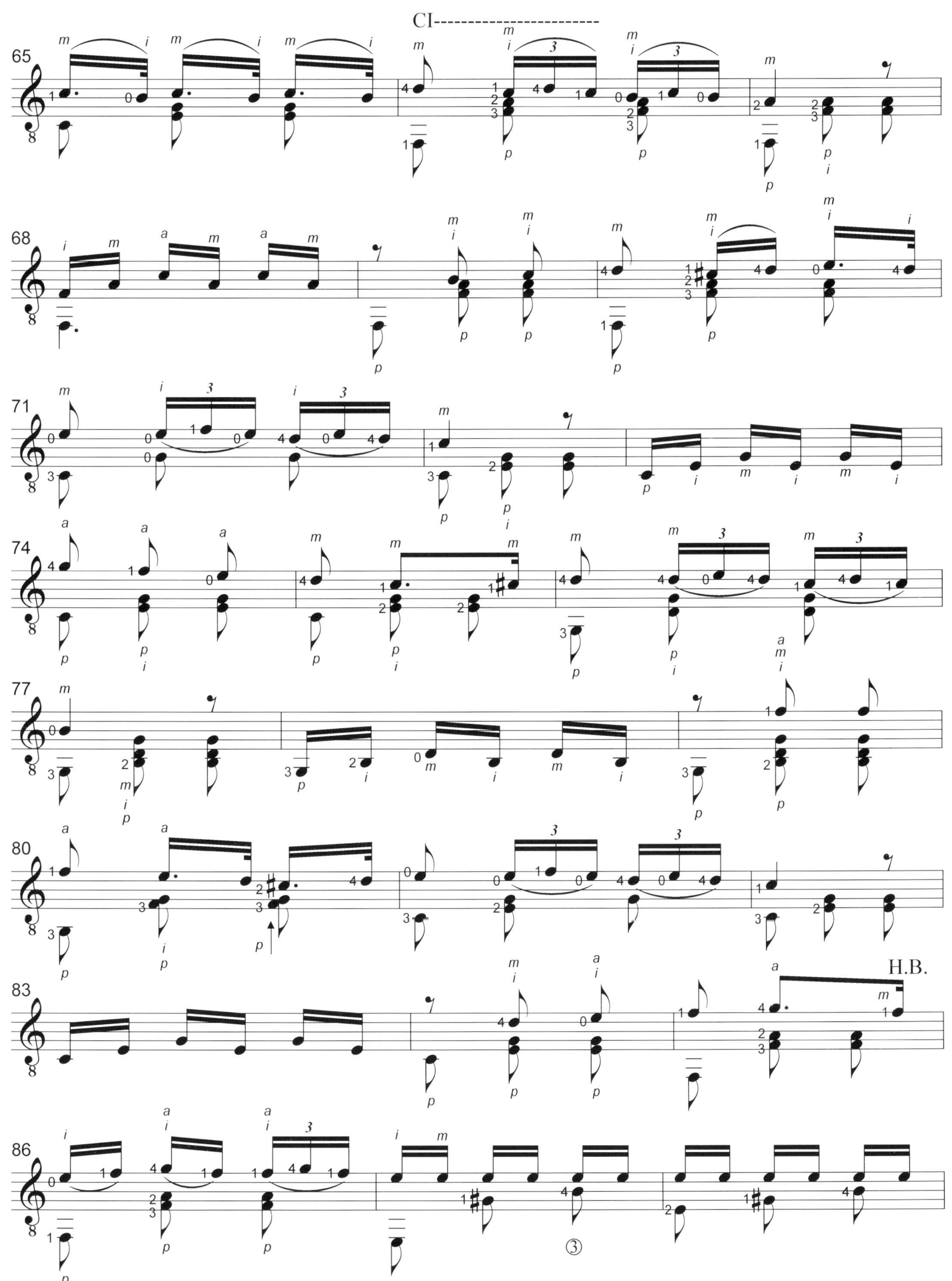

CI
H.B.

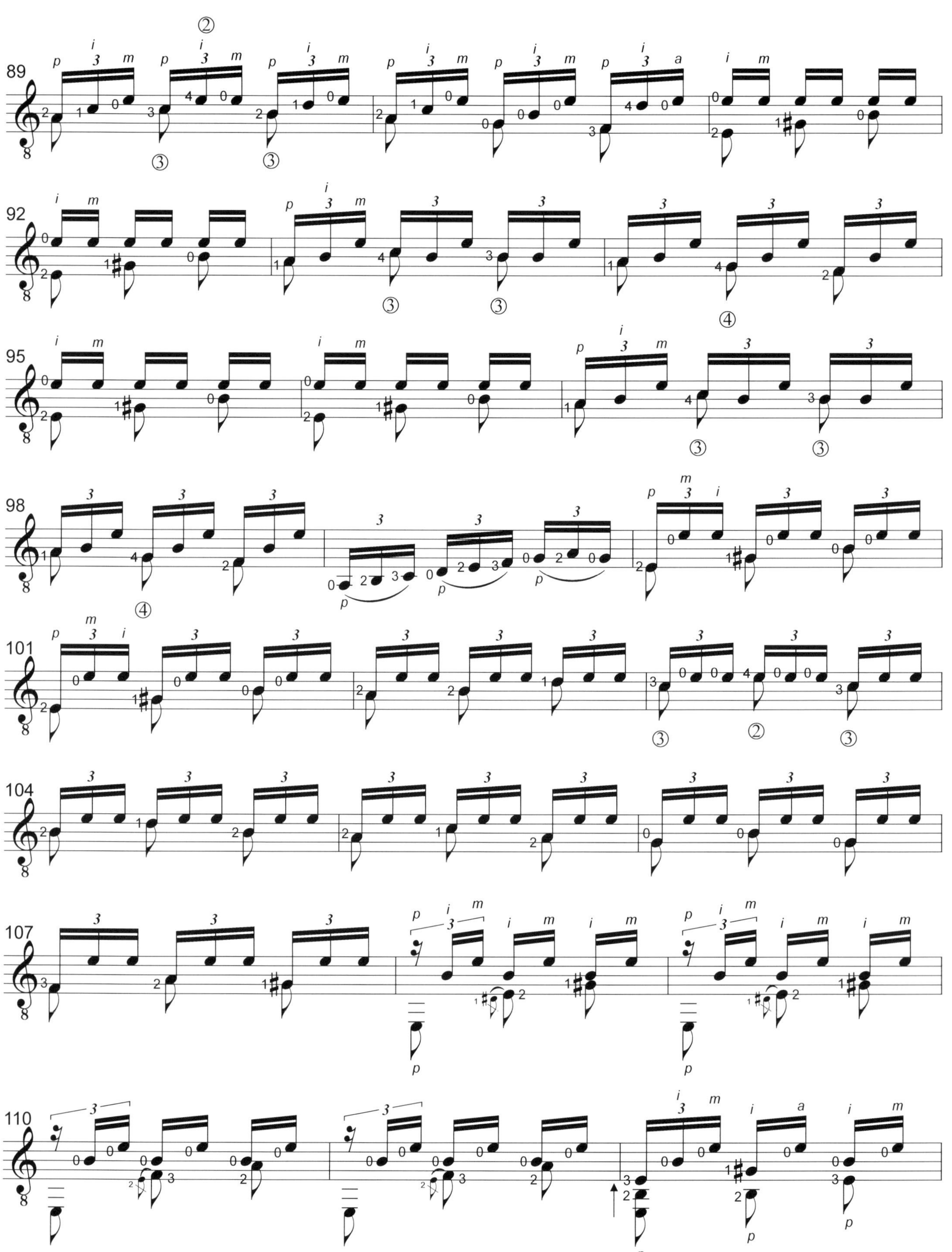

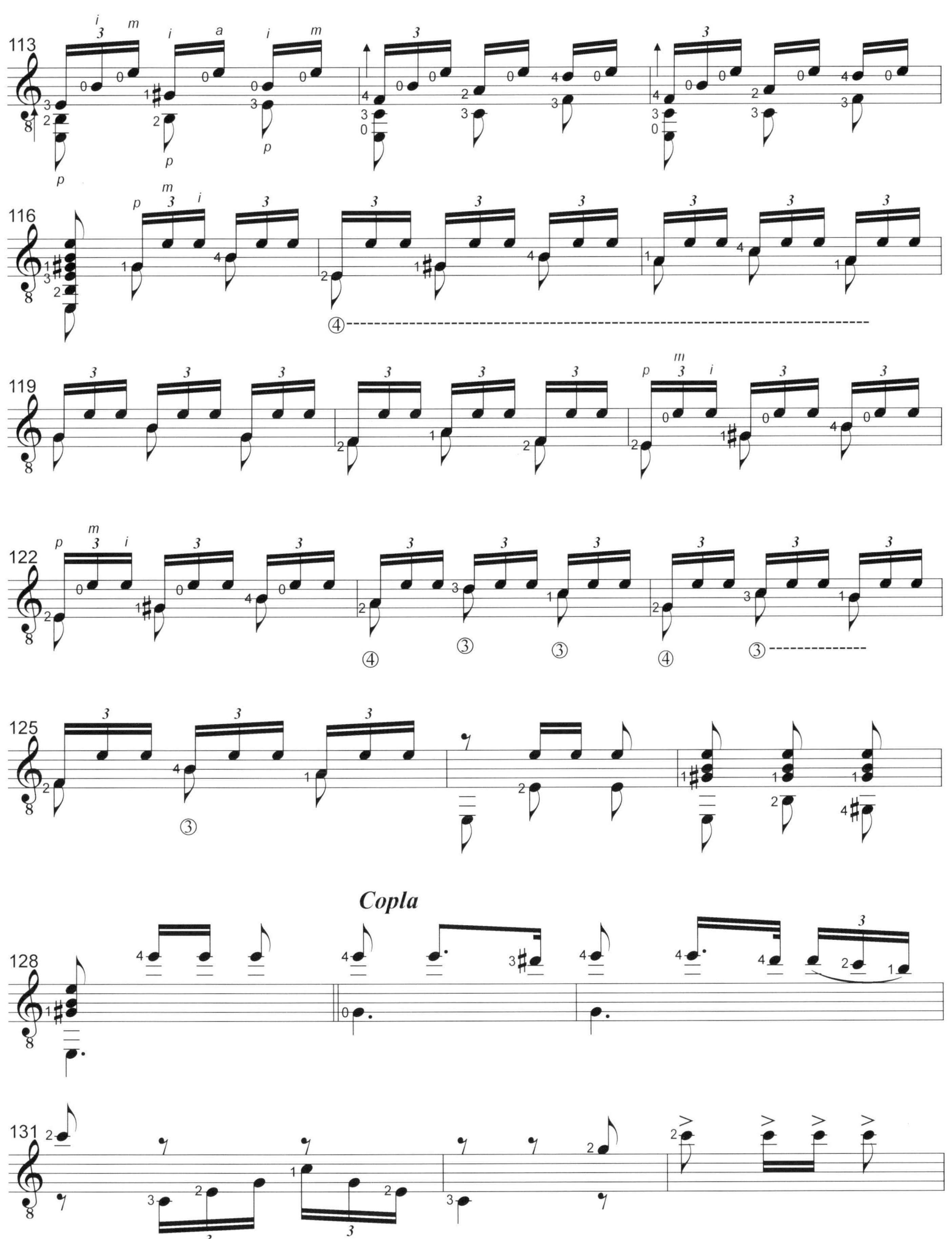
Copla

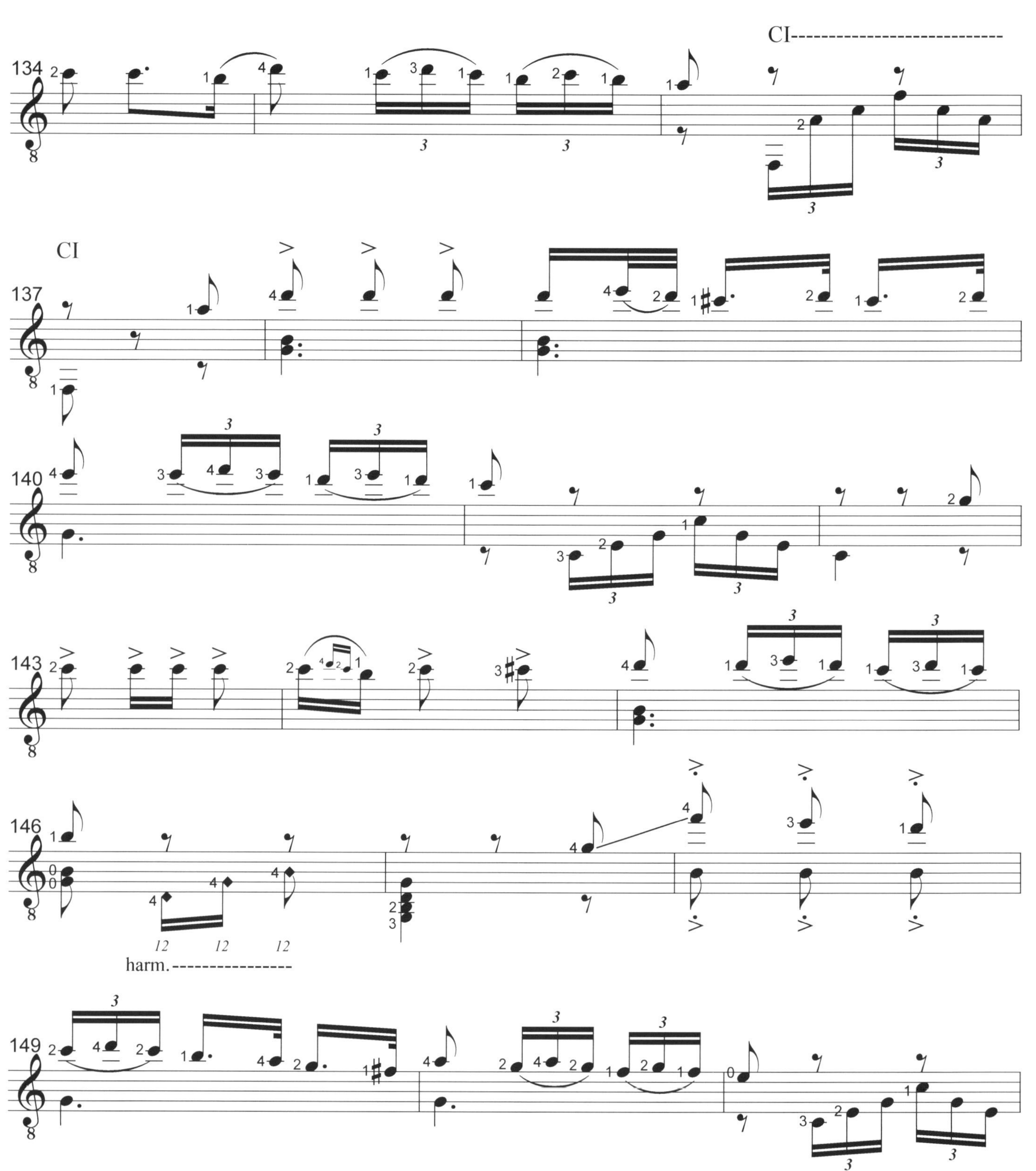
CI
CI
harm.

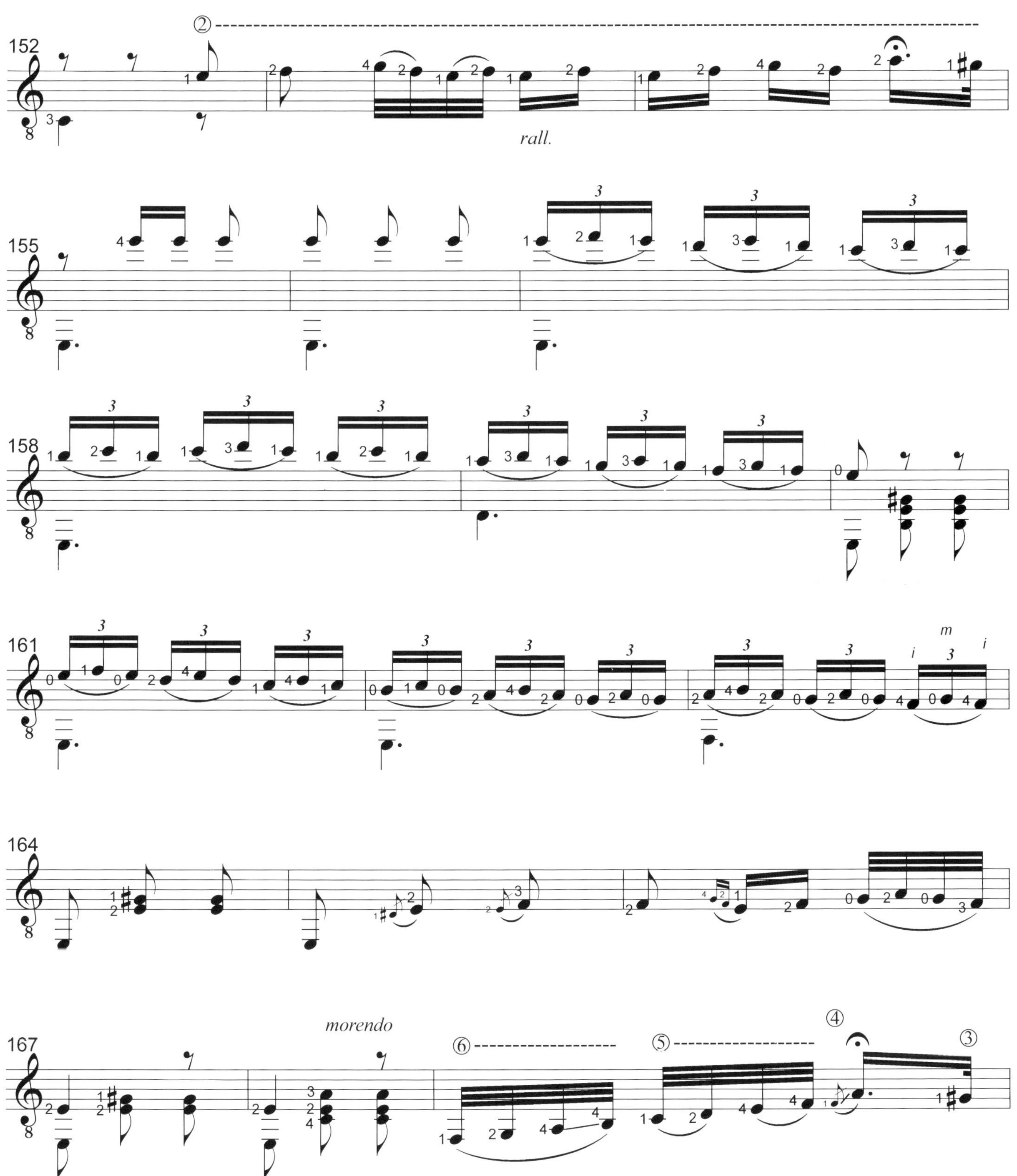
rall.
morendo

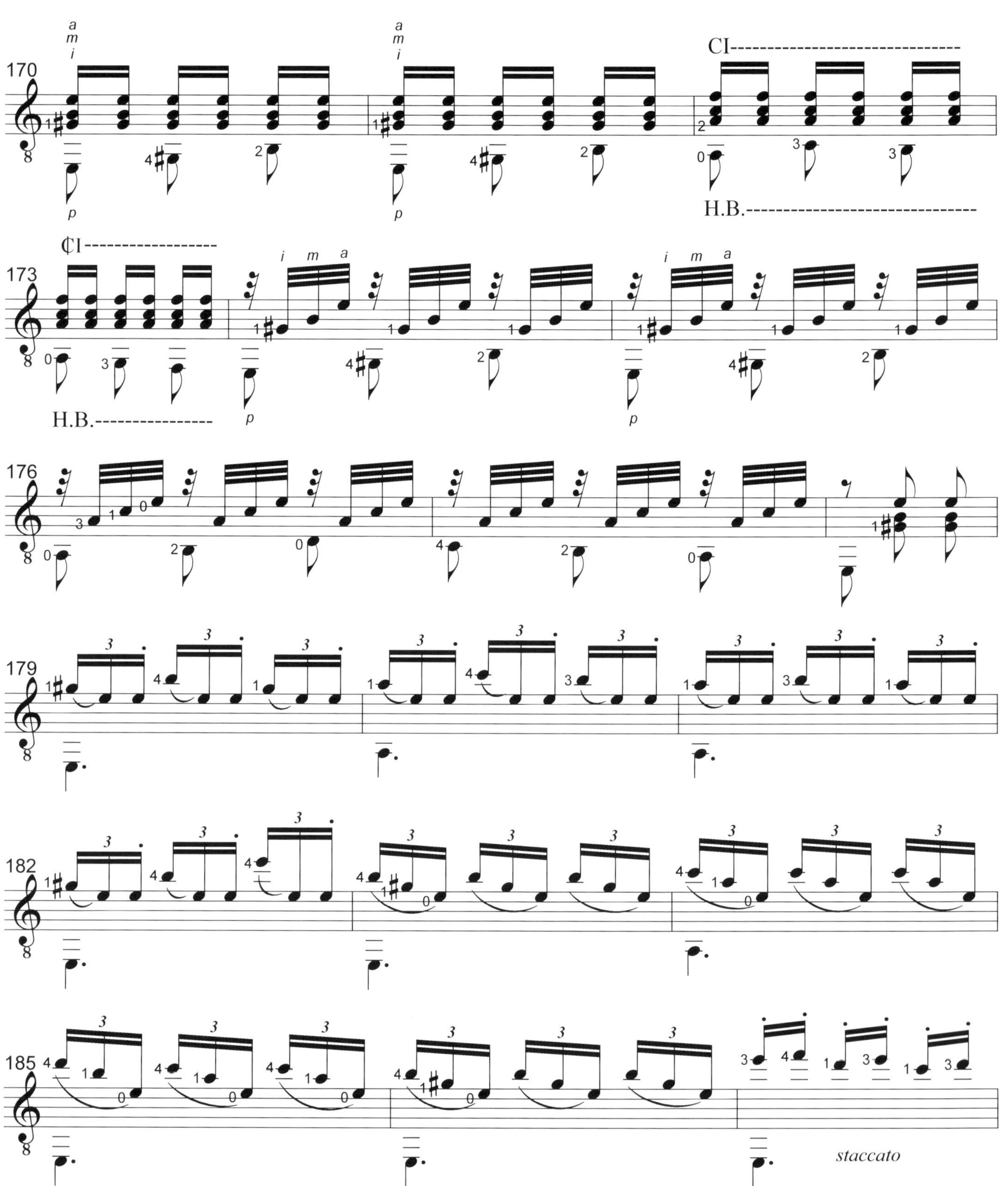
a
m
i
170
CI
H.B.
173
CI
H.B.
i m a
p
176
179
182
185
staccato

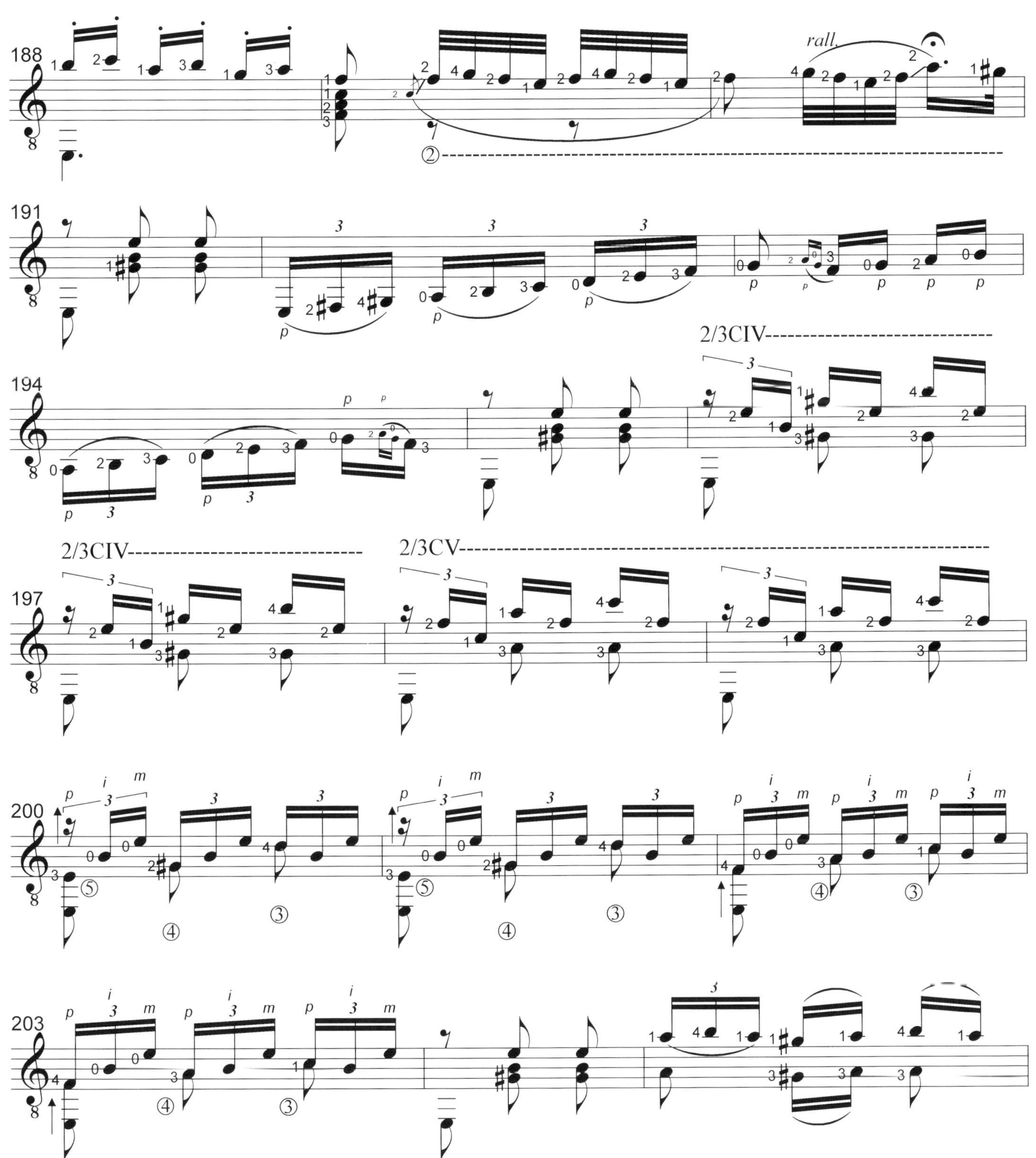
188
rall.
191
194
2/3CIV
197
2/3CIV
2/3CV
200
203

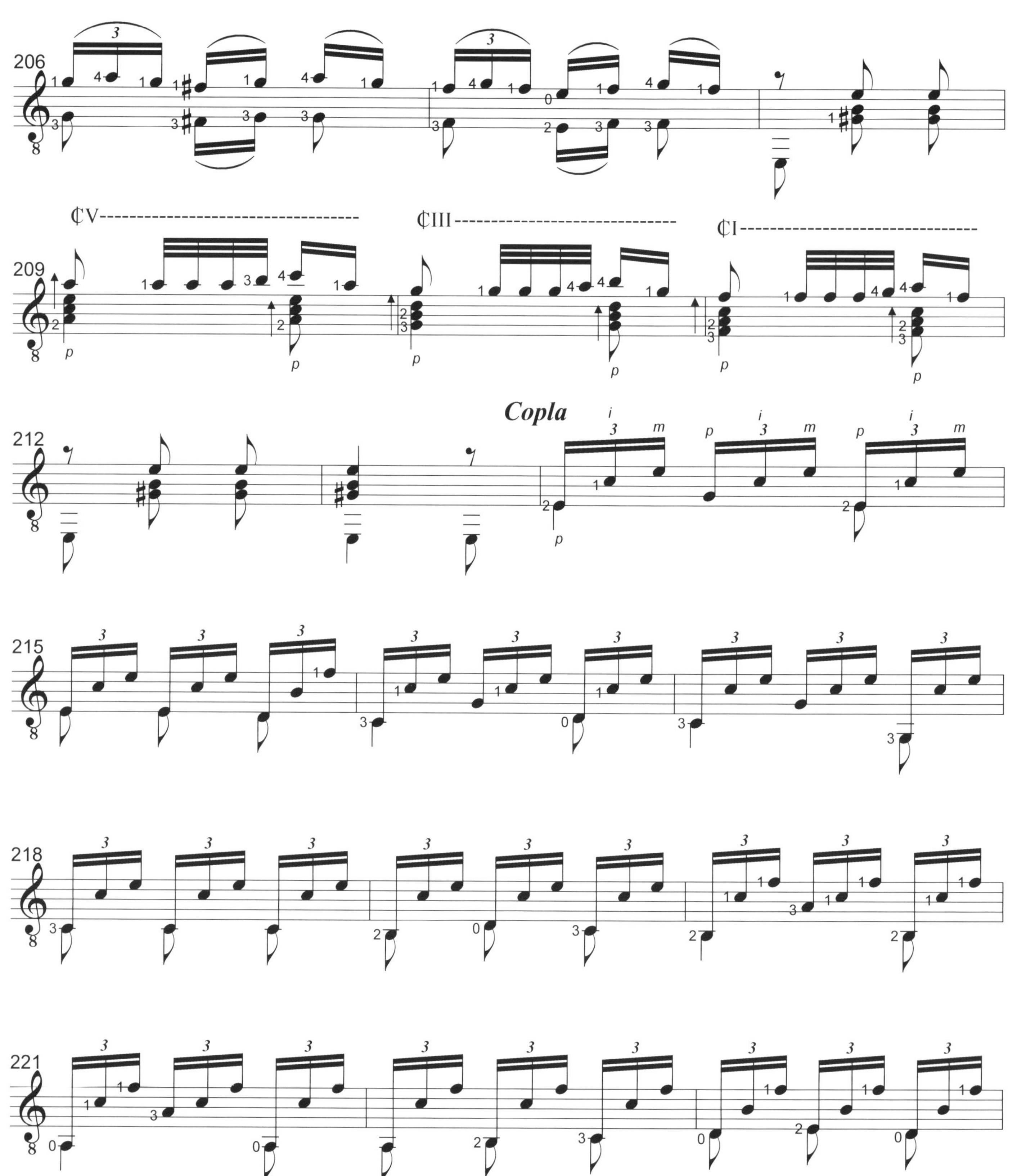

206
209
¢V
¢III
¢I
212
Copla
215
218
221

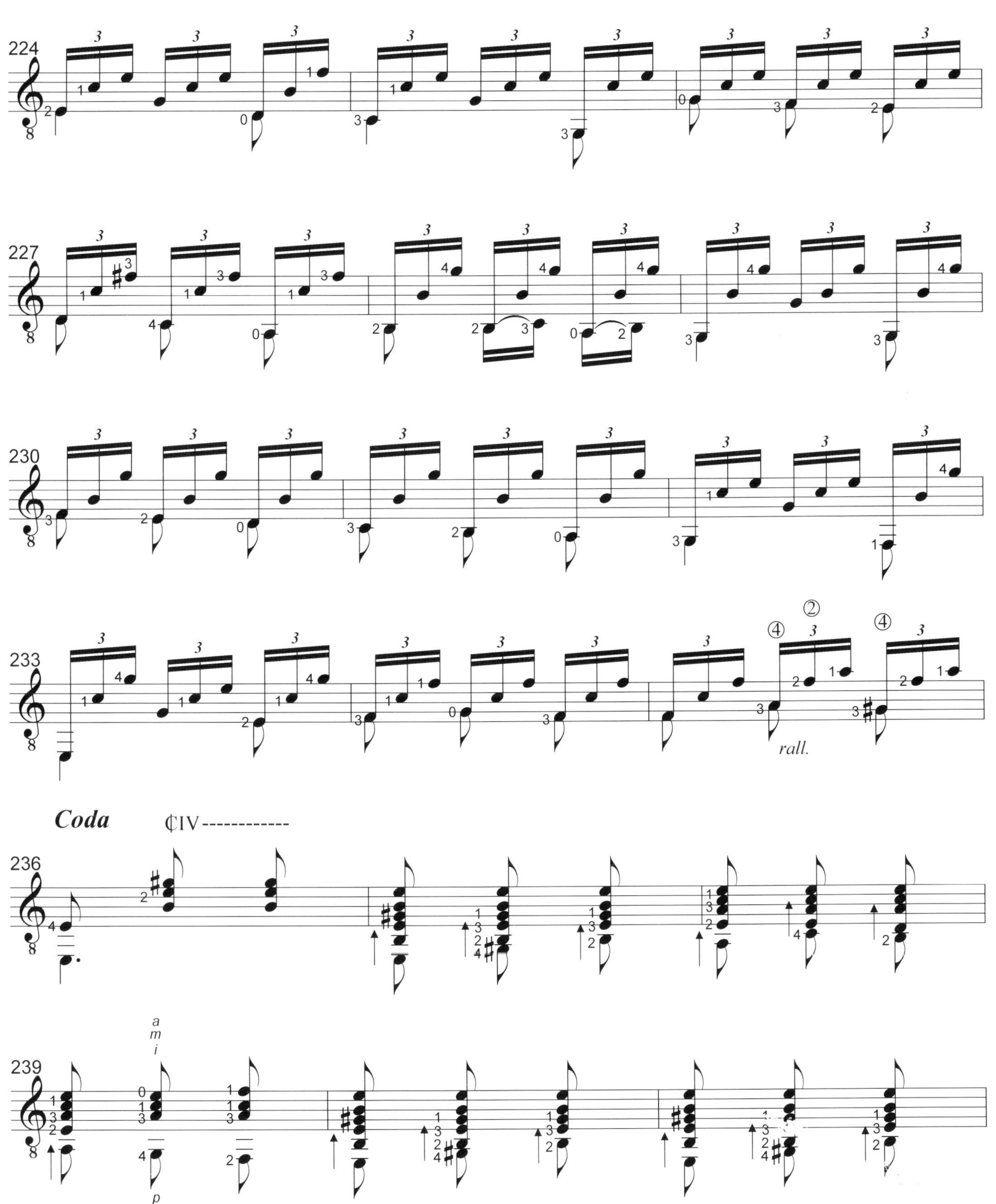
rall.
Coda
CIV
a
m
i
p

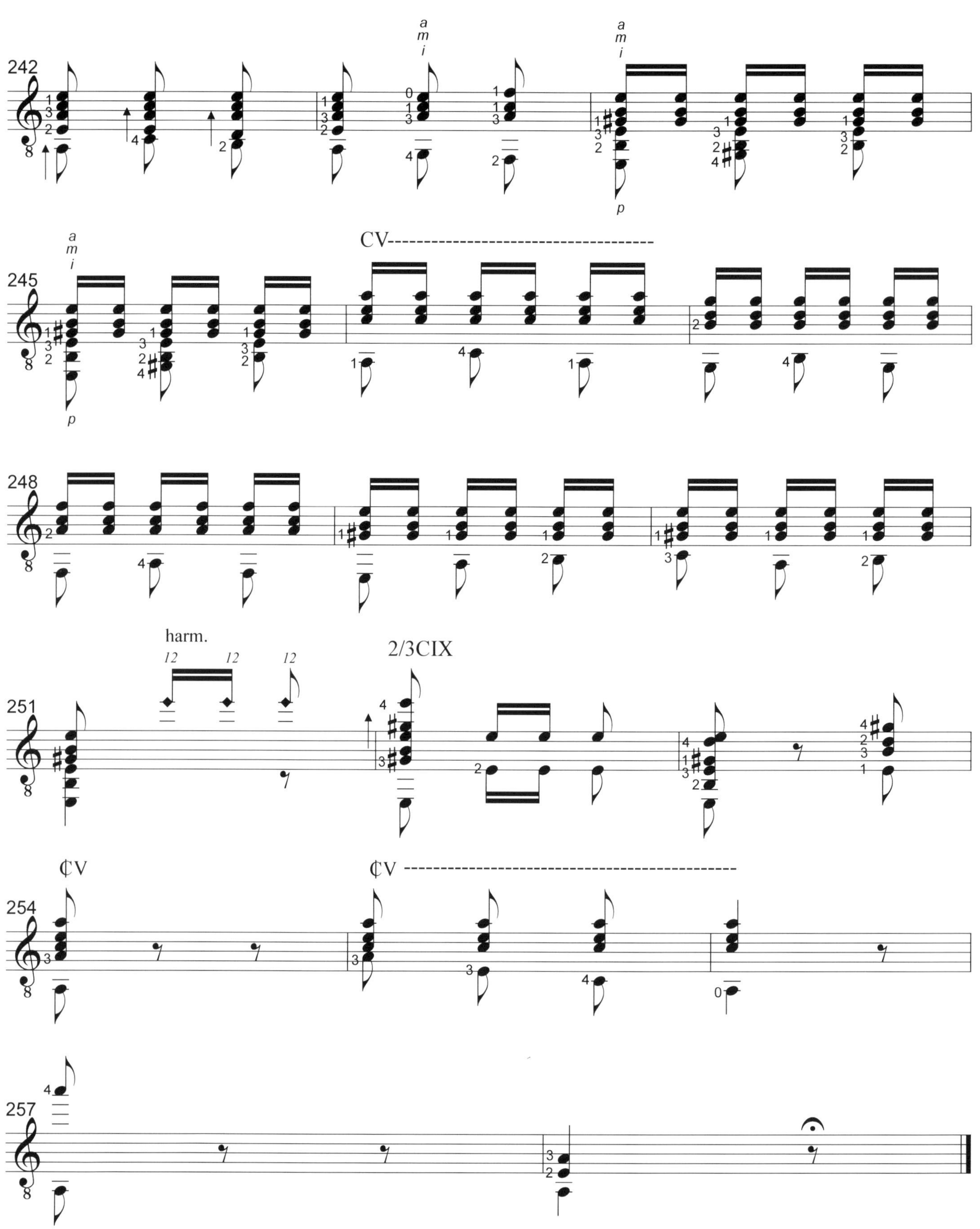
242
a m i
a m i
p
245
a m i
CV
p
248
251
harm.
12
12
12
2/3CIX
254
CV
CV
257

Los Panaderos

Julian Arcas

Edited by Corey E. Whitehead

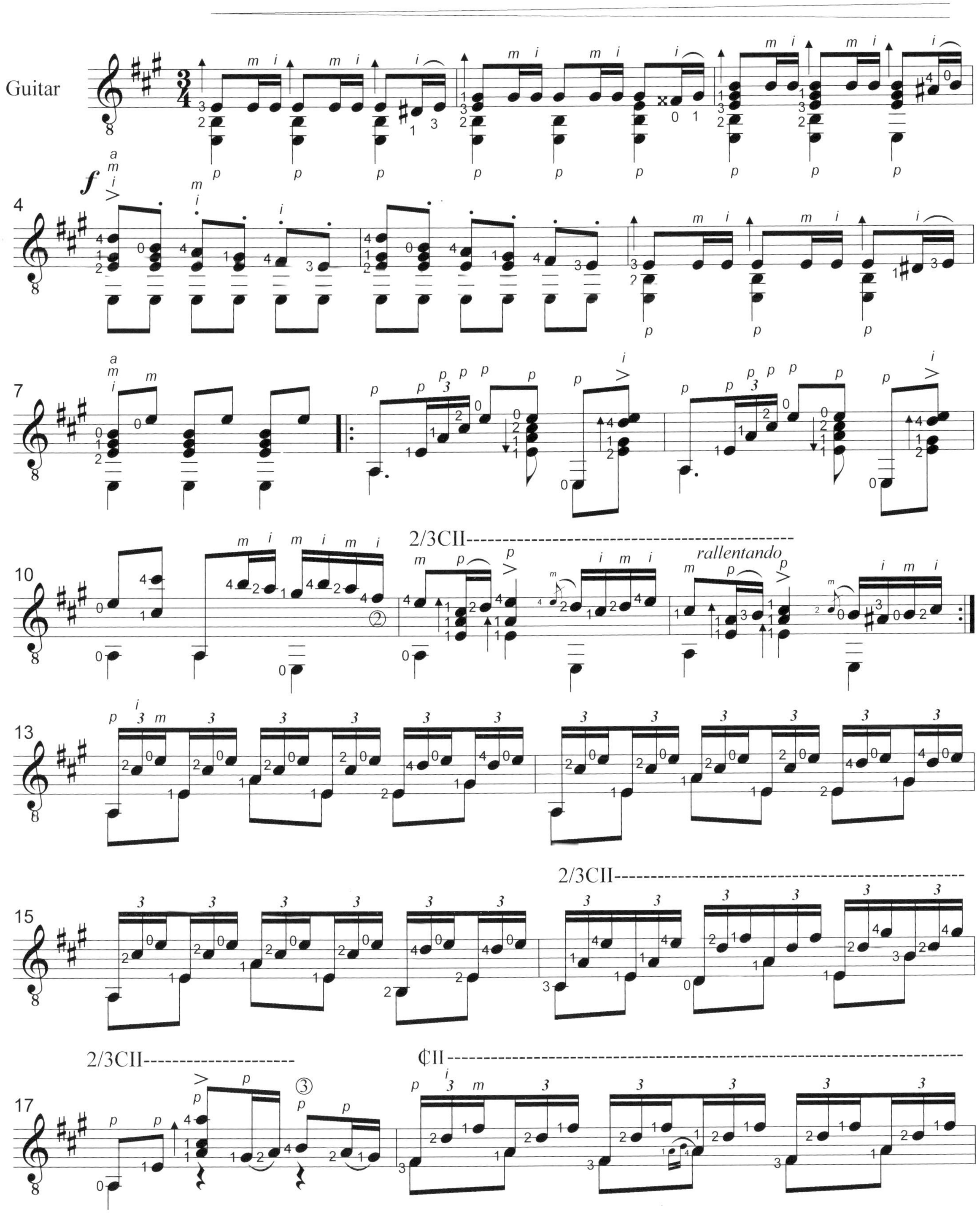

Guitar

rallentando

2/3CII

¢II

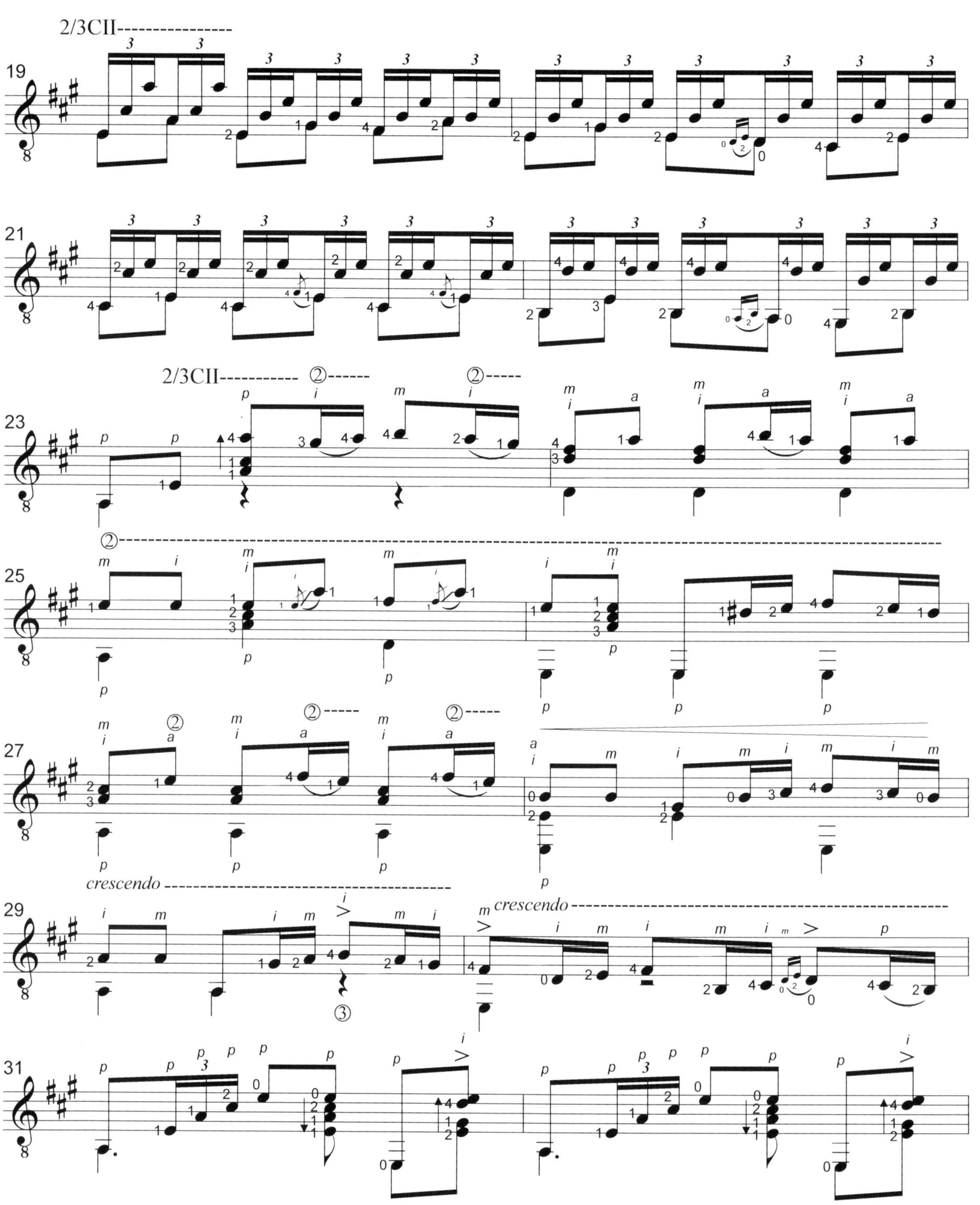
2/3CII
2/3CII
crescendo
crescendo

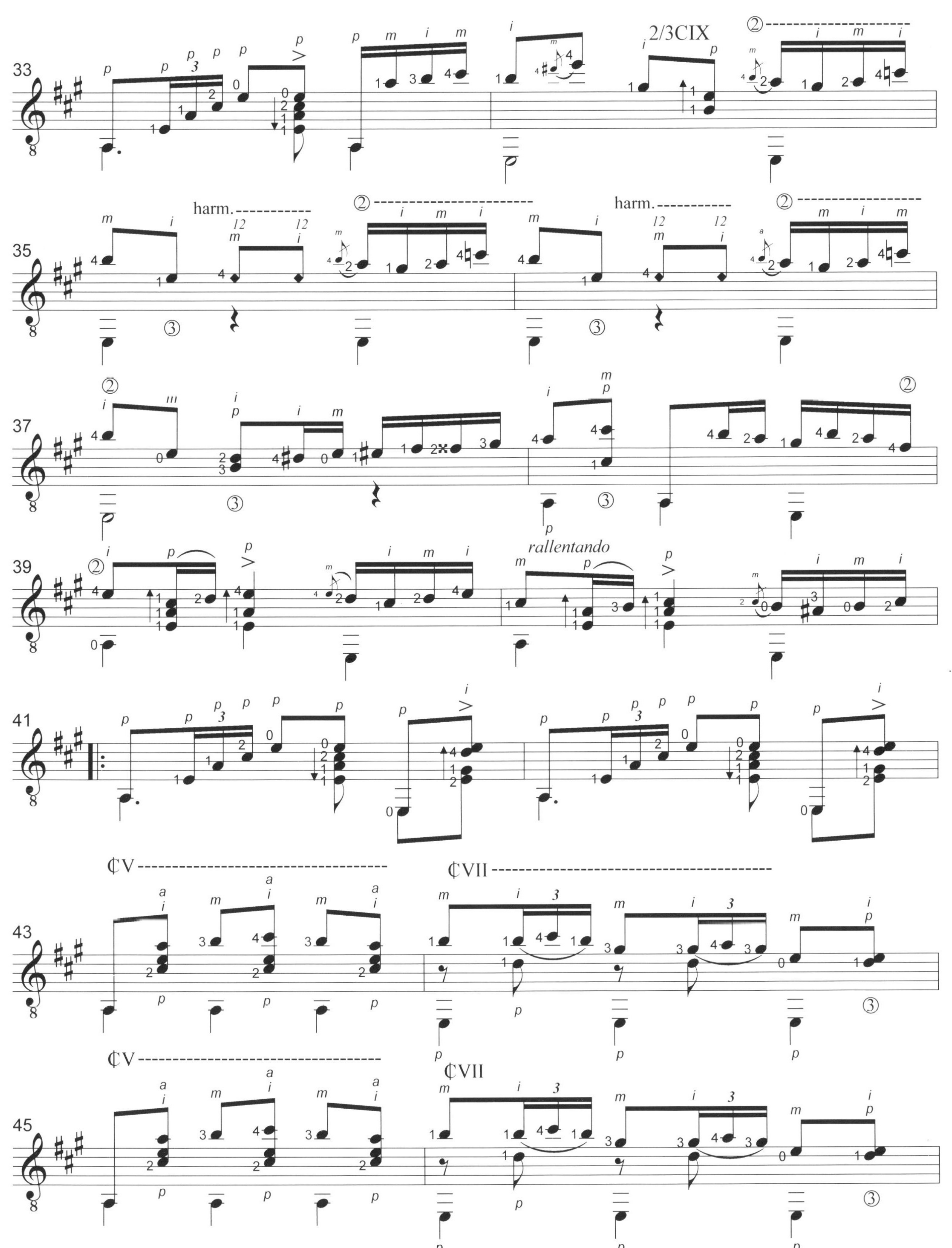
2/3CIX
harm.
harm.
rallentando
CV
CVII
CV
CVII

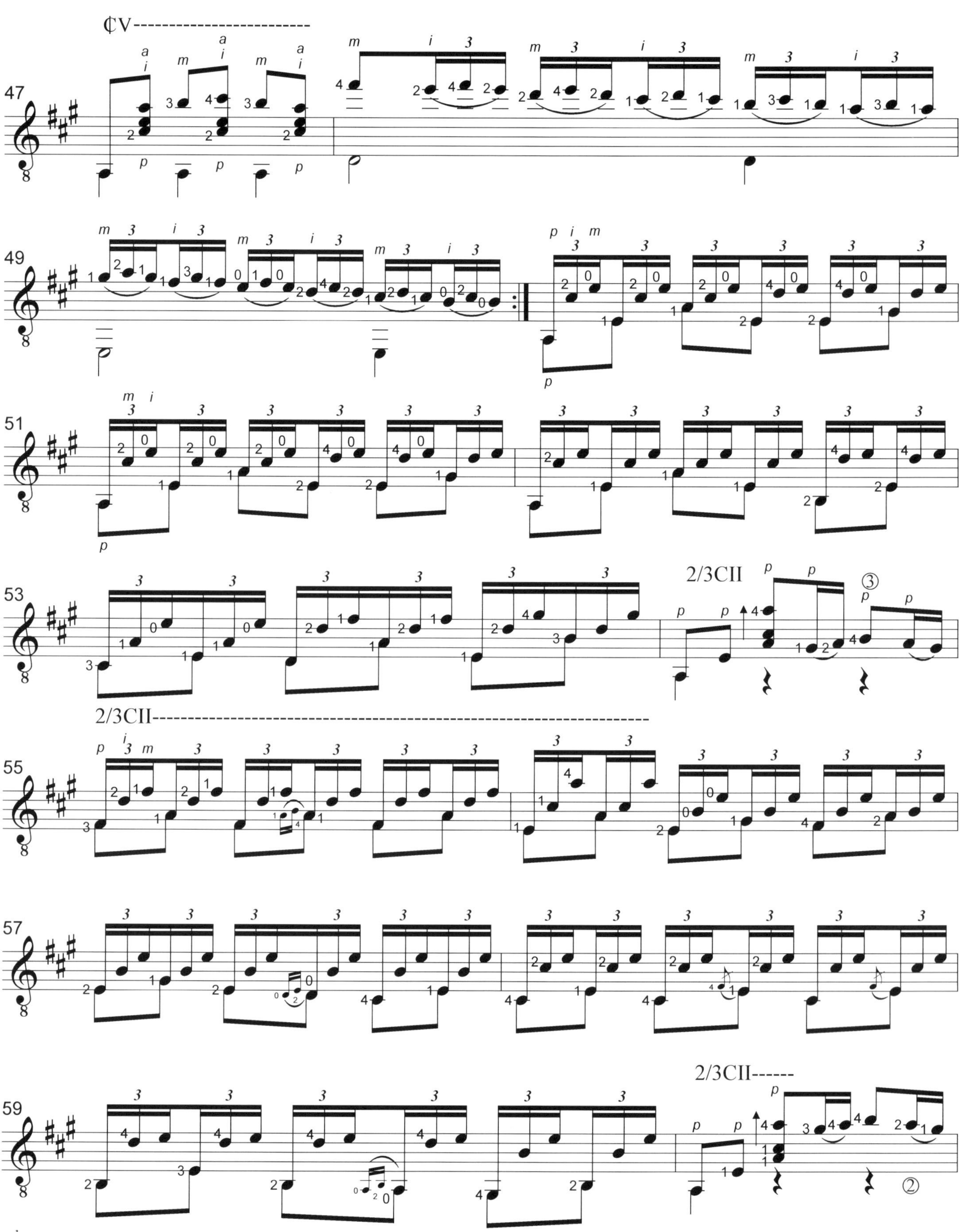

CV
47
49
51
53
2/3CII
2/3CII
55
57
2/3CII
59

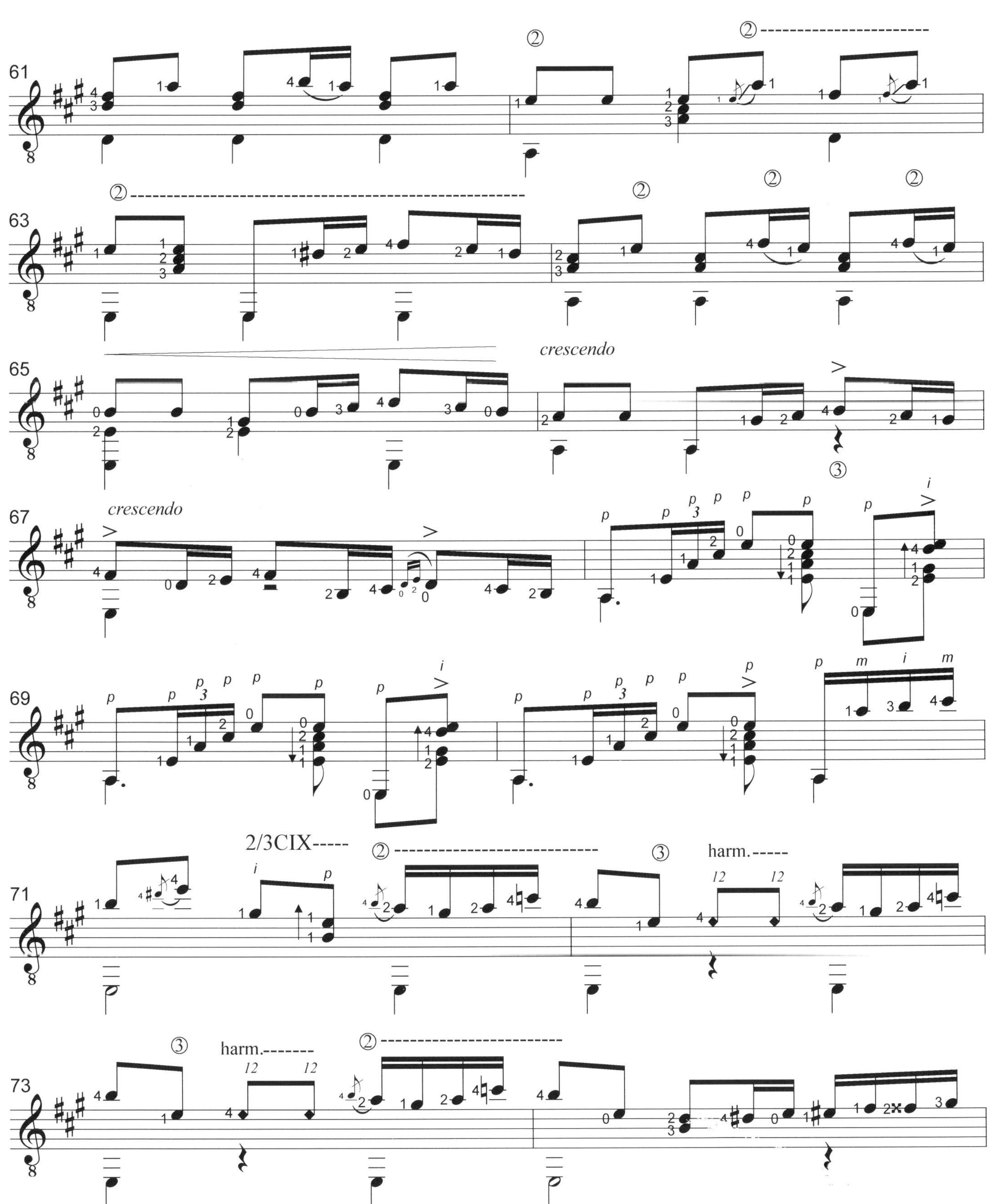
61
63
65
crescendo
67
crescendo
69
2/3CIX-----
71
harm.-----
73
harm.-------

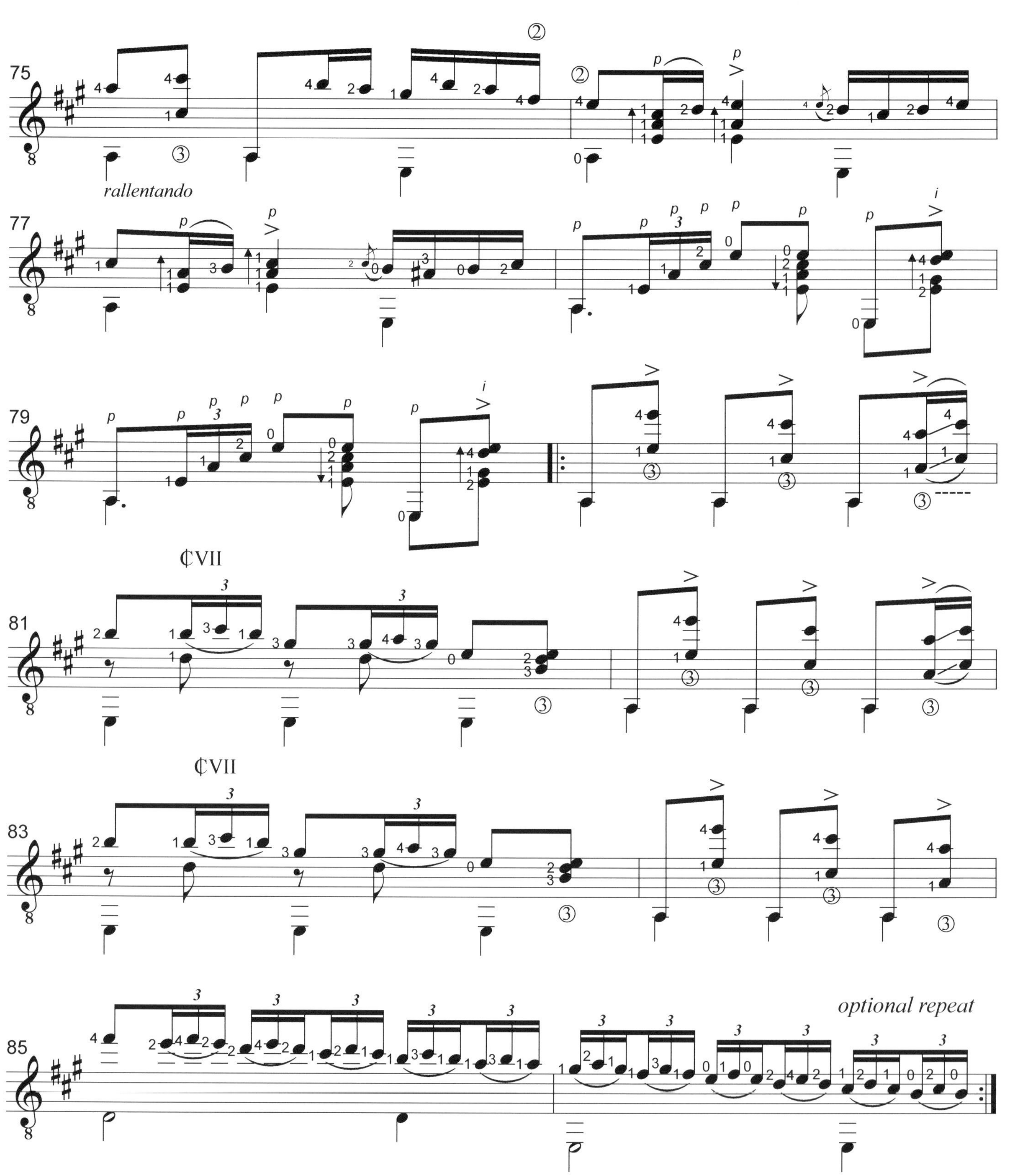
rallentando
¢VII
¢VII
optional repeat

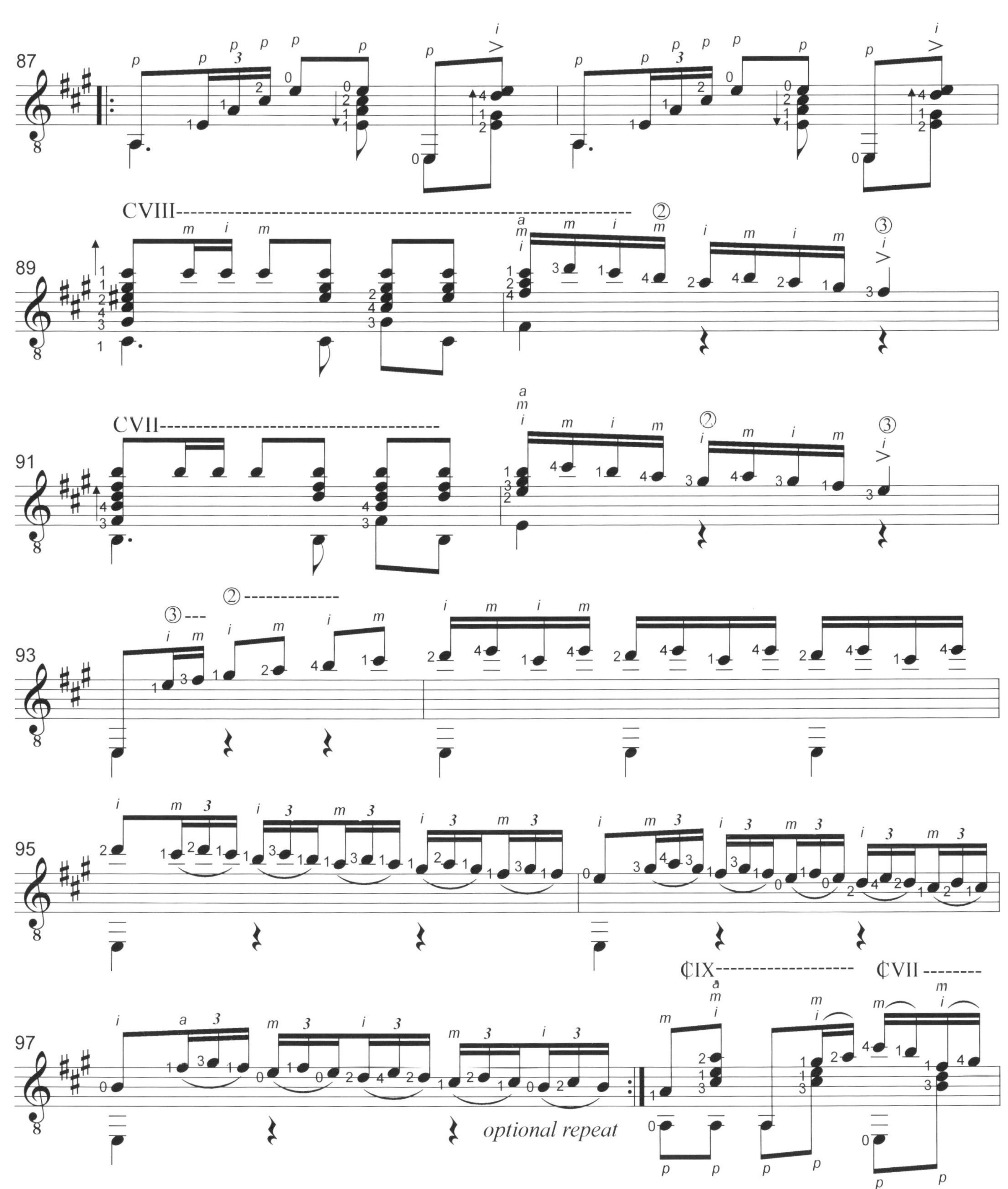
87
89
CVIII
91
CVII
93
95
97
optional repeat
¢IX
¢VII

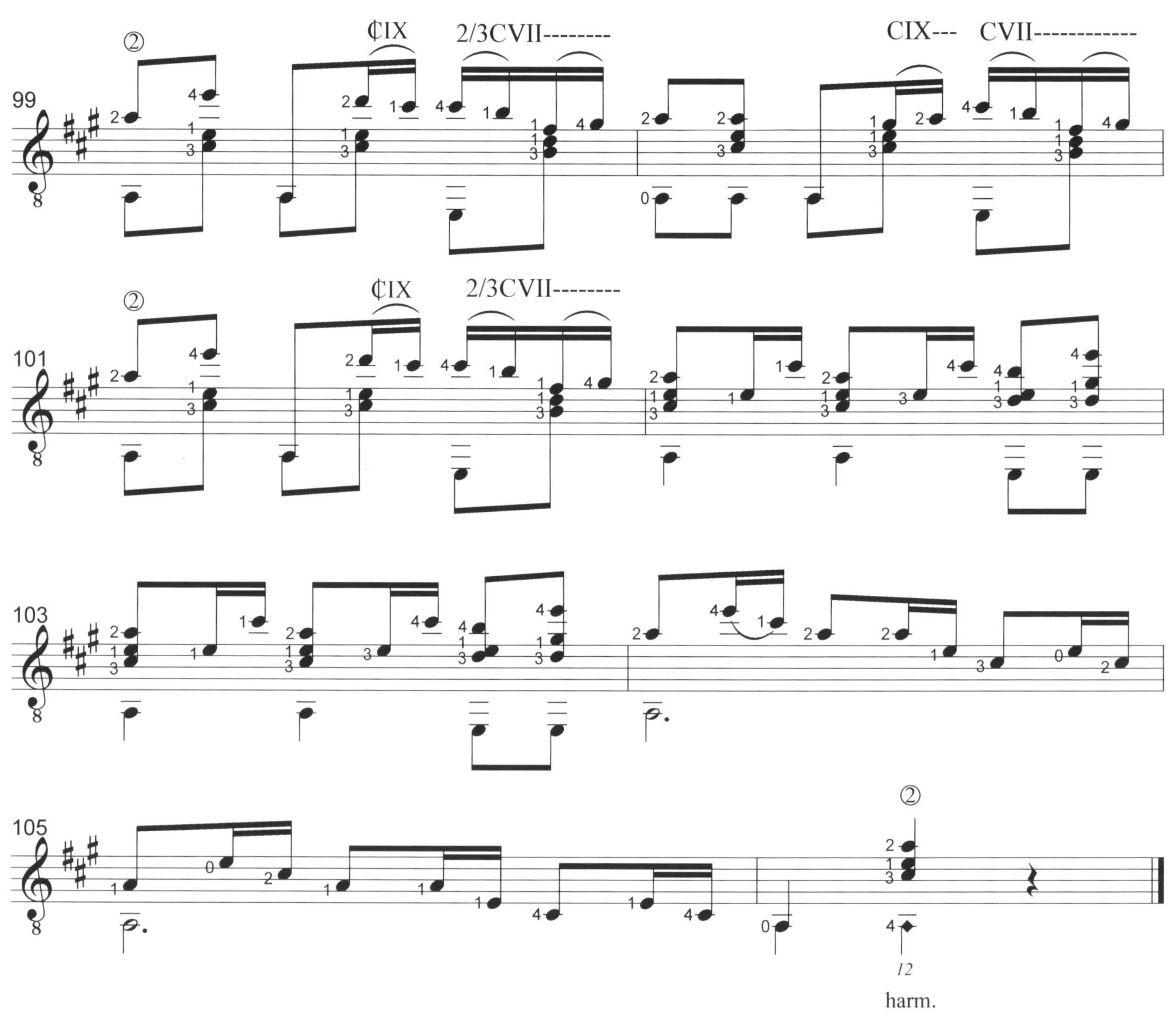
₵IX
2/3CVII--------
CIX---
CVII------------
harm.

Unit II, Part I

Soleá

Unit II, Part I
Soleá

The introduction to Unit I, Part II mentioned the form of the *Soleá* being dictated by the *cantaor* (singer) and that is true. However, when no singer is present, the form is dictated by the guitar soloist, or by the dancer or dancers. The form of *Soleá* still has "laws and canons." There are modular parts for the guitarist in the accompaniment of *cante* or *baile*.

The form of the *Soleá* will differ depending upon the situation. When accompanying a singer, one follows the form dictated by the rules of accompanying a singer. When accompanying a dancer, or dance ensemble, the form is dictated by the choreography. When performing as a soloist, one is expected to incorporate the traditional formal elements, but at the same time has the liberty to write themes and harmonies that do not resemble the traditional canons of *Soleá*. This concept also applies to other *palos* such as *Tangos*, *Fandangos*, *Siguiriyas*, and their related rhythmic sub-forms.

The accompaniment of *cante* of course requires a singer and the accompanist must adjust to the singer. One can practice accompanying with singers on old recordings, playing along with the guitar accompaniment on the recording as a guide. One can first attempt to copy the accompanist exactly, and then later compose or improvise a second guitar part as if two guitarists are accompanying the singer on the recording.

If you cut the accompaniment section from the following works, the compositions work as solos for the concert stage, or for the formation of technique for playing Spanish music. The understanding and synthesis of flamenco performance practice, assists the classical guitarist in the interpretation and performance of Spanish music, and of Baroque music in general.

"Soleá por arriba (baso)" by Richard Marlow and Corey Whitehead

1) This work begins with a ***llamada*** or "call" to the singer or dancer. Then the ***salida*** and ***paseo*** follow, each having a specific chord progression. Sometimes these sections are referred to by their chord names, for example: ***La, Do, Fa, or Mi.***
2) This is followed by another *llamada* to close the rhythmic section and introduce the first melody.
3) The first melody is introduced in measure 21. This section features a pedal tone F (Fa). This pedal tone is "fixed" as the left-hand finger does not lift from this note. This technique and *falseta* section are referred to as a *posicion fija "fa"* wherein all notes ring over one another and the pedal tone as much as possible to create dissonant tension.
4) Several *falsetas* follow, each using the thumb *(pulgar)* in some way, leading to a slower section called the *falseta* or *silencio* which is a solo for the dancer and for the guitarist. This usually features *tremolo* and *arpeggio*. In this section, the dancer (even if imaginary) shows off hand and arm movements and does not do complex footwork.
5) This is followed by an uplift in the tempo, a *subida* in the subsequent section called the *escobilla* as the dancer resumes footwork, in an *accelerando* buildup of volume and tempo.
6) The work ends with a *macho falseta por alzapúa* and a *final por bulerías.*
7) These parts are all likewise present in the *Alegrías* form found later in the book.

"Soleá de Utrera" by Richard Marlow and Corey E. Whitehead

1) This work is in A (La) Dórico (Phrygian) and is somewhat less complex than the previous arrangement of *Soleá* which was following the form used to accompany *baile.* This example provides an introduction to an accompaniment of the singer in measures 29-48. The *cante* accompaniment is for only one *letra* (lyric). Typically in a performance with a singer there are 3 or 4 verses (*letras).* One may play variations similar to this for the remaining *letras* depending on the singer. Technically these recordings demonstrate *tercios* of *letras*, or in other words, one verse. The term *letras* most often refers to a verse of four lines or *tercios*, with one of the lines being repeated. The *soleá* may also use a five-*tercio* lyric scheme.
2) The guitar responds with a final *falseta* from measures 50-70.

"Bulería por soleá" by Richard Marlow and Corey E. Whitehead

1) This short work demonstrates some of the typical kinds of techniques and harmonies associated with a *Bulería por soleá* which is often misunderstood. This *palo is* often incorrectly called *Soleá por bulerías.* **The *Soleá por bulerías* does not exist.** The reason the *Soleá por bulerías* does not exist is that it is unnatural to accompany the verses of the *soleá* with the rhythm of the *bulerías.* What does exist is the *letra* of the *bulería* sung with the rhythm of the *soleá.*
2) There may be some solo works performed and/or recorded by artists with the title *Soleá por bulerías*, but the singers, musicologists and flamencologists would disagree with the use of that title as it is a *palo* that does not exist.

Soleares por arriba (baso)

Richard Marlow and Corey E. Whitehead
(Edited by Corey Whitehead)

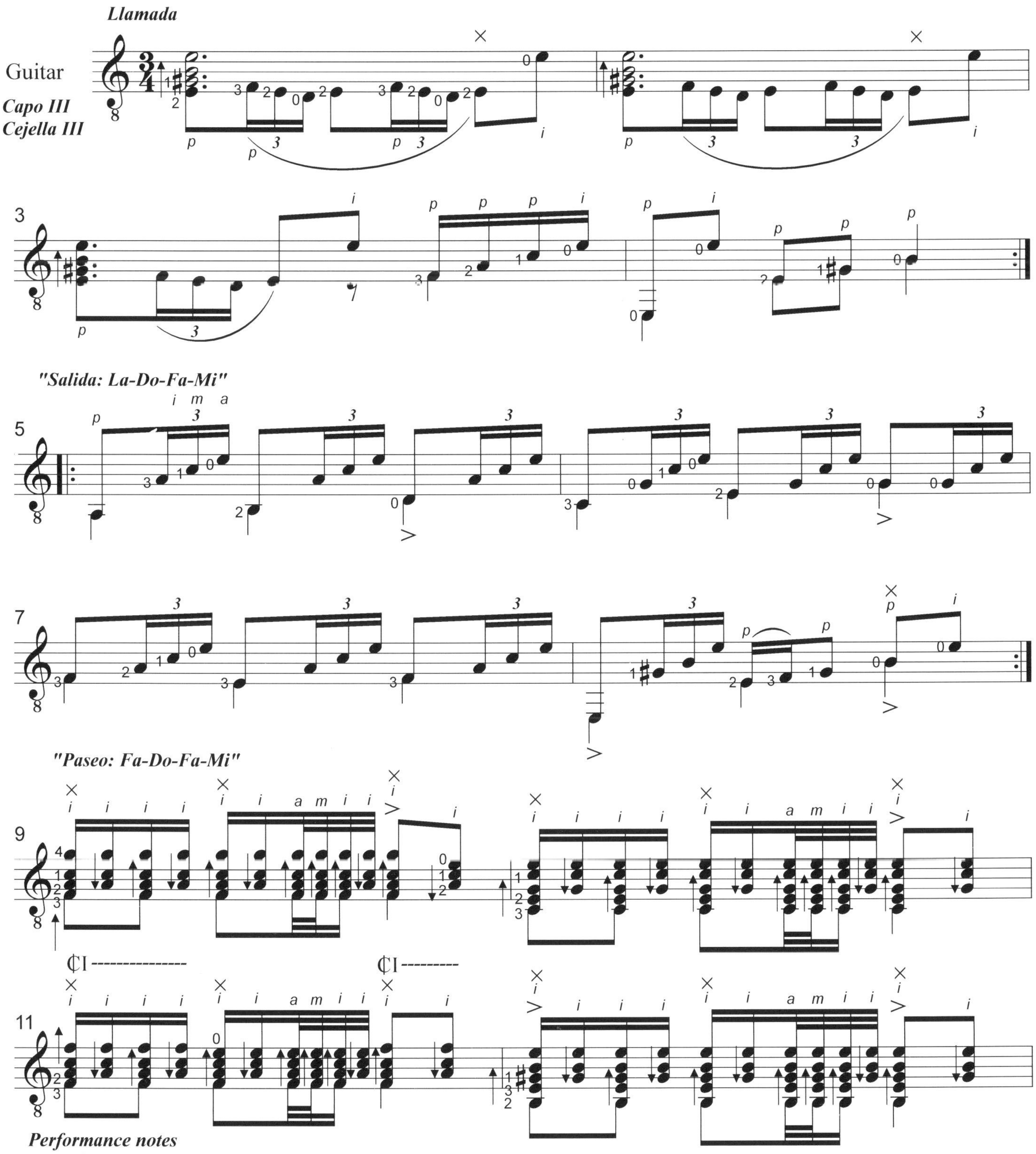

Llamada

Guitar

Capo III
Cejella III

"Salida: La-Do-Fa-Mi"

"Paseo: Fa-Do-Fa-Mi"

Performance notes

1) Anchor the thumb on the sixth string throughout.
2) The "x" symbol signifies a "golpe" with the "a" finger simultaneously as the "i" finger plays.
3) The R.H. fingers "a-m-i" should touch the thumb lightly before strumming downward.
4) "Apagar con la mano derecha" *means to stop or mute the strings with the right-hand palm.*

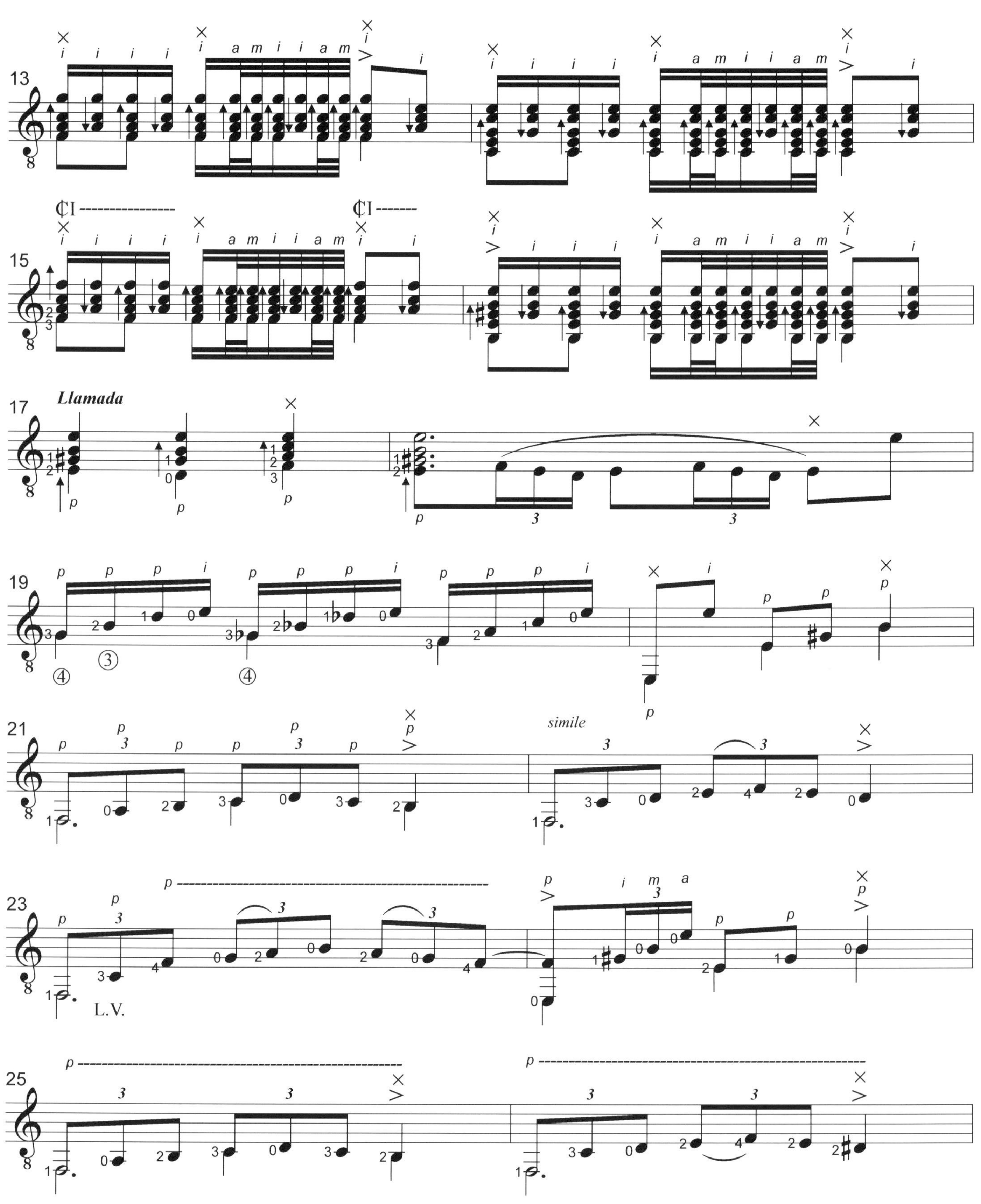

Llamada
simile
L.V.

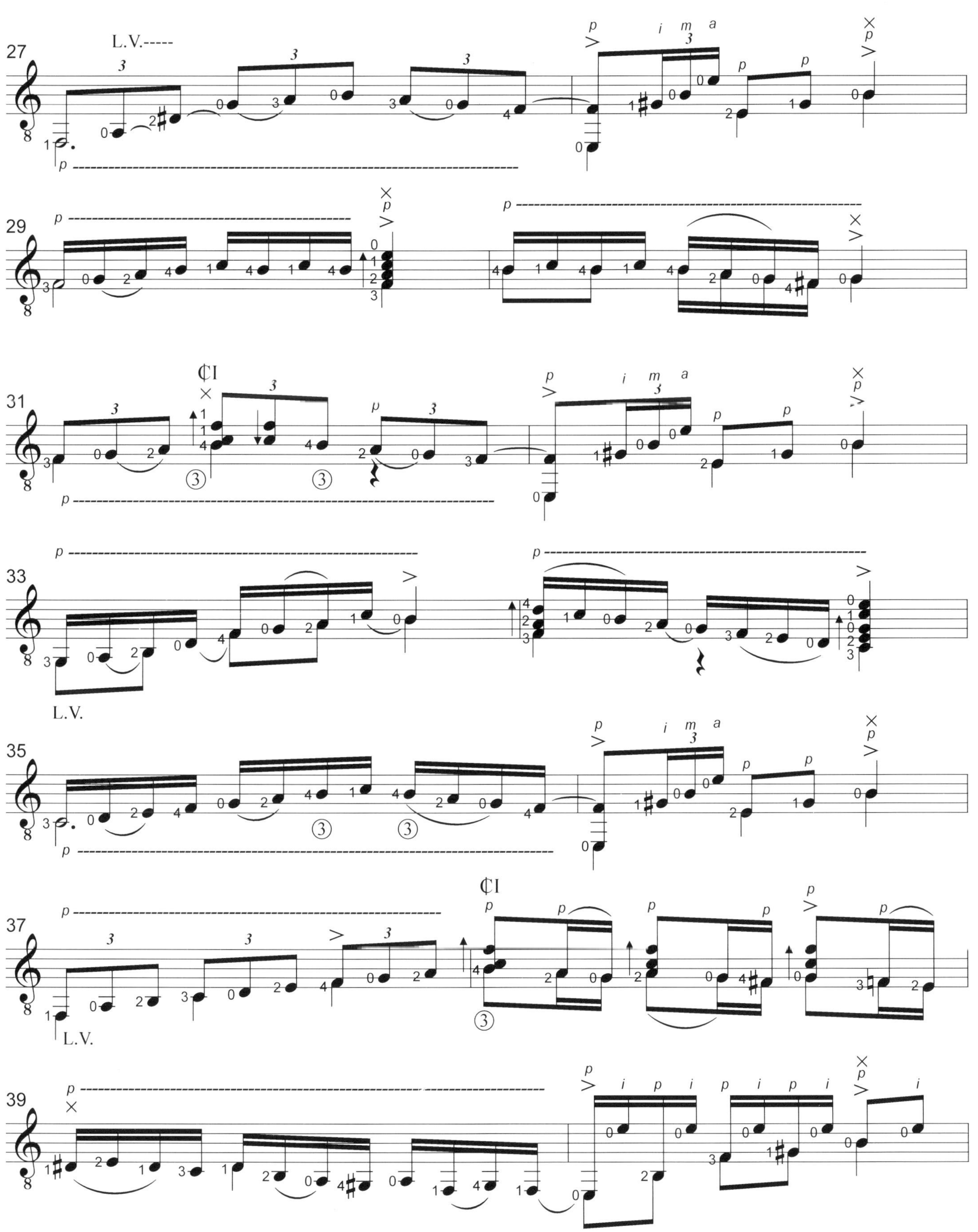
L.V.-----
L.V.
L.V.
ȻI
ȻI

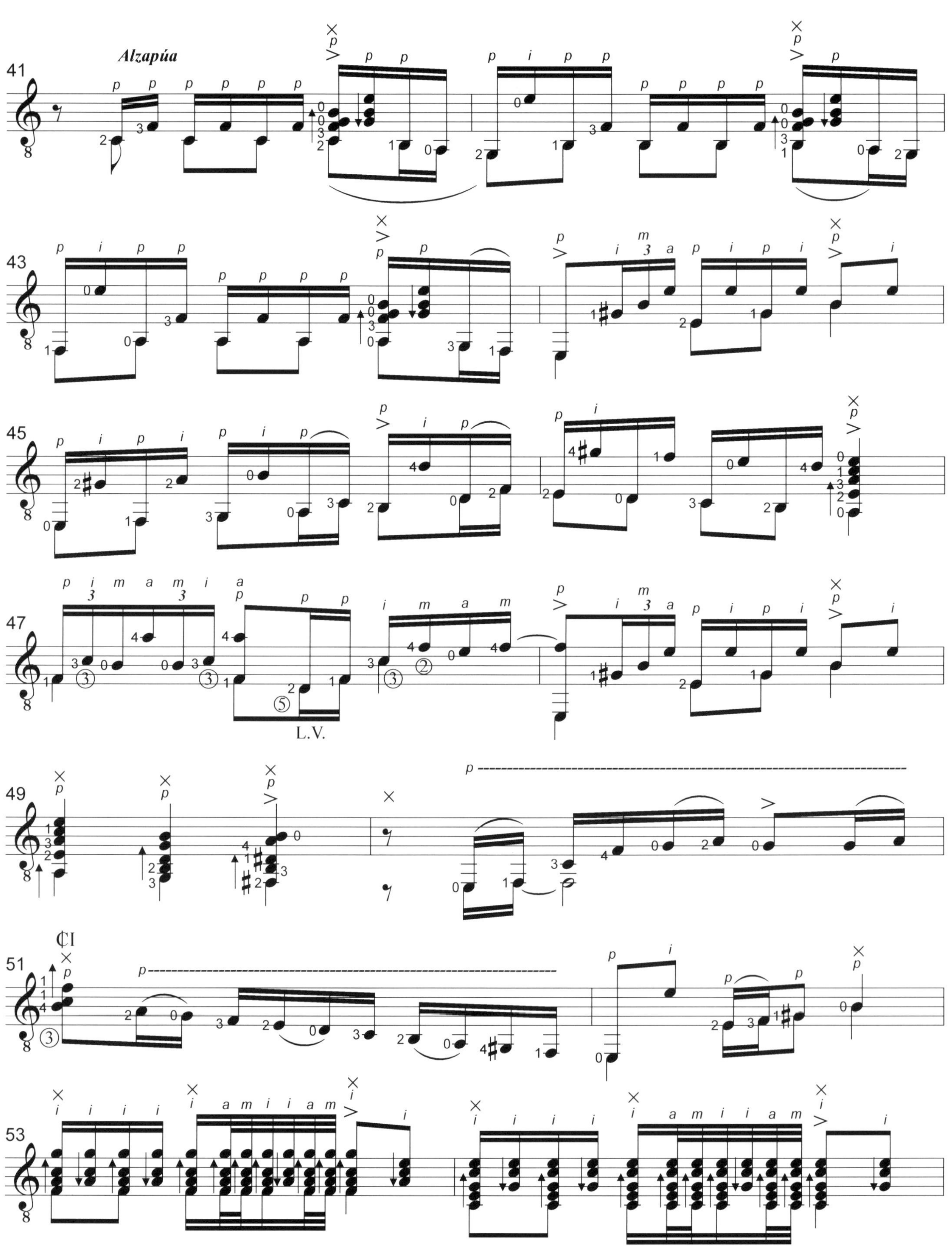

Alzapúa
L.V.
CI

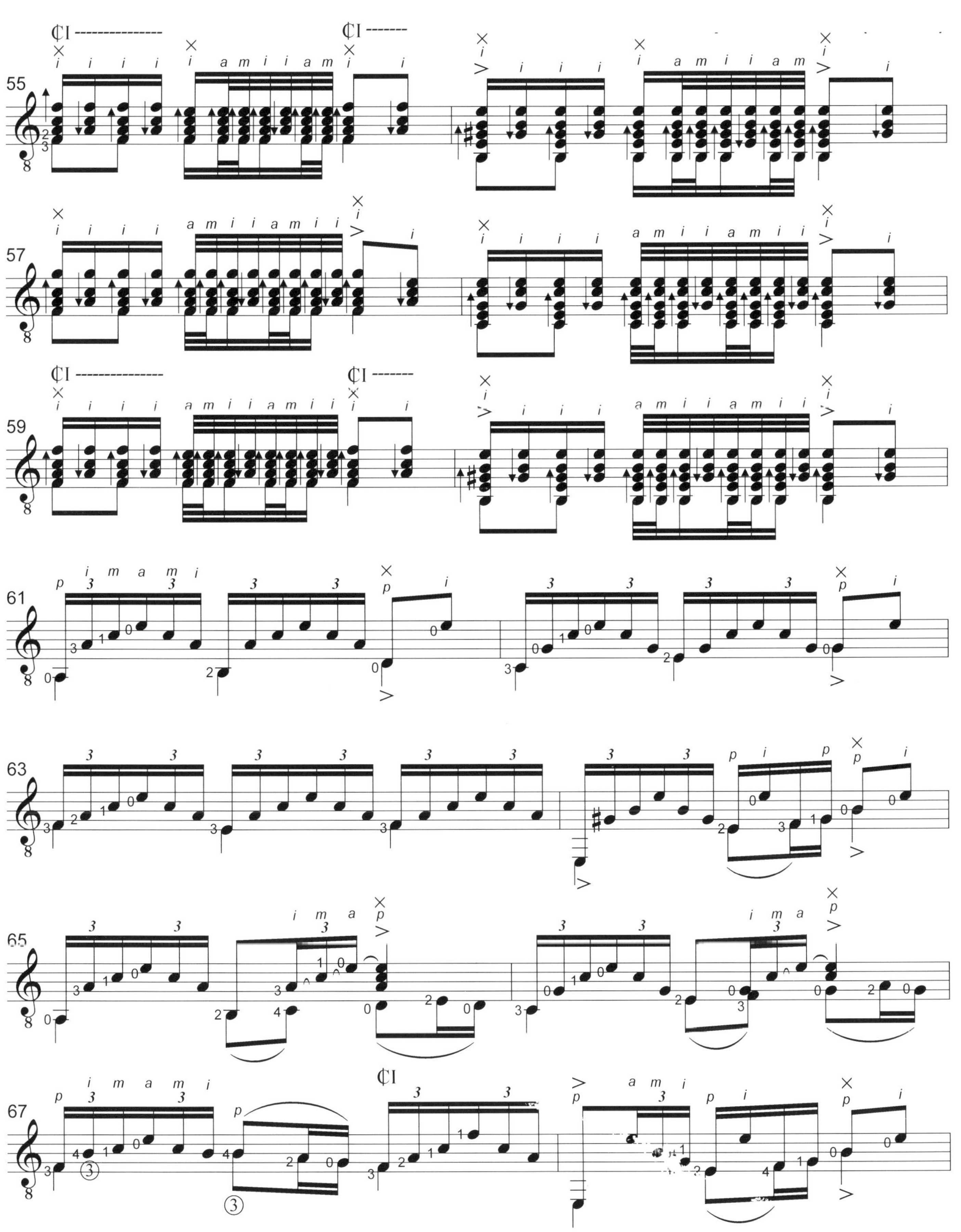

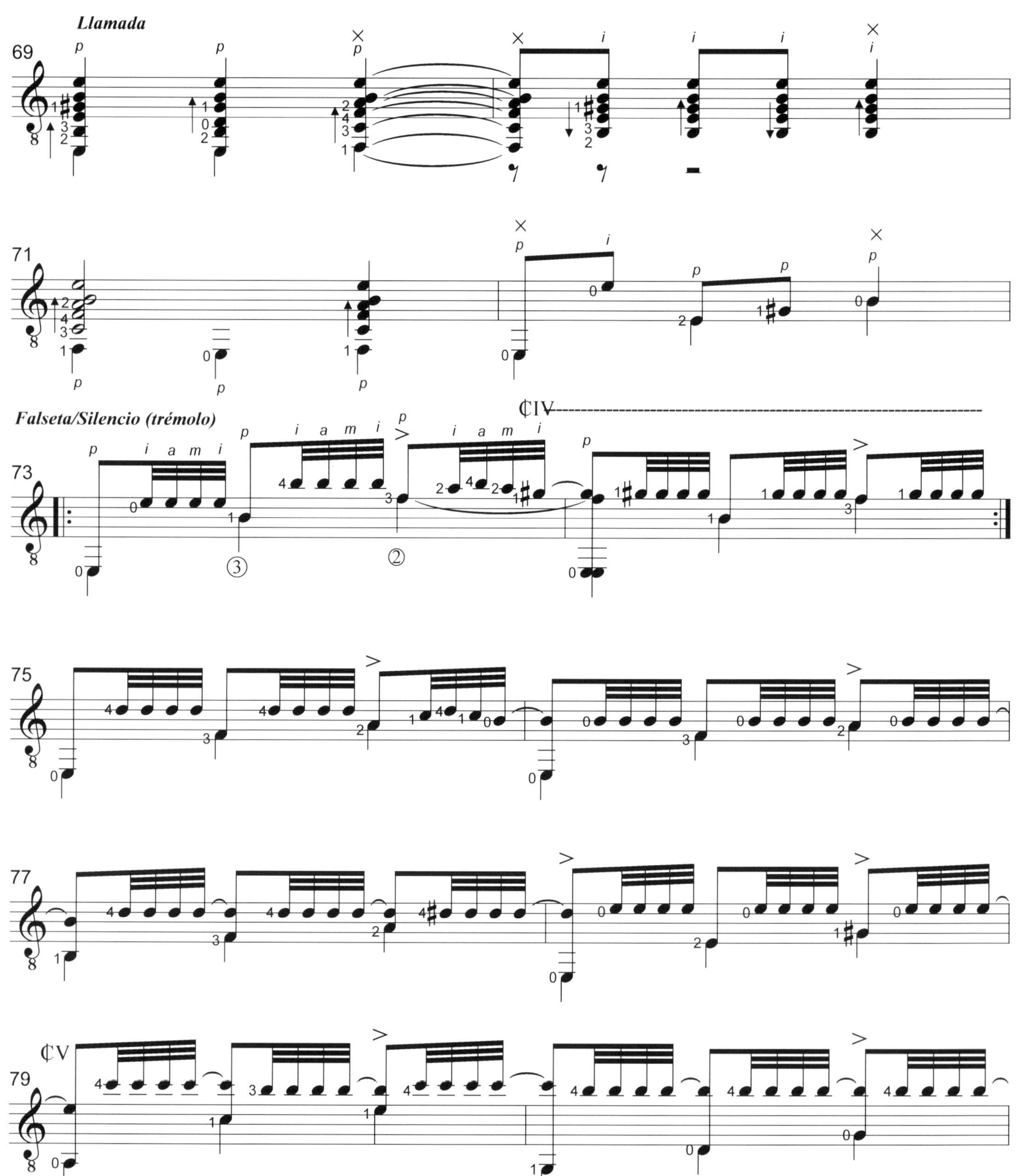

Llamada
Falseta/Silencio (trémolo)
CIV
CV

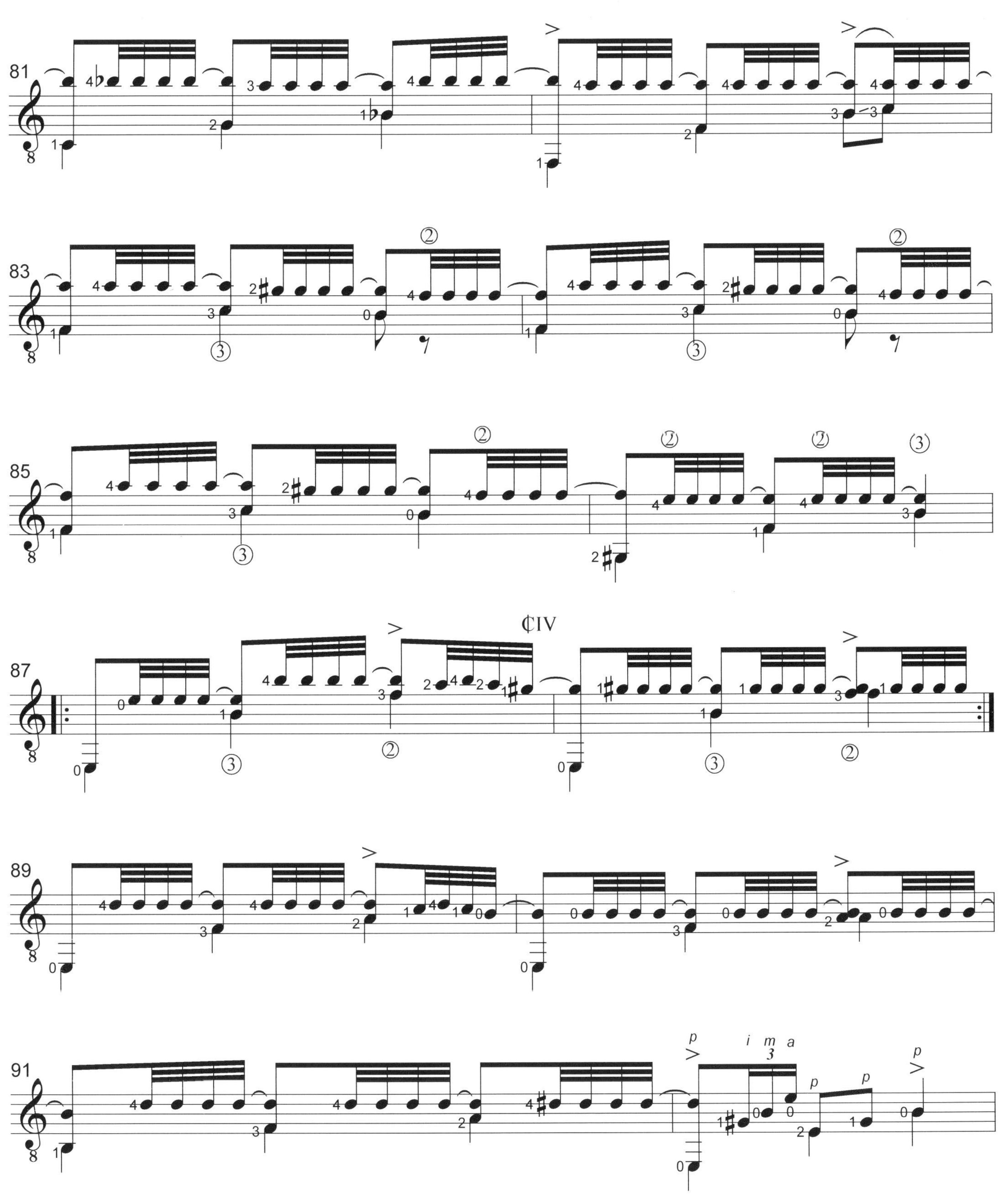
81
83
85
87
ȻIV
89
91
p
i m a
3
p
p
p

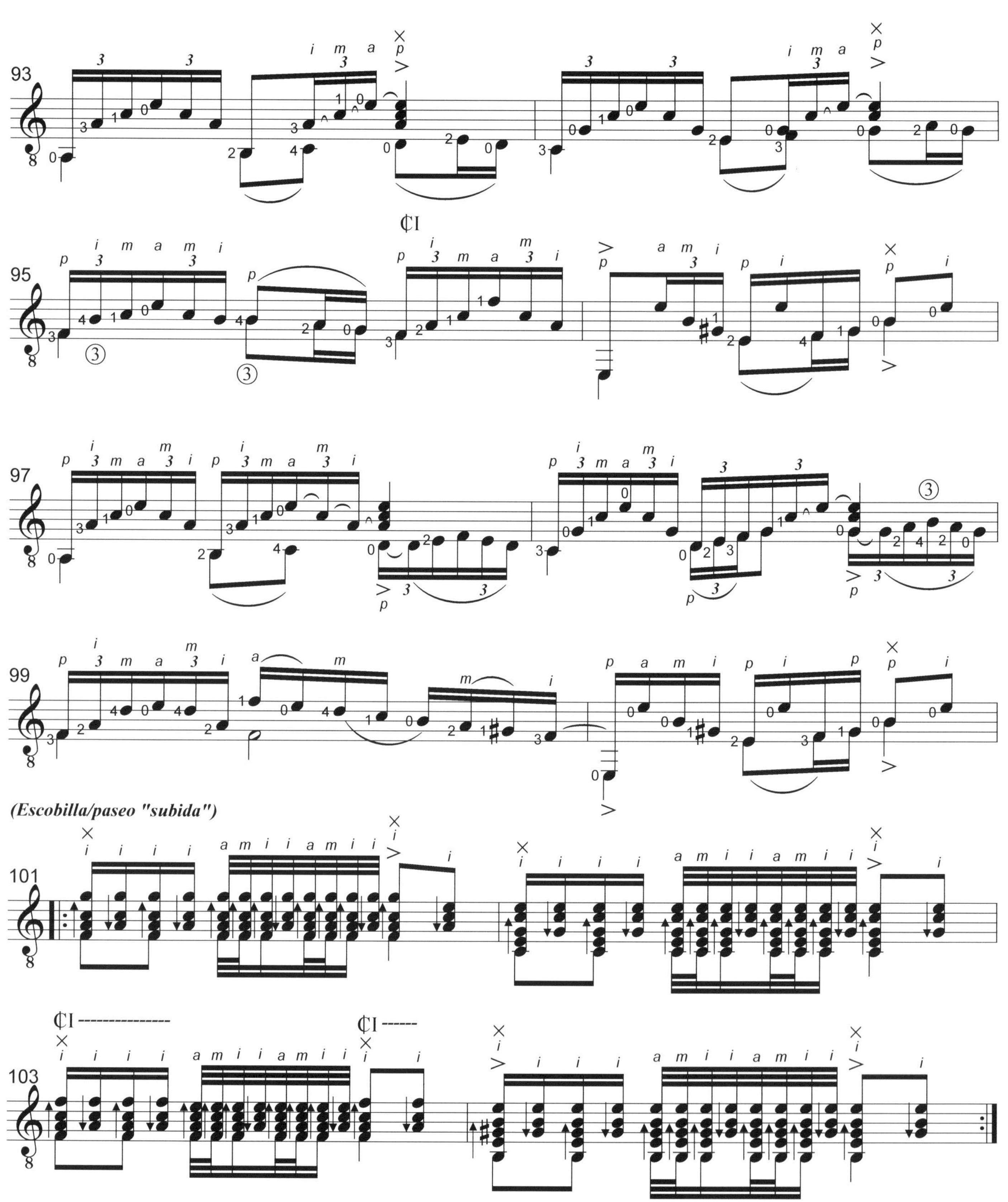
93
95
97
99
(Escobilla/paseo "subida")
101
103

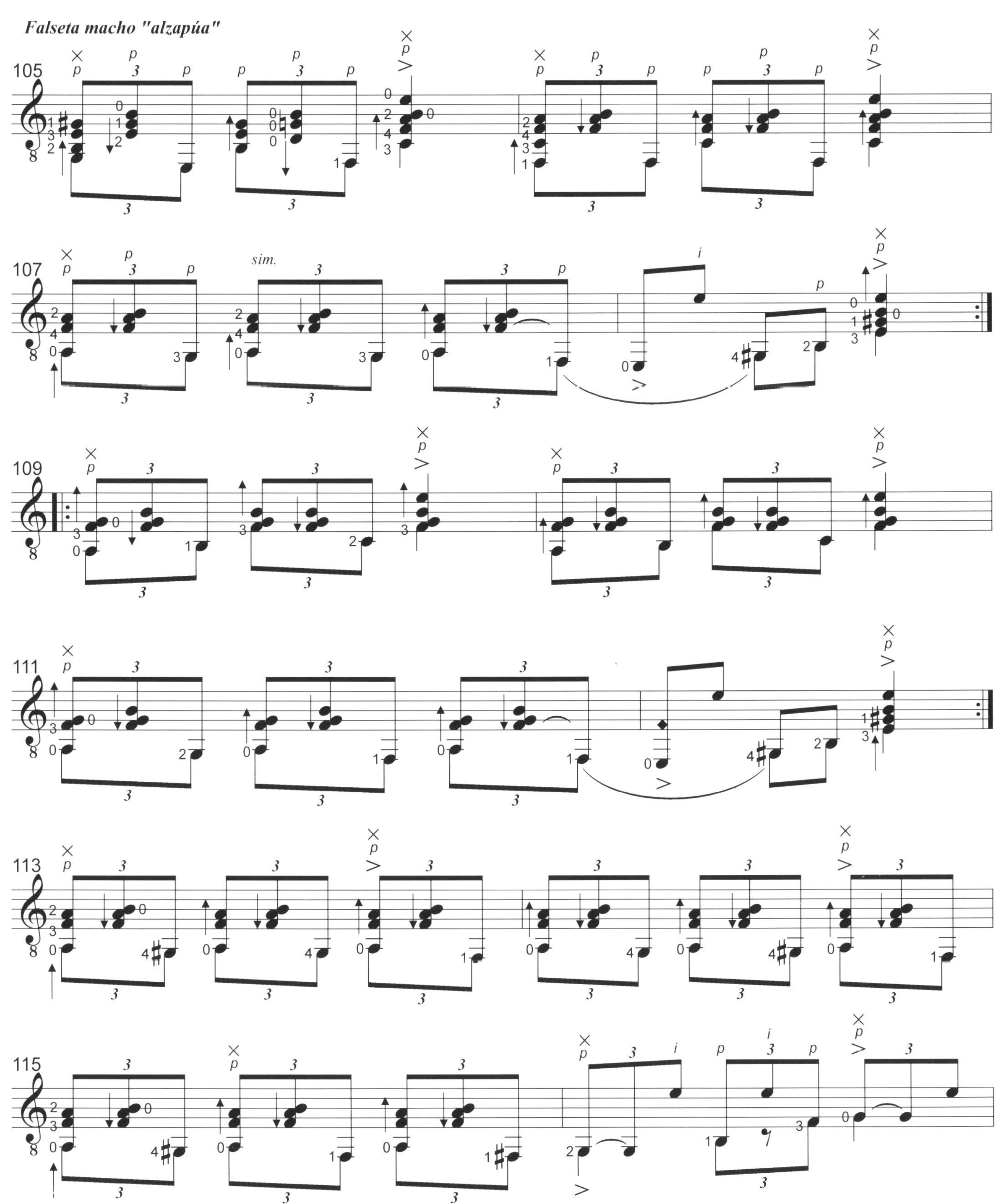

Falseta macho "alzapúa"
sim.

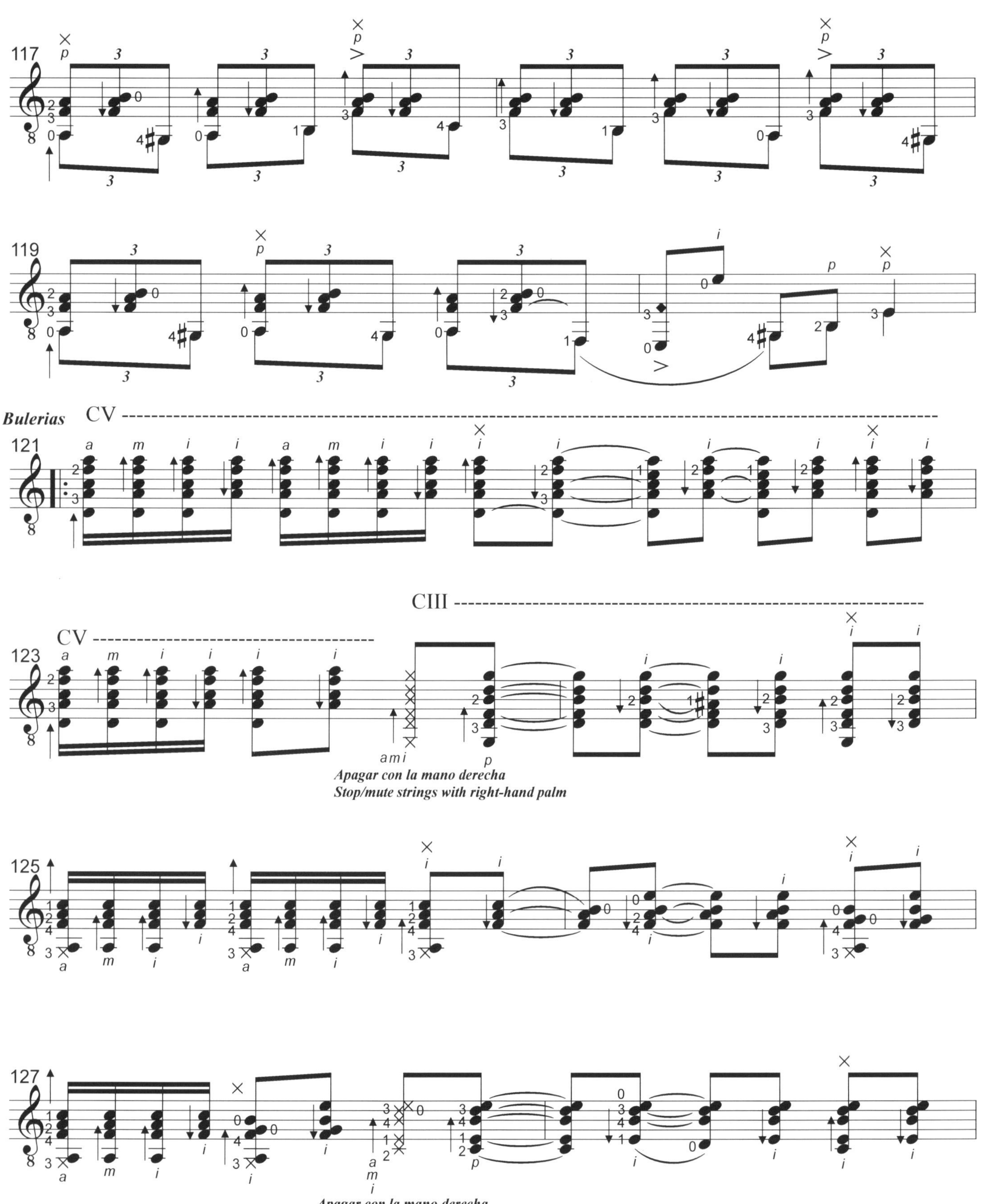
Bulerias
CV
CIII
Apagar con la mano derecha
Stop/mute strings with right-hand palm
Apagar con la mano derecha
Stop/mute strings with right-hand palm

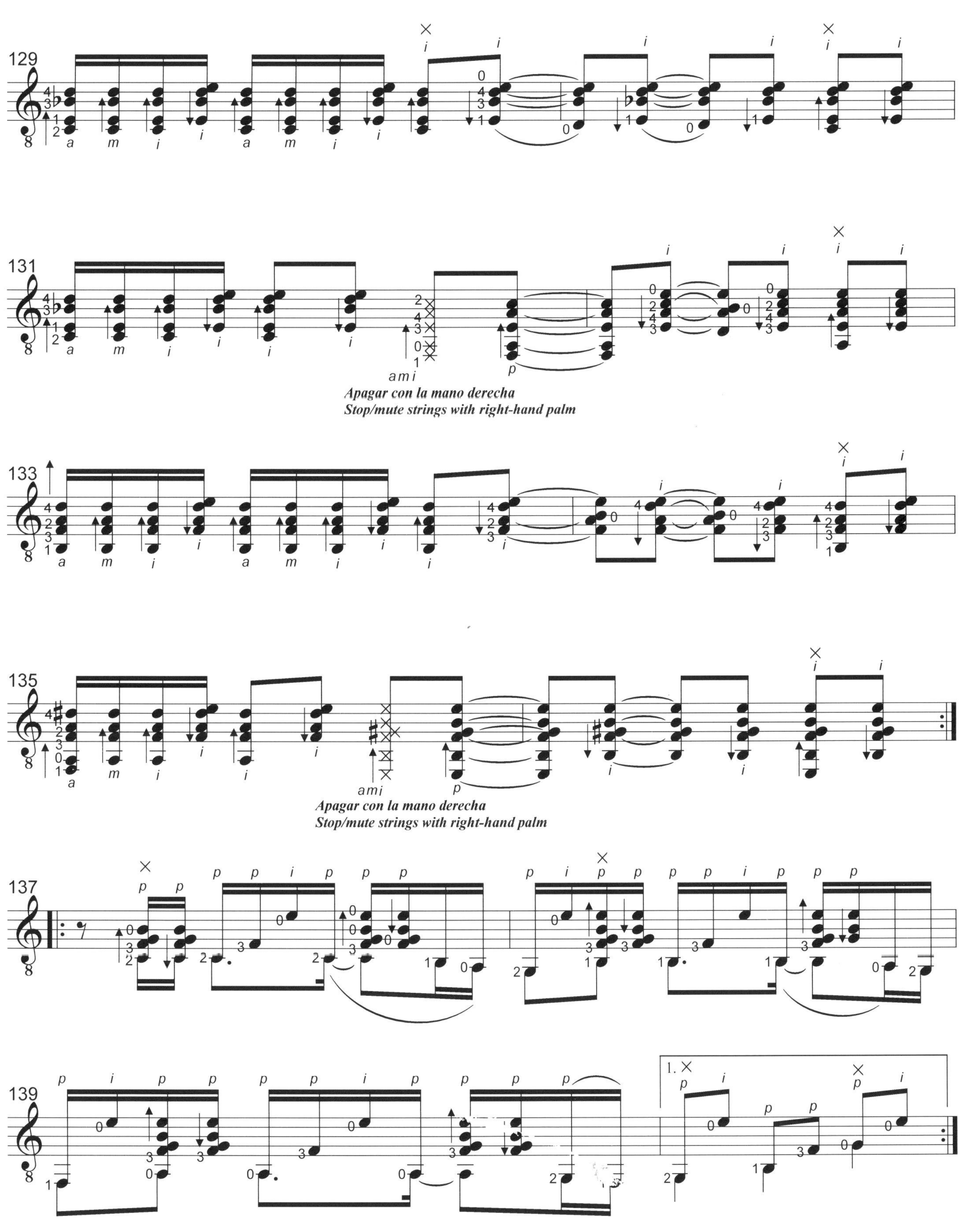
Apagar con la mano derecha
Stop/mute strings with right-hand palm
Apagar con la mano derecha
Stop/mute strings with right-hand palm

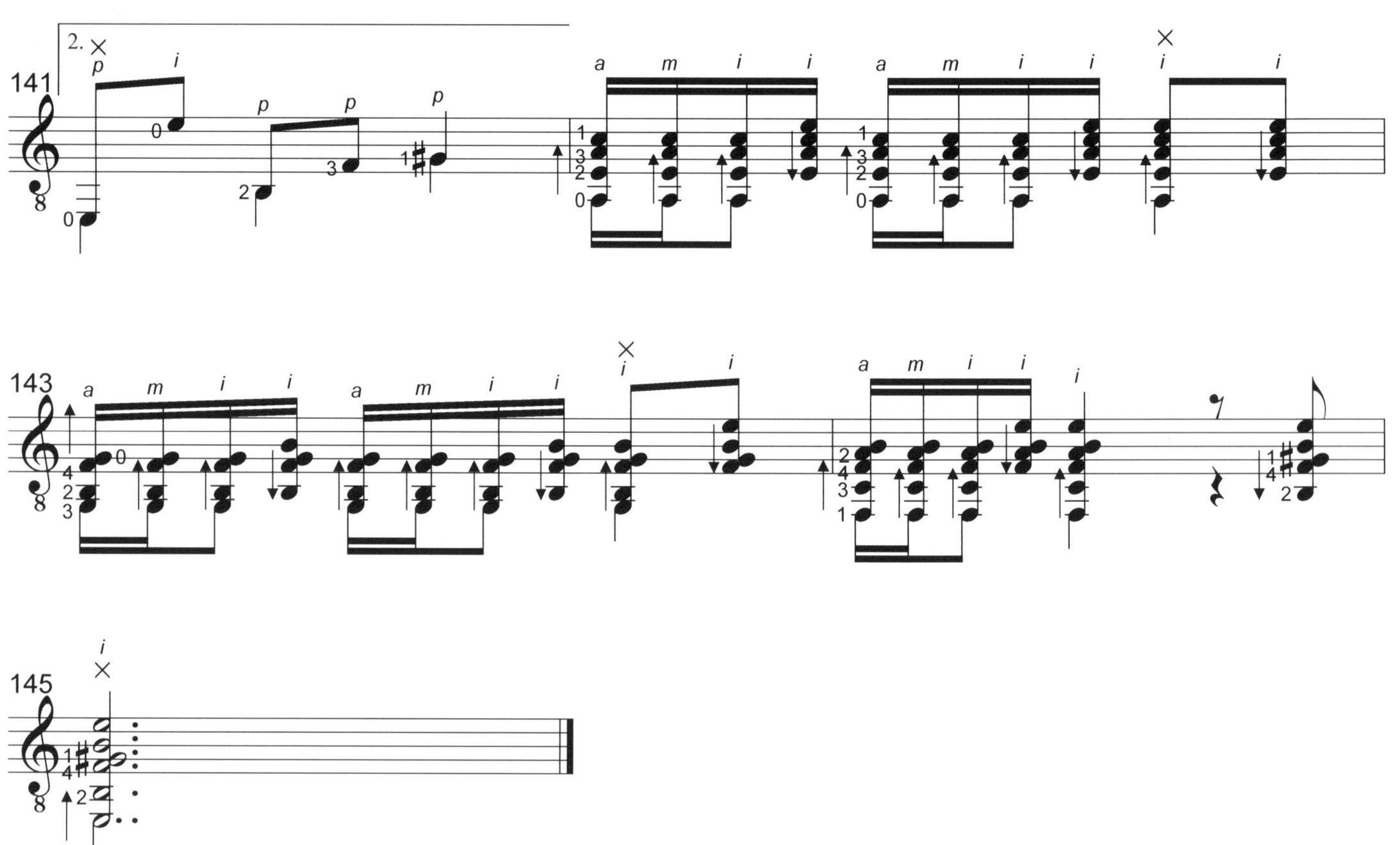
141
2.
143
145

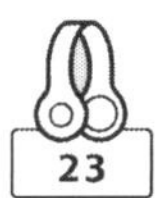

Soleá de Utrera

Richard Marlow and Corey Whitehead
(Edited by Corey Whitehead)

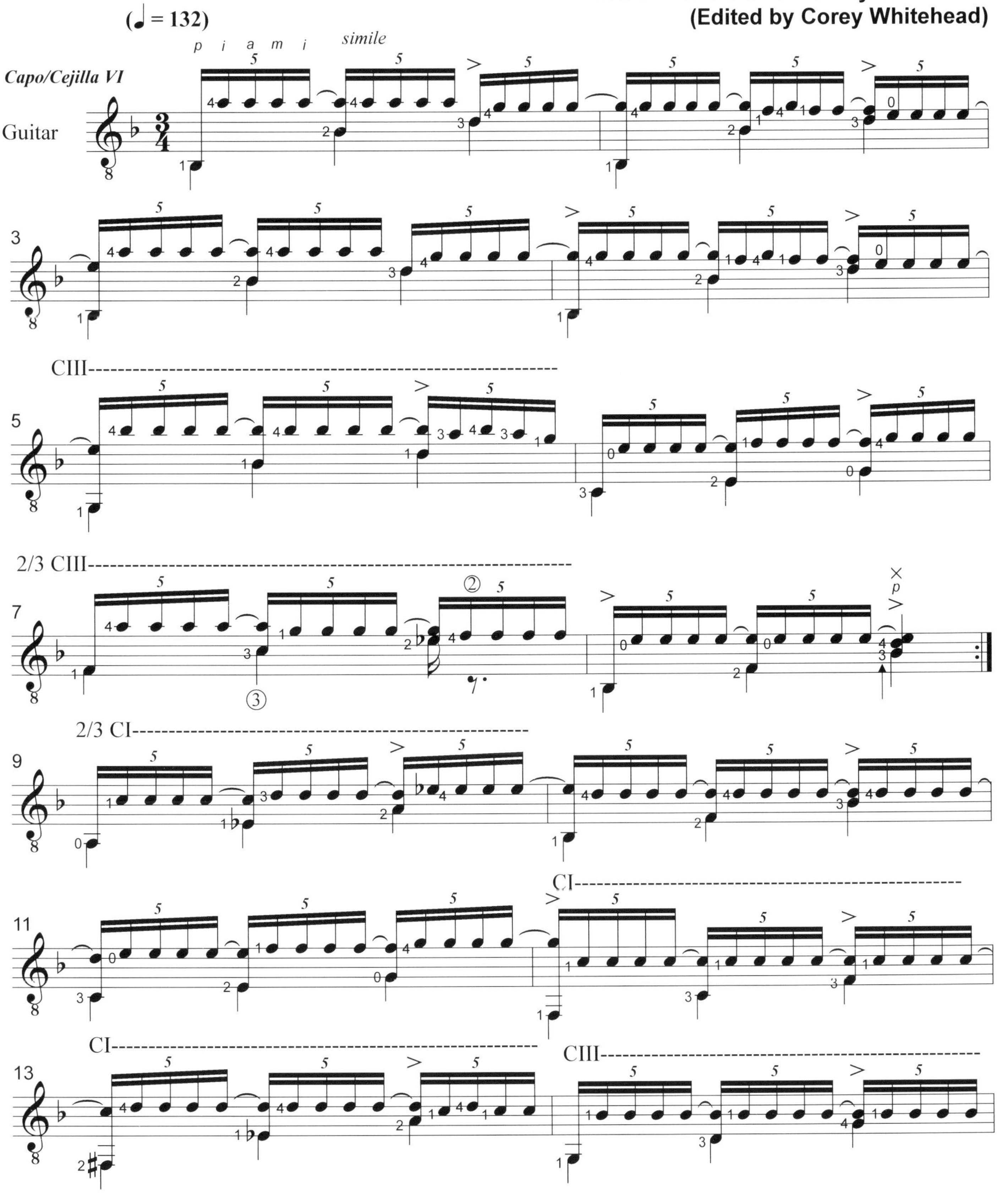

(♩ = 132)

p i a m i simile

Capo/Cejilla VI

Guitar

CIII

2/3 CIII

2/3 CI

CI

CI

CIII

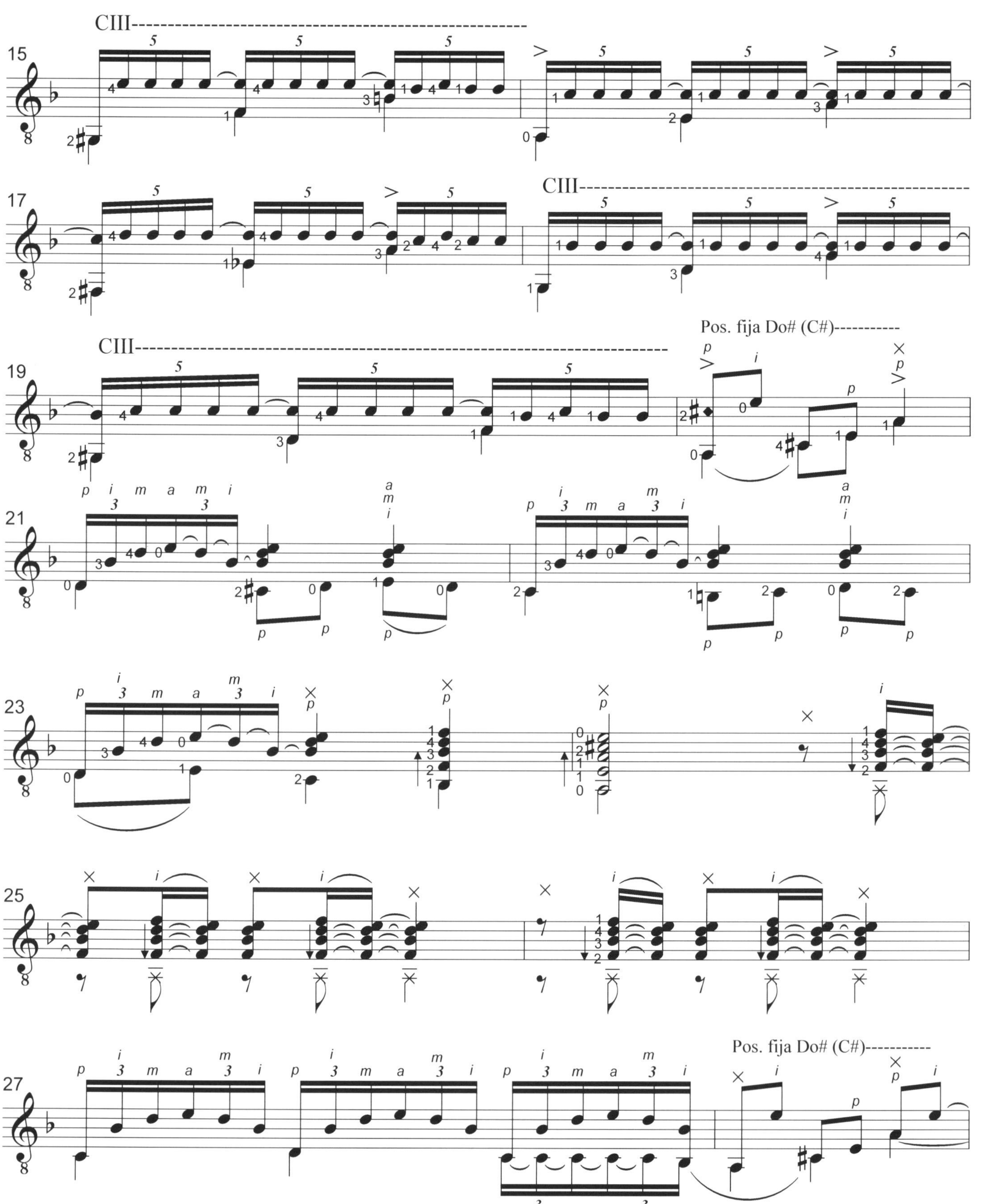
CIII
CIII
CIII
Pos. fija Do# (C#)
Pos. fija Do# (C#)

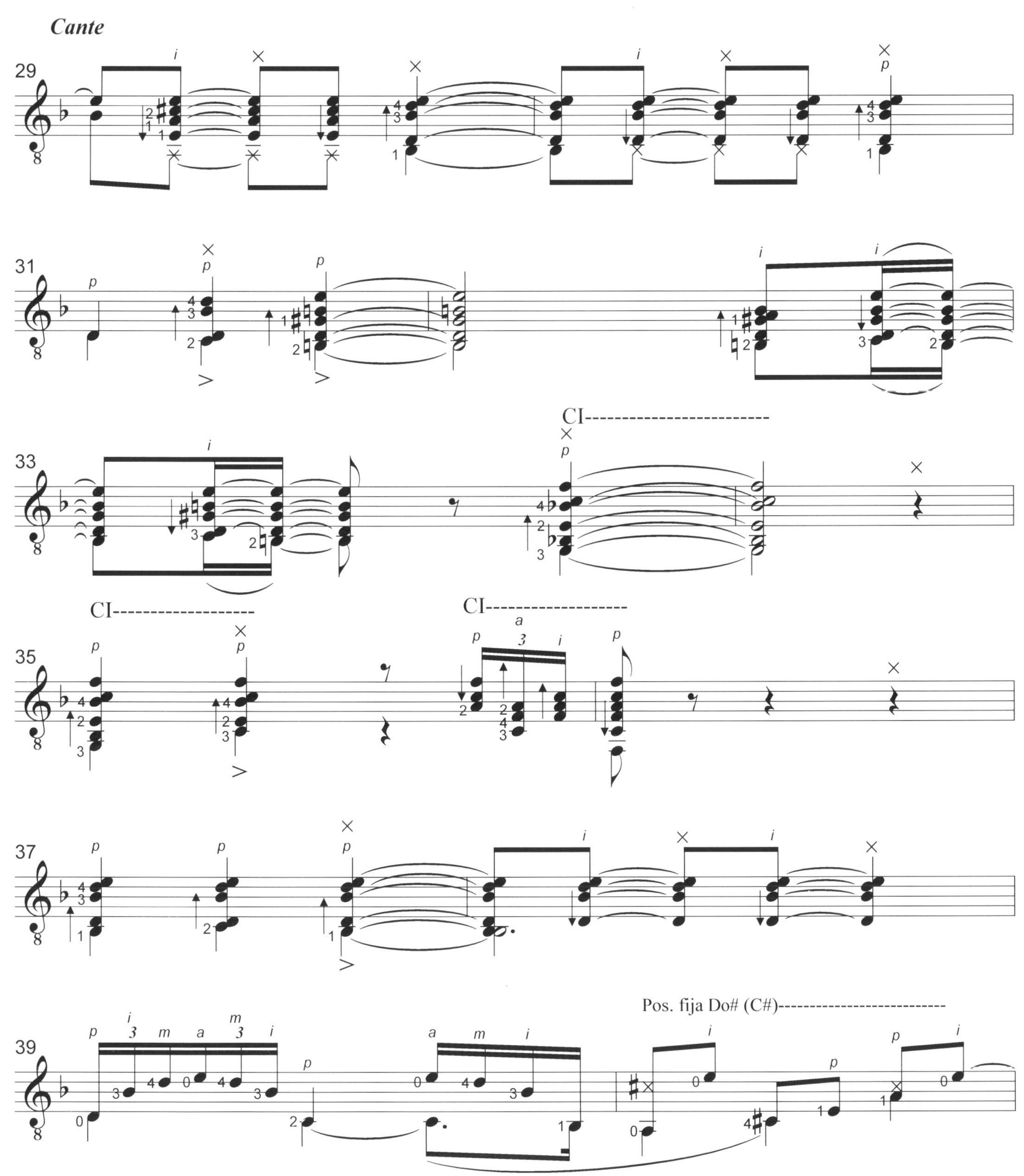
Cante
CI---------------------------
CI--------------------
CI--------------------
Pos. fija Do# (C#)----------------------------

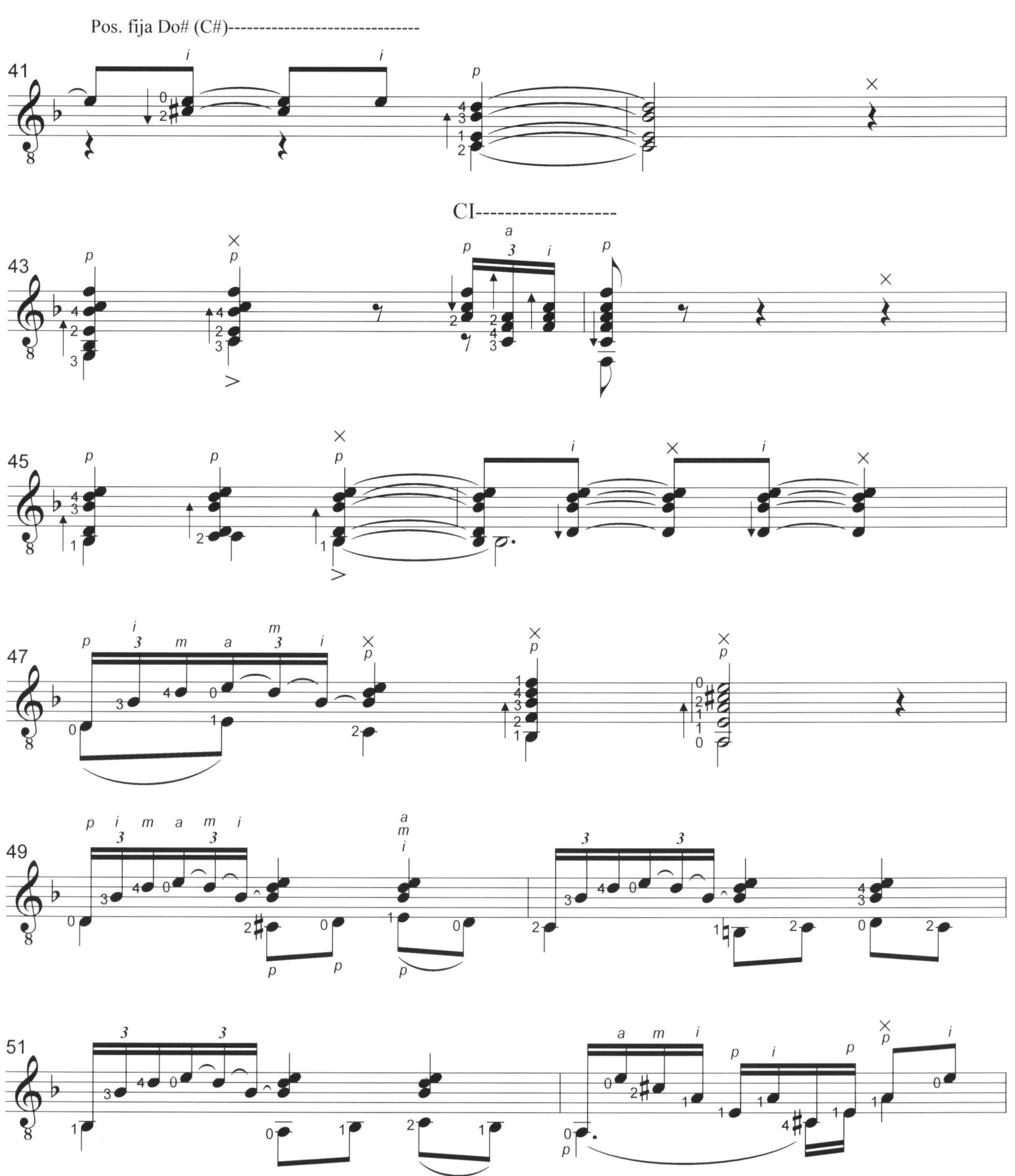
Pos. fija Do# (C#)--------------------------------
CI-------------------

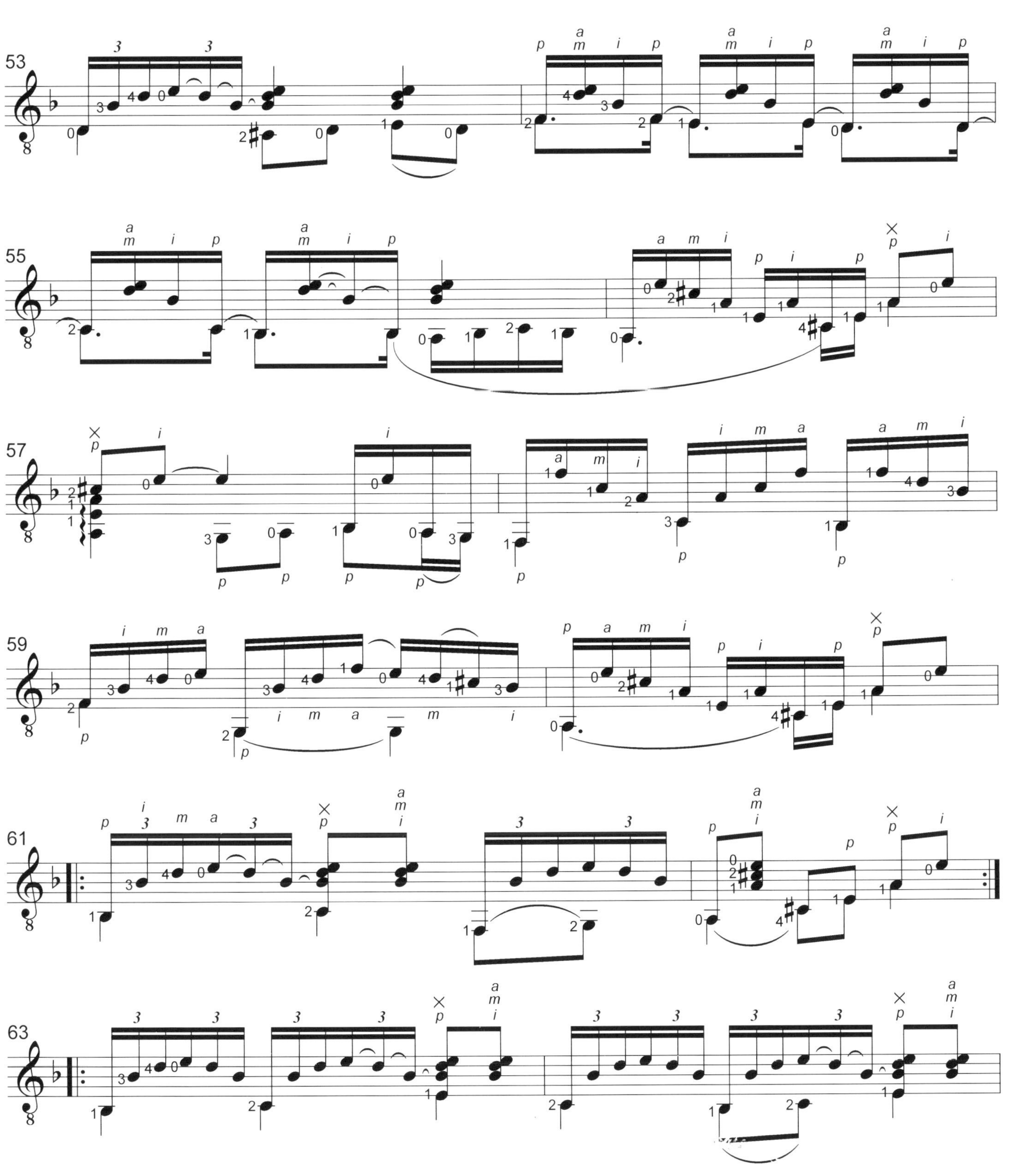
53
55
57
59
61
63

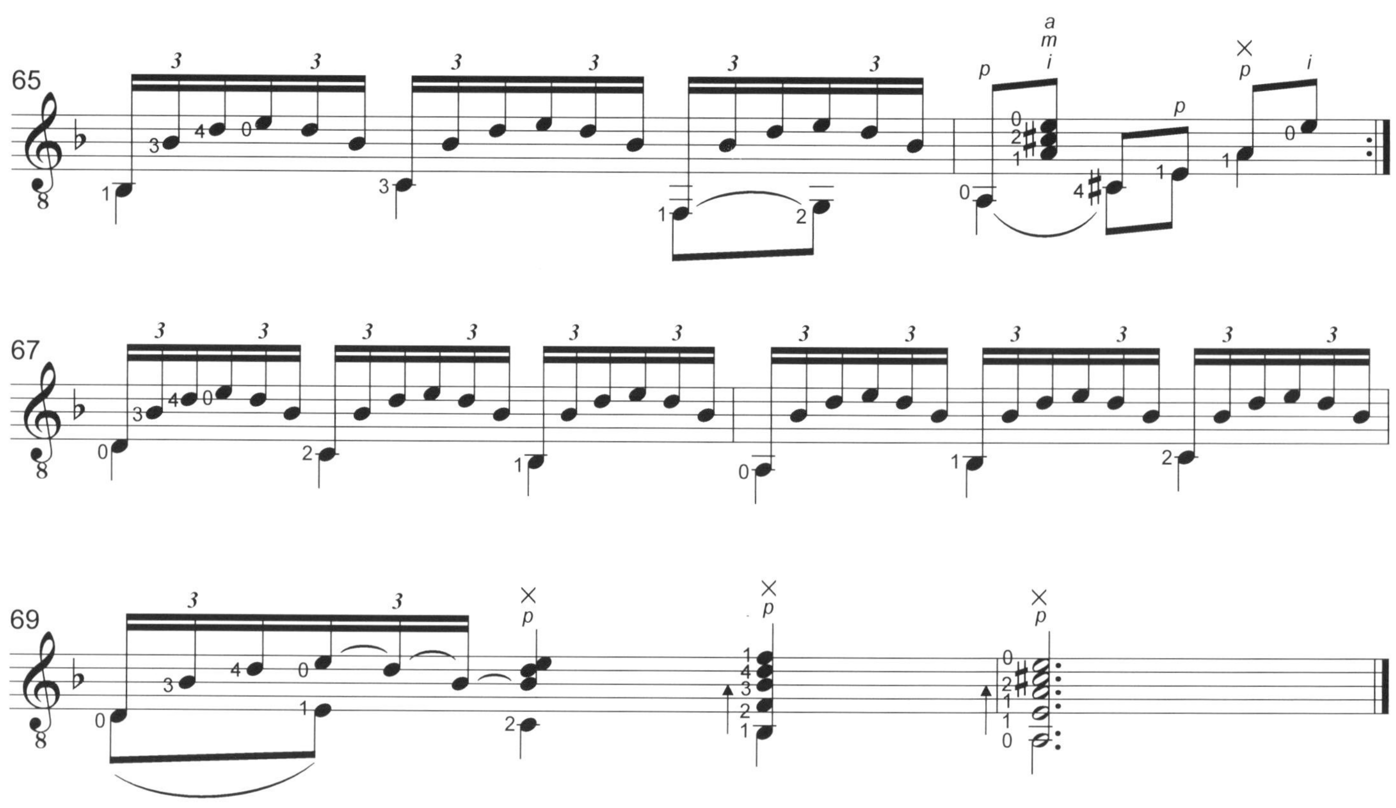

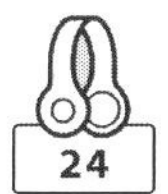

Bulerías por soleá

Richard Marlow and Corey Whitehead
(Edited by Corey Whitehead)

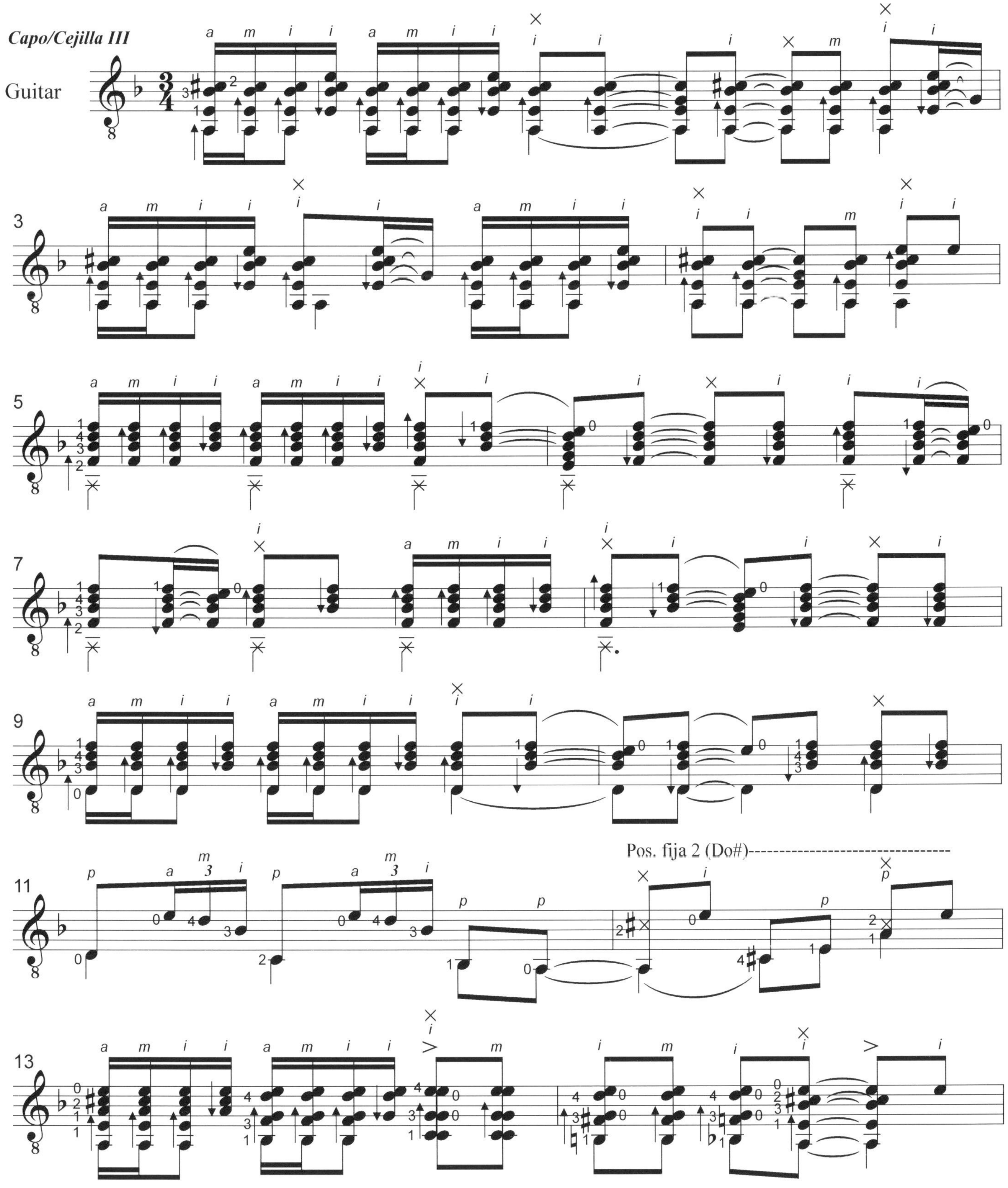

Capo/Cejilla III

Guitar

Pos. fija 2 (Do#)

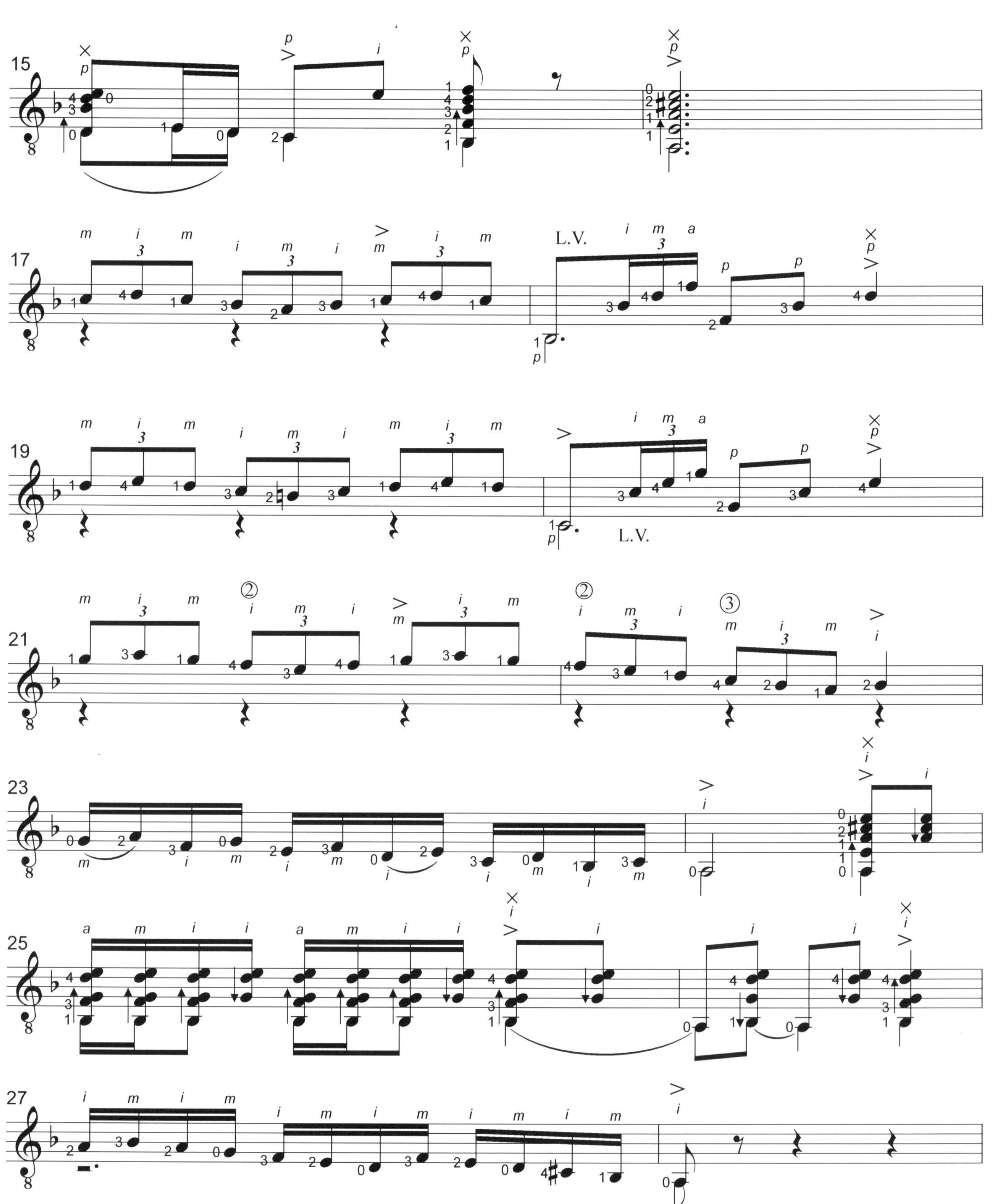
15
17
L.V.
19
L.V.
21
23
25
27

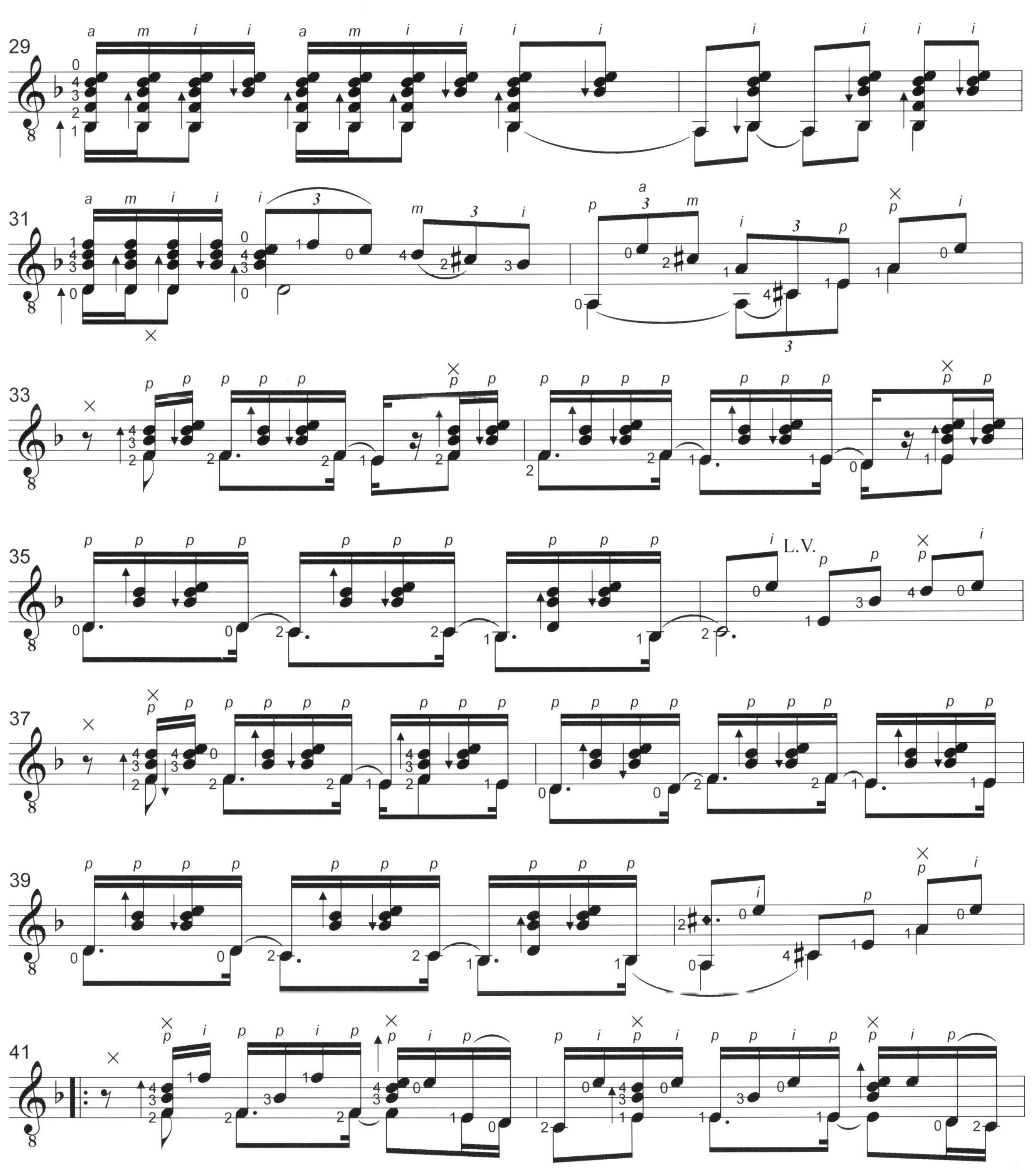

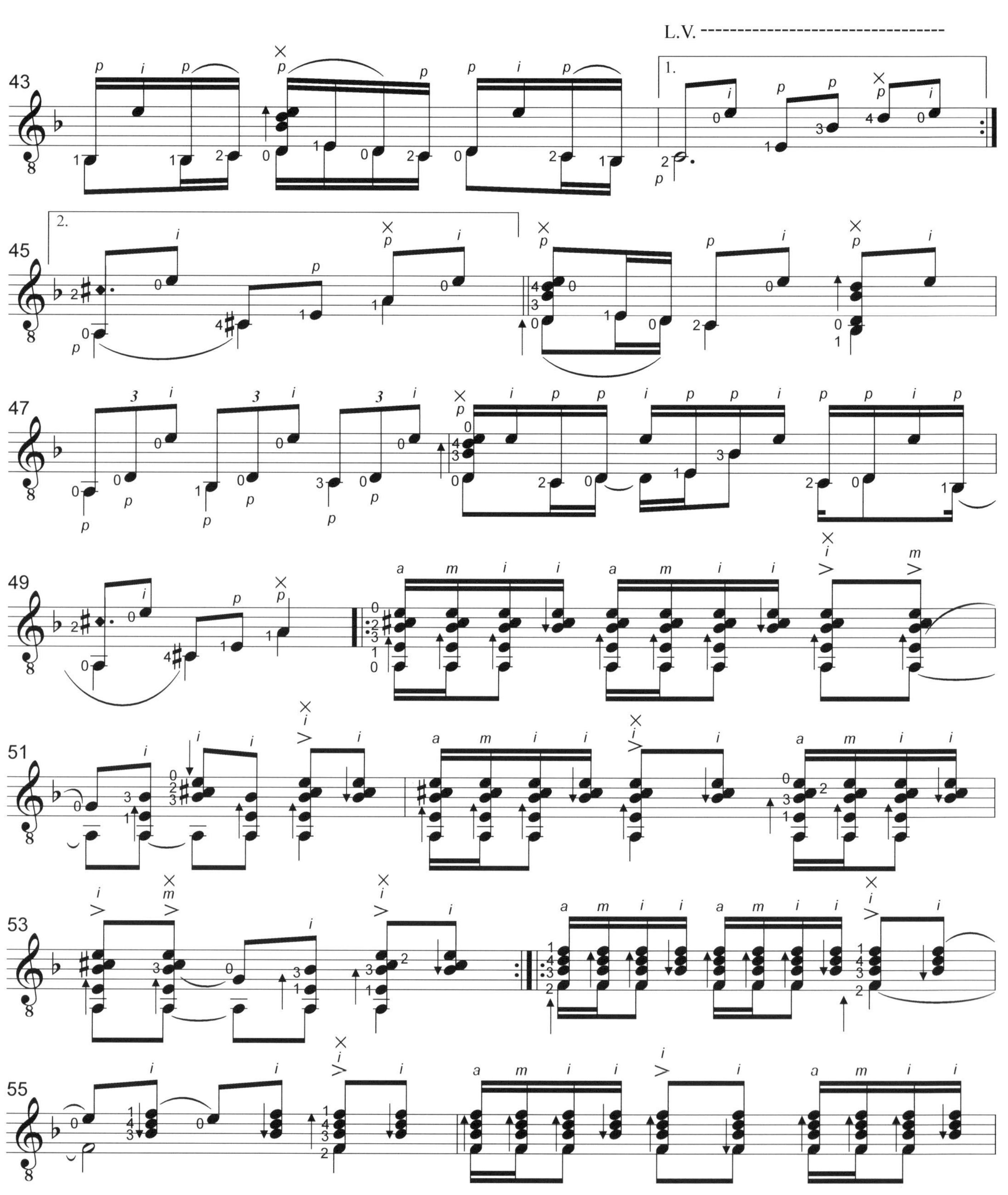
L.V.

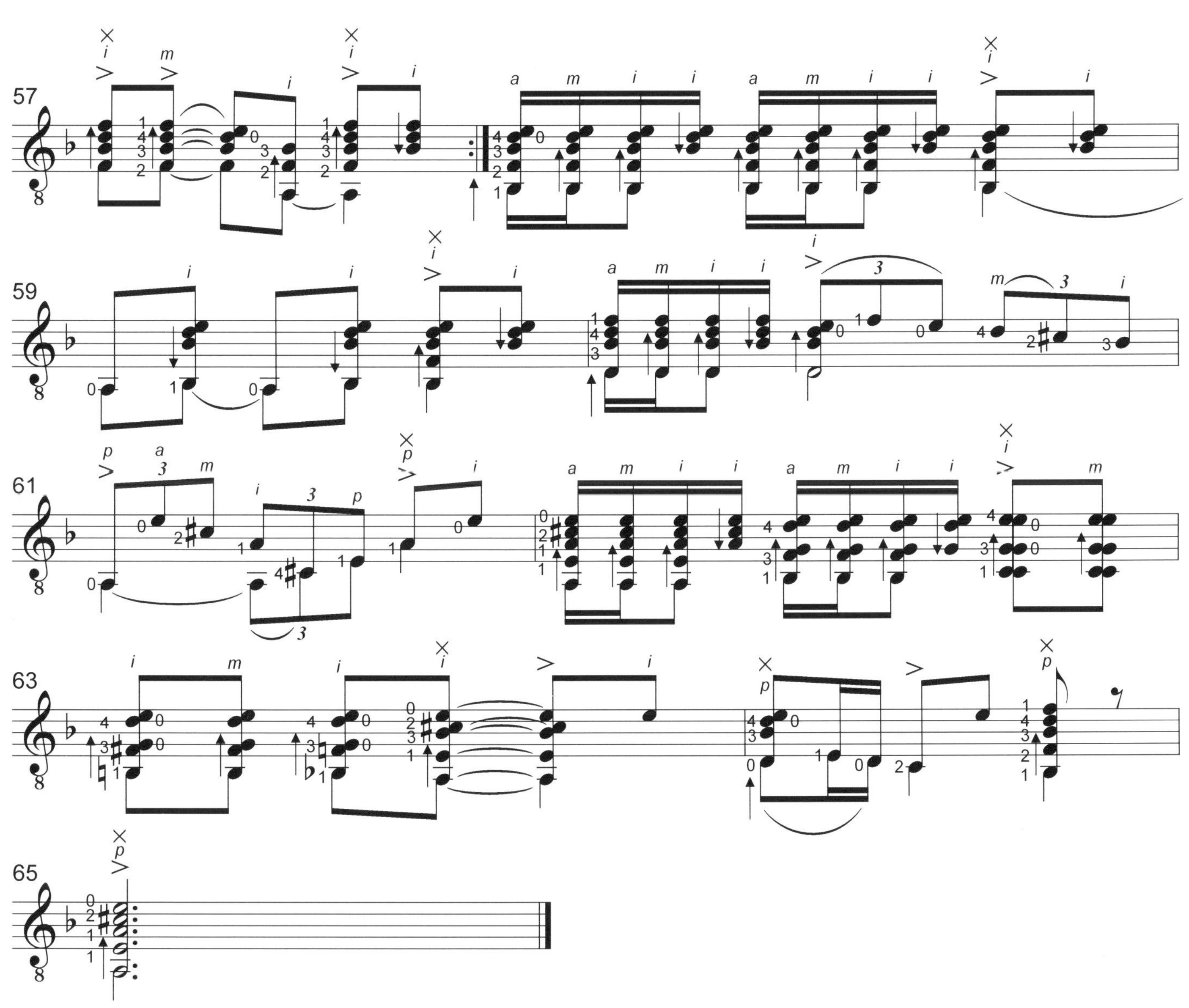
57
59
61
63
65

Unit II, Part II

Tientos and Tangos

Unit II, Part II
Tientos and Tangos

"Tientos" by Richard Marlow and Corey Whitehead

1) The first eight (8) measures of solo guitar introduction are followed by *cante* accompaniment from measures 9 to 45.
2) Measures 46-61 offer a series of guitar solo *falsetas.*
3) If one accompanies more than one verse, play a *falseta* following each verse. Before the entrance of the singer on the 2nd and 3rd verses, play a *llamada*. A *llamada* in this form would be any chord accompaniment in *compás* (in the rhythm and meter of the palo) with the chords: Dm (iv), C (♭III), B♭ (♭II), A (I).
4) The roman numerals indicate scale degree by their numerical value and chord quality in the use of capitalization. Capitalized numerals indicate chords of a major quality. Lower case numerals indicate chords of a minor quality. Lower-case numerals followed by a small circle indicate a diminished chord. The use of the flat symbol preceding a roman numeral indicates that the root note of the chord is one semitone (half-tone or half-step) lower than normal when using the roman numerals to represent the intervallic structure of the major scale.
5) For example, the chords of the C major scale (or any major scale) represented by roman numerals would be written as follows: C Major (I), D minor (ii), E minor (iii), F Major (IV), G Major (V), A minor (vi) and B-diminished (vii°).
6) The chords of the C natural minor scale would be represented with roman numerals that reflect their altered root note positions as follows: C minor (i), D diminished (ii°), E-flat Major (♭III), F minor (iv), G minor (v), A-flat major (♭VI), and B-flat major (♭VII).
7) Throughout this work, the written eighth notes are not played evenly, but rather with "swing 8ths" as in jazz or in Baroque music *(notes inégales)*. This unequal division of the two notes gives 2/3 of the beat to the first 8th note and 1/3 of a beat to the second 8th note.
8) To accurately play a quarter-note triplet: Divide two beats into triplet 8th notes (three-part or ternary beat division): Count and play as follows; play the quarter-note triplet on the boldface number count: **1** 2 **3** 1 **2** 3.
9) Read the notes on the *Tientos* study from Mel Bay's *Formative Works for the Flamenco/Classical Guitar Tradition* by Corey Whitehead and Richard Marlow, Mel Bay, 2024.

"Tangos Extremeños" by Richard Marlow and Corey Whitehead

1) Extremadura is a Spanish province situated between Huelva, and the southeast border of Portugal. The *Bulería* and *Tango* from this region have a particular flavor and grammar, just as the dialect of Spanish from this region is unique.
2) *Extremeño* refers to anything from the province of Extremadura.
3) This example begins with a five-measure solo guitar introduction. A short introduction is not uncommon in jazz, and the practice is sometimes used when the singer wants to enter right away.

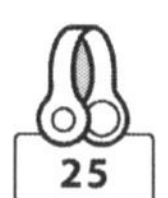

Tientos

Corey Whitehead and Richard Marlow
Edited by Corey Whitehead

Capo/Cejilla V

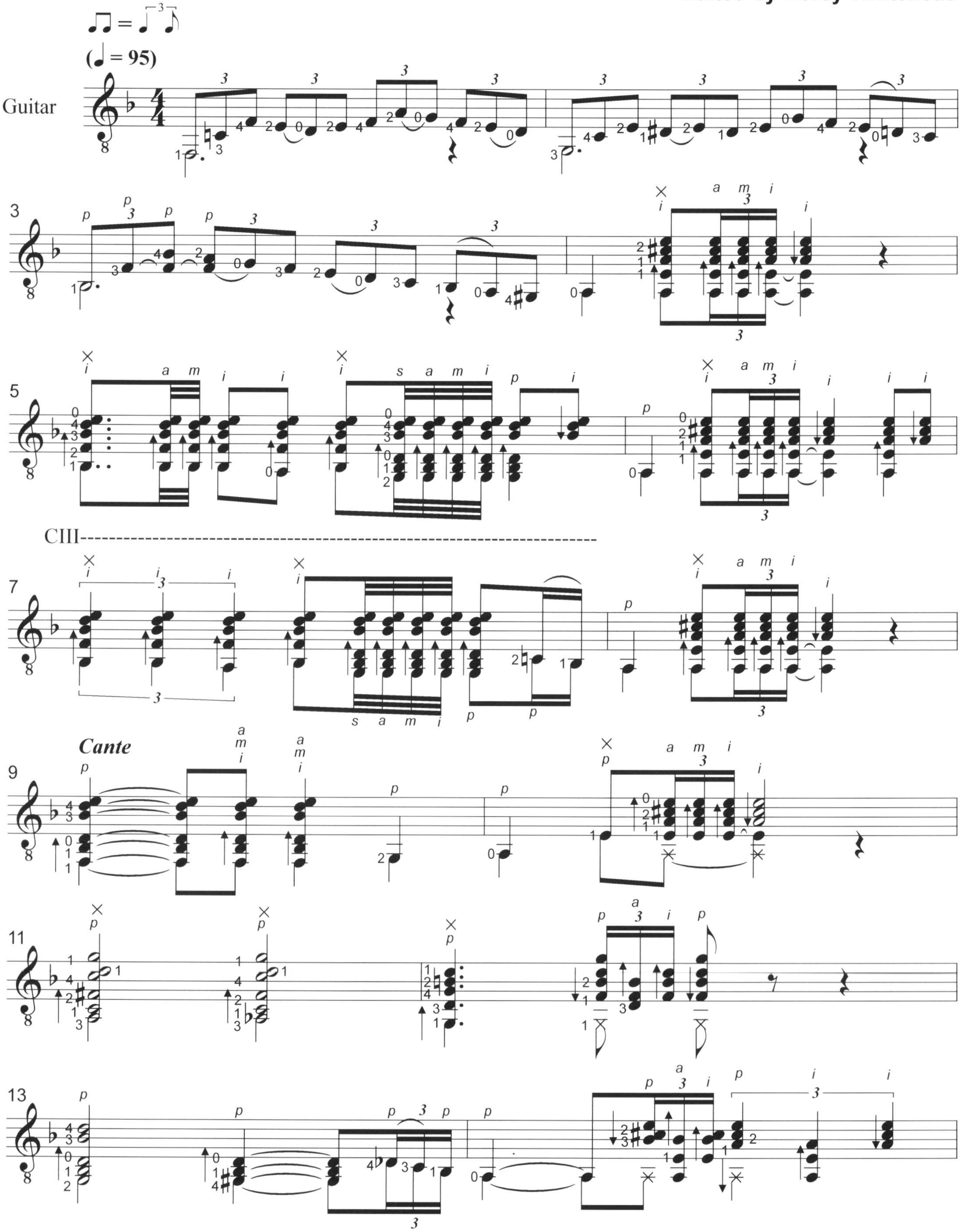

(♩ = 95)

Guitar

CIII

Cante

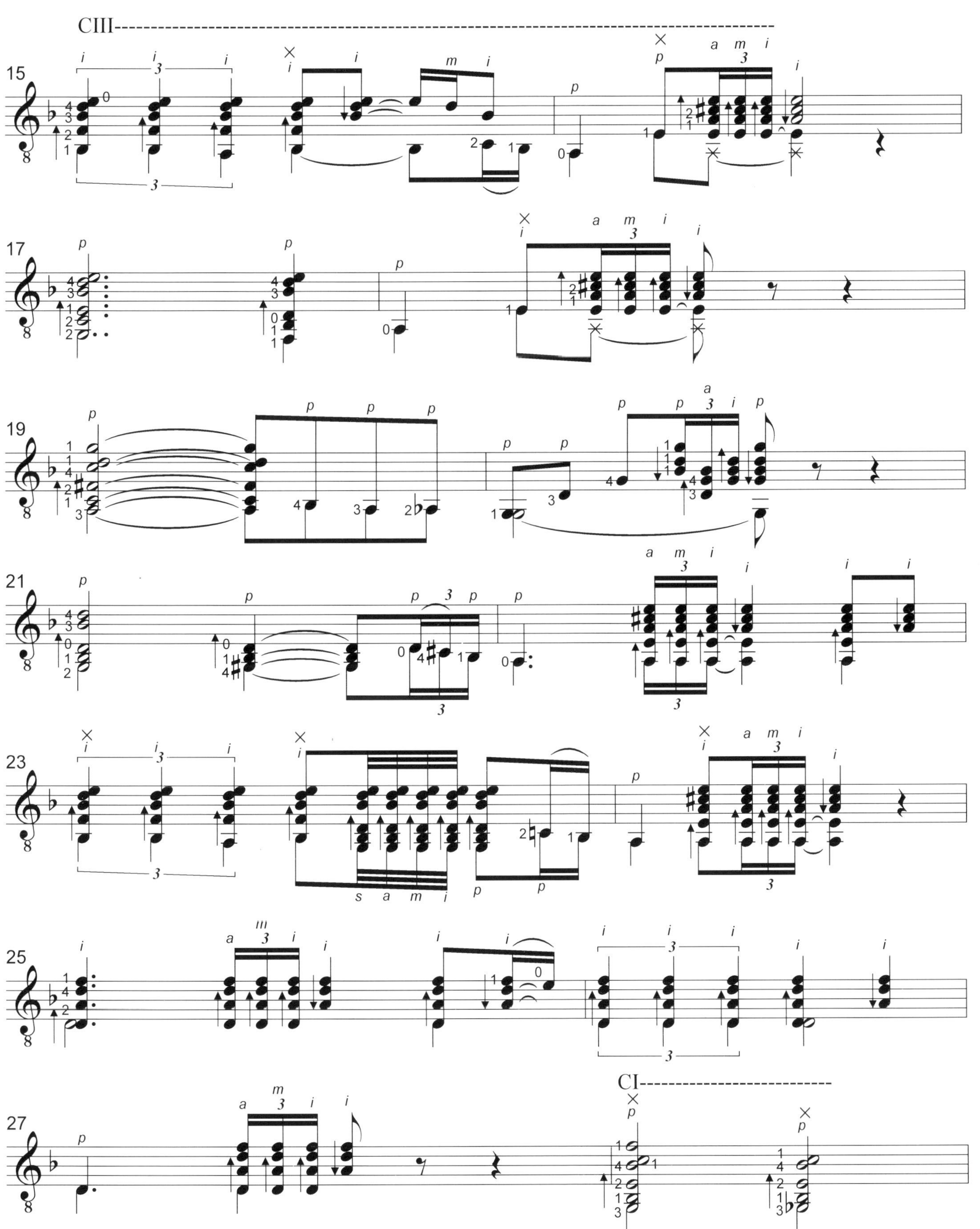
CIII
CI

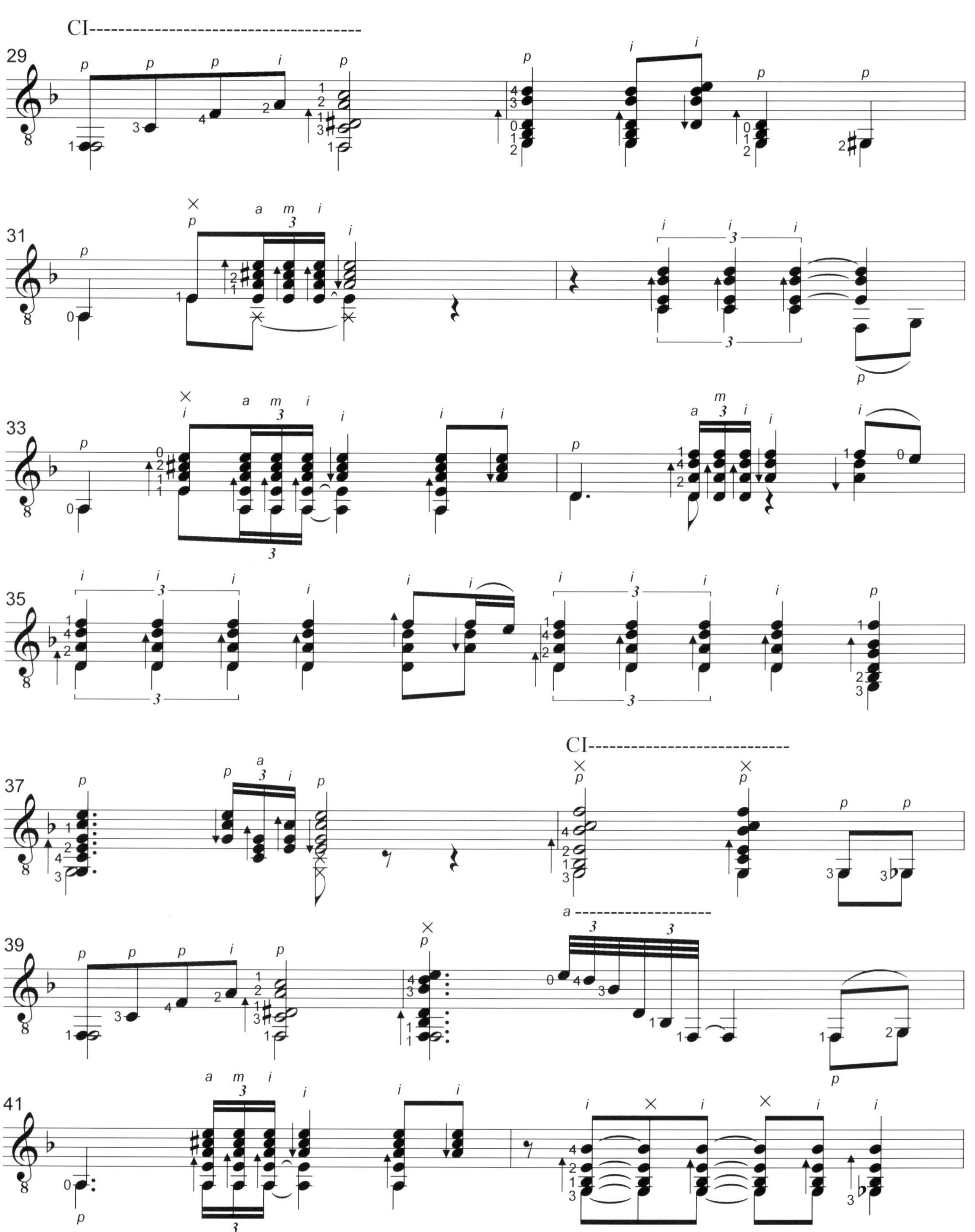
CI
29
31
33
35
37
CI
39
a
41

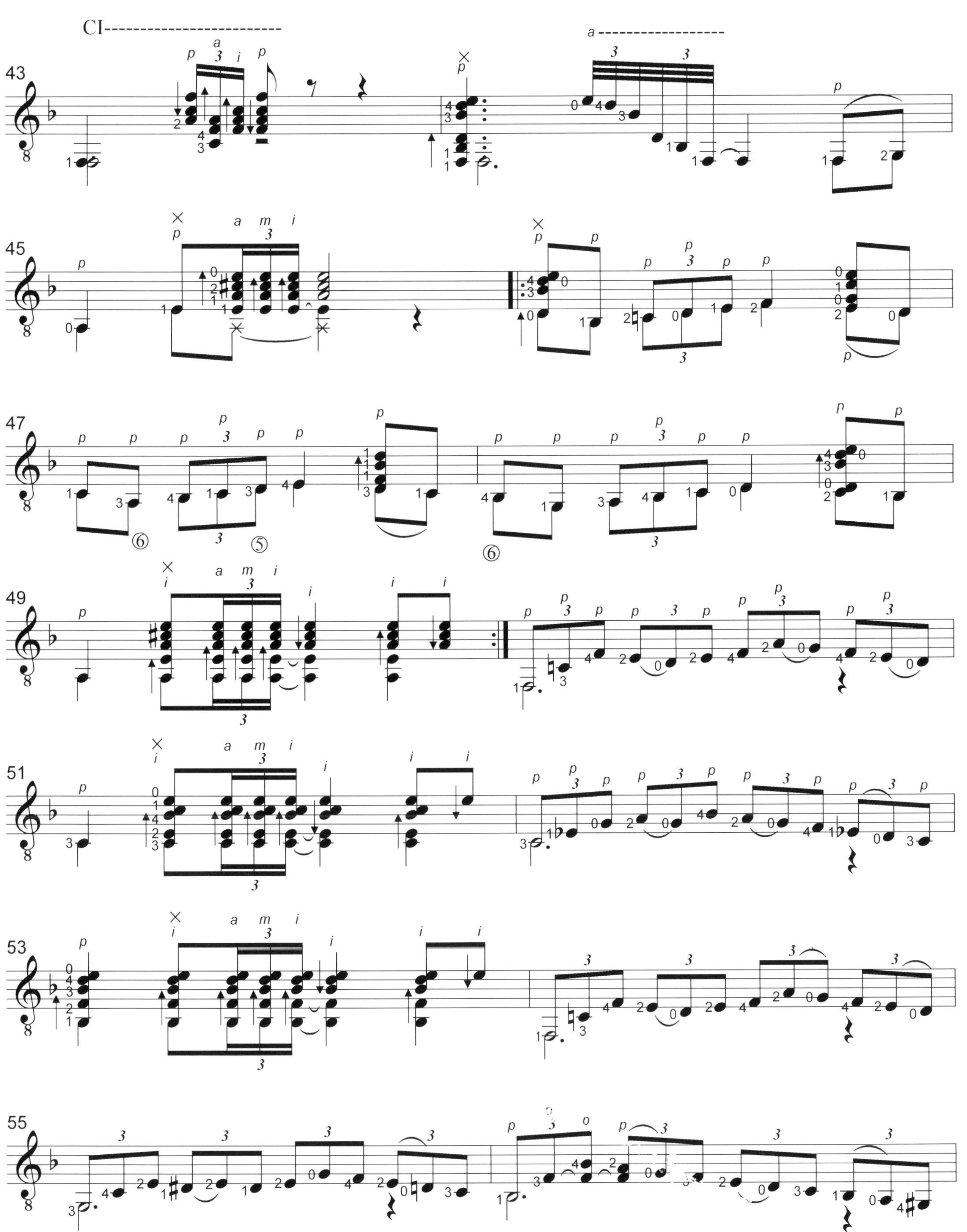

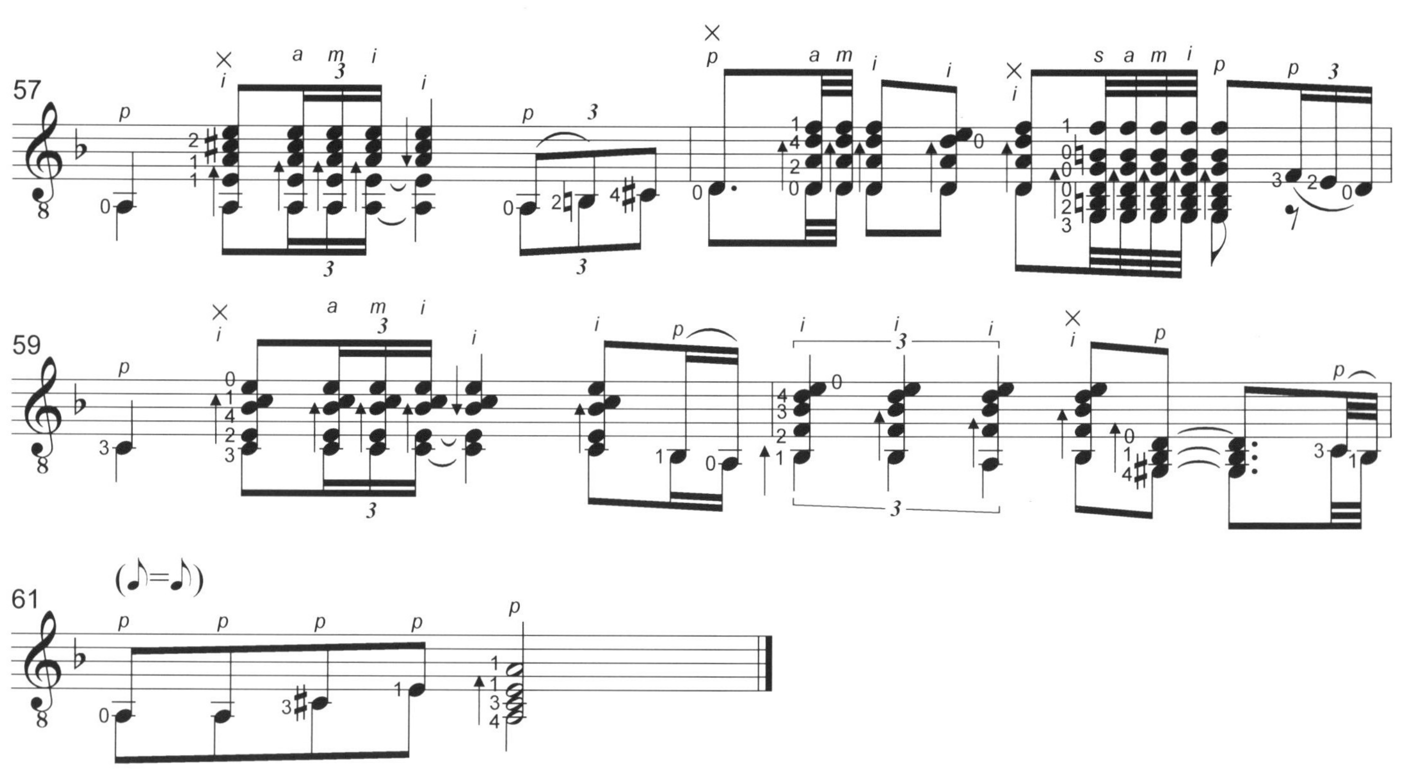

57
59
61

Tangos Extremeños

Richard Marlow and Corey Whitehead
Edited by Corey Whitehead

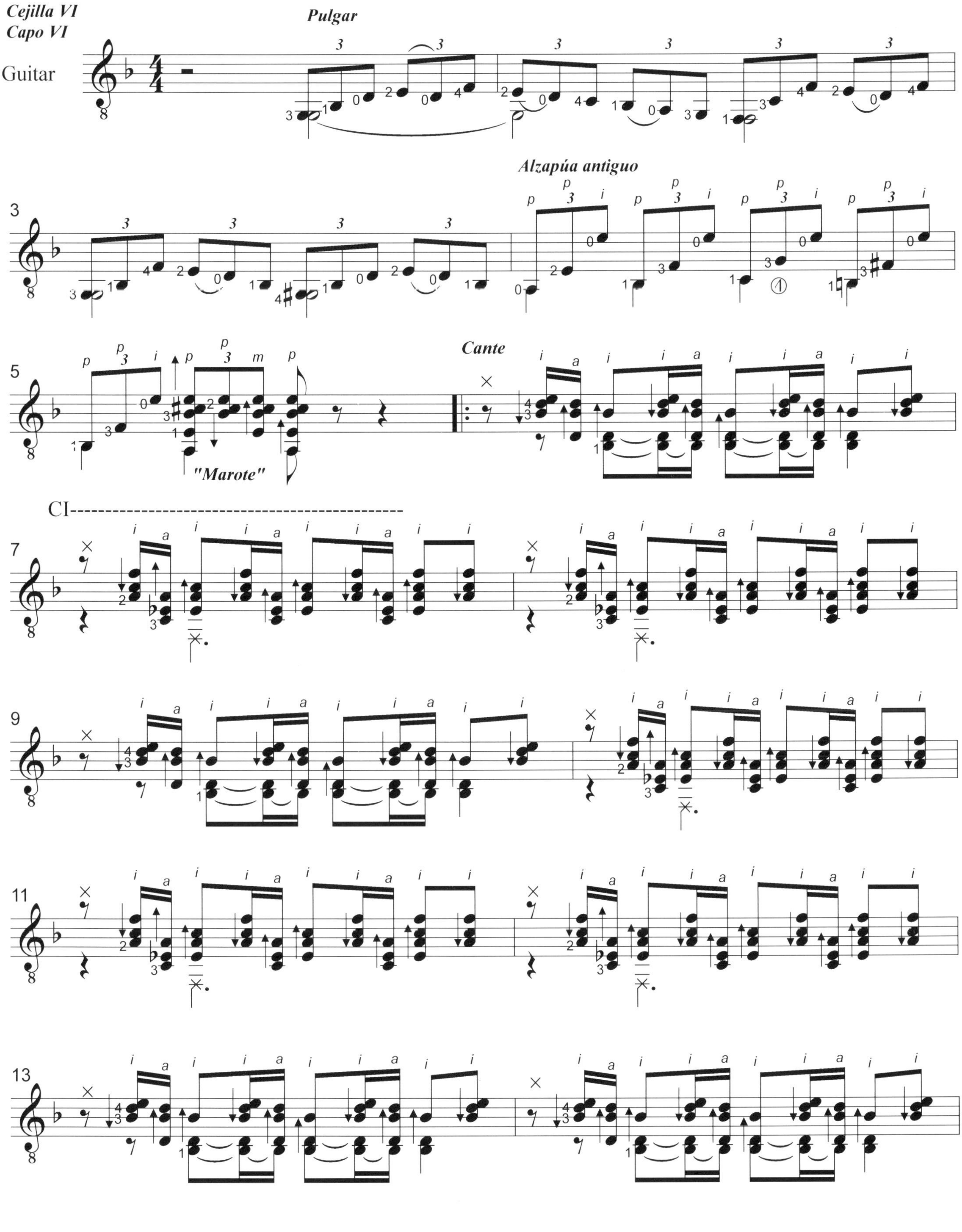

Cejilla VI
Capo VI

Pulgar

Guitar

Alzapúa antiguo

Cante

"Marote"

CI

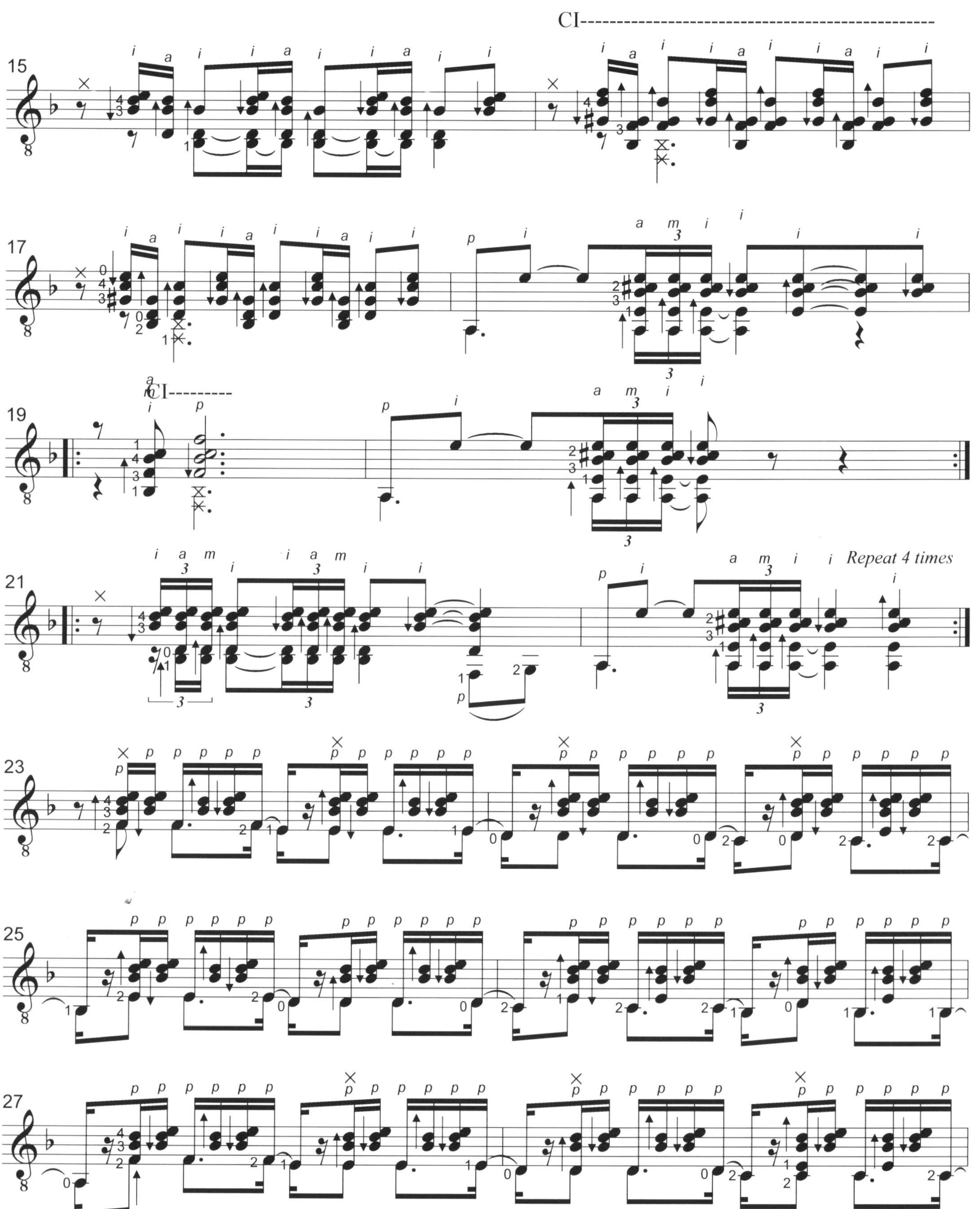
CI
CI
Repeat 4 times

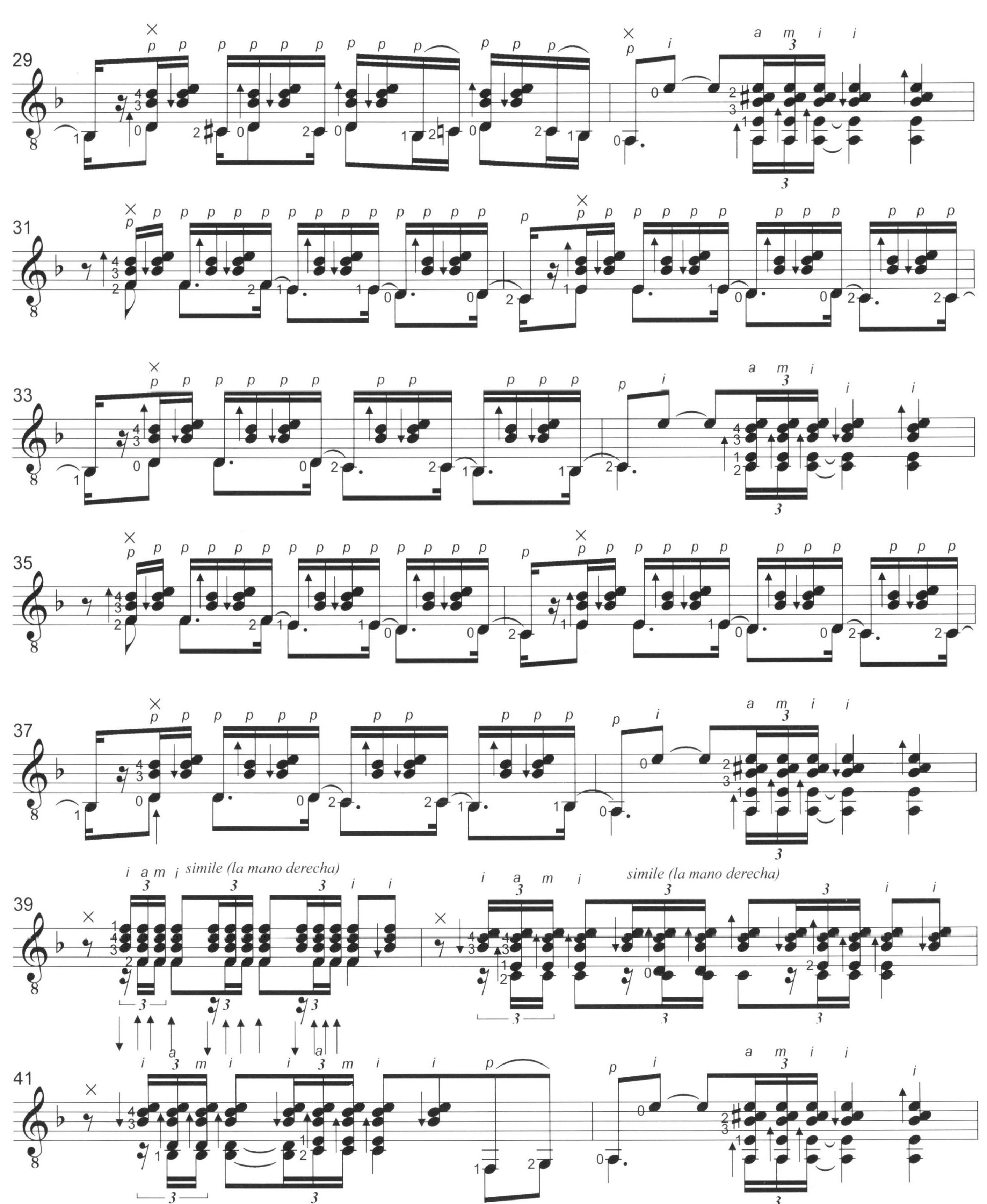

simile (la mano derecha)
simile (la mano derecha)

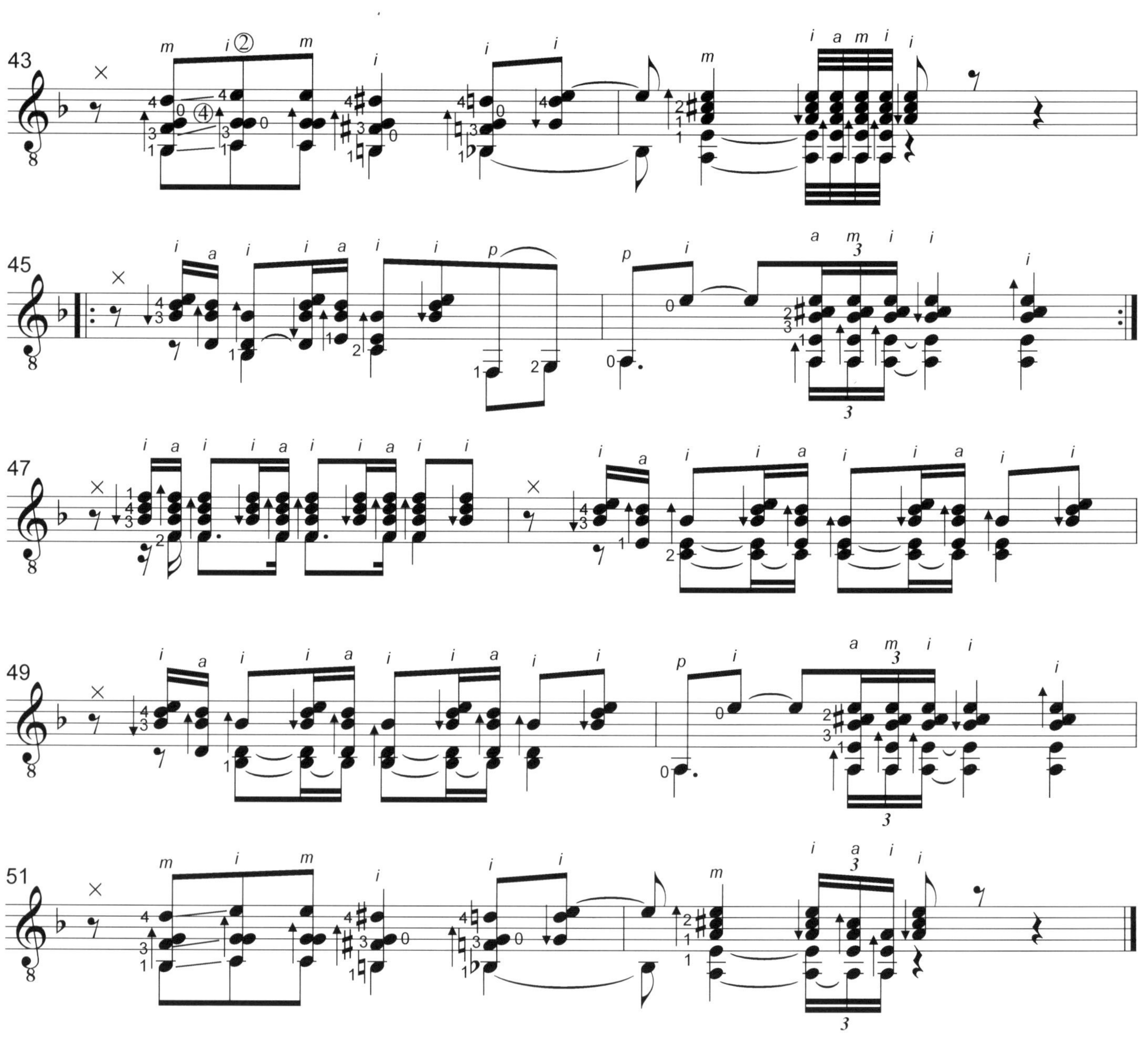

Unit II, Part III

Fandangos

Unit II, Part III
Fandangos

"*Fandangos de Manuel Torre*" by Manuel Torre, Richard Marlow and Corey Whitehead.

1) This work begins with a 19-measure solo guitar introduction, followed by the *cante* in measures 20-43.
2) Measures 44-73 are a solo guitar section that features a popular *copla,* played as a chord-melody solo by the guitarist, just as a jazz player would play chord-melody arrangements that included conversational call-and-response between the melody and accompaniment.
3) Measures 74 to the end presents a final guitar solo *falseta* that does not feature a *cante* section played by the guitar.
4) In order to perform this work with the proper technique and feeling (*aire),* read the detailed performance notes on the *Fandangos* study from *Formative Works for the Flamenco/Classical Guitar Tradition* by Corey Whitehead and Richard Marlow, Mel Bay, 2024.

Fandangos de Manuel Torre

Manuel Torre, Richard Marlow and Corey Whitehead
Edited by Corey Whitehead

(♩ = 140)

Cejilla III
Capo III

Guitar

The right hand is always the same
La mano derecha siempre lo mismo

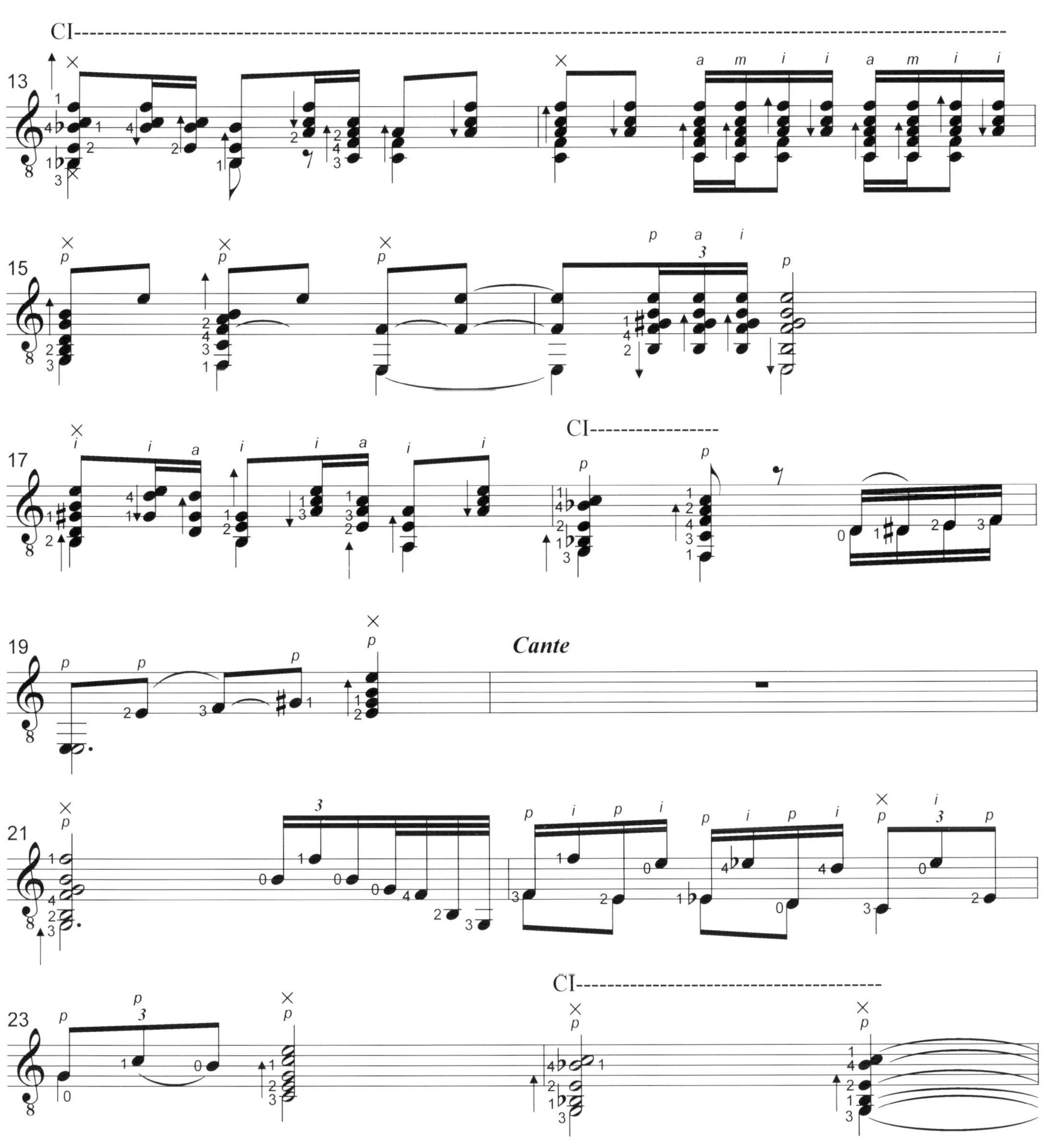
CI
Cante
CI
CI

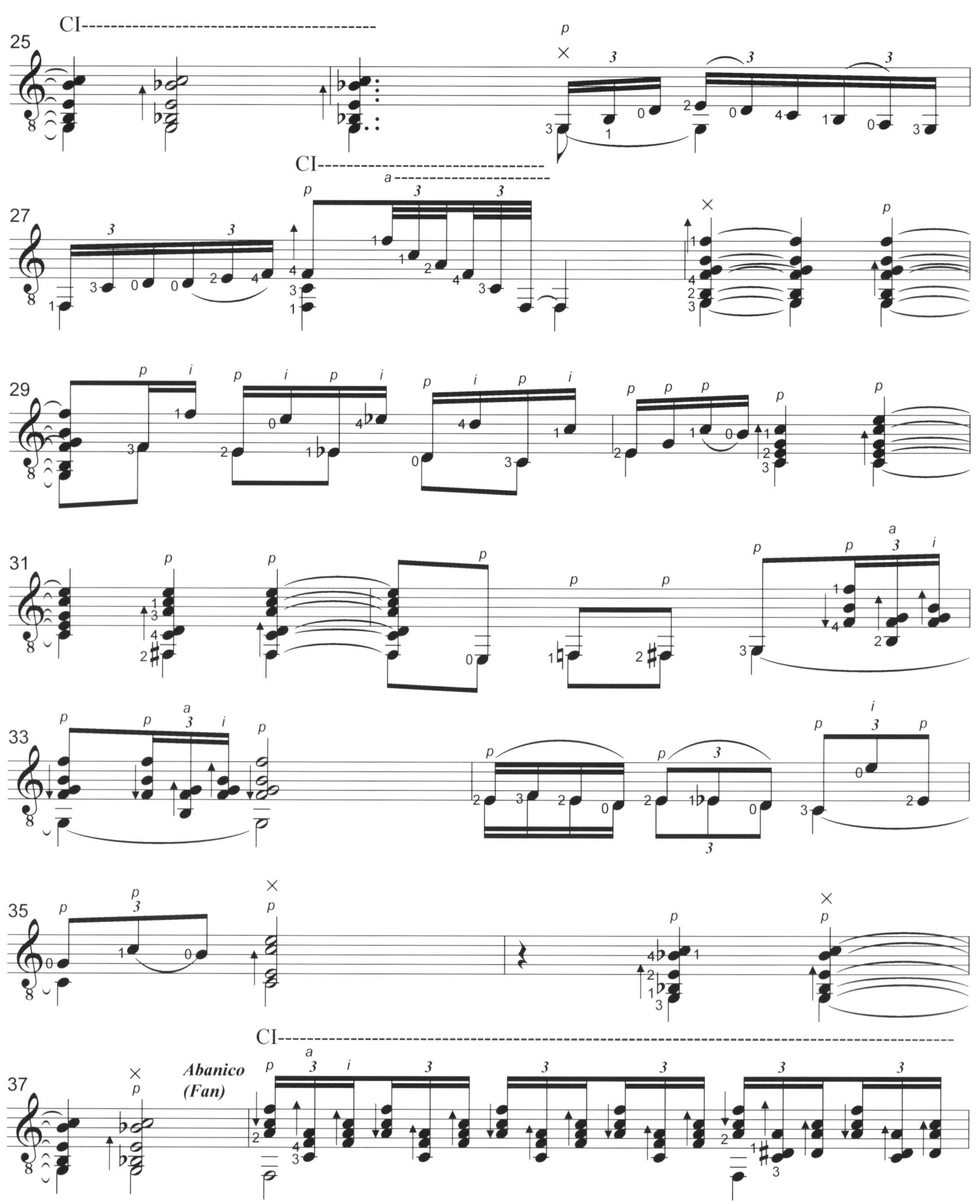
CI
CI
Abanico
(Fan)
CI

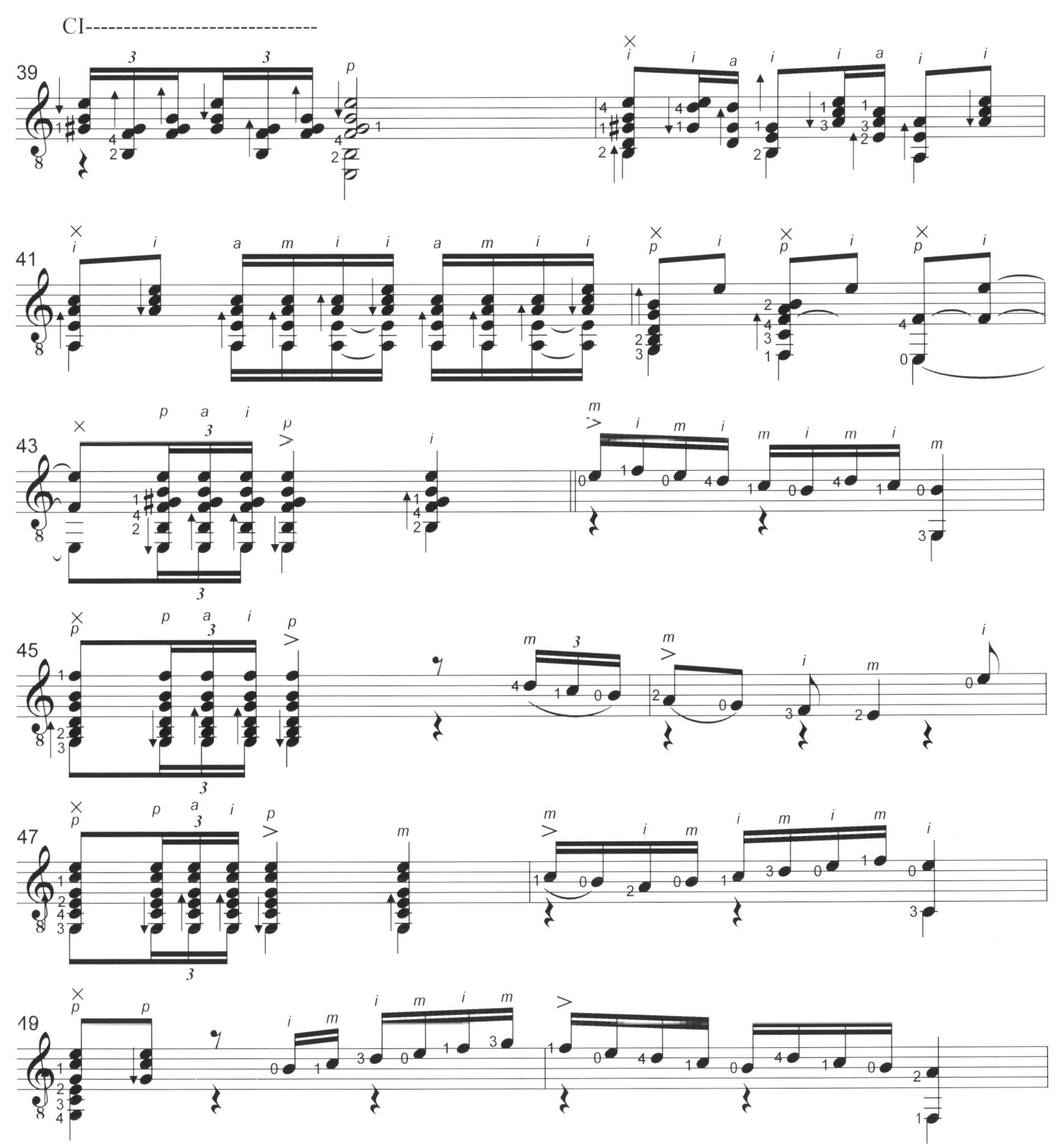
CI------------------------------

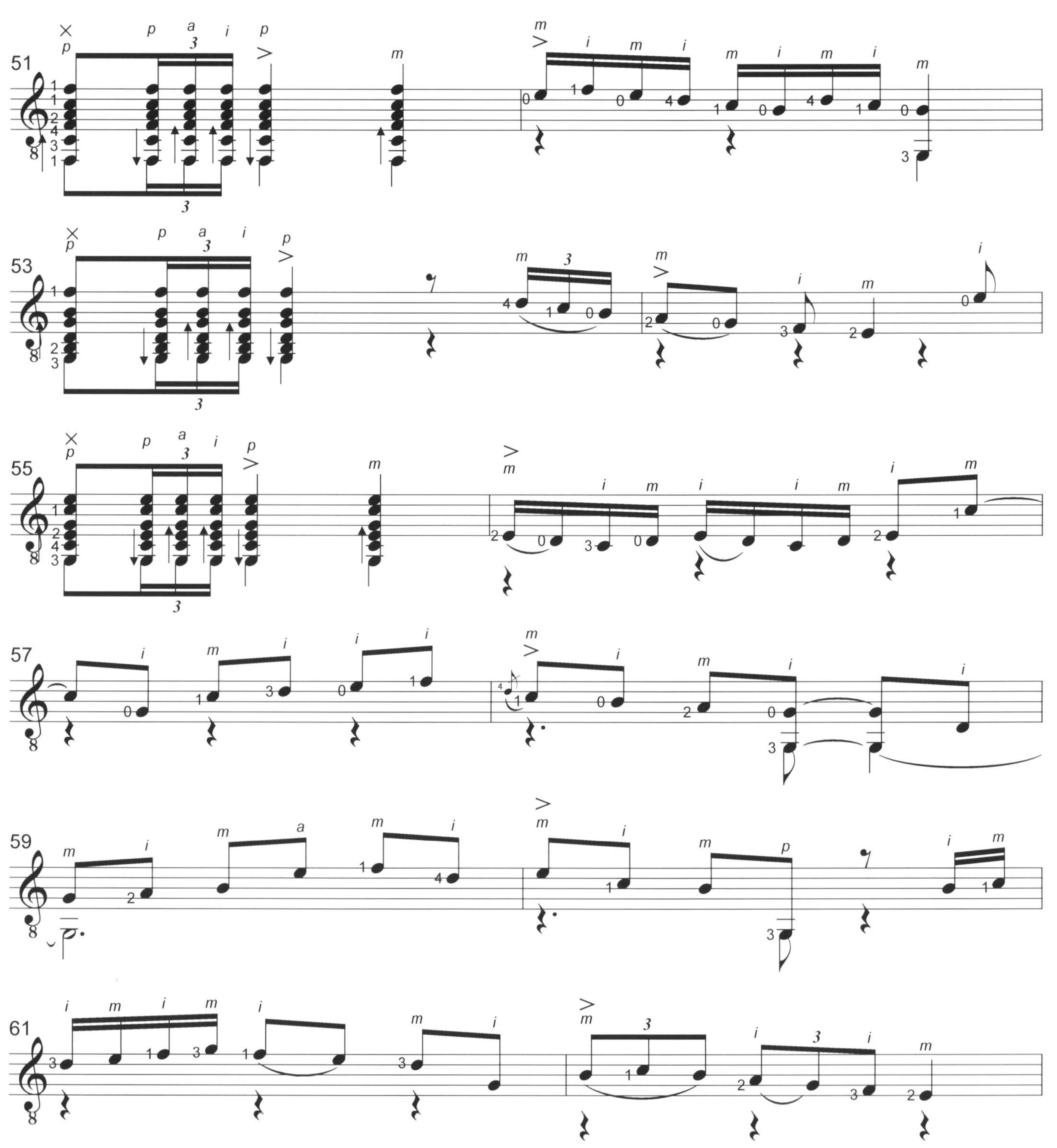

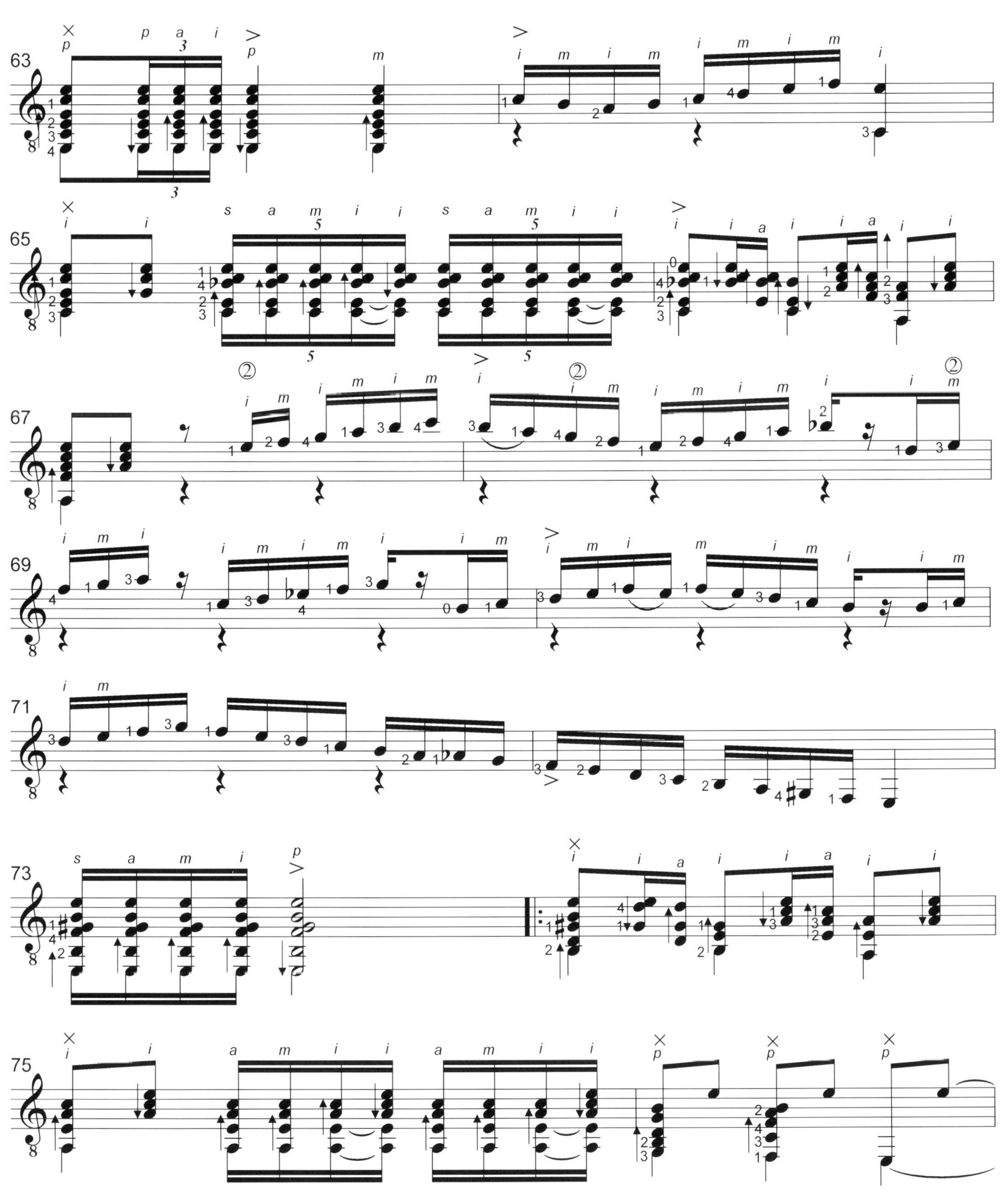
63
65
67
69
71
73
75

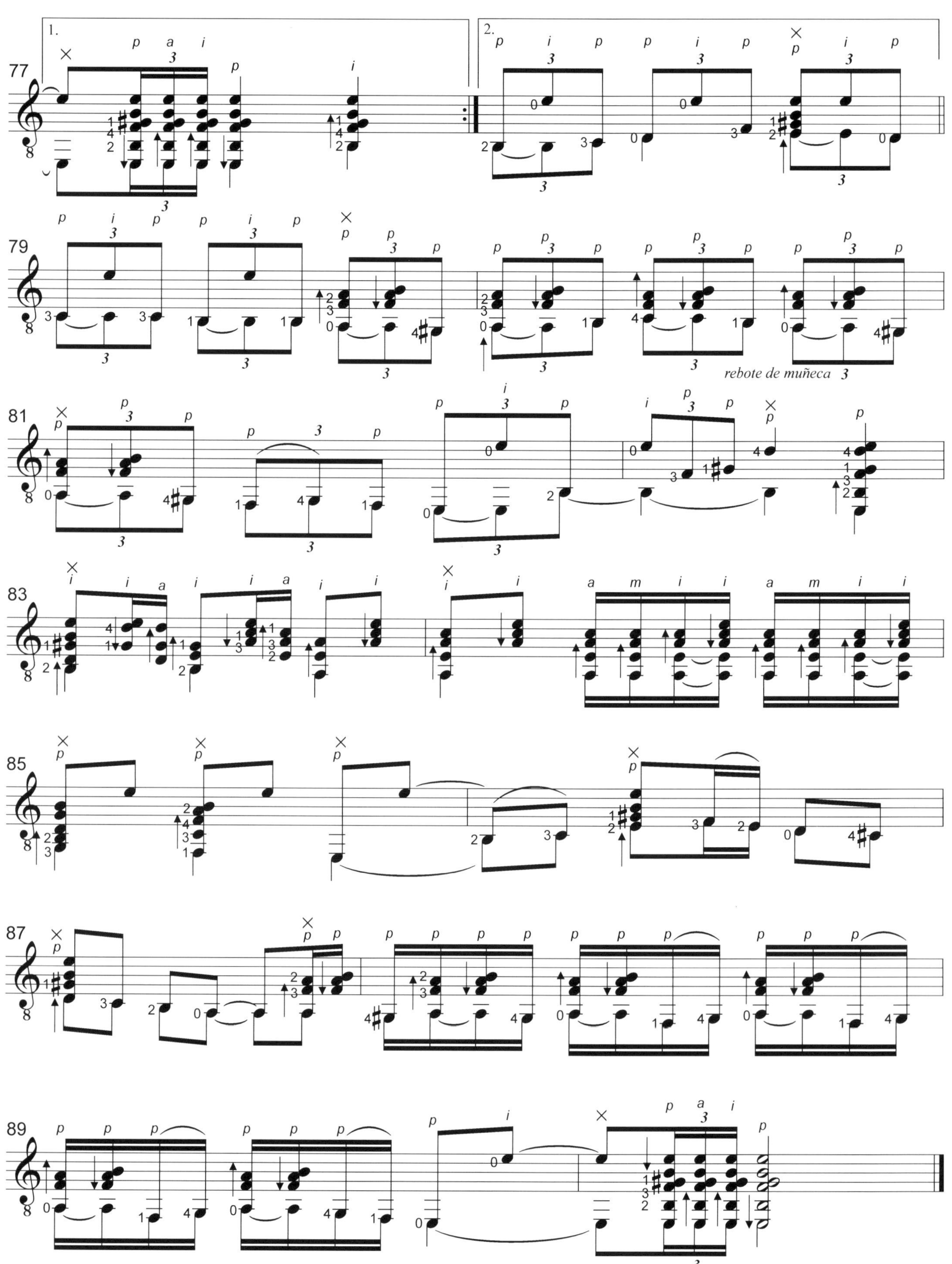
rebote de muñeca

Unit II, Part IV

Siguiriyas

Unit II, Part IV
Siguiriyas

"Siguiriyas de Jerez" by Richard Marlow and Corey Whitehead

1) The *cante* enters in measure 12 on *"Ay"* which ends at the *llamada,* the *cante* continues at the *letra* in measure 53.
2) A guitar solo is played to the end of the work.
3) The "Ay!" is always the opening exclamation preceding the lyrics of a profound or deep flamenco song (*cante jondo*). It is a painful cry on a single syllable which the singer "intonates" around of the first note of the song, often singing quartertones above and/or below the central pitch. The singer also may choose to sing *melismas* or in other words, many notes on this single syllable "Ay!"
4) The "a" finger is dragged from the first string to the fourth string in measure 5. This is a technique called "*retraste*."
5) Notes with a diamond-shaped head indicate that a note is pressed and held by the left hand without sounding or being played with the right hand.
6) Although the key signature indicates D minor with one flat, the work consistently uses a C-sharp to create an A major chord at the end of phrases. Using the C-sharp here in this way is like the use of the raised seventh scale degree in harmonic minor in Baroque music. The difference between the use of this chord in flamenco versus in the Baroque period, is that in the Baroque period the song or phrase mostly ends on the *tonic,* or D minor chord, whereas in flamenco one terminates the song or phrase on the *dominant,* or A Major chord.
7) The tonality of this work is centered on A, using the D minor scale mostly, except at the ends of phrases where the C-sharp enters and suggests what sounds like harmonic minor. Starting and ending the work on A while using the key signature for D minor creates the sound of the modern Phrygian mode. However, flamenco uses not only the C-sharp, but also the D-flat. This is an important distinction between flamenco and classical music. This use of the enharmonic version of the C-sharp is one of the differences between flamenco and modern modal music.
8) Before attempting to play this work, it is very helpful to study the notes on the *Siguiriyas* study from *Formative Works for the Flamenco/Classical Guitar Tradition* by Corey Whitehead and Richard Marlow, Mel Bay, 2024.

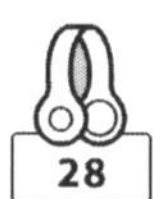

Siguiriyas de Jerez

Richard Marlow and Corey Whitehead
(Edited by Corey Whitehead)

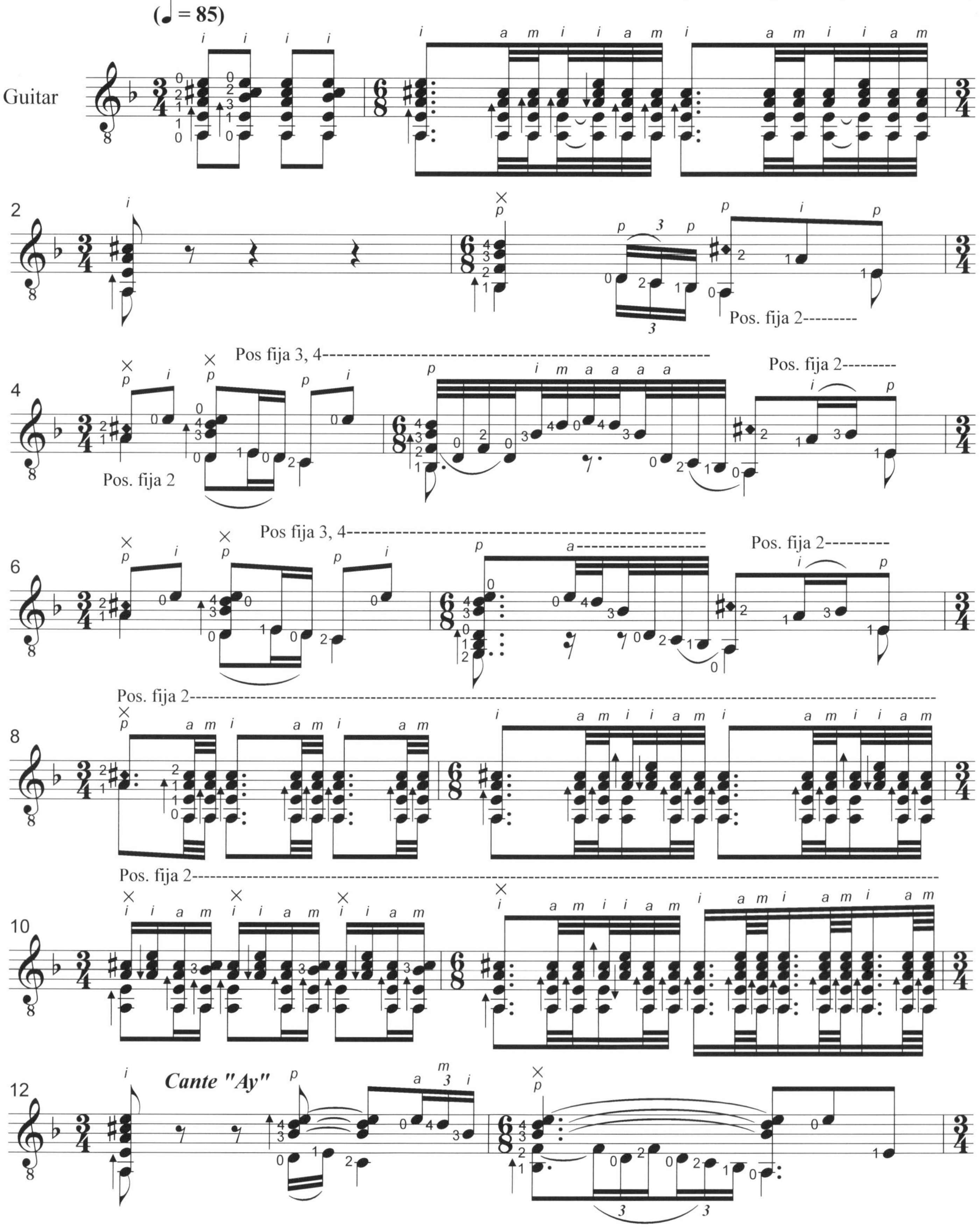

(♩ = 85)

Guitar

Pos. fija 2

Pos fija 3, 4

Pos. fija 2

Pos fija 3, 4

Pos. fija 2

Pos. fija 2

Pos. fija 2

Cante "Ay"

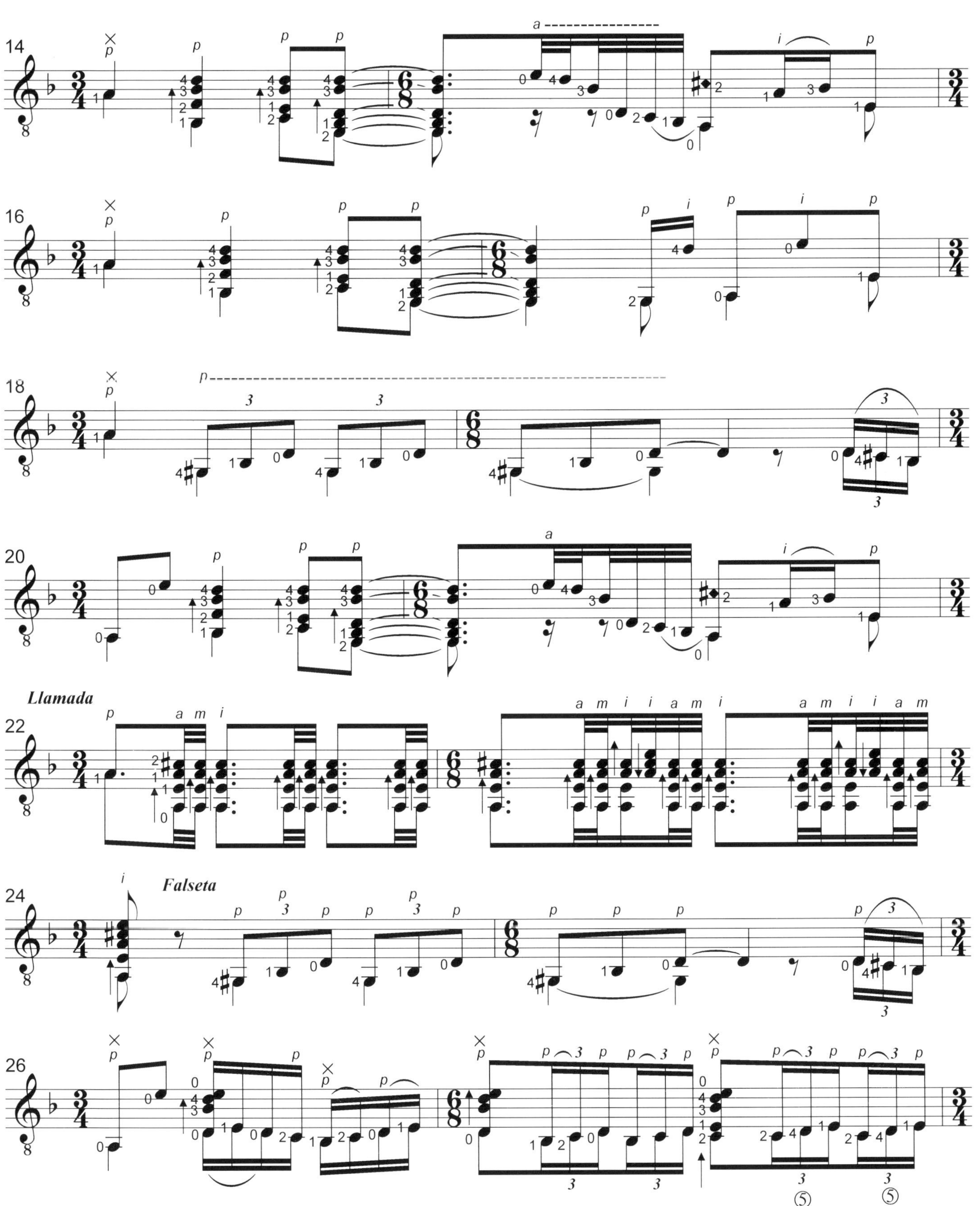
Llamada
Falseta

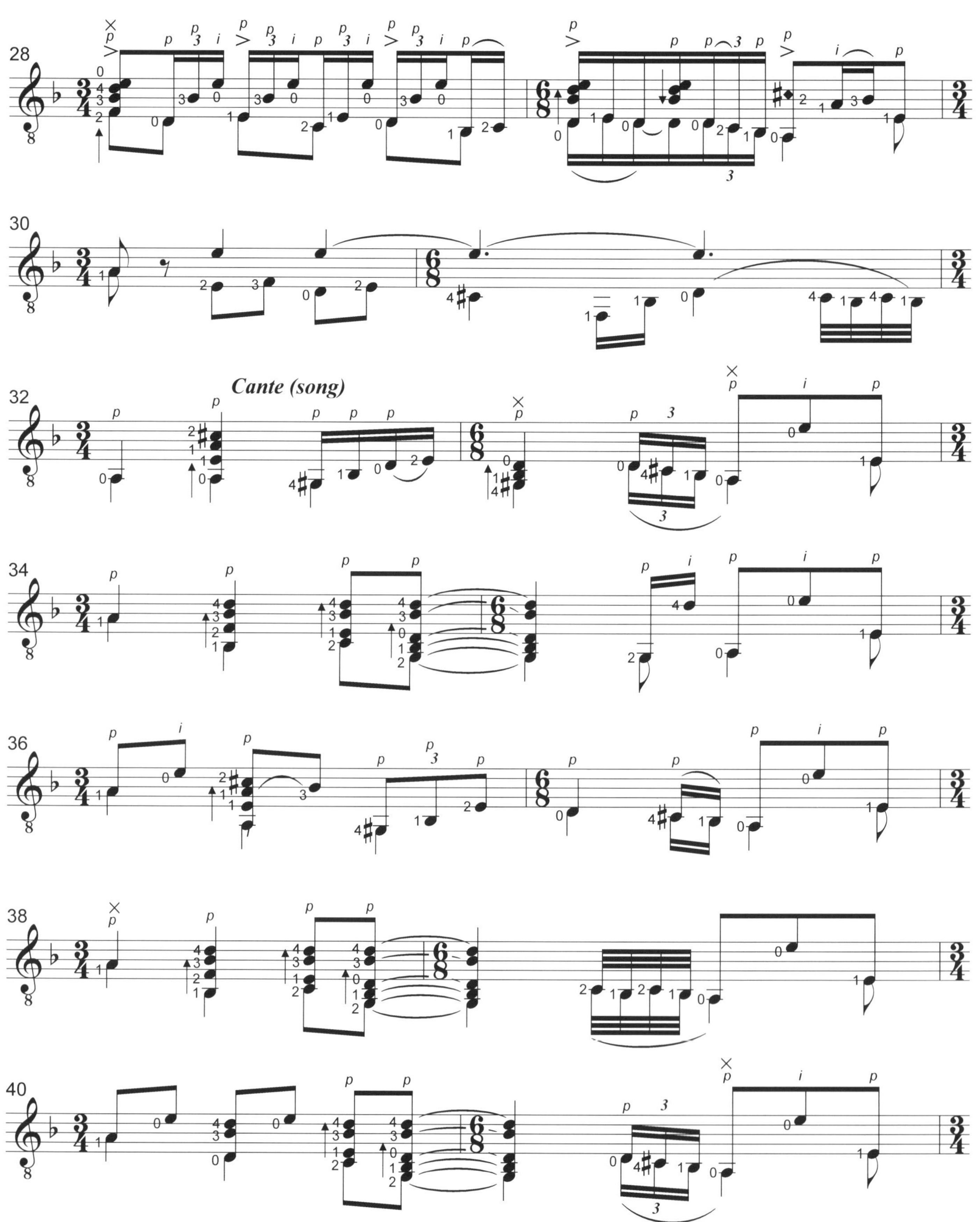
Cante (song)

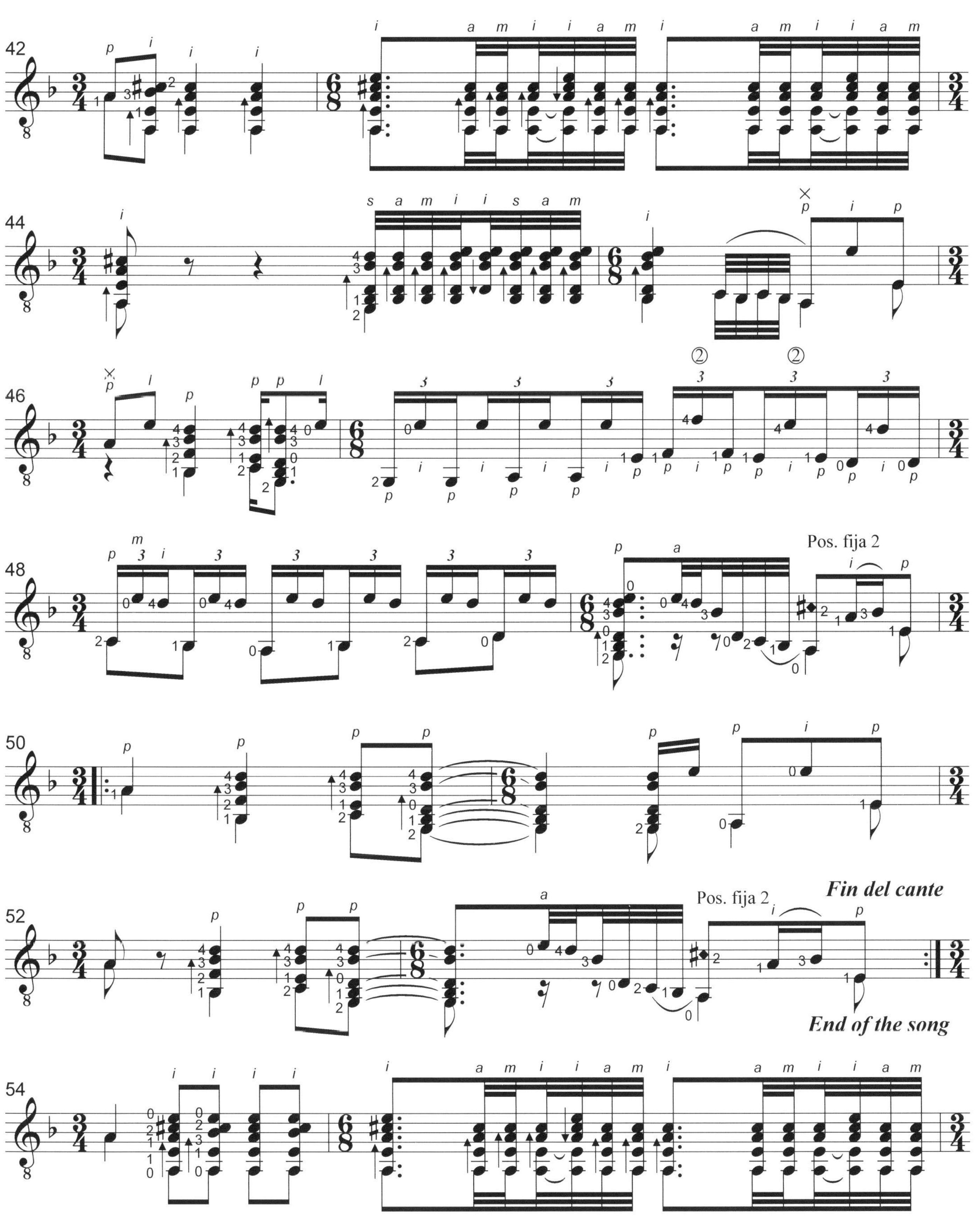
Pos. fija 2
Pos. fija 2
Fin del cante
End of the song

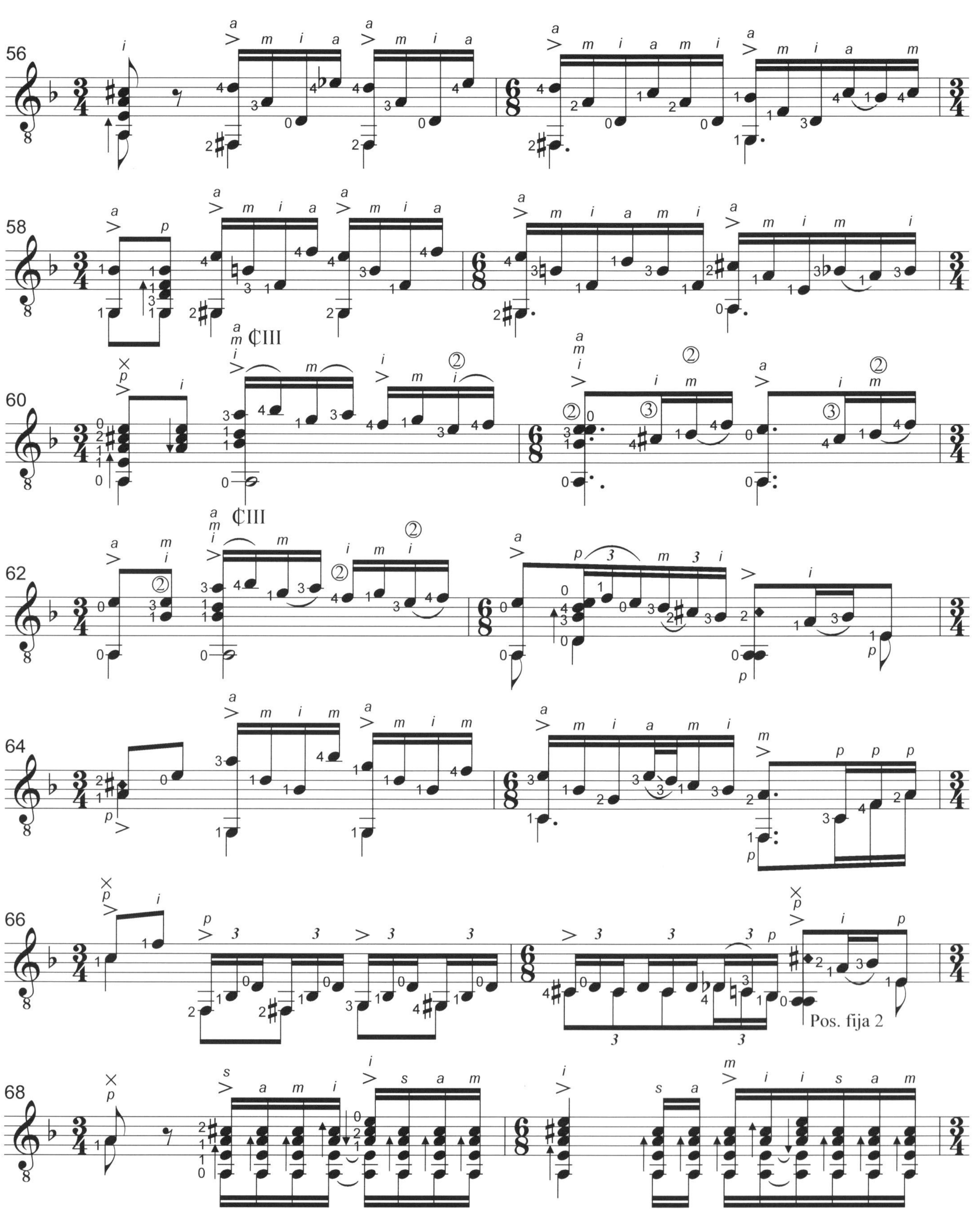

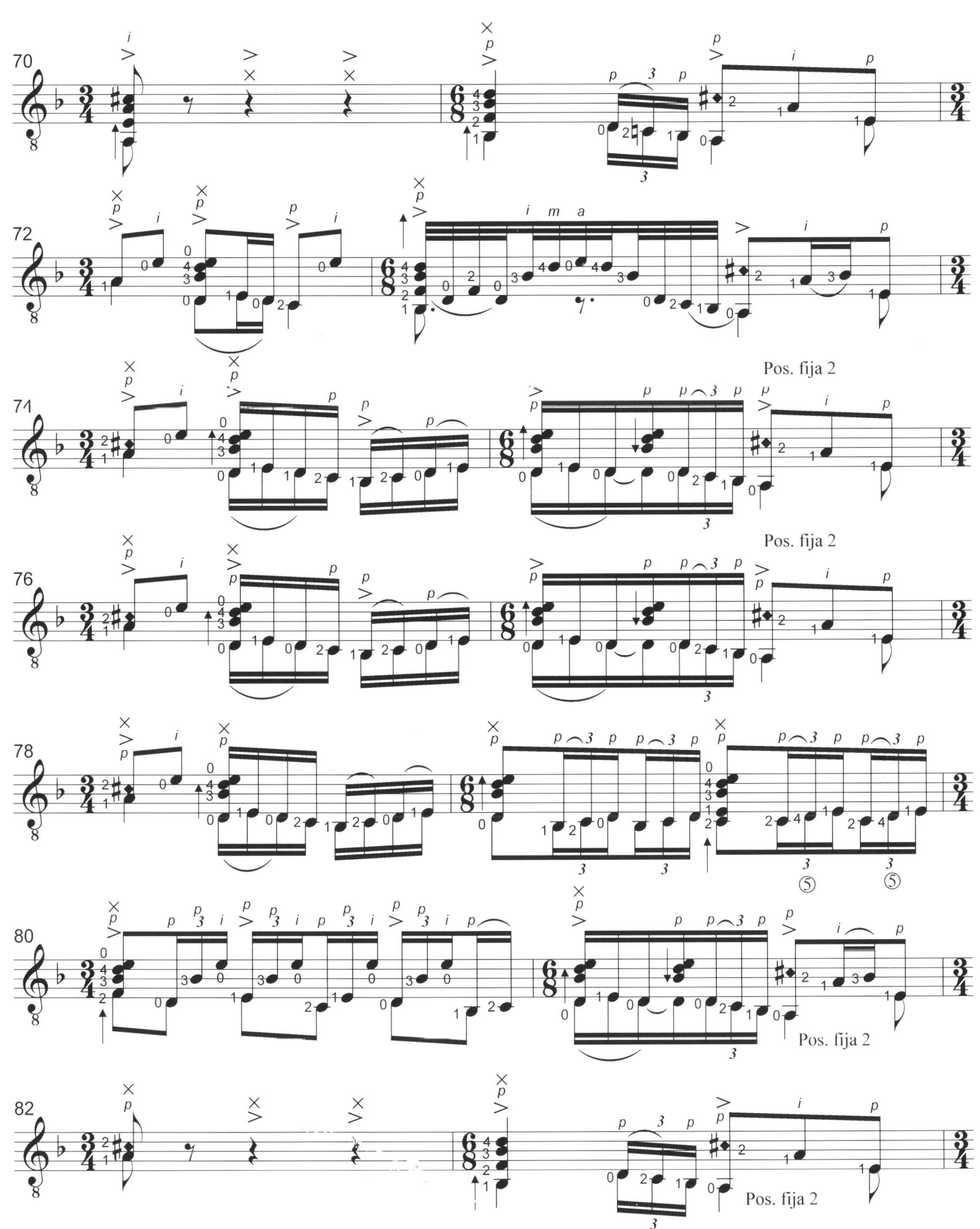
70
72
Pos. fija 2
74
Pos. fija 2
76
78
80
Pos. fija 2
82
Pos. fija 2

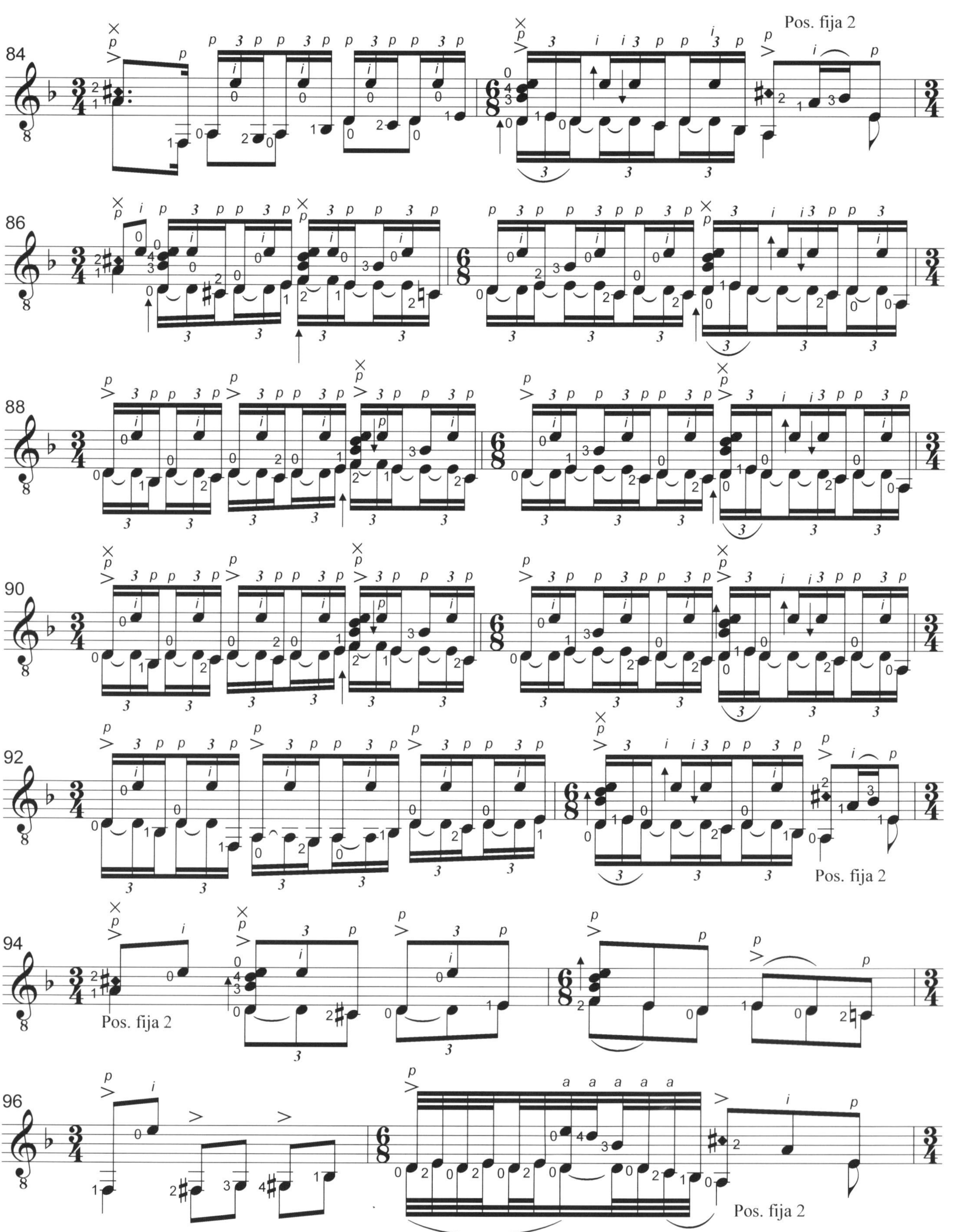

84
Pos. fija 2
86
88
90
92
Pos. fija 2
94
Pos. fija 2
96
Pos. fija 2

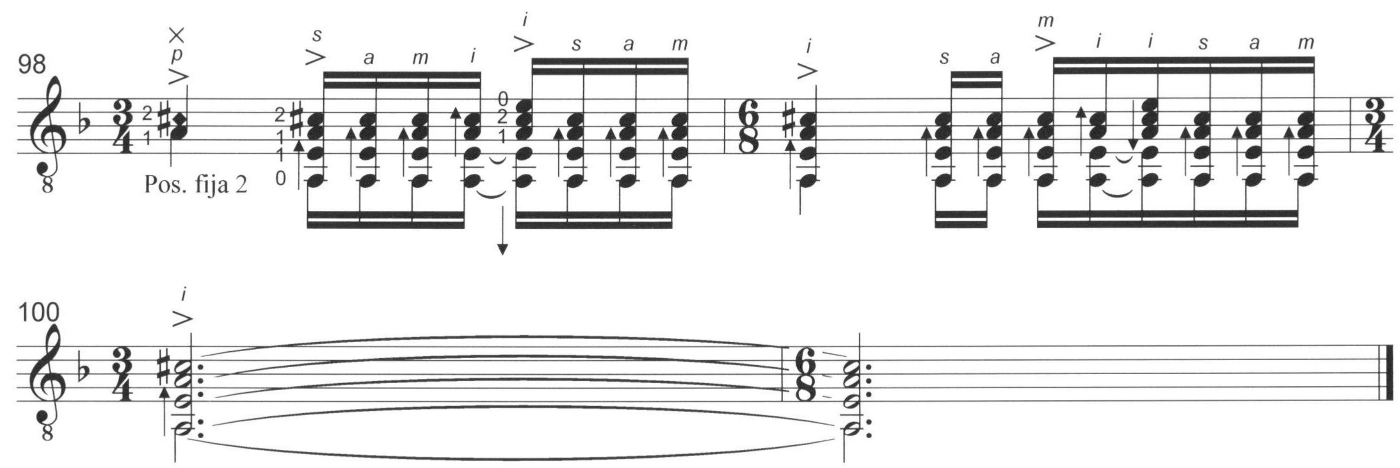
98
Pos. fija 2
100

Unit II, Part V

Alegrías, Caracoles, Bulerías

Unit II, Part V
Alegrías, Caracoles, Bulerías

"Bulerías de Jerez" by Richard Marlow and Corey Whitehead

1) The performance notes from the *Bulerías* study from the *Formative Works for the Flamenco/Classical Guitar Tradition* by Corey Whitehead and Richard Marlow, Mel Bay, 2024 are helpful in performing this work with the correct technique and feeling *(aire).*
2) The two alternating 6/8 to ¾ measures comprise a full phrase, each beat being of 8th-note duration. The beats of 8th-note duration are grouped into 3-3-2-2-2
3) The work begins with a 24-measure introduction to the *cante.*
4) As in the previous examples, this form may be expanded when the singer performs more than one verse of the *letras.* In this case, the guitarist often plays a very short *falseta* of one or two phrases maximum, and then continues the accompaniment of the *cante.* This solo of two phrases.
5) The accompaniment of the *cante* begins with a two-measure figure in the guitar accompaniment (mm. 25-26) which is typical in Jerez. This strumming pattern comprises a full twelve-beat phrase. One may apply the same technique to other chords and create an Andalusian cadence from Dm, C, B♭, A.
6) The *golpe* (x) symbol is used sometimes in the place of a rest, or to keep percussive time during the sounding of a chord. Some of these *golpe* (x) symbols are not placed above a note, chord, or rest and should be played in time on the beats as a chord is sustained.
7) Many variations of the *rasgueado* patterns are included in this work, however, one may use a pattern that is familiar in the place of some of these advanced or unfamiliar strum patterns. Playing a strum pattern that fits within the desired beat is what matters first, then the particular expression and *aire* may be developed as one masters one strum pattern, they may begin to add new patterns to their "toolbox" of expressive techniques.

"Alegrías de Córdoba" by Richard Marlow and Corey Whitehead

1) For further information on the *Alegrías de Córdoba* and *Alegrías in Em,* study the *Formative Works for the Flamenco/ Classical Guitar Tradition* by Corey Whitehead and Richard Marlow, Mel Bay, 2024. The first 23 measures of this work were presented as an etude in the repertoire series.
2) The tempo suddenly changes in measure 25 after this slow introduction (mm.1-24).
3) The final solo guitar *falseta* continues from measure 81 to the end.
4) In general, in this work and all others in this book, adhere as strictly as possible to the marked accents, and *golpes.*

"Caracoles: (Alegrías in C)" by Richard Marlow and Corey Whitehead

1) For detailed information on performance of this *palo,* read the notes on the *Alegrías in C* in the studies from the *Formative Works for the Flamenco/Classical Guitar Tradition* by Corey Whitehead and Richard Marlow, Mel Bay, 2024.

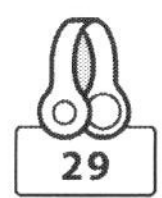

Bulerías de Jerez

Richard Marlow and Corey Whitehead
Edited by Corey Whitehead

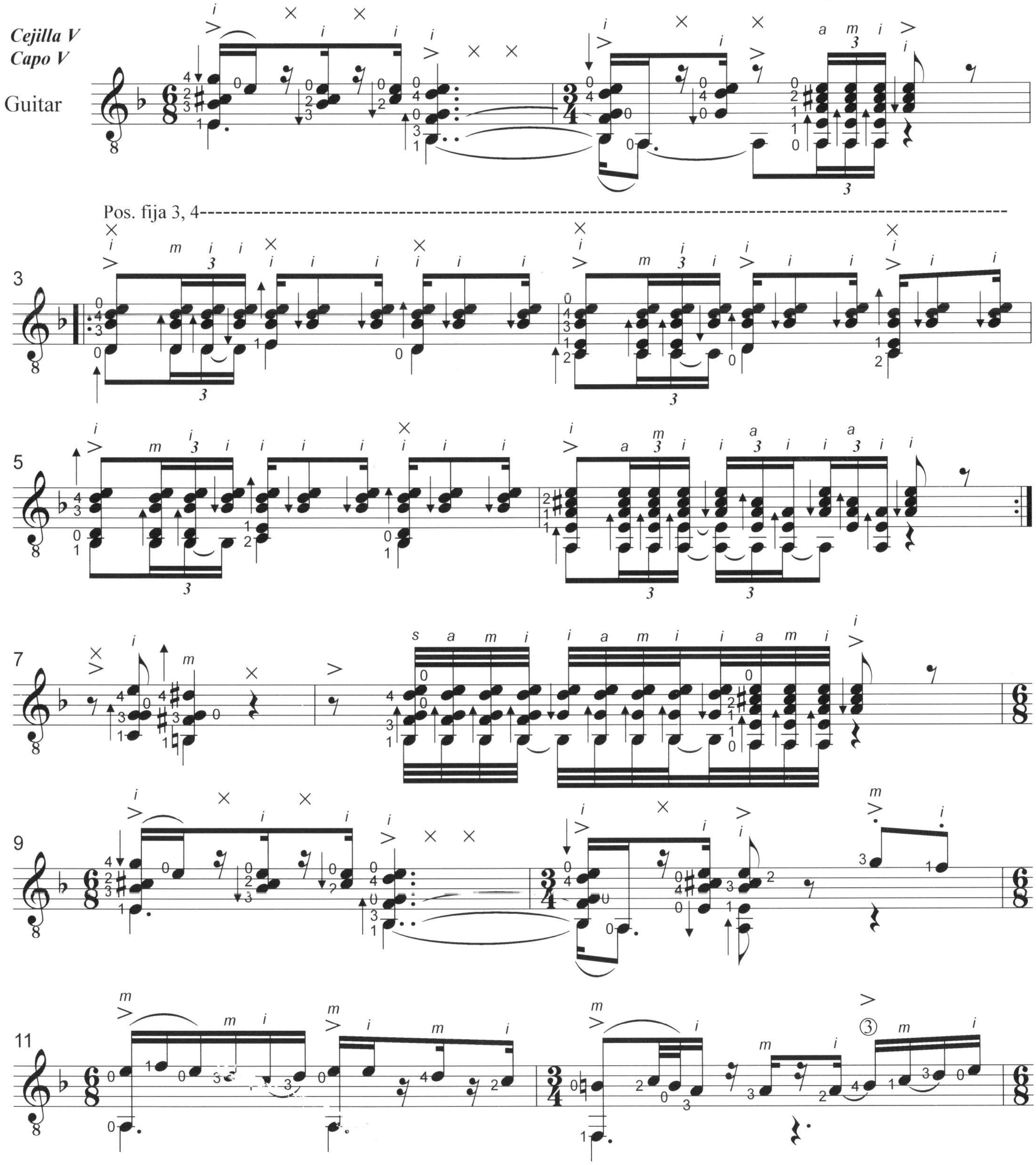

Cejilla V
Capo V

Guitar

Pos. fija 3, 4

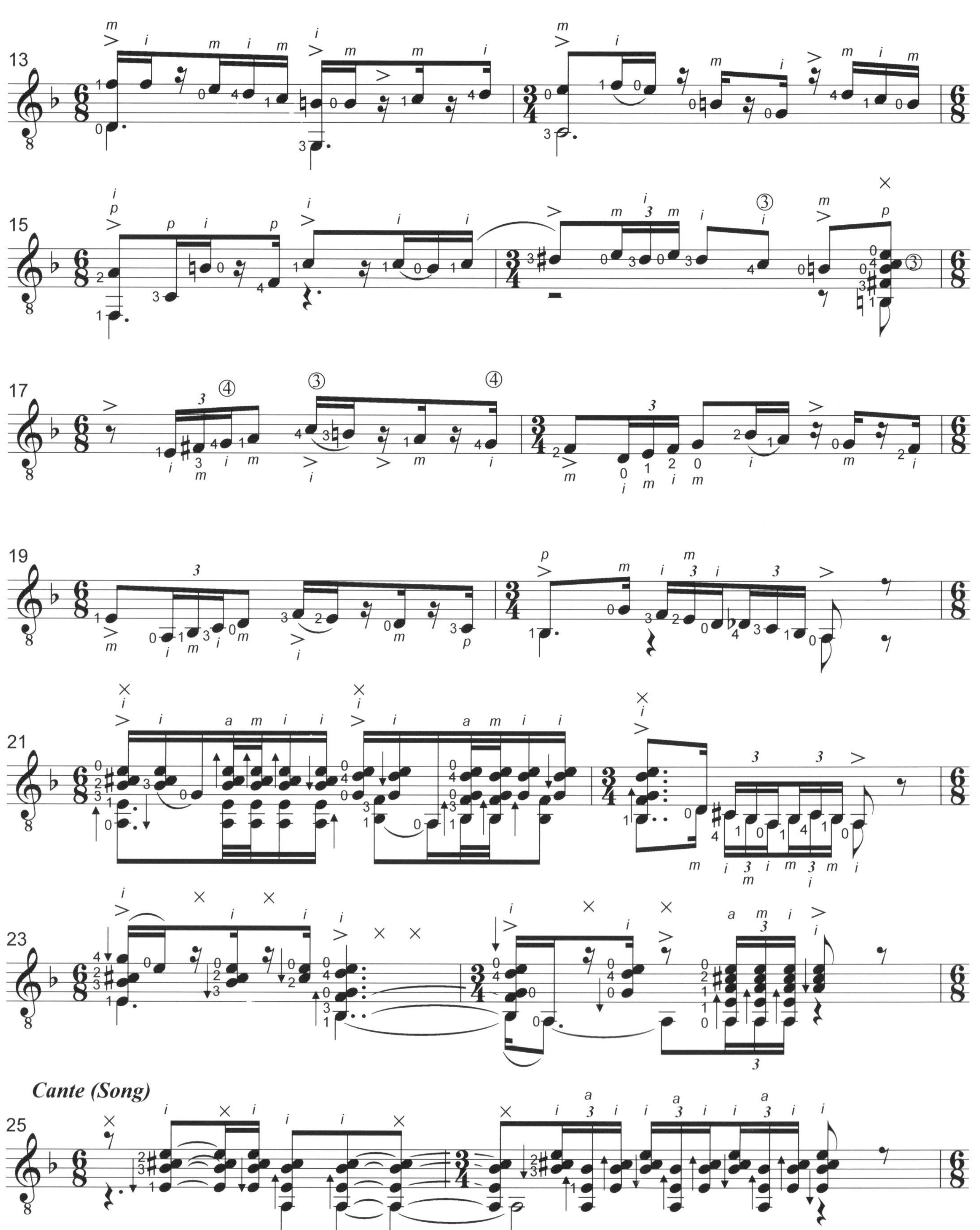
Cante (Song)

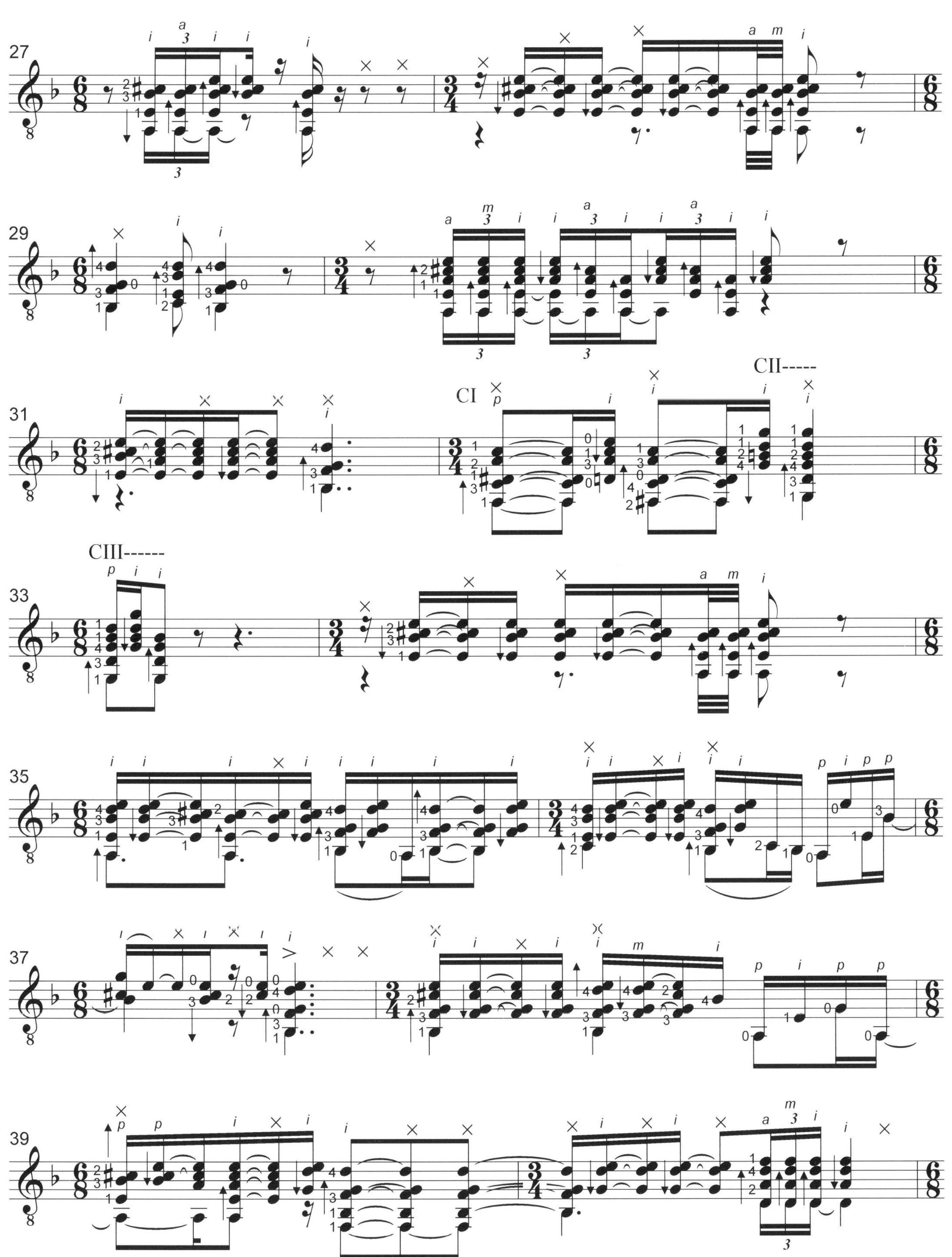
27
29
31
CI
CII-----
33
CIII------
35
37
39

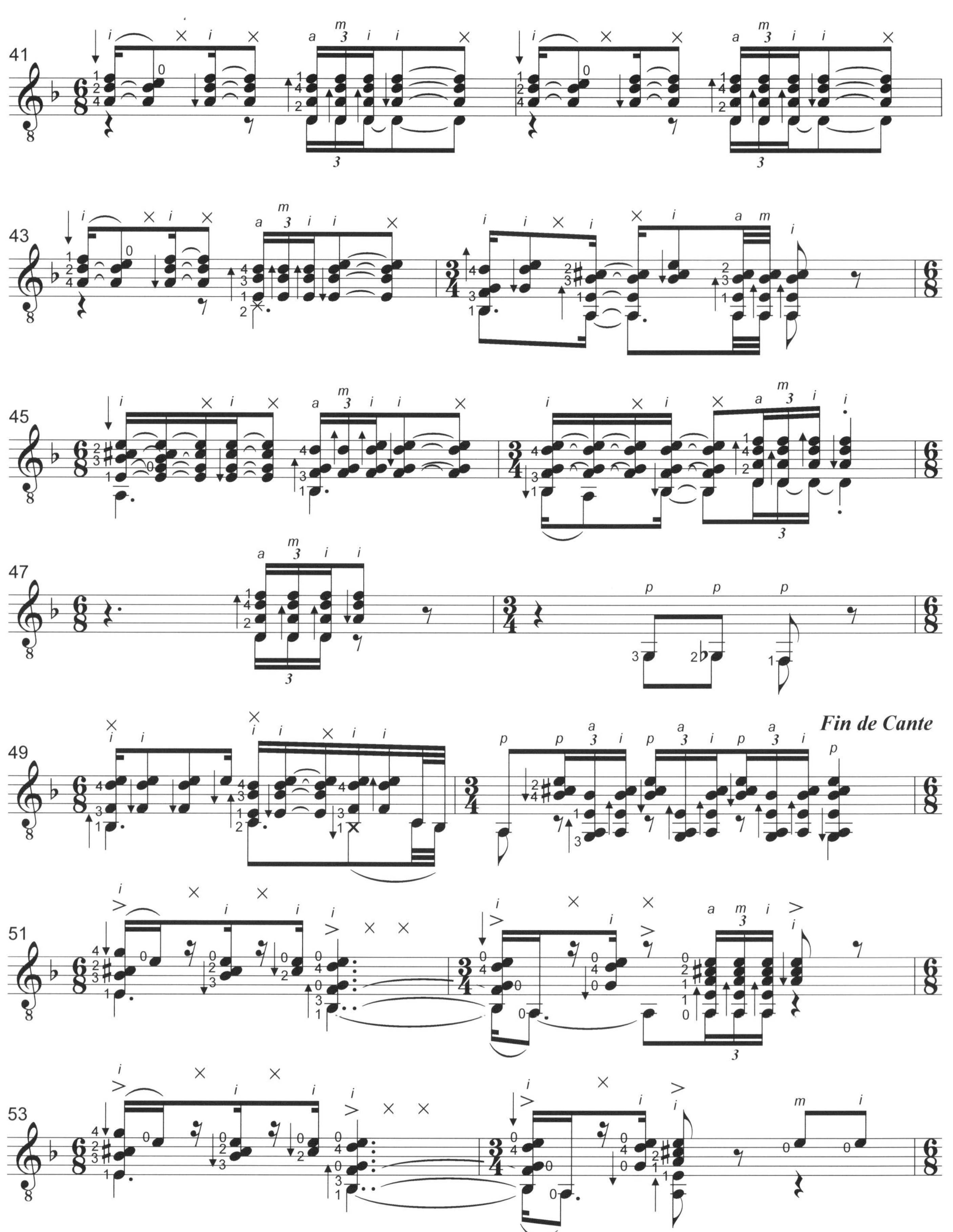
41
43
45
47
49
51
53
Fin de Cante

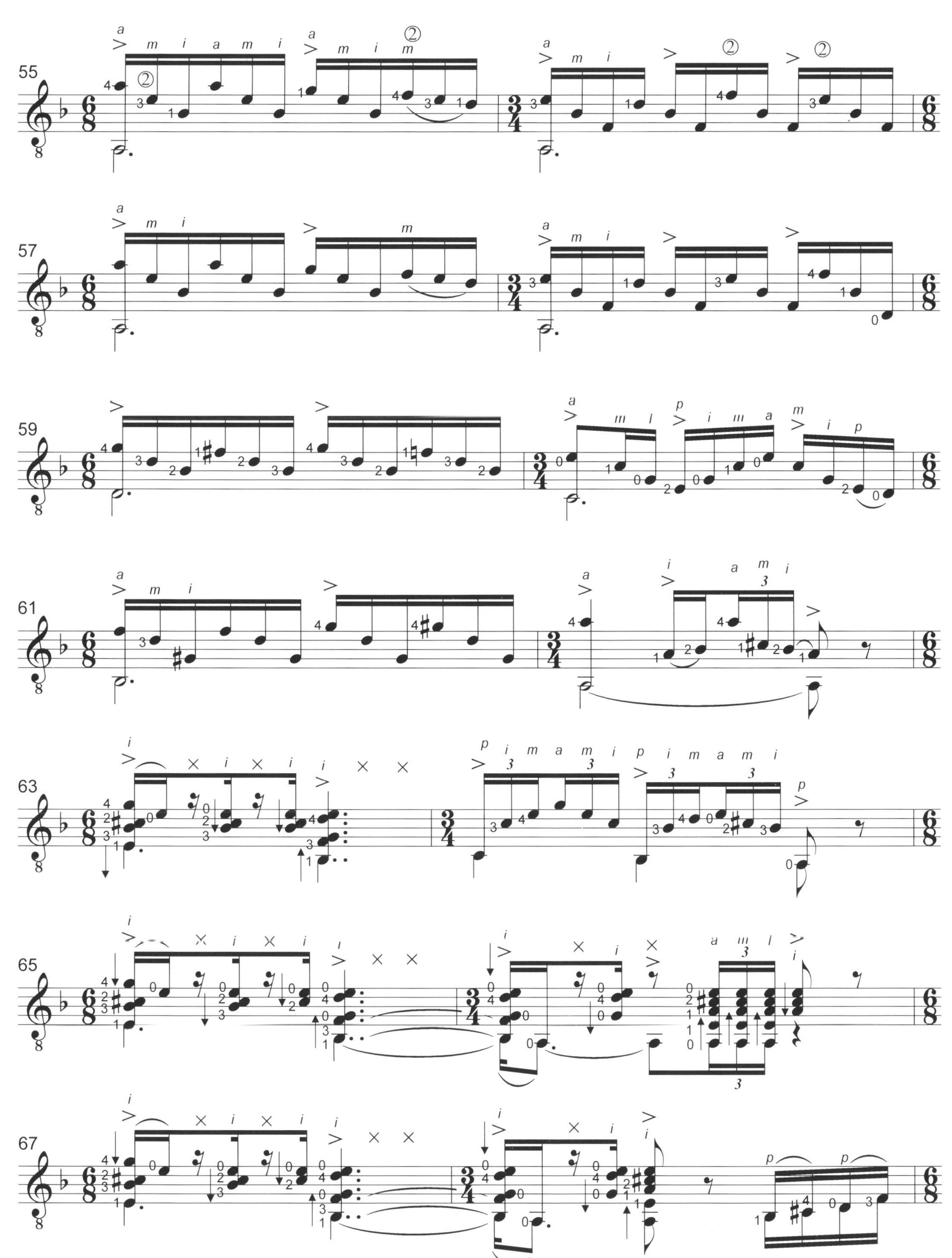

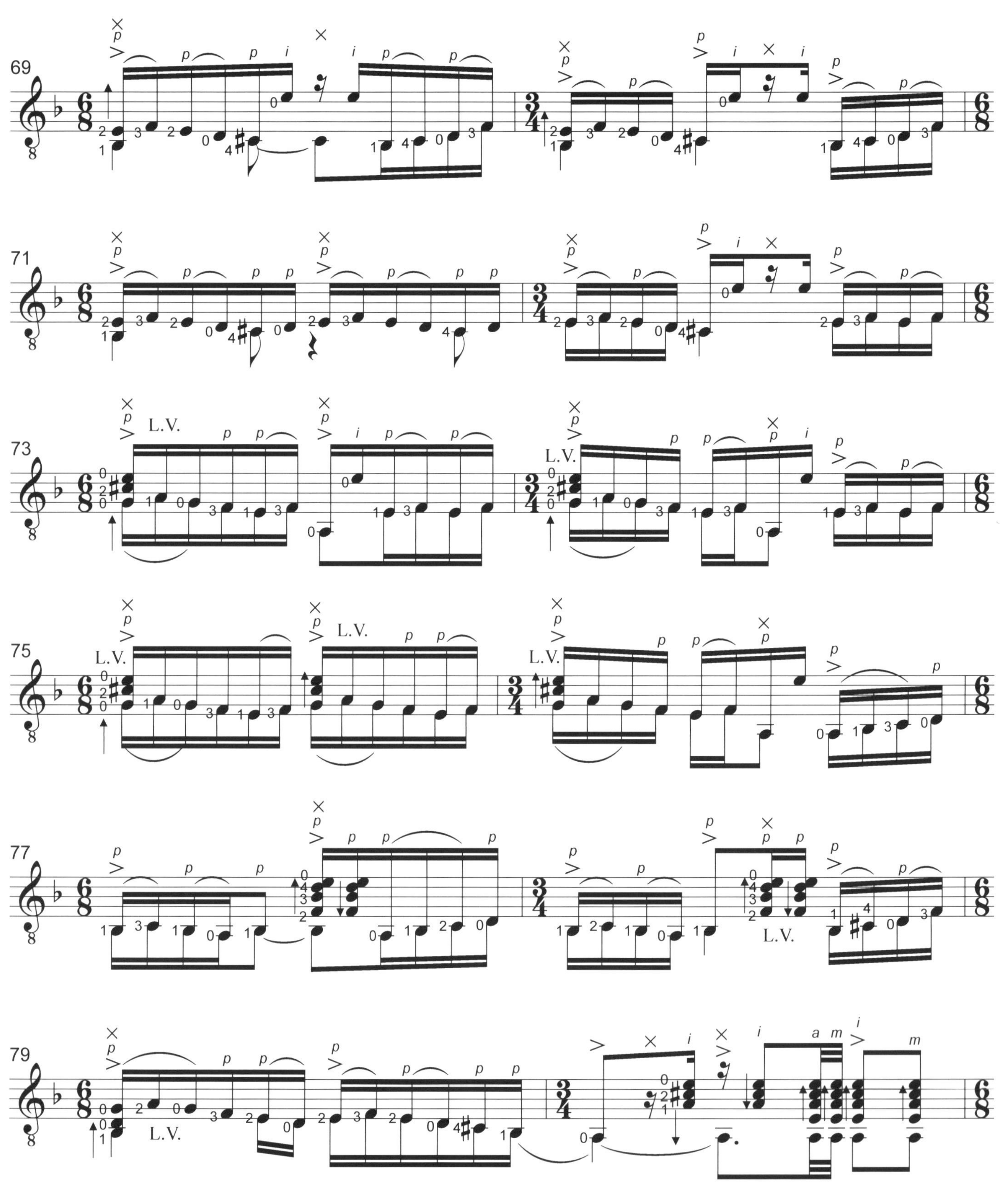
69
71
73
L.V.
75
L.V.
77
L.V.
79
L.V.

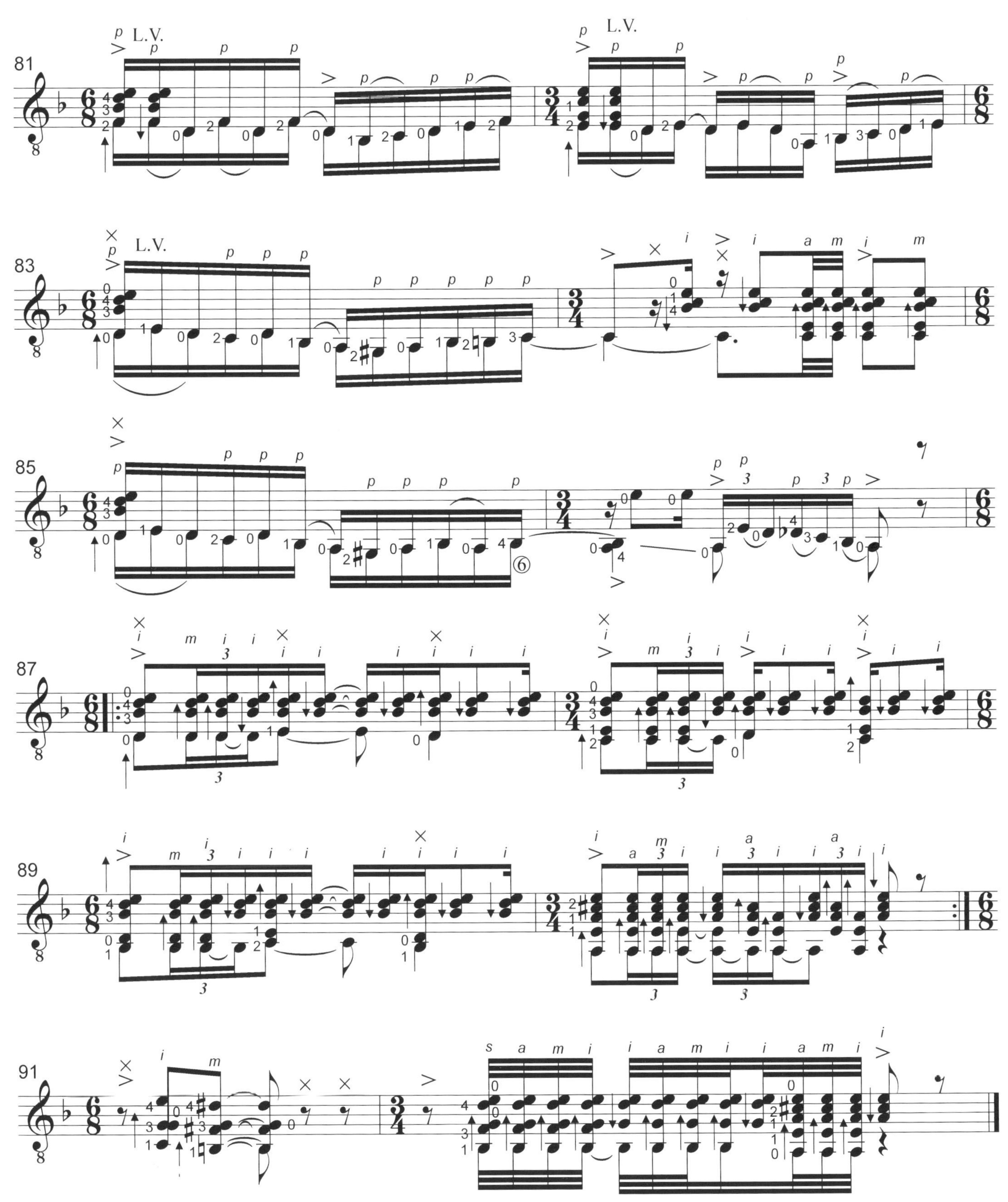
L.V.
L.V.
L.V.

Alegrías de Córdoba (Mi menor)

Corey Whitehead and Richard Marlow
Edited by Corey Whitehead

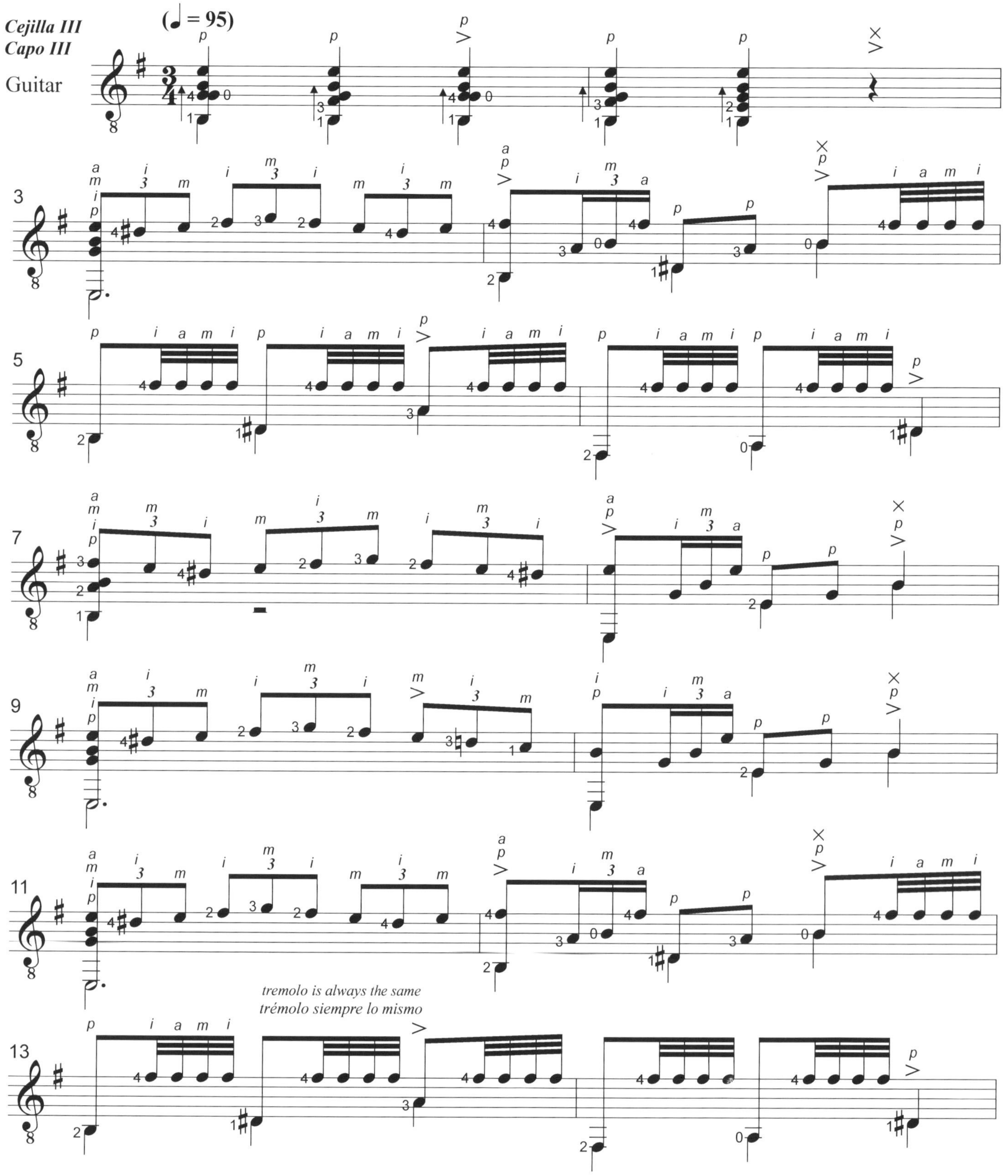

Cejilla III
Capo III

(♩ = 95)

Guitar

3

5

7

9

11

tremolo is always the same
trémolo siempre lo mismo

13

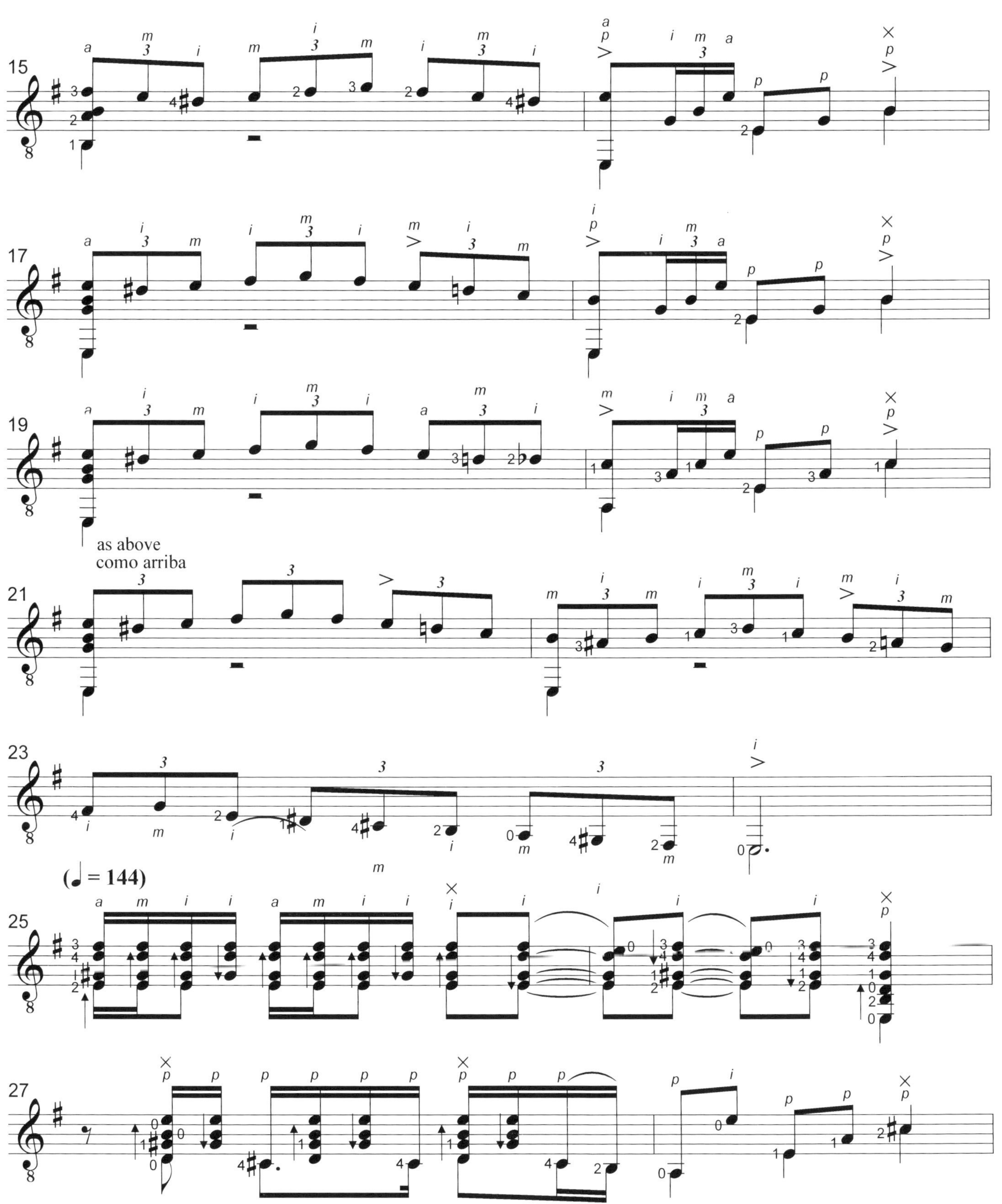
as above
como arriba
(♩ = 144)

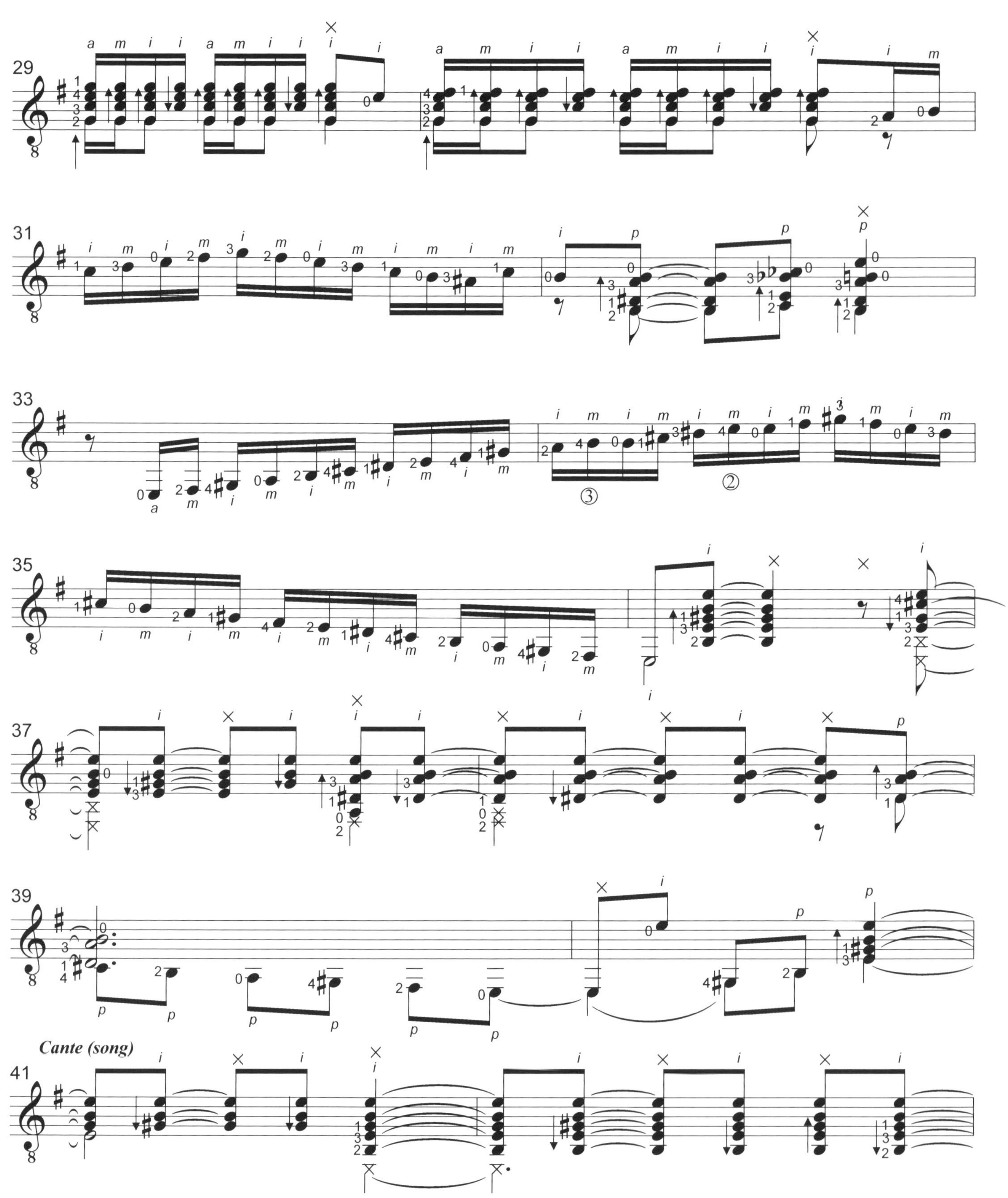
Cante (song)

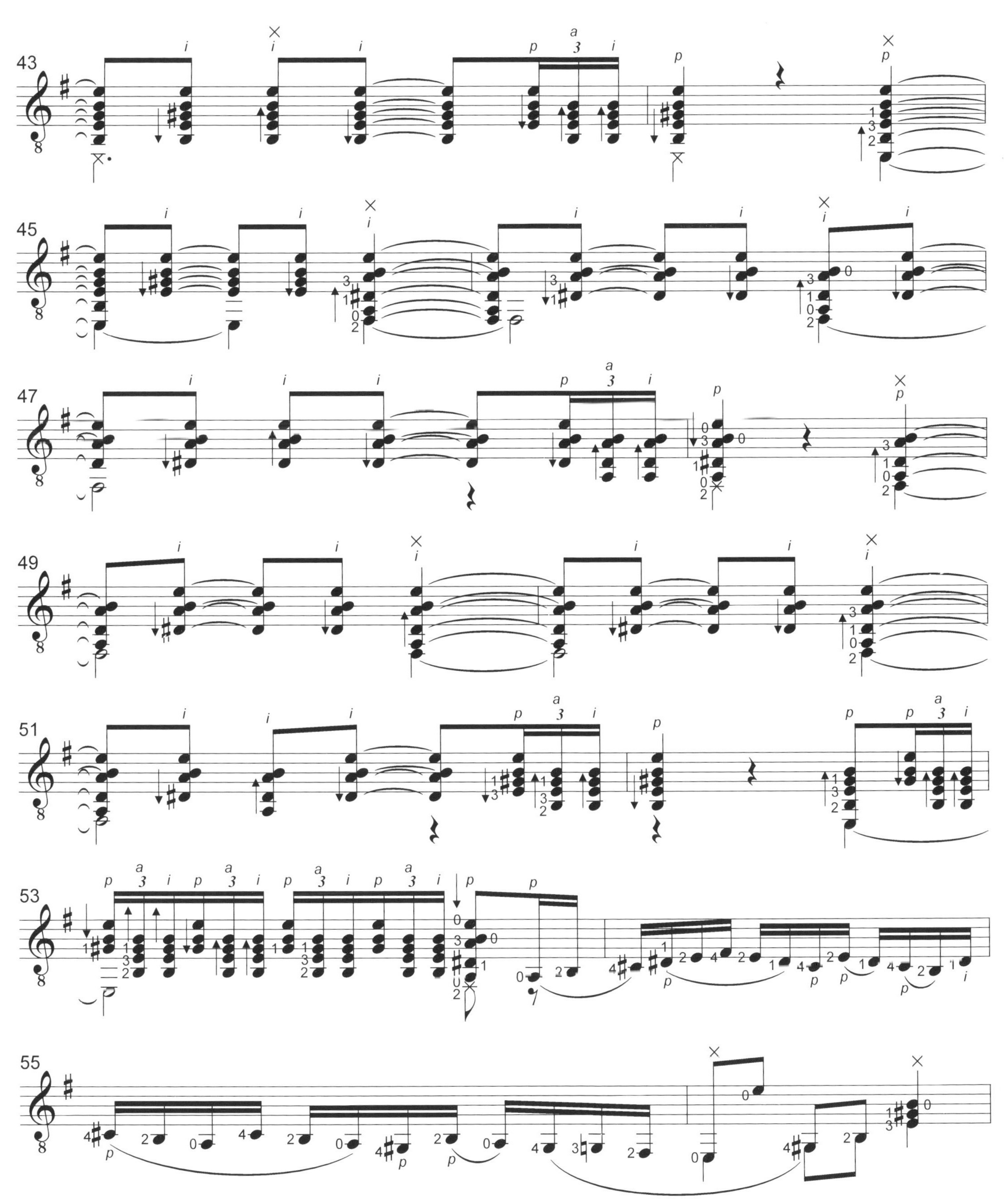

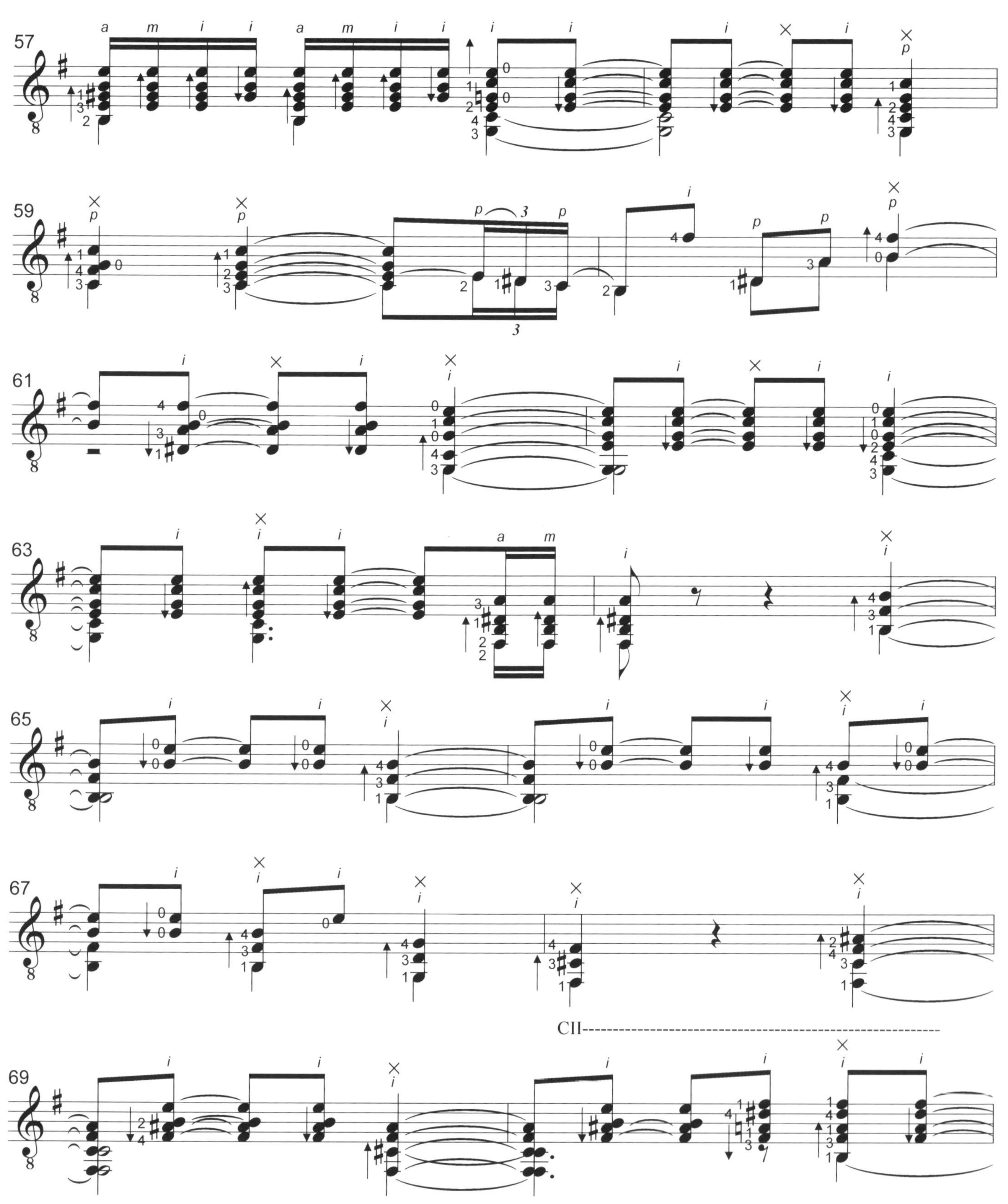
CII

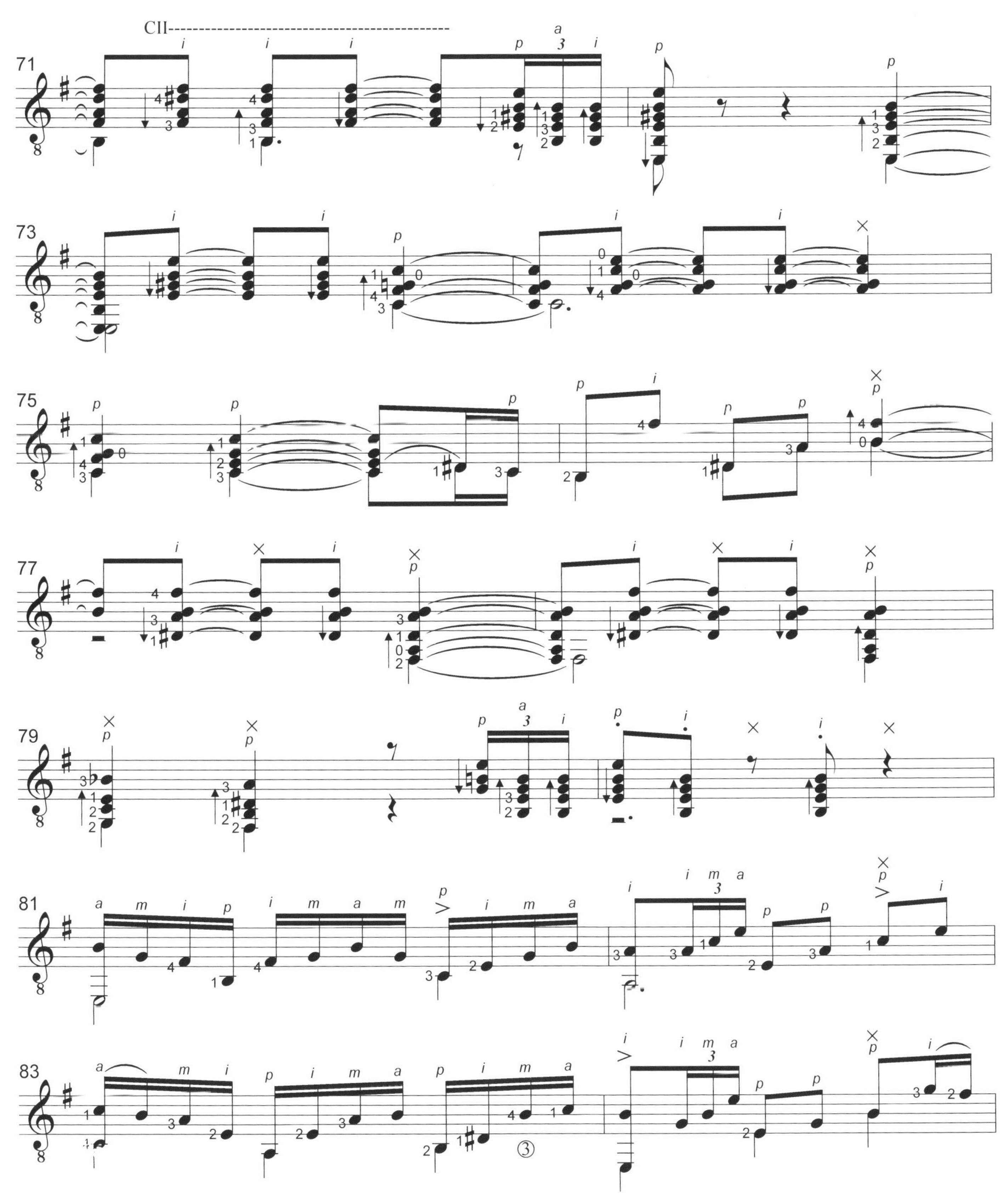
CII
71
73
75
77
79
81
83

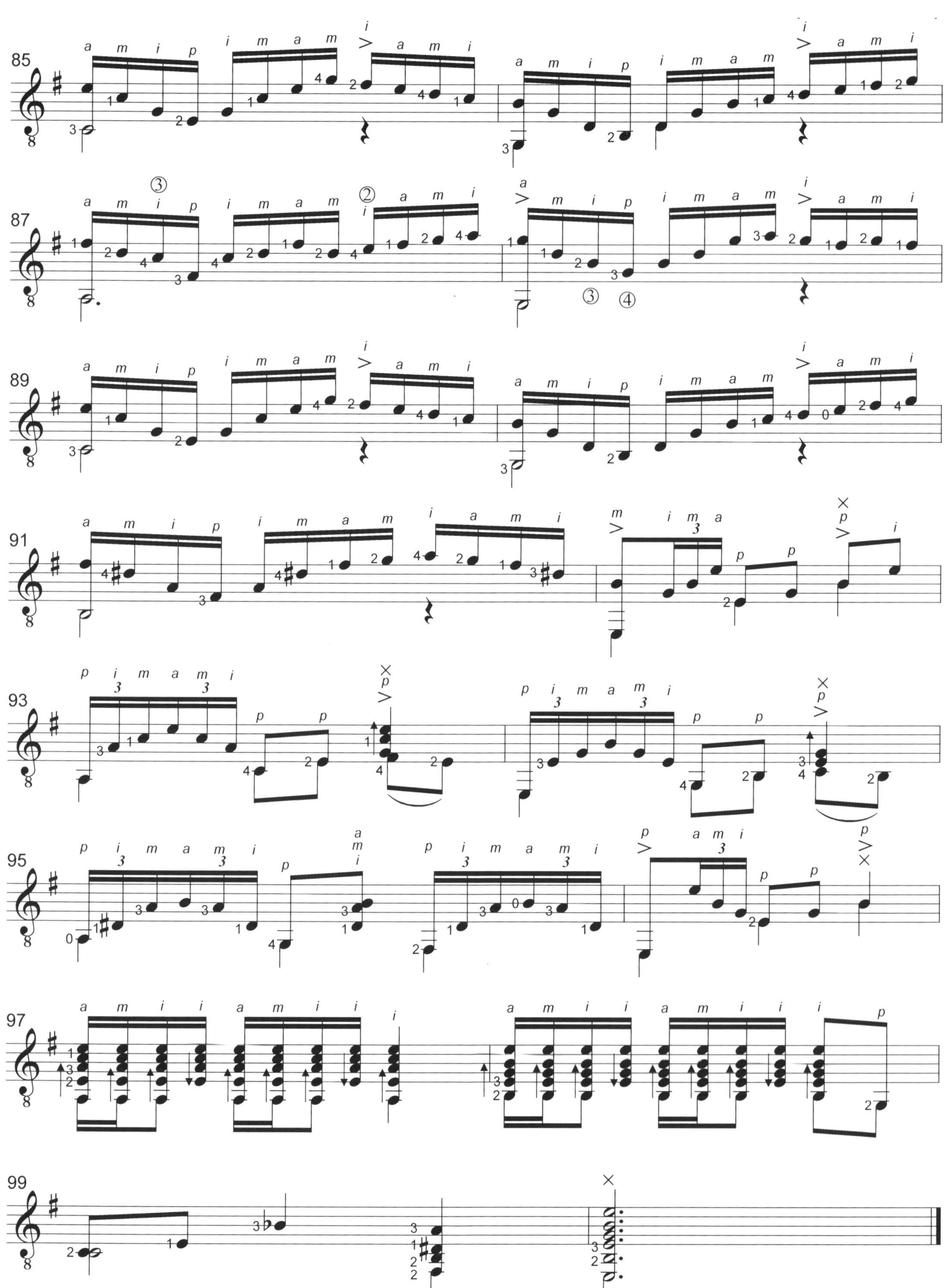

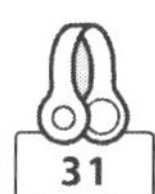

Caracoles (Cantiñas/Alegrías en Do)

Corey Whitehead and Richard Marlow
Edited by Corey Whitehead

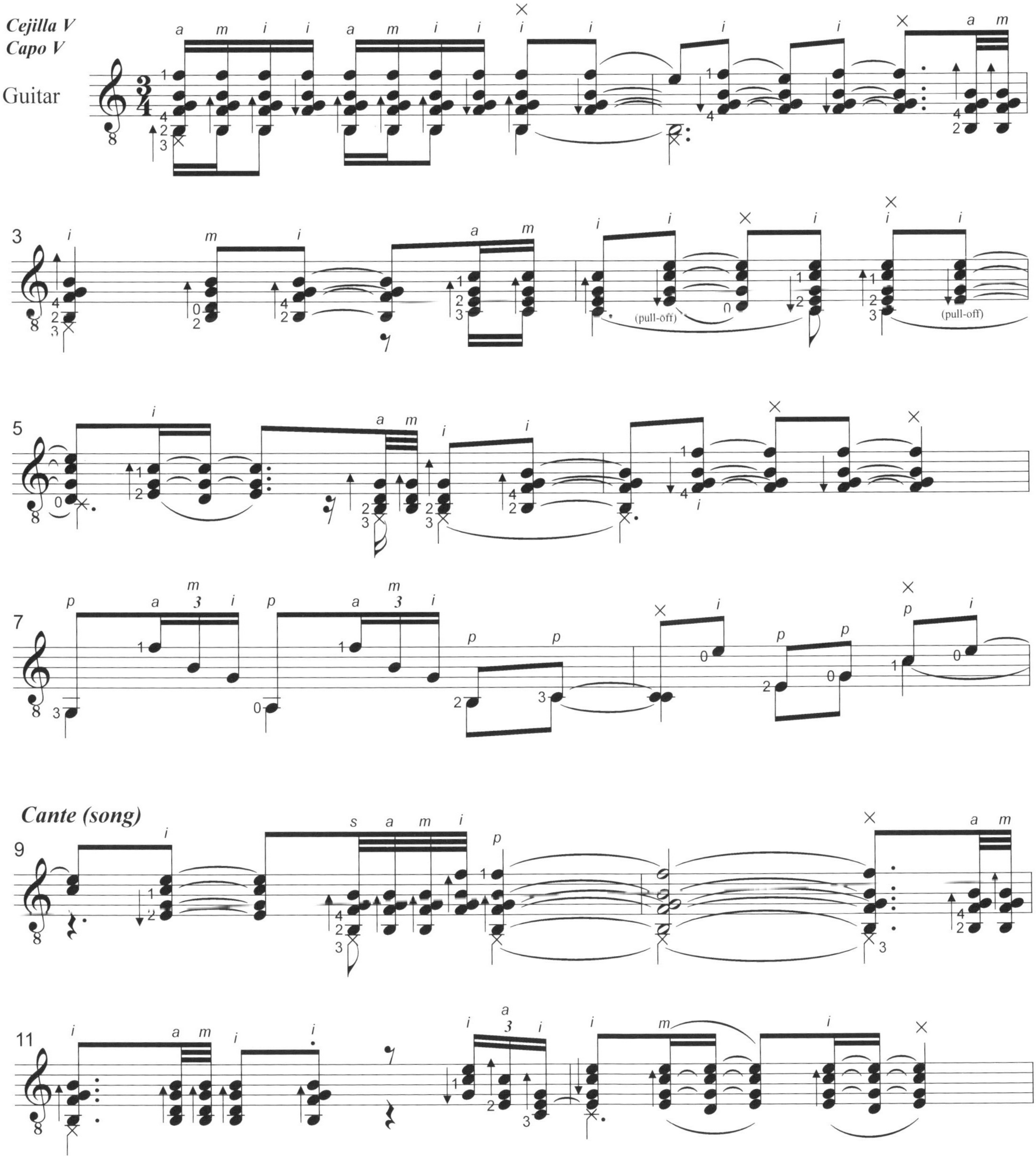

Cejilla V
Capo V

Guitar

(pull-off)

(pull-off)

Cante (song)

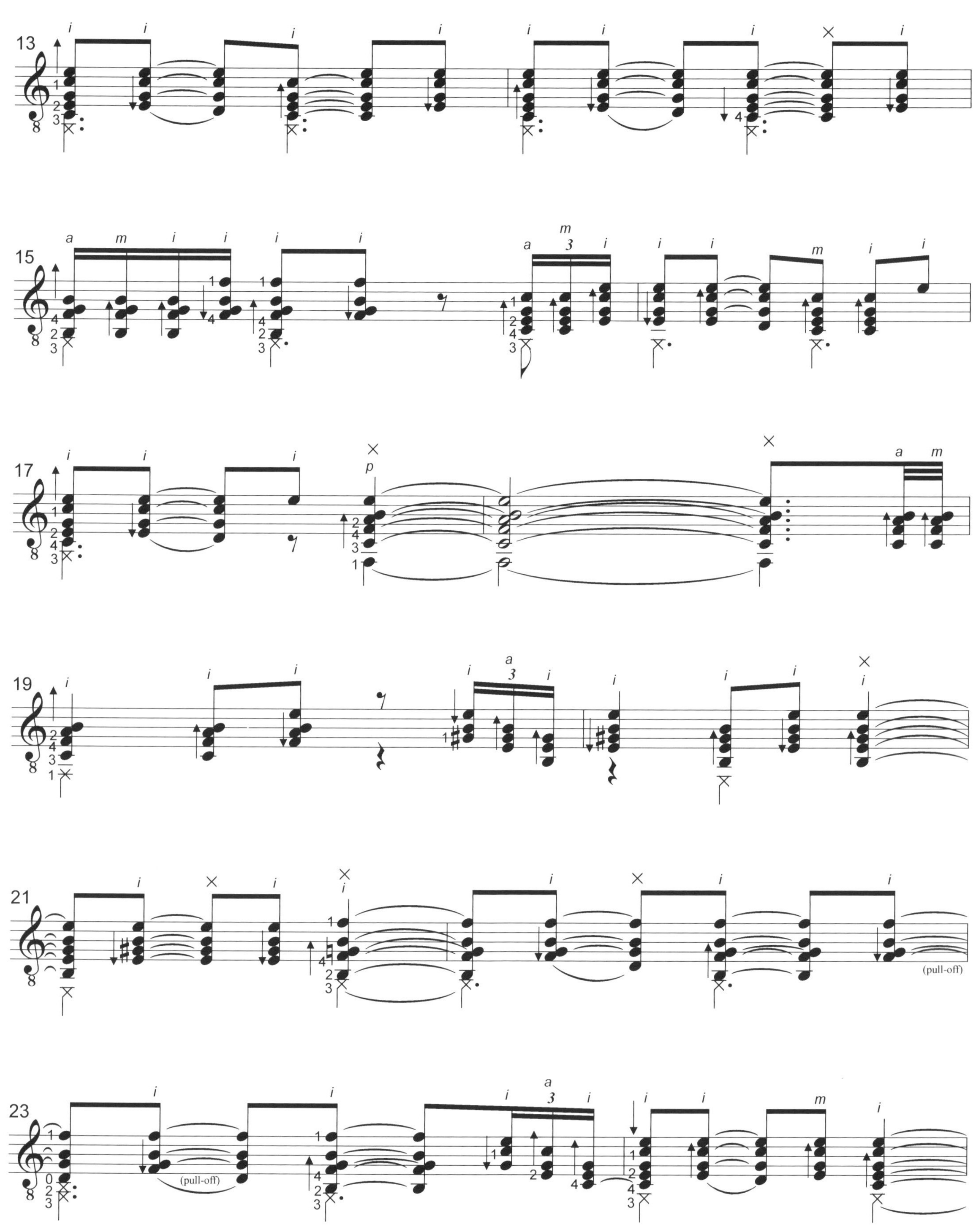
(pull-off)
(pull-off)

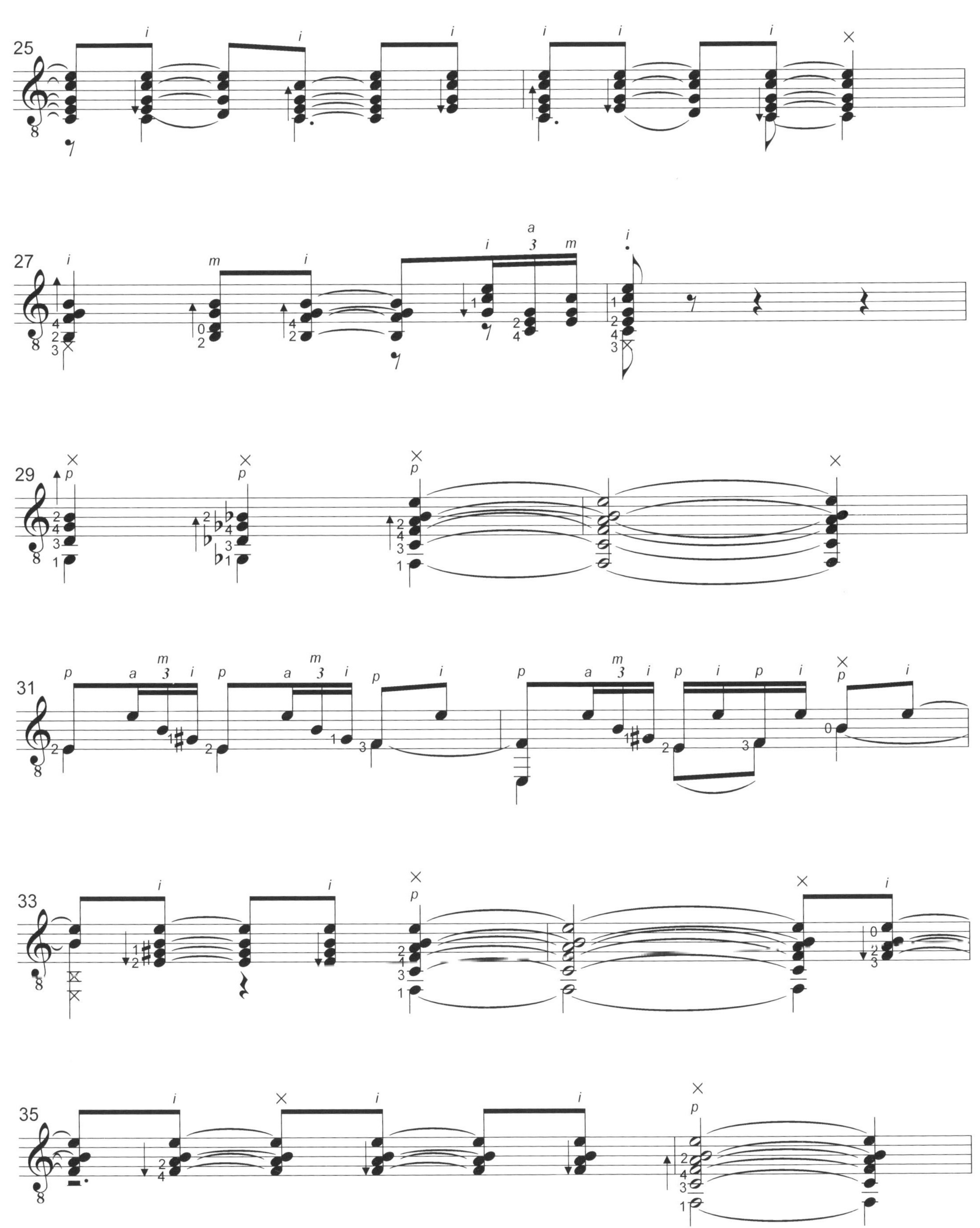

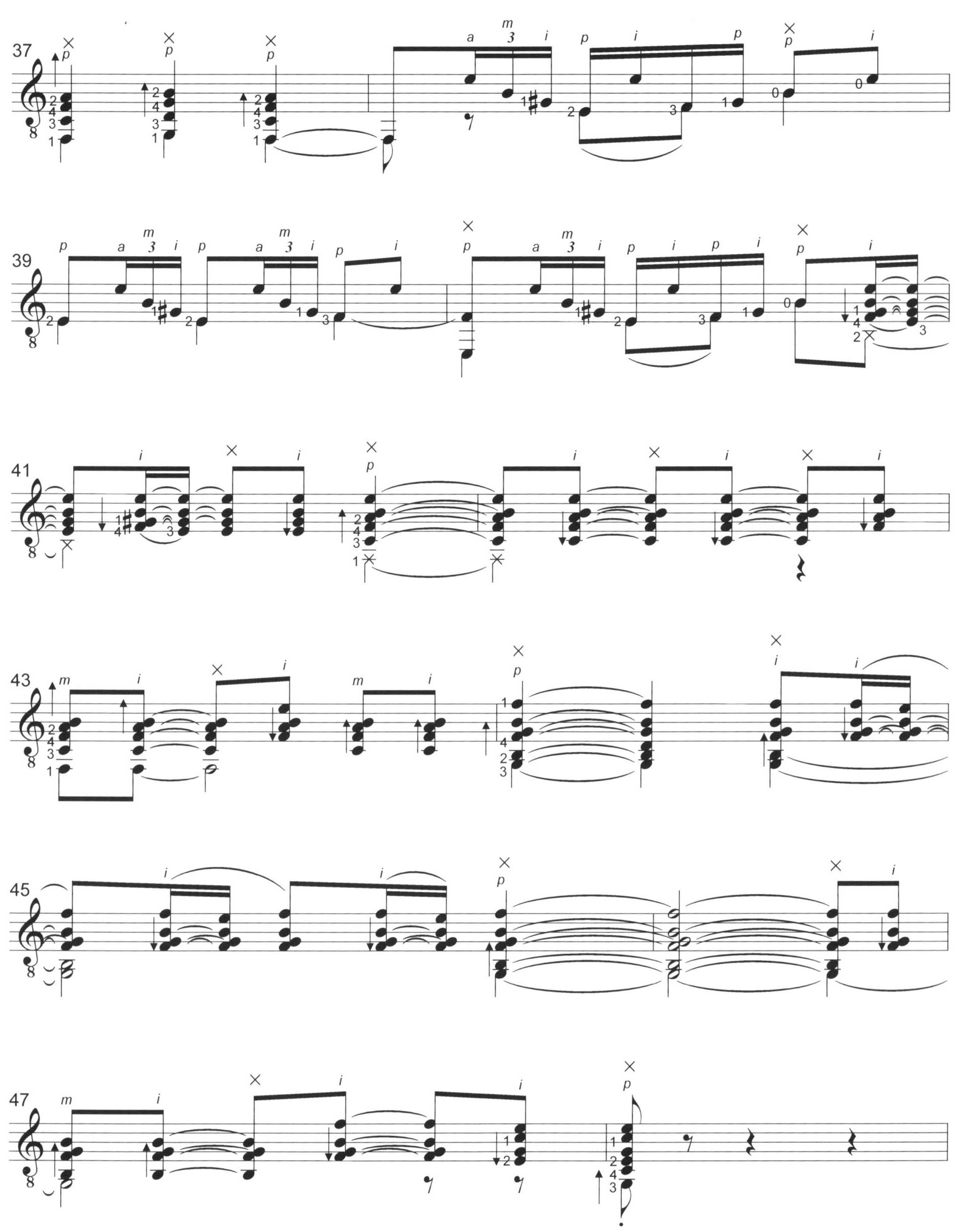

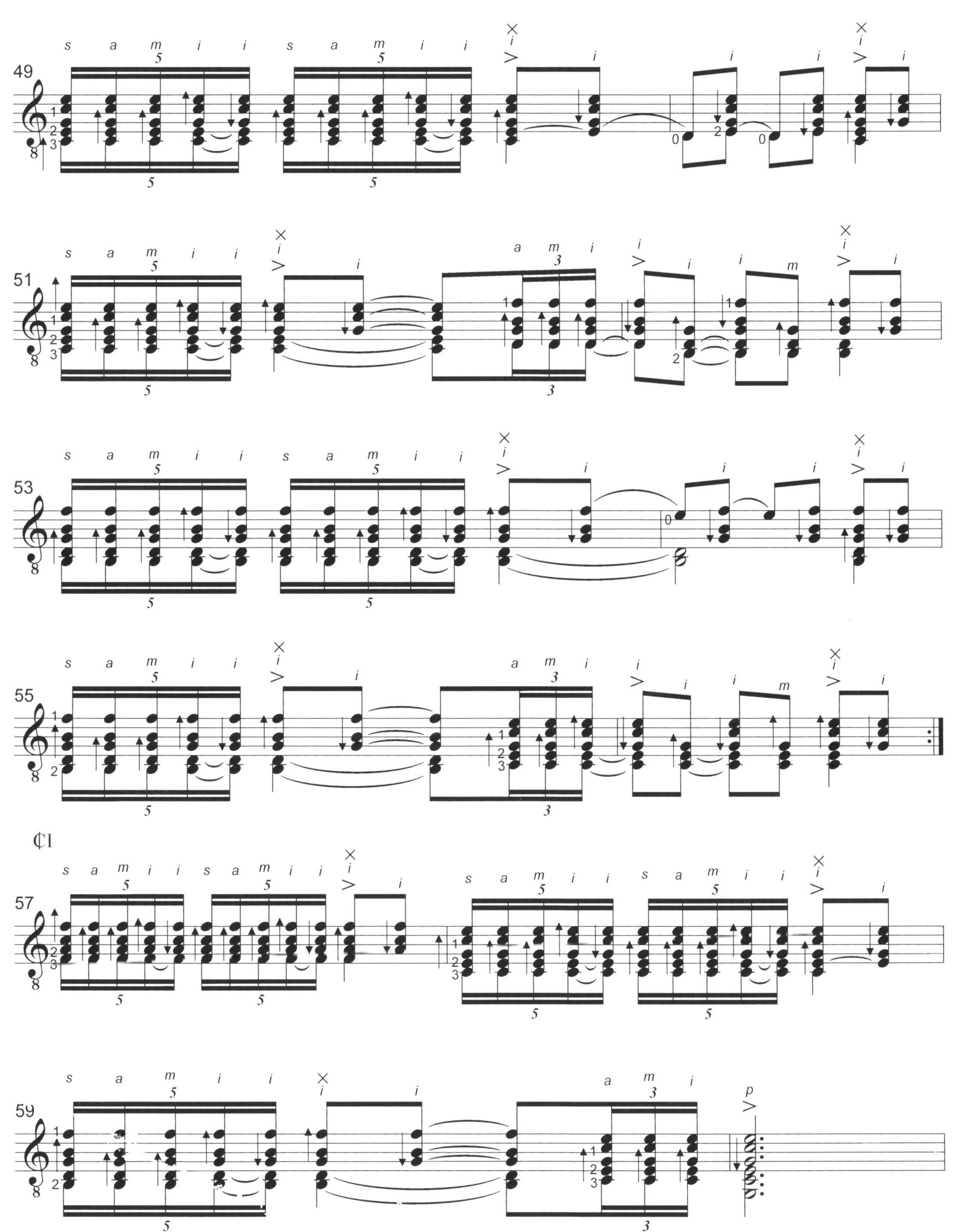
49
51
53
55
¢I
57
59
p

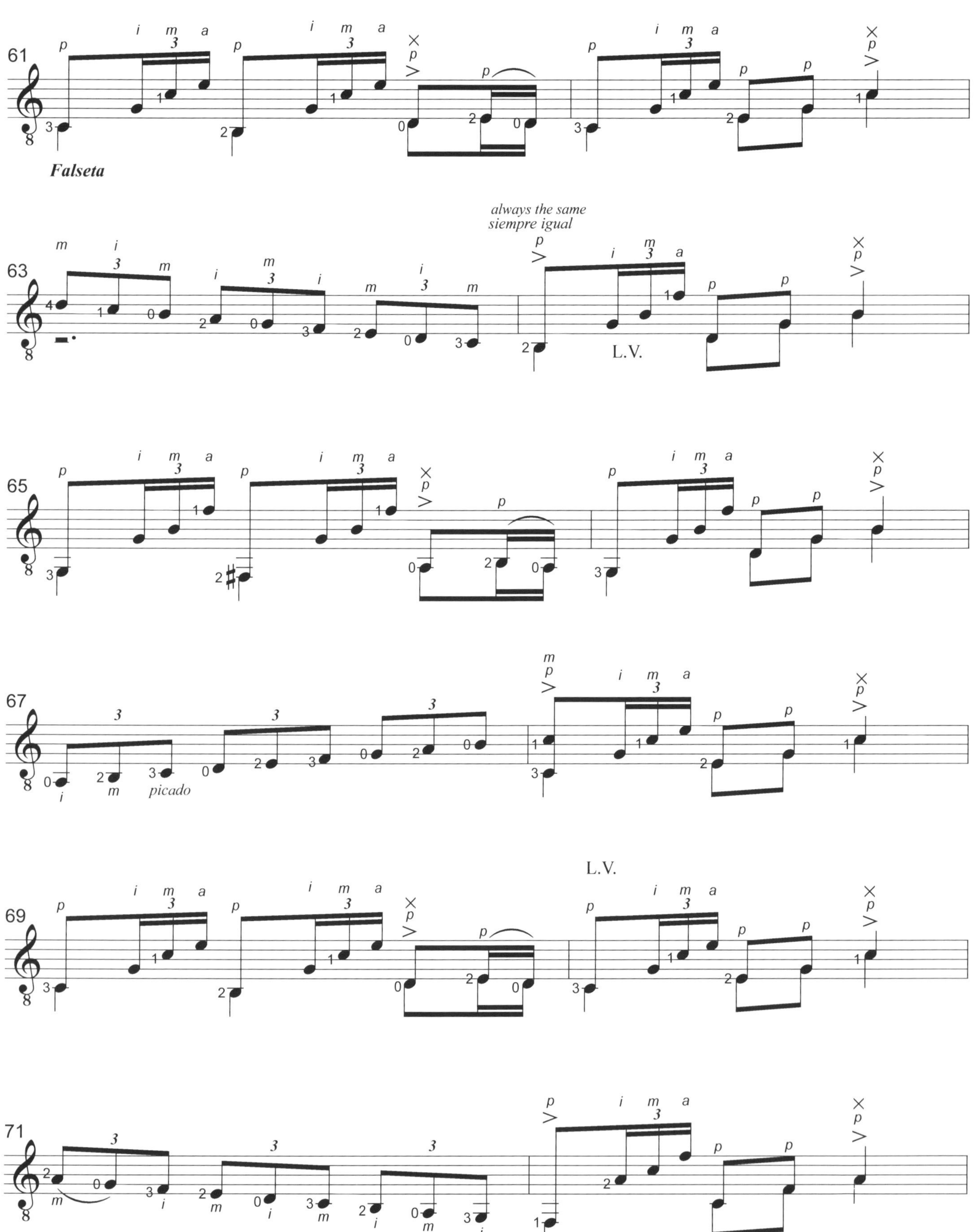
Falseta
always the same
siempre igual
L.V.
picado
L.V.

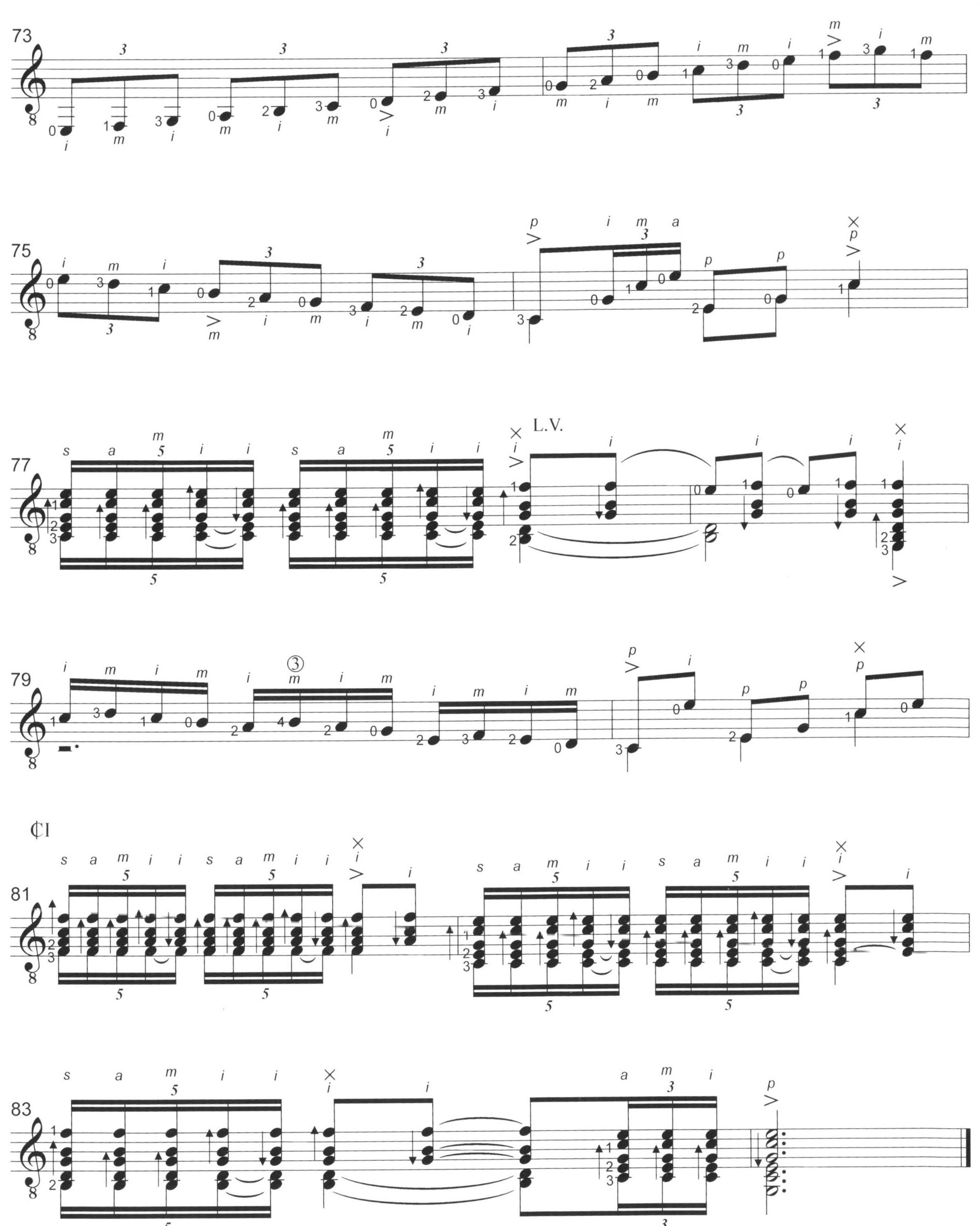
L.V.
CI